The Singularity of Western Innovation

Leonard Dudley

The Singularity of Western Innovation

The Language Nexus

Leonard Dudley
Montreal, Canada

ISBN 978-1-137-40317-9   ISBN 978-1-137-39822-2 (eBook)
DOI 10.1057/978-1-137-39822-2

Library of Congress Control Number: 2017946893

© The Editor(s) (if applicable) and The Author(s) 2017
This work is subject to copyright. All rights are solely and exclusively licensed by the Publisher, whether the whole or part of the material is concerned, specifically the rights of translation, reprinting, reuse of illustrations, recitation, broadcasting, reproduction on microfilms or in any other physical way, and transmission or information storage and retrieval, electronic adaptation, computer software, or by similar or dissimilar methodology now known or hereafter developed.
The use of general descriptive names, registered names, trademarks, service marks, etc. in this publication does not imply, even in the absence of a specific statement, that such names are exempt from the relevant protective laws and regulations and therefore free for general use.
The publisher, the authors and the editors are safe to assume that the advice and information in this book are believed to be true and accurate at the date of publication. Neither the publisher nor the authors or the editors give a warranty, express or implied, with respect to the material contained herein or for any errors or omissions that may have been made. The publisher remains neutral with regard to jurisdictional claims in published maps and institutional affiliations.

Cover image © FALKENSTEINFOTO / Alamy Stock Photo
Cover design by Samantha Johnson

Printed on acid-free paper

This Palgrave Macmillan imprint is published by Springer Nature
The registered company is Nature America Inc.
The registered company address is: 1 New York Plaza, New York, NY 10004, U.S.A.

Preface

On the bookshelf of Western history, the modern period is bounded by two solid bookends in the form of "tions"—the Reformation in the sixteenth century and globalization in the twentieth. Between them stands a sequence of three stout "isms"—*nationalism*, *industrialism* and *imperialism*—each emerging in a separate century.

The seventeenth century marked the beginning of *nationalism*—a series of movements whose aim was to promote the interests of "a sufficient number of people in each state who consider(ed) themselves to form a nation", to use the definition of Hugh Seton-Watson (1977, 3–5). The bitter mid-century rivalry between the Dutch and the English for mercantile pre-eminence was a sign that a new kind of nation had emerged within boundaries that approximated those of a political state. There followed three centuries of bitter rivalry between the British nation state and its continental counterparts.

With the eighteenth century came *industrialism*, the appearance of societies organized not on the basis of agriculture, commerce and craftsmanship, but rather of industries powered by machines. New technologies shifted the locus of production from the household and workshop to the smelter and factory. During the century and a half prior to 1850, as Joel Mokyr (1990) has shown, all but a few of the most important innovations were developed in just three states—Britain, its American offshoot and France. We shall see that these states were precisely the first to have experienced language standardization a century earlier.

As for the nineteenth century, it was the age of a new form of the third "ism", *imperialism*. Previously, the Portuguese and Spanish had built colonial empires in less-developed regions based on the pillage of human and natural resources. However, in the half century after 1815, there emerged a new imperialism under the leadership of Britain and France that aimed to integrate the more advanced civilizations of Asia and North Africa by force into Western-dominated commercial networks. Daniel Headrick (2010) has described the new technologies that permitted this more intensive type of exploitation. Yet there was something more. As we shall see, a sense of a common identity gave the expeditionary forces of the West a cohesiveness that Asian armies lacked.

Most of the events in these three long centuries had their own distinct causes. However, the sequential timing of the three "isms" suggests the possibility of some underlying causal relationship. I happen to live in Montreal where for two and a half centuries of daily skirmishes, the languages of the two dominant European powers in the period to be studied in this book have struggled against each other. Recently, however, political and demographic movements have increased the linguistic homogeneity of the city. A standardized French is clearly establishing itself as the vernacular, while English is used for contact with the outside world. At the same time, the city has become culturally and technologically one of the most dynamic centers in North America. It comes almost intuitively to one living in this environment to ask whether linguistic change could have played a role in the Eurasian dramas of the past three centuries. Consider then the three "isms" mentioned above—nationalism, industrialism and imperialism—along with some facts that suggest how language might have played a role in their emergence.

First, during the seventeenth century, did something happen to the languages of England and France that failed to occur elsewhere in Europe or Asia at the time? One possible indicator of such a change is a new type of publication. In 1658 and 1678 appeared the first monolingual dictionaries of the English and French languages, respectively, that were not simply lists of hard words to spell (Green 1996). It would take another century or more before equivalent dictionaries were published for other north-European vernacular languages. The Asian civilizations would have to wait until the twentieth century for such vernacular dictionaries to appear.

Second, during the eighteenth century, did the linguistic changes in question somehow make it easier for groups of innovators to come up with ideas for new technologies and to develop them into products that were useful? Consider, for example, the letter written in 1773 by an English manufacturer to a Scottish engineer proposing a partnership to develop an efficient steam engine (Marsden 2004, 84). A century earlier, Matthew

Boulton and James Watt would have had great difficulty in communicating with each other, let alone working together productively on a path-breaking industrial technology.

Third, in the nineteenth century, did the technologies incorporated into Western factories and their machines also have applications that dramatically reduced the cost of waging war against states equipped with earlier generations of military techniques? An example of the military impact of such new technologies occurred in 1827, during the Greek War of Independence. A small British-built steamship firing explosive shells destroyed an Ottoman sailing fleet (Abney-Hastings 2011). The event would mark the beginning of the end for wooden sailing warships.

In the following study, each of these three questions will be discussed in a separate section. Part 1 below will concentrate on the seventeenth century. During this period, Western Europe experienced the beginning of a remarkable acceleration in the flow of information—what historian Steven Marks (2016) has called the "Information Nexus". It will be shown that this discontinuity is attributable in part to language standardization in two of the largest states, in what will be termed the Linguistic Revolution. Part 2 will go on to describe three of the most important industrial innovations of the eighteenth century—the steam engine, machine tools and interchangeable parts—and their initial downstream extensions. It will become clear that the key innovations of this technological disruption, the familiar Industrial Revolution, were made possible by cooperation within networks of innovators sharing a common language. Finally, Part 3 will examine three important military innovations of the nineteenth century that stemmed from these earlier civilian breakthroughs; namely, the steamship, shell-firing cannon and mass-produced firearms. Here was a Military Revolution that, combined with the aggressive cohesiveness of the nation state, assured Western dominance over Asia until the end of the millennium.

The sequential timing of these three revolutions suggests that there may be causal links between them. Indeed, the presence of such ties has been proposed in several recent studies of the rise of the West. As we shall see, however, there is more than one way to interpret the direction of causality. In the concluding chapter, we will confront a networking hypothesis emphasizing language standardization with a popular alternative—the tournament model of interstate conflict described by Philip T. Hoffman (2015). The basic issue in explaining the rise of the West will be rephrased in terms of the importance of intergroup *competition* relative to intragroup *cooperation*.

I am grateful to Ulrich Blum and Ulrich Witt for their support during the long gestation of the ideas in this book. I wish to thank Sarah Lawrence, Allison Neuburger and their colleagues at Palgrave Macmillan for their helpful guidance in the preparation of the manuscript. I am also grateful to Ramaraj Britta for her excellent work in editing the text. And last but not least, many thanks to Brigitte for her patience and for the many excellent suggestions she has offered over the last three years.

Montreal, Canada   Leonard Dudley

Contents

1 **Introduction** 1
   1.1 *The Challenge* 1
   1.2 *Beyond Supply and Demand* 3
   1.3 *The Seventeenth Century* 7
   1.4 *The Eighteenth Century* 9
   1.5 *The Nineteenth Century* 15
   1.6 *Outline of the Book* 18
   References 25

Part 1 The Linguistic Revolution 29

2 **1600: The Dynastic Cycle** 31
   2.1 *The End Is Nigh* 31
   2.2 *Elizabeth I* 33
   2.3 *Mehmed III* 38
   2.4 *Akbar* 44
   2.5 *The Wanli Emperor* 48
   2.6 *Whither the Dynastic Cycle?* 54
   References 55

3	Printing	59
	3.1 Which Was More Important: Paper or the Printing Press?	59
	3.2 Printing in England	60
	3.3 Printing in the Ottoman Empire	67
	3.4 Printing in India	71
	3.5 Printing in China	73
	3.6 The Asymmetric Diffusion of Two Macro-inventions	77
	References	78

4	Literacy	81
	4.1 Literacy in Britain	81
	4.2 Literacy in the Ottoman Empire	84
	4.3 Literacy in India	85
	4.4 Literacy in China	88
	4.5 Comparing Literacy Rates	92
	References	96

5	Language Standardization	99
	5.1 Language, Nationalism and the Willingness to Pay Taxes	99
	5.2 Linguistic Convergence in Britain	100
	5.3 Linguistic Divergence in the Ottoman Empire	107
	5.4 Linguistic Divergence in India	110
	5.5 Linguistic Divergence in China	112
	5.6 States of Confusion	119
	References	121

Part 2	The Industrial Revolution	125

6	1700: Financing the Imperial State	127
	6.1 The Cycles' End	127
	6.2 England in 1700	128
	6.3 The Ottoman Empire in 1700	133
	6.4 India in 1700	137

	6.5	China in 1700	142
	6.6	The Fiscal Dilemma	146
	References		147

7	**Steam Makes Waves**		151
	7.1	An Innovative Dead End	151
	7.2	Who Invented the Steamboat?	151
	7.3	Cooperating with Steam	154
	7.4	Practical Steam Transport	158
	7.5	Cruising the Hudson	161
	7.6	A Steam-Powered Warship	163
	7.7	Language Standardization and Innovation	163
	References		165

8	**Machines to Make Machines**		167
	8.1	An Uninnovative Invention	167
	8.2	Machines for Making Things	167
	8.3	John Wilkinson	169
	8.4	Henry Maudslay	171
	8.5	Richard Roberts	175
	8.6	Machines at the Great Exhibition of 1851	178
	References		178

9	**Cloning the Industrial Revolution**		181
	9.1	Of Muskets and Horse Pistols	181
	9.2	From Cannon to Clocks	182
	9.3	Eli Whitney	185
	9.4	Simeon North	186
	9.5	John Hall	189
	9.6	The American System of Production	191
	References		192

Part 3 The (Second) Military Revolution 193

10 1793: A Geopolitical Watershed 195
  10.1 An Unstable Equilibrium 195
  10.2 Britain in 1793: Gentlemanly Imperialism? 196
  10.3 The Ottoman Empire in 1793: A New Order 199
  10.4 India in 1793: The Apogee of a Hegemon 203
  10.5 China in 1793: A Delicate Mission 205
  10.6 The Shifting Borders of Imagined Communities 209
  References 212

11 Steamships 215
  11.1 Steam at Sea 215
  11.2 Steam Versus the Ottoman Empire 216
  11.3 Steam Versus the Qing Dynasty 220
  11.4 The Imagined Community Adopts Steam Technology 224
  11.5 The Industrial Revolution Goes to War 226
  References 227

12 Rifled Artillery 229
  12.1 From Bows and Arrows to Nuts and Bolts 229
  12.2 The Ottoman Empire: The End of the Wooden Warship 230
  12.3 India: Redcoat Against Redcoat 232
  12.4 China: If at First You Don't Succeed 237
  12.5 From Conquest to Control 241
  References 242

13 Mass-Produced Firearms 243
  13.1 The Marginal Cost of Victory 243
  13.2 The Crimean War 245
  13.3 The Indian Rebellion of 1857 250
  13.4 Lances Versus Rifles 257
  13.5 The Toolbox for Empire 261
  References 262

14	Conclusion	265
	14.1 The Great Game	265
	14.2 The Tournament Model	267
	14.3 The Language-Standardization Hypothesis	270
	14.4 Competition or Cooperation?	275
	14.5 Six Arrows of Geopolitical Change	278
	14.6 Persistence	279
	References	284

References 287

Index 305

List of Figures

Fig. 1.1   The looting of the Old Summer Palace, Beijing, 1860. The British justified the subsequent burning of the palace complex as a collective punishment for the ill-treatment of prisoners by the Qing authorities (Reproduced from Wikipedia Commons)   2

Fig. 2.1   Queen Elizabeth I in 1595 by Marcus Gheeraerts the Younger. The queen was the fifth and last ruler of the Tudor dynasty (Reproduced from Wikipedia Commons)   34

Fig. 2.2   The initial coat of arms of the British East India Company. The motto "Deo ducente nil nocet" may be translated as "If God leads, nothing can harm us." Granted a trading charter in 1600 by Queen Elizabeth I, the commercial firm by 1850 would control territory that accounted for a fifth of the world's population (College of Arms, MS I. 9 f. 84r. Reproduced by permission of the Kings, Heralds and Pursuivants of Arms)   38

Fig. 3.1   Copy of a 1647 newsbook, the predecessor of the newspaper. Published in quarto format regularly during the English Civil War, *The Moderate Intelligencer* contained both domestic and foreign news (Reproduced from *Folger Shakespeare Library*)   65

Fig. 4.1   Title page of the first edition of the King James Bible, 1611. This vernacular translation of the Bible has been the best-selling book in English since the seventeenth century (Reproduced from *Wikipedia Commons*)   93

xvi   LIST OF FIGURES

Fig. 5.1   Title page to *The New World of English Words*, 1658. Though plagiarized in part from an earlier compilation of hard words to spell, Edward Phillips's publication was the first English vernacular dictionary to include common words (Reproduced from *Folger Shakespeare Library*)   105

Fig. 6.1   The emperor Aurangzeb was a pious Muslim who abstained from alcohol and studied the Quran and treatises on Islamic law. However, during his reign, the fiscal regime put in place by Akbar gradually collapsed (Reproduced from *Wikipedia Commons*)   139

Fig. 7.1   Engraving of the *Charlotte Dundas II* by the son of William Symington. Built in 1802, this boat was the first steam-powered vessel able to perform practical work (Reproduced by permission of *alamy.com*)   160

Fig. 8.1   James Nasmyth's drawing showing an old lathe and a modern lathe. The machine tools developed by Henry Maudslay and his associates were able to produce metal parts to a tolerance that was without precedent (Reproduced from Robertson Buchanan, *Practical Essays on Mill Work and Other Machinery; Revised into a Third Edition with Additions by George Rennie, Esq., C.E., F.R.S.*, J. Weale, London, 1841, 396)   174

Fig. 9.1   Harpers Ferry Armory in 1865, looking downstream. The combined currents of the Shenandoah and Potomac Rivers provided ample power for turning metal-working machinery (Reproduced from *Wikipedia Commons*)   188

Fig. 10.1   In 1793, the young sultan Selim III introduced new army units, the *Nizam-i Djedid*, intended to bring the Ottoman army up to European standards (Reproduced from *Wikipedia Commons*)   200

Fig. 10.2   A memorial near Pune, India, commemorating Mahadaji Shinde, ruler of the Maratha state of Gwalior in central India (Reproduced from Wikipedia Commons)   204

Fig. 10.3   Caricature of the reception of British delegate Lord Macartney by the Chinese emperor Qianlong in 1793 (Reproduced from the National Portrait Gallery)   207

Fig. 11.1   The *Karteria*, the first steam-powered vessel to be used in combat. In the Battle of Itea in September 1827, the Hellenic Navy ship's explosive shells penetrated the wooden hulls of the opposing Ottoman fleet, setting the ships on fire (Reproduced from *Wikipedia Commons*)   217

Fig. 12.1	Interior of the Taku North Fort immediately after its capture, 1860. The explosive shells fired by British 12-pound Armstrong guns proved deadly for the fort's Chinese defenders (Reproduced from Wikipedia Commons)	240
Fig. 13.1	The 93rd Highlanders at the storming of the Sikandar Bagh. During the second relief of Lucknow in November 1857, the powerful Enfield rifle provided a significant firepower advantage to British troops (Reproduced from Wikipedia Commons)	255
Fig. 14.1	The tournament model	267
Fig. 14.2	The language-standardization hypothesis	273

LIST OF TABLES

Table 5.1	Intelligibility of Scandinavian dialects to Danes from Copenhagen	102
Table 5.2	First monolingual vernacular dictionary by country	106
Table 5.3	Intelligibility of Chinese dialects to rural residents of the Suzhou area	118
Table 14.1	Great breakthroughs by country, 3000 BCE–1699 CE	280
Table 14.2	Great breakthroughs by country, 1700–1849	281
Table 14.3	Great breakthroughs by country, 1850–2000	282

CHAPTER 1

Introduction

1.1 THE CHALLENGE

The middle decade of the nineteenth century saw a series of spectacular events that underlined the dominance of the West relative to the major Asian civilizations. In 1853, Russian warships equipped with French-designed cannon firing explosive shells set the wooden sailing ships of an Ottoman fleet ablaze at Sinop in northern Anatolia. Some 3000 Ottoman soldiers and sailors burned to death, while only 37 Russians lost their lives (Clodfelter 2008, 195). Four years later, after a siege of over 3 months, British troops and their Indian employees blasted through the walls of Delhi, the former Mughal capital, and massacred thousands of its inhabitants. Finally, in 1860, French and British soldiers armed with rifled cannon and mass-produced rifles crushed a Chinese army at the gate to Beijing. They then looted and set fire to the Qing emperor's Summer Palace complex just outside the Chinese capital, destroying 200 buildings and priceless works of art (see Fig. 1.1). Was this sudden dominance of the West simply a question of more effective military technology, or was there some more profound underlying explanation?

In the most recent years, there has been a rough balance of economic and military power between the major regions of Eurasia. China, India and Europe have all been viable enough economically to require little outside financial aid and have been sufficiently strong militarily to have few fears of attack from outside their region. Even in the Middle East, Turkey and Iran have been economically and militarily strong enough to discourage external

Fig. 1.1 The looting of the Old Summer Palace, Beijing, 1860. The British justified the subsequent burning of the palace complex as a collective punishment for the ill-treatment of prisoners by the Qing authorities (Reproduced from Wikipedia Commons)

aggression. A century and a half ago, however, the situation was remarkably different. As William McNeill (1963, 565–567) observed in *The Rise of the West*, by the 1850s one region of Eurasia—Western Europe, along with its American offshoot—had reached a degree of military and economic superiority over the societies of Asia that had no precedent since the beginning of historical records.

A sequence of international agreements imposed on Asia by the Western Great Powers in the mid-nineteenth century signaled the henceforth unequal nature of East-West relations. In 1856, the Treaty of Paris closed the Black Sea to warships and fortifications, thereby confirming that the crumbling Ottoman Empire would survive only as long as Britain and France saw it as a useful bulwark against Russian expansion. Two years later, by the Government of India Act, the entire south Asian subcontinent was placed under direct rule of the British Crown. Finally, in October 1860, the Convention of Beijing brought to an end the Second Opium War, obliging the Chinese Empire to make a series of humiliating concessions to Britain, France and Russia. In effect, by 1860 the three great Asian empires had been put under Western trusteeship.

Two and a half centuries earlier, in the first quarter of the seventeenth century, such one-sided outcomes would have been as unthinkable as they are today. At that time also, there had been a rough geopolitical equilibrium between the main civilizations of Eurasia. The principal conflicts were internal to each region. In the West, the Catholic powers of Southern Europe were busy contesting the strength of their Protestant rivals to the north. In the Middle East, the Sunni Ottoman Empire was up against the Shia Safavid dynasty of Iran. Meanwhile, in India, the Mughal emperor Akbar was attempting to suppress the autonomy of dissident Shia sultanates in the Deccan. At the same time in China, the Ming dynasty had barely succeeded in blocking an invasion of Korea by the Japanese when it was confronted by the rise of a powerful Manchu state on its northern frontier. The one important example of inter-civilization conflict at that time, the Long War between Austria and the Ottoman Empire, had ended in a stalemate. What had happened?

1.2 Beyond Supply and Demand

The aim of this study is to contribute an element that has been missing from previous accounts of the rise of the West, namely, the impact of language standardization. According to the consensus among economists and historians, the lead acquired by the West over the great Asian civilizations by the mid-nineteenth century was due to two advantages. First was the efficiency of Europe's liberal, democratic institutions. Second was the wealth of resources to which it had access, owing to its own geography and to its conquests in America and Africa. While the competitive states of Western Europe were opening up vast hitherto-unexploited territories in these continents, the autocratic regimes of Asia were experiencing the pressure of population on limited agricultural land. The inevitable Malthusian consequences followed. However, in the most recent decades, the success of South Korea, Singapore, Taiwan and China itself—countries with institutions very different from those of the West and lacking abundant resources—might lead us to ask whether some element is missing from the familiar story.

At the same time, there has been a reexamination of the Industrial Revolution in Britain and France. There is a growing body of evidence to indicate that underlying the acceleration of industrial production in the

West was the formation of new social groups. As towns and cities expanded, people came together with strangers to form new associations. The spread into the provinces of the dialect of each nation's capital was accompanied by an unprecedented increase in citizens' willingness to cooperate with one another. As a result, collaboration between specialists from different areas of expertise permitted a number of crucial breakthroughs that opened up new trajectories of technical progress. Explanations of the East-West gap that focus solely on institutions and resources would therefore seem at best to be incomplete.

The point of difference that distinguishes this book from previous studies of the rise of Europe and the decline of Asia since 1600 is its emphasis on the effect of language standardization on people's willingness to cooperate with strangers. In a word, while linguistic divergence was undermining the autocratic regimes of Asia, the increasing standardization of the British and French vernaculars was facilitating the cooperation required to develop new technologies and apply them in warfare.

All of us have had probably the experience of meeting a stranger who spoke our first language with an accent. Even though one might generally understand what the other person was saying, imagine the difficulty of working intensely with such a person on an important project. Moreover, could one really trust such a person to be as reliable as someone from one's own background? In the year 1600, virtually everyone in Eurasia, from Ireland to Japan, was in this situation whenever she ventured any distance from her home community. However, in the second half of the seventeenth century, with the publication of the first true monolingual English and French dictionaries, the literate citizens of these nations began to have access to a standard medium of everyday communication. As a result, over the following century in England, its American offshoot and northern France, people increasingly found that when they traveled away from their homes, they could communicate well in this standard vernacular with those they met. With growing ease of contact came a greater willingness to cooperate.

Recent research in social psychology and linguistics provides support for the importance of language in building trust[1]. When two strangers meet, empirical studies have shown, the crucial issue for each person is whether the other can be trusted (Wojciszke et al. 1998; Fiske et al. 2007). Experiments by Shiri Lev-Ari and Boaz Keysar (2010) indicate that one of the measures people use to evaluate trustworthiness is accent. The stronger one's accent, the less credible one sounds. Moreover, annoyance with accents applies not only to those using a second language but also to those speaking variants of the same language (Sumner and Samuel 2009). Heblich et al. (2015) found that in Germany, a person's readiness to cooperate with a stranger from another region fell when the latter spoke with a strong regional phonology instead of the standard pronunciation. In short, one's willingness to trust was found to depend negatively on the strength of the accent of the other person. "Just as the colour of one's skin or education level might, however unjustly, influence our behaviour, voice cues activate the same social biases and influence behaviour in a similar manner" (Sumner 2015, 239).

If so, then the tendency for languages to drift apart over time might help explain why Chinese innovation rates fell after the fourteenth century, especially for those complex innovations whose development demanded two or more individuals with complementary skills. As the frontier of knowledge expanded outward in the late Middle Ages, it had become becoming increasingly difficult for a single individual to span the range of knowledge required to produce something both new and useful. Developing novelty was no longer simply a matter of a clever artisan coming up with a bright idea about how slightly to improve existing techniques. Increasingly, to yield the breakthroughs that were to give the West its technological lead, the necessary ingredient was *cooperation* among people with different skill sets. Yet such cooperation was likely to yield results only if large numbers of people shared a common language and writing system. Thus without a heightened willingness to cooperate within large networks, a society's capacity to innovate was severely constrained.

Meanwhile, in Britain and northern France during the sixteenth century, single entrepreneurs were trying to master the complex challenges that blocked further technological advance. In the West Midlands, Dud Dudley was struggling unsuccessfully to smelt iron with coal. In Devonshire, Thomas Savery was discovering that his ingenious atmospheric pump was unable to extract water from deep mines. Finally, no one had been able to replace the hand-turned spinning wheel for producing thread from the short fibers of wool and cotton (Dudley 2012, ch. 1).

However, as the sixteenth century proceeded, the societies of Britain and France were gradually being transformed by the standardization of the way people wrote and spoke. Under the effects of what Benedict Anderson (2006, 36) has called "print-capitalism", printers and educators were approaching a consensus concerning how the English and French languages were to be written and spoken. The period between the end of the Middle

Ages and the beginning of the Industrial Revolution saw an unprecedented integration of language networks at the national level in Britain and France. A sharp rise in literacy rates followed by growing standardization of the English and French languages allowed potential innovators from different regions to communicate easily with one another. In both societies, by collaborating with strangers who possessed complementary skills, entrepreneurs could obtain the knowledge that they themselves lacked.

As the new information technologies lowered the cost of generating trust among strangers from different regions, these two European societies were able to create the complex technological breakthroughs that led to self-sustaining innovation. For example, with the cooperation of Birmingham metalworkers, Devonshire natives Thomas Newcomen and his colleague John Calley were able to pump water from a deep coalmine at Dudley Castle in the West Midlands (Rolt and Allen 1977, 46). Thanks to the insights of his Welsh apprentice, John Thomas, Abraham Darby from Staffordshire in the Midlands was able to produce pots from coke-smelted iron at a fraction of the price of the brass equivalent. Lewis Paul the son of a London pharmacist collaborated with a Birmingham carpenter, John Wyatt, to produce the first functioning cotton-spinning factory. In France, the process for producing sodium carbonate (soda ash) from salt patented by Loire valley native Nicolas Leblanc's would not have been possible without the collaboration of chemist Jean Darcet, who came from the Landes in the southwest of France.

Meanwhile in Asia, not only did the high cost of signaling willingness to cooperate curtail innovation itself but also it limited the capacity to adopt the inventions of others. In short, the global shift in economic and military power had its origins in an integration of communications networks that was unique to the West.

This study breaks the rise of the West relative to Asia into three distinct steps. First, beginning in the seventeenth century, came what might be called the *Linguistic Revolution*. Owing to the phonetic character of European writing systems, printing with movable characters came into general use in the West three centuries earlier than in Asia. For the first time in history, it became possible for millions of ordinary people to have access to the world's accumulated knowledge. Equally important, in the two most centralized large states, the appearance of the first monolingual vernacular dictionaries and grammar texts enabled them to learn to communicate with one another in a standardized form. The new English and

French vernaculars served not only as channels for efficient flows of information but also as signals of trustworthiness.

Second, over the following century, a resulting increase in people's readiness to cooperate gave rise to a transformation in the way new ideas were generated. In a change that was termed the *Industrial Revolution*, expanding social networks in Britain, France and the United States permitted the development of complex manufacturing technologies whose absence had previously threatened to block economic progress.

Third, in the nineteenth century, a small number of breakthrough technologies developed initially for civilian use were extended into the military domain in a development that could be called a *(Second) Military Revolution*. This transformation, compressed into a few decades, involved the application of three new mechanical devices, namely, the steamship, shell-firing artillery and the mass-produced rifle. The asymmetric diffusion of these techniques across Eurasia initiated a long period of divergence in military capacity between East and West that would last until the end of the millennium.

Although the individual components of this three-part story are for the most part well known, their assembly into a powerful chain of causality is the element of novelty proposed in the present study. Before proceeding to a chapter-by-chapter preview of the book, let us examine some of the main previous contributions to the study of these three disruptive centuries.

1.3 The Seventeenth Century

In the West, the century after 1600 saw not only the continued diffusion of the printing press but also a continued rise in literacy rates and, in certain regions, the beginnings of standardized speech and writing in the vernacular. No analogous development occurred in the great Asian civilizations.

The introduction of printing with movable type in the late Middle Ages was only the latest in a series of mutations in the processing of information that had occurred since the beginning of the Upper Paleolithic period some 50,000 years ago. Linguists Gilles Fauconnier and Mark Turner have proposed the concept of a "double-scope network", a concept that takes as inputs two different organizing frames of thought. It then combines them to form a blend that has properties of each of the original frames but also an "emergent structure of its own" (Fauconnier and Turner 2002, 131). This new structure of thought made possible the metaphor, whereby a familiar set of ideas is applied in novel way. Art, science and religion, the authors argued, were all the result of a discrete step in the evolution of the human brain perhaps 50,000 or more years ago that permitted complex language (Fauconnier and Turner 2002, 186–187).

Recent research on the origins of writing has made clear that this linguistic development was only one of the revolutions in communications that have shaped human society over the past 200,000 years. In the late fourth millennium BCE, an anonymous Sumerian scribe had a remarkable idea. Historian of writing Barry Powell (2009) has explained that it was becoming increasingly difficult to find a separate symbol for each word that the scribe wished to record. One day the scribe realized that the symbol used for one object could be used for a concept with similar-sounding name. For example, he could use a drawing of an arrow, pronounced *ti* in Sumerian also to represent the word for life, pronounced *til* or the word for rib likewise pronounced *ti* (Powell 2009, 71–72). The context in which the character appeared would enable the reader to determine which of the multiple meanings was intended. It now became possible to record virtually unlimited quantities of information, such as people's names, historical events and tax records, by using a limited number of symbols to represent the corresponding syllables as pronounced in the Sumerian language. In practice, Sumerian logosyllabic cuneiform writing used about 600 distinct characters.

Additional steps were required, however, before an accurate record of human speech could be made. In an initial great leap, traders along the eastern Mediterranean coast selected a small subset of phonetic symbols from the large set of logosyllabic symbols that Egyptian scribes used. Possibly the Egyptians had used these phonetic characters to write foreign words such as the names of Semitic workers. This West Semitic "consonantal syllabary" reduced the number of symbols to be learned from several hundred to about 22–30 (Powell 2009, 154). Then around 800 BCE, a Greek scribe decided to assign some of these rarely-used consonantal symbols in order to represent the vowels in his own language, adding a few other signs where necessary. The result was the first true alphabet.

Although the people of East Asia may have learned about logosyllabic writing through their trade with the peoples of the Middle East, most of the phonetic structure was subsequently abandoned. As William Hannas (1997, 9–19) explained, because of the weakening of this link, for many centuries there has been considerably less connection between the script and the spoken language in China than in societies with alphabetic writing.

Did this dichotomy between writing and speech matter? It might be argued that a society's writing system can have no appreciable long-term economic impact. For example, Japan, with one of the world's most complex writing systems, was able to catch up with the West once its regime removed the policy barriers that impeded economic growth. The country today has virtual universal literacy and its citizens have been awarded the Nobel Prize on over 20 occasions.

Even if we admit that the choice of writing system can have an effect on the structure of a society, we are not much closer to explaining why there was innovation in the West but not in the East in the eighteenth and nineteenth centuries. After all, the branching of phonetic Indo-European writing systems from the earlier logosyllabic and consonantal trees occurred almost 3000 years ago. Something much more recent must have happened to explain the sudden success of the West during the modern period in combining elements of existing information to create something new.

It will be suggested in Part 1 below that the key development was not the printing press but a subsequent mutation that occurred in the seventeenth century. Printers in London and Paris gradually *standardized* their written grammar and spelling to correspond to the spoken language of educated people in these capital cities. As literacy rates in these standardized languages rose beyond the levels attained in Asia, there emerged networks comprising millions of people who were able to correspond and converse easily with each other in a language close to their everyday speech—provided that each had learned Standard English or Standard French. To understand the impact of such expanding social networks on innovation, we must now turn to the conditions under which people are willing to cooperate with those who are neither kin nor neighbors.

1.4 The Eighteenth Century

How can we explain the growing disparity in income levels between Europe and Asia after 1700? This accelerated continuation of Eric Jones's (1981) "European Miracle" led to what Samuel Huntington described as "The Great Divergence" between East and West.[2] During the later Middle Ages and the early modern period, Europeans had developed few new technologies themselves, although they had been able to adapt Asian inventions such as the decimal system, paper, the compass and printing with movable type (Mokyr 1990, 215–218). Then in the eighteenth century, the people of several regions of Western Europe and North America began to innovate at a rate that was unprecedented in world history. The discoveries during this period would allow the West to dominate the rest of the world militarily and economically over the two centuries that followed.

For half a century, Western historians have been debating the causes of an apparent decline in Asian—particularly Chinese—innovation after the fourteenth century.[3] It is now clear that the Chinese, Indians and Muslims did not altogether stop inventing; for example, the bristle toothbrush, bronze movable type and petroleum lamps all appeared in China under the Ming Dynasty between 1368 and 1644 (Bowman 2000, 601). The more important issue in discussing the Great Divergence may be stated as follows: *what changed in the modern period to allow a small number of regions in the West to innovate at a rate that was without precedent?* In exploring this question, we may also discover why Asia failed to make the same leap.

What does it take for a society to be able to innovate? The conventional wisdom emphasizes the *supply* side. This approach has a long history. In his famous 1884 defense of liberalism, *The Man* versus *the State*, the British political philosopher, Herbert Spencer ([1884] 1981, 9), argued that increases in the welfare of British citizens since the English Civil Wars of the seventeenth century were due to the removal of state restrictions on private actions. More recently, Nobel prize-winner Douglass North extended this reasoning, affirming that the key to economic progress has been the reduction of transactions costs (North 1981). With Barry Weingast, he identified England's Glorious Revolution of 1688, with its introduction of credible constraints on the power of the monarch to modify property rights, as the key to the acceleration of economic growth that occurred during the Industrial Revolution (North and Weingast 1989).

Daron Acemoglu and James Robinson (2012) have also pointed recently to the institutions that protect property rights and contracts as a key consideration to explain why Britain outpaced Spain in the eighteenth century. A corollary put forth by Joel Mokyr (2002, 2009) after comparing the British and continental Enlightenments is that in addition, the innovating society must have a set of beliefs—an ideology—that favors the practical application of new knowledge.

An alternative approach also dating from the nineteenth century contends that institutions and ideology are not enough to explain the West's technological lead over the East. Rather, this second line of reasoning attributes Europe's success in innovating to a change in incentives that affected the *demand* for innovation. Stanley Jevons (1865, 69) noted that many of Britain's inventions from the beginning of the eighteenth century were dependent on the availability of inexpensive coal. In the first volume of *Capital*, Karl Marx ([1867] 1990, part VIII) applied an analogous argument to what he called *"ürsprungliche Akkumulation"*, an expression that is usually translated into English as "Primitive accumulation". By this term, he meant the extra resources to which the West had access by exploiting the silver and gold of the Americas, the slave labor of Africa and the lands and people of the Indian subcontinent. Marx did not mention specifically the effect of these supplementary resources on the incentive to innovate, arguing instead that they allowed the capitalist class to appropriate the surplus labor of those so dispossessed. More recently, however, Kenneth Pomeranz (2000, 23) revived Marx's argument, affirming that Europe's extraction of overseas resources can be compared to the exploitation of its coal deposits in reducing the cost of land and energy. Without the resulting lifting of the land constraint, Pomeranz (2000, 32) asserted, Europe's technological inventiveness would not have been sufficient to propel it into self-sustaining growth.

In a recent contribution, Robert Allen (2009) returned to Stanley Jevons's hypothesis of the effect of coal on the incentive to develop labor-saving and land-using innovation. The principal stimulus to innovation in Britain, Allen argued, was inexpensive energy relative to labor. New technologies were developed through the response of entrepreneurs to the opportunities signaled by changes in factor prices.[4] In the case of eighteenth-century Britain, the rising costs of labor and conventional sources of energy led skilled artisans and their backers to develop new processes that replaced labor with machinery and substituted coal for charcoal, wind and water.[5]

Taken together, these two lines of attack, capturing both supply and demand forces, would seem to offer a complete explanation of innovation during the Industrial Revolution. However, the combined effects of institutions and factor prices are unable to explain why over the course of the eighteenth and early nineteenth centuries only a small number of regions in the North-Atlantic community were able to innovate, while others with similar institutions and factor prices were not. In England, Steve Pincus (2009) has shown, a political consensus emerged only during the last decade of the eighteenth century. It is difficult to believe that this understanding among the elites was the factor that stimulated the investigations of Newcomen and Darby and their associates a mere 10 years later. Regarding

France, as mentioned below, the first important innovations in the 1720s preceded the Revolution by over a half century.

The factor-price argument makes good sense. Eric Jones (2010) observed that in England over the eighteenth century, improvements in transport and communication led to increasing regional specialization, with the coal-rich north specializing in manufacturing and the south England in agriculture. Yet a low price of energy relative to labor cannot explain why despite plentiful cheap coal, the northeast of England along with Wales contributed few innovations prior to 1850.

Two observations from the early eighteenth century suggest that there is something more to innovation than protecting property rights under appropriate factor prices. The first case is a false positive. In 1706, experienced Dutch metal-workers employed by Abraham Darby in Bristol were unable to cast a thin-walled pot of iron, whereas the inexperienced Darby and a young apprentice subsequently succeeded and went on to develop a process for smelting iron with coke (Percy 1864, 887). Yet the institutions and factor prices of southern England were no more favorable to innovation than those of the Netherlands were.[6] The other case is a false negative. Between 1726 and 1728, two French artisans, Basile Bouchon and Jean-Baptiste Falcon, developed the first process for controlling production numerically—a loom that used perforated tape or punched cards to select the appropriate warp threads for weaving a pattern in silk (Daumas 1980, 609). However, neither France's autocratic institutions nor its combination of low wage rates and high energy costs was particularly favorable to this type of innovation (Allen 2009, 123, 125). These two examples are not isolated cases. While the Netherlands contributed no important innovation between 1700 and 1850, France was second only to Britain in the number of new technologies produced during this long period. These prediction errors therefore suggest that something may be missing from current accounts of the Industrial Revolution.

Both Mokyr (1990, 291) and Allen (2009, 136) made a distinction between rare "macro-inventions" and more numerous micro-inventions. In defining macro-inventions, Mokyr emphasized the originality of the technology, while Allen focused on the usefulness of its applications and those of its subsequent extensions. However, neither of these two features alone is sufficient to account for the divergence between the East and the West, as the Chinese inventions of the petroleum lamp (original) and the toothbrush (useful) illustrate. Three examples of Western "General Purpose Technologies" that were not only highly original but also generated numerous downstream spillovers are the steam engine, machine tools and interchangeable parts.[7] Reference to institutions, ideology and factor prices alone cannot explain why these complex technologies, the core of the West's technological lead, were developed near Birmingham, London and Philadelphia, respectively, rather than near Shanghai, Kolkata and Istanbul.

It has been realized for several hundred years, ever since Adam Smith's ([1776] 1977, 145, 158) *The Wealth of Nations*, that competition can improve the efficiency of a market for a product or service. As for cooperation, it is often associated with cartels or collusion to defraud—behavior that reduces welfare. However, when it comes to innovation, cooperation may be at least as important as competition.

A recent current of research develops this point of view by studying the effect of communication on strategic behavior; that is, in social situations where the outcome for each individual depends on the actions of others. In a survey article, Eric Alden Smith (2010) observed that there are numerous ways in which communication through language may facilitate cooperation. Language allows collective goods to be distributed in ways that motivate voluntary cooperation. If information is costless, "cheap talk" may allow individuals with convergent interests to coordinate their strategies (Farrell and Rabin 1996). In addition, language permits information concerning the past behavior of individuals to circulate in large groups, thereby facilitating the punishment of those who deviate from social norms (Smith 2010, 236–237). For these reasons, Robert Boyd and Peter J. Richerson (2009, 3281–3282) argued, the language of humans allows them to cooperate and innovate on a scale without equal among other animals.

If acquiring a standardized language has a cost and this cost is higher for those less willing or able to cooperate, the ability to speak and write "correctly" may be used as a signal to identify potential collaborators. Michael Spence (1973, 358–359) argued that signaling of this type is feasible if the cost of sending a message is negatively correlated with the competence and willingness to cooperate of the players. For example, if those who have received a formal education can solve problems at a lower cost than those less well-trained, a diploma is a credible signal of ability. If so, we would expect to find a direction of causality that runs from communication technologies to cooperation and then to industrial technology. In concrete terms, the linguistic conditions that favored the extension of social networks in the decades prior to the eighteenth century may help explain the technological breakthroughs that sparked the Industrial Revolution.

Is there any evidence that cooperation has become more important in the innovation process over the most recent centuries? Joseph Schumpeter ([1942] 2008, 101–102) observed that since the nineteenth century, large corporations that have formed through the process of "creative destruction" have been able to make invention part of their routine. Empirical support for this position comes from a study of United States patent data compiled by Tom Nicholas (2010, 57–58). In 1880, over 90 percent of all patents were granted to individual inventors. By 1930, their share had fallen to 53 percent and by 2000 to under 20 percent of the total. By the latter year, American firms accounted for over 40 percent of all patents, with about the same share going to foreign firms.[8] However, these data may still be understating the importance of cooperation, since often the patents of independent inventors went to individuals who listed co-inventors. For example, Thomas Mctighe, who had over forty patents, named two co-inventors in his patent for the dial telephone (Nicholas 2010, 66). Such co-invention may help explain why the quality of patents going to independent inventors, as measured by subsequent citations, remained high in the American data.

There is an additional reason why Nicolas's figures may underestimate the actual degree of cooperation. There is a difference between inventing something original enough to be granted a patent and the successful launching of a new product or service. The most successful independent inventors were those located in or near large urban centers. There they could maintain contact with agents and patent lawyers who could sell their patents to large corporations that had the resources necessary to exploit the ideas. In other words, successful innovation often involved collaboration between independent inventors and corporations, with the market for patents as the intermediary (Nicholas 2010, 59–60). This conclusion is consistent with recent evidence on learning networks in the biotechnology sector, a young industry with a rapidly changing technology. In a survey of some 225 dedicated biotechnology firms, Walter Powell (1996) and his associates found that rapidly growing firms were more likely to be involved in networks of cooperation that spread beyond firm boundaries.

Further evidence of the significance of cooperation in innovation comes from the study of innovation contests sponsored by firms looking for new ideas. For example, in 2009 BMW Motorrad sponsored a contest to search for new ideas in motorcycle design. Angelika Bullinger et al. (2010, 296) and her colleagues reported the results of such a contest sponsored by a university in which 214 teams, each with three to five members, took part.

The degree of cooperation relative to competition was measured by the extent to which the participating teams took account of the comments posted by others, either by searching for information or by reacting to suggestions. The authors found a U-shaped curve, with the most innovative teams having either a high or a low willingness to cooperate. An intermediate level of cooperative orientation was associated with less innovativeness (Bullinger et al. 2010, 296).

In summary, since the 1920s, cooperation would seem to be at least as important as competition in stimulating innovation. Schumpeter's argument that a large monopolistic corporation may have the most incentive to innovate may not convince everyone. However, the fact remains that independent inventors have in recent decades accounted for only a small fraction of all patents issued, with by far the largest share granted to corporations. And even among individual patents, many inventors list co-inventors. Particularly in sectors where the technology is changing rapidly, the optimal research team may spread beyond the borders of a single corporation or agency.

How far back can we push this need for cooperation in order to innovate? Accounts of innovation during the Industrial Revolution generally describe each invention as the work of a single person.[9] However, as we shall see in Part 2, three key breakthroughs leading to the rise of the West—those that were at the same time strikingly innovative and generators of multiple downstream military spillovers—involved teamwork. In each case, there were at least two people who made essential contributions and whose services could not be bought on the open market.

1.5   The Nineteenth Century

The problem for Asian societies as the nineteenth century began was deeper than a mere slowdown in their rates of innovation. As Part 3 below will show, the Qing dynasty in China, the Maratha Confederation in India and the Ottoman Empire in the Middle East had been able to take power because they had been the most effective groups in their regions in exploiting military techniques developed in Europe. However, over the nineteenth century, Asian societies began to fall increasingly far behind militarily, unable successfully to borrow new military technologies as rapidly as the West was creating them. The East's delay in standardizing its vernacular would finally begin to have geopolitical consequences. The financing and organization of a modern army and navy demanded a degree of social integration that was impossible with pre-modern communications networks.

When a quarter century of warfare in Europe came to an end in 1815, each of the principal combatants was equipped with the latest developments in military technology. However, soldiers or sailors who had fought in the wars between Spain and France almost three centuries earlier would have had little difficulty in recognizing the weapons and tactics being used. Infantrymen still fought in tight formation with smoothbore firearms that were ineffective at a distance of over 100 yards (91 m). They were supported by cavalry whose main weapons in shock combat were the sword or lance. Infantry and cavalry were both backed up by smoothbore artillery firing a solid round shot with an effective range of less than a kilometer. At sea, wooden sailing ships fought one another at close range with broadsides from the same types of cannon firing the same cast-iron spherical projectiles. Nothing fundamental had changed in the intervening centuries, except perhaps for the replacement of pikes by bayonets as the infantry's principal defense against cavalry charges. As the Maratha had shown in India, an Asian army with equipment only a few decades out of date by European standards could make up for any technological shortcomings by committing greater numbers of soldiers.

By the 1860s, a half century later, there had been profound changes in both weapons and tactics in the more advanced Western states. Infantrymen now carried rapid-firing rifles accurate at a range of up to 600 yards (550 m) and fought in much looser formations than before. Cavalrymen were armed with repeating handguns as well as swords. Rifled artillery could fire explosive shells with a range of two miles (3.2 km) or more. Meanwhile, iron-hulled armored steamships with cannon that fired explosive shells had rendered wooden sailing ships obsolete. As both Russia and the Ottoman Empire had found during the Crimean War, other things being equal, the side with the more modern equipment and training had an enormous advantage.

These nineteenth-century developments should be distinguished from a "Military Revolution" of the early modern period that has been identified by some military historians. Michael Roberts (1956) was the first to suggest this concept, applying it to the period from 1560 to 1660. Geoffrey Parker (1996) argued that the beginning of the revolution should be pushed back to the late fifteenth century. However, Jeremy Black (1991) asserted that since there were also important changes in the century after 1660, the "revolution" was better described as a long period of gradual evolution.

This early-modern transformation consisted of a long period of transformation in the way armies, navies and fortifications were equipped and structured—changes that were either developed independently or copied by Asian states with the assistance of European mercenary advisors.

In contrast, the nineteenth-century transformation, which we will call the (Second) Military Revolution, was compressed into a few decades. The changes involved the application of a small number of mechanical devices, namely, the steamship, rifled artillery and the mass-produced rifle. The rapid diffusion of these techniques in the West and obstacles to their application in the East initiated a long period of divergence in military capacity that would last for the rest of the millennium.

Daniel Headrick (2010) has described the impact of these developments on European imperialism. The most important of the three technologies was undoubtedly the steamship. "Steam was both the means and the incentive for Britain to take over parts of the Middle East" (Headrick 2010, 195)—along with the rest of southern and eastern Asia. Steamships reduced transport costs, making trade and investments more profitable. In addition, shallow-draft iron-hulled armed steamboats now had access to the interior of the Asian continent and to bodies such as the Persian Gulf and the Red Sea, thereby greatly increasing the quantity of resources that could be exploited. Steam also increased the value of hitherto unexploited territory by changing the paths of maritime transport. For example, as shipping that had previously passed by the Cape of Good Hope began to take the Red Sea route, Egypt suddenly became of considerable potential value to Britain as a link in its trade routes (Headrick 2010, 197).

Developments in artillery and firearms technology gave European armies further immense advantages over Asian forces, reducing the cost of capturing and holding additional territory. The new rifled cannon and mass-produced rifles had much greater range and destructive power than earlier smoothbore weapons. As a result, small European expeditionary forces leveraged with hired local troops could defeat Asian armies many times their size.

However, the divergence between the Western imperialist powers and their Asian rivals was not limited to technology. The superiority of Britain and France was also due in part to their capacity to coordinate infantry, cavalry and artillery on the battlefield, to project and supply their forces overseas and to finance these efforts from their own resources. This degree of integration required a willingness to cooperate among citizens of the same nation that the Ottoman, Indian and Chinese empires were unable to replicate. As we shall see in the following chapters, the development of this level of engagement at the national level coincided with the standardization of the English and French languages. In Asia, there was no comparable degree of linguistic standardization before the twentieth century.

1.6 Outline of the Book

If we admit that some influence in addition to institutions and factor prices is required to explain the rise of Europe and its offshoots relative to Asia in the years between 1600 and 1860, there are three questions that must be asked.

First, apart from better protection of property rights and a fall in the relative cost of energy, what was it that changed in the West during the seventeenth century, increasing Europeans' capacity to innovate successfully over the three centuries that followed? This question is the subject of Part 1.

Second, in the eighteenth century, how exactly did this change enable the West to overcome the obstacles that continued to block innovation by artisans elsewhere across Eurasia? Part 2 will study this topic.

Third, why in the nineteenth century were the Chinese, Indian and Ottoman states no longer unable to defend themselves against the military innovations of the West as they had over the two preceding centuries, namely, by purchasing Western arms and advice while compensating for any weakness by the weight of greater numbers? Part 3 will seek an explanation for this crucial divergence in military capacity.

Part 1: The Linguistic Revolution The first four chapters of the book describe the linguistic situation across Eurasia in the seventeenth century. In the year 1600, Chap. 2 shows, the symptoms of dynastic decline were evident in the autocratic regimes that ruled over England, the Ottoman Empire, India and China. Their problems were not only political but also military and fiscal. In each state, the customary rule for succession was questioned. In addition, powerful internal interest groups opposed the sovereign's power. Militarily, each of the four states had a tenuous hold over its acquired territory, each being threatened from both within and without. Finally, with the spread of the market economy, the need to find cash regularly for the wages of the regime's sailors and soldiers had become a sword of Damocles that hung over the head of each ruler, ready to fall at any scheduled payday.

Until the end of the sixteenth century, we learn in Chap. 3, English publishers had been slower than their Continental counterparts in adopting the printing press. Then suddenly, in the middle decades of the seventeenth century, there was a great increase in the number of titles published—not only books and pamphlets but also newspapers. At that time in China, under the late Ming dynasty, printed copies of literary works and popular writings were inexpensive. However, because of the high cost of preparing each page under block printing, there were many fewer titles available than in Europe. As for the Muslim world, prior to the nineteenth century, the Mughal and Ottoman Empires made little use of either block printing or movable type, in part because the potential markets were too small to justify the high fixed cost of reproducing Perso-Arabic script mechanically.

Chapter 4 compares the resulting changes in relative literacy between West and East. We first join James I early in his reign over England, Scotland and Ireland. Seeking a way to bind his three kingdoms together, he ordered his scholars to work on a new translation of the Bible into English. The resulting publication was one of the most important factors explaining the rise of literacy in Britain over the following two centuries. Indeed, the King James Bible has been the best-selling book in the English language since the seventeenth century. Its effects were felt first in the dissenting denominations, which put great emphasis on literacy for all men and women. However, literacy soon spread widely throughout British society, as it did elsewhere in Northern Europe. Meanwhile, in the Hindu and Muslim worlds, where printing had not been introduced, literacy rates stagnated. By 1750, even China could no longer compete with the West in terms of effective literacy, despite its centuries-old tradition of block-printed classical and vernacular literature.

We turn in Chap. 5 to the resulting divergence in degrees of language standardization. The year of publication of the first monolingual dictionaries in the vernacular by private publishers offers a rough measure of the extent of a society's linguistic standardization. A shared ability to speak and write a formally learned vernacular offered a powerful signal by which individuals could select strangers likely to be trustworthy. By the middle of the eighteenth century, both Britain and northern France had linguistic networks consisting of millions of people able to speak and write in a standardized vernacular. These nations were at least a century ahead of other European societies and almost three centuries in advance of China, India and the Ottoman Empire in this respect. In each of these Asian societies, there were multiple dialects for oral communication at the local level. However, few people had mastered the written and spoken languages used for communication between members of the elite who came from different regions.

Part 2: The Industrial Revolution In the second part, the discussion turns to the technological innovations of the eighteenth century. We begin in Chap. 6 with a description of the fiscal and military situation in 1700. The years between 1600 and 1700 had seen the creation of the first British Empire, but the beginning of the end for the Ottoman and Mughal Empires and the complete collapse of the Ming Empire. These events coincided with differences in these societies' capacity to realize three essential administrative transformations that were made necessary by the evolution of military technology. These changes were (i) military spending, from organizing small cavalry armies paid in kind to financing ever-larger gunpowder armies and fleets of warships whose personnel had to be paid in cash; (ii) fiscal structure, from direct taxes levied on property to indirect taxes on trade and commerce; and (iii) organizational control, from decentralized households of the nobility to the centralized administration of state bureaucracies.

In Chap. 7, we learn how the first industrial energy source was applied to transportation. Although the steam engine had been invented in the first decades of the eighteenth century, it did not begin to transform transportation in Europe until the century's end, when engineering advances allowed the production of more efficient steam engines. The first area to be affected was water transport, with the development of steamships. Subsequently, terrestrial transport was revolutionized with the spread of railways. Meanwhile, manufacturing was gradually shifting from water to steam power. Do cheap coal and expensive labor explain the West's advance over the Asian civilizations? If so, one must first clarify why before 1850 only two of Europe's numerous coal-producing regions (namely, the English Midlands and Lancashire) were characterized by rapid innovation. Moreover, as Needham (1965, 378–390) observed, at the end of the Middle Ages, China had a lead of several centuries over the West in most areas of technology. Why had this advance disappeared by 1750?

Chapter 8 describes the development of the first machine tools. With the hand-held tools in use across Eurasia until the last decade of the eighteenth century, it had been virtually impossible to produce precision metal parts, such as screws of fine tolerance. With the invention of the slide-rest lathe, it became possible for the first time to make metal parts to a precise specification. Was it the establishment in Britain of institutions to protect the property rights that led to such technological developments? If so, why should the engineers of France, where protection of private interests was considerably weaker, have also been remarkably inventive in the design of machine tools? As for Asia, one of the greatest weaknesses of manufacturers in the other three great civilizations was their inability to develop precision machine tools.

With increasingly ingenious designs of machine tools, as Chap. 9 explains, it became possible to mass-produce identical metal parts for the first time. In 1801, Eli Whitney demonstrated to an audience of powerful Americans the advantages of "uniformity" in manufacturing by assembling pistols from randomly selected parts. However, the show was a sham: each component of the pistols had previously been carefully cast and filed by hand. It was not until a quarter of a century later that the efforts of two ingenious New England machinists, Simeon North and John Hall, led to the development of machinery capable of producing identical rifles. Yet credit should also go to a long list of people including officials of the American War Department, all of them linked together by a standardized American vernacular. Nowhere in Asia did such a network of collaboration exist. Could the drift of Asia's spoken languages away from the classical written standards be part of the explanation for this growing East-West technological divergence?

Part 3: The (Second) Military Revolution The third section explores the impact of language standardization on the development of three military innovations—the steam warship, rifled artillery and mass-produced firearms—that played critical roles in the wars between Europe and the Asian empires over the half century after 1815. Chapter 10 provides a snapshot in the year 1793 of the four societies being studied. The rulers of the three great Asian civilizations were each developing strategies for dealing with the threat posed by the European powers' growing military strength. North of Beijing, as his court looked on, the Qianlong emperor reacted skeptically to the request of Lord Macartney that China's ports be opened to British traders. Meanwhile in India, Mahadaji Shinde, the powerful military commander of the Maratha Confederation that dominated most of the subcontinent, felt confident that his Western-trained army could halt any attempts by the British to expand beyond the territories they held. At the same time, in the Ottoman Empire, the young sultan, Selim III was decreeing a series of reforms to modernize his army, with the goal of bringing its organization and equipment up to European standards.

In Chap. 11, we follow the history of three privately owned steamships that played important roles in the military decline of the Orient during the five decades following the Congress of Vienna of 1815. In each case, cooperation among strangers belonging to the same language network was the key to the success of the West.

The first vessel, the *Karteria*, was financed in part by the London Greek Committee, a group of private individuals dedicated to aiding the new Greek rebel government and in part by the ship's captain, Frank Abney Hastings, a former British navy officer. The small steam-powered warship virtually single-handedly demolished a small Ottoman squadron in 1827 during the Greek War of Independence. Three weeks later, Britain and its allies destroyed the Ottoman fleet in the Battle of Navarino. The second ship, the *Nemesis*, was a 184-foot (56 m) steam-powered paddle frigate purchased by the East India Company in 1840 during the First Opium War. She was built in 3 months at Birkenhead, Cheshire, with two 60 hp engines made across the Mersey in Liverpool by the firm of Scottish engineer George Forrester. With an iron hull and a draft of only five feet (1.5 m), it could sail inland up rivers that were too shallow for ocean-going wooden ships to navigate. In 1841, it destroyed the Chinese fleet and shore batteries that guarded the Boca Tigris, the entry to the Pearl River and the port of Canton. A half century after Lord Macartney's visit to Beijing, the Qing dynasty had lost its gamble: the West's military technology was so far in advance of China's that Britain was able to impose its will on a once-proud civilization. Meanwhile, in India, since the final defeat of the Sikhs in 1849, no local power had dared oppose the British. The saga of the *Sarah Sands*, a British merchant ship recruited to transport troops during the Indian Rebellion of 1857, illustrates that the advantages of the West were not limited to its technology. Britain's considerable social cohesion, made possible by high literacy and a standardized vernacular, was a factor that no Asian society could rival prior to the twentieth century.

Chapter 12 describes a series of conflicts between European and Asian forces in the 1850s that demonstrated not only the superiority of weapons manufactured with Western machine tools but also the remarkable cohesion of Western forces in battle. In 1853, the shocking Russian destruction of a Turkish fleet at Sinop indicated clearly that French-designed guns firing explosive shells at close range were fatal for the wooden ships of Asian navies. Four years later, during the Indian Rebellion, the British were victors in the siege of Delhi despite being greatly outnumbered and outgunned by artillery teams they had trained and that were using the latest British weapons. The British had the advantage of a standardized written and spoken language, whereas the rebels, most of whom were illiterate, lacked a common mother tongue. The Indians, without trained officers, were obliged to communicate in a military-camp lingua franca that was the first language of no one. Finally, in China in August 1860 during the Second Opium War, the rifled Armstrong gun in the hands of disciplined, trained troops played an important role in the British-French victory at the Third Battle of the Taku Forts.

Chapter 13 describes a third advantage of European armies over their Asian opponents, namely, their access to individual firearms that had been mass-produced through the military application of a technology designed initially to manufacture wooden clocks. In May 1857, sepoy troops at Meerut in northern India rebelled and marched on Delhi, calling on the surviving head of the Mughal dynasty to lead them against the British. The spark that provoked this uprising was the introduction of the new Enfield rifle. Soldiers were required to bite off the end of the cartridge—an act that was anathema to both Hindus and Muslims, since the exterior was reported to be coated with the grease of both cows and pigs. Although it took 2 months for word of the rebellion to reach England and another 4 months for British reinforcements to reach Calcutta, the outcome was inevitable. Rifled firearms, produced in volume with interchangeable parts, had been the immediate cause of the revolt. However, once most of the sepoys had been disarmed and the Empire mobilized, the accuracy and range of the new weapons in the hands of Europeans brought the rebellion to a quick end.

This study, with its emphasis on communication within a society, is at odds with recent explanations of the Great Divergence, most of which focus on interstate competition. The last chapter therefore compares alternative causal chains that link warfare, language and innovation, one approach emphasizing competition and the other cooperation. It is argued that the competitive *tournament* model, applied recently to this period by a number of historians, cannot explain why the rise of the West was in essence the emergence of two societies—Britain, along with its American offshoot, and France—relative to the rest of the world. Rather, it is the cooperative *language-standardization hypothesis* presented in this study that enables us to understand why the asymmetric spread of common spoken and written vernaculars conferred on these three states a lead in developing military applications of a few breakthrough cooperative innovations.

Notes

1. Francis Fukuyama (1995) argued that societies differ in the degree to which people trust those outside their family or clan. Since trust is necessary for cooperation, these cultural differences determine the scale of corporations and accordingly the extent of a society's economic success. He contrasted high-trust societies such as Japan and the United States with low-trust societies like France and China. However, Fukuyama did not consider the role of a standardized vernacular language as a medium for the creation of trust.
2. The attribution appears in Frank (2001, 180).
3. Joseph Needham (1969, 190) noted that China had been more efficient than the West "in applying human knowledge to meet practical human needs" until the fifteenth century but then for some reason failed to maintain its lead. Eric Jones (1981) also drew attention to the divergence phenomenon in the "European Miracle". For a review of the "Great Divergence" question, see Duchesme (2011, 170–181).
4. Broadberry and Gupta (2009) extended this argument, suggesting that differences in initial factor prices can explain not only the direction, but also the *rate* of factor-saving technical change.
5. Van Zanden (2009, 154) argued that a low wage premium for skilled craftsmen in Western Europe during the period studied provided an incentive to replace unskilled labor by relatively inexpensive skill-intensive machines. However, since in the industrial areas of southern China, the skill premium was similar to that of Western Europe (Ibid., 200), this consideration cannot explain the observed East-West divergence in innovation rates.
6. See Allen (2009, 123) along with de Vries and van der Woude (1997, 161–163).
7. Bresnahan and Trajtenberg (1995) defined a General Purpose Technology (GPT) as one that may be adapted for use in a variety of applications in a number of industries. The atmospheric steam engine was one such development. See Dudley (2012, Tables 2.1, 3.1 and 4.1) for 11 other GPTs, all cooperatively developed.
8. In their study of Italian patents between 1861 and 1913, Alessandro Nuvolari and Michele Vasta (2013, 22) also found a sharp rise in the proportion of patents granted to firms and a fall in the share of independent inventors.
9. See, for example, Cardwell (1991) or Mokyr (1990).

References

Acemoglu, D., & Robinson, J. A. (2012). *Why nations fail: The origins of power, prosperity and poverty.* London: Profile Books.

Allen, R. C. (2009). *The British industrial revolution in global perspective.* Cambridge, UK: Cambridge University Press.

Anderson, B. (2006). *Imagined communities: Reflections on the origin and spread of nationalism* (Revised ed.). London: Verso.

Black, J. (1991). *A military revolution? Military change and European society 1550–1800.* London: Macmillan.

Bowman, J. S. (2000). *Columbia chronologies of Asian history and culture.* New York: Columbia University Press.

Boyd, R., & Richerson, P. J. (2009). Culture and the evolution of human cooperation. *Philosophical Transactions of the Royal Society B, 364,* 3281–3288.

Bresnahan, T. F., & Trajtenberg, M. (1995). General purpose technologies: 'engines of growth'? *Journal of Econometrics, 65,* 83–108.

Broadberry, S., & Gupta, B. (2009). Lancashire, India, and shifting competitive advantage in cotton textiles, 1700–1850: The neglected role of factor prices. *Economic History Review, 62,* 279–305.

Bullinger, A. C., Neyer, A.-K., Rass, M., & Moeslein, K. M. (2010). Community-based innovation contests: Where competition meets cooperation. *Creativity and Innovation Management, 19,* 290–303.

Cardwell, D. S. (1991). *Turning points in western technology.* Canton: Science History Publications.

Clodfelter, M. (2008). *Warfare and armed conflicts: A statistical reference to casualty and other figures, 1500–2000.* Jefferson: McFarland.

Daumas, M. (1980). *A history of technology and invention, vol. III, The expansion of mechanization 1725–1860.* London: John Murray.

de Vries, J., & van der Woude, A. (1997). *The first modern economy: Success, failure and perseverance of the Dutch economy, 1500–1815.* Cambridge: Cambridge University Press.

Duchesme, R. (2011). *The uniqueness of western civilization.* Leiden: Brill.

Dudley, L. (2012). *Mothers of innovation: How expanding social networks gave birth to the industrial revolution.* Newcastle upon Tyne: Cambridge Scholars.

Farrell, J., & Rabin, M. (1996). Cheap talk. *Journal of Economic Perspectives, 10*(3), 103–118.

Fauconnier, G., & Turner, M. (2002). *The way we think: Conceptual blending and the mind's hidden complexities.* New York: Basic Books.

Fiske, S. T., Cuddy, A. J., & Glick, P. (2007). Universal dimensions of social cognition: warmth and competence. *Trends in Cognitive Sciences, 11,* 77–83.

Frank, A. G. (2001). Review of the great divergence: Europe, China, and the making of the modern world economy by Kenneth Pomeranz. *Journal of Asian Studies, 60*, 180–182.

Fukuyama, F. (1995). *Trust: The social virtues and the creation of prosperity.* New York: Free Press.

Hannas, W. C. (1997). *Asia's orthographic dilemma.* Honolulu: University of Hawaii Press.

Headrick, D. R. (2010). *Power over peoples: Technology, environments, and western imperialism, 1400 to the present.* Princeton: Princeton University Press.

Heblich, S., Lameli, A., & Riener, G. (2015). The effect of perceived regional accents on individual economic behavior: A lab experiment on linguistic performance, cognitive ratings and economic decisions. *PLoS One, 10*, 1–16.

Jevons, S. (1865). *The coal question: An inquiry concerning the progress of the nation and the probable exhaustion of our coal-mines.* London: Macmillan.

Jones, E. L. (1981). *The European miracle.* Cambridge, UK: Cambridge University Press.

Jones, E. L. (2010). *Locating the industrial revolution: Inducement and response.* Singapore: World Scientific.

Lev-Ari, S., & Keysar, B. (2010). Why don't we believe non-native speakers? The influence of accent on credibility. *Journal of Experimental Social Psychology, 11* (2), 77–83.

Marx, K. (1990 [original 1867]). *Capital: A critique of political economy* (Vol. 1). London: Penguin.

McNeill, W. H. (1963). *The rise of the West.* Chicago: University of Chicago Press.

Mokyr, J. (1990). *The lever of riches: Technological creativity and economic progress.* Oxford: Oxford University Press.

Mokyr, J. (2002). *The gifts of Athena: historical origins of the knowledge economy.* Princeton: Princeton University Press.

Mokyr, J. (2009). *The enlightened economy: An economic history of Britain 1700–1850.* New Haven: Yale University Press.

Needham, J. (1965). *Science and civilisation in China, vol. 4, physics and physical technology, part II, mechanical engineering.* Cambridge, UK: Cambridge University Press.

Needham, J. (1969). *The grand titration.* Toronto: University of Toronto Press.

Nicholas, T. (2010). The role of independent invention in U.S. technological development, 1880–1930. *Journal of Economic History, 70*, 57–82.

North, D. C. (1981). *Structure and change in economic history.* New York: Norton.

North, D. C., & Weingast, B. R. (1989). Constitutions and commitment: The evolution of institutions governing public choice in eighteenth century England. *Journal of Economic History, 49*, 803–832.

Nuvolari, A., & Vasta, M. (2013). *Independent invention in Italy during the liberal age, 1861–1913.* Pisa: Sant'Anna School of Advanced Studies.

Parker, G. (1996). *The military revolution: military innovation and the rise of the West, 1500–1800* (2nd ed.). Cambridge, UK: Cambridge University Press.
Percy, J. (1864). *Metallurgy: Iron and steel.* London: John Murray.
Pincus, S. (2009). *1688: The first modern revolution.* New Haven: Yale University Press.
Pomeranz, K. (2000). *The great divergence: China, Europe, and the making of the modern world economy.* Princeton: Princeton University Press.
Powell, B. B. (2009). *Writing: Theory and history of the technology of civilization.* Chichester: Wiley-Blackwell.
Powell, W. W., Koput, K. W., & Smith-Doerr, L. (1996). Interorganizational collaboration and the locus of innovation: Networks of learning in biotechnology. *Administrative Science Quarterly, 41,* 116–145.
Roberts, M. (1956). *The military revolution, 1560–1660.* Belfast: M. Boyd.
Rolt, L. T., & Allen, J. S. (1977). *The steam engine of Thomas Newcomen.* Hartington: Moorland Pub. Co.
Schumpeter, J. A. (2008 [original 1942]). *Capitalism, socialism and democracy.* New York: HarperCollins.
Smith, M. R. (1977). *Harper's Ferry Armory and the new technology: The challenge of change.* Ithaca: Cornell University Press.
Smith, E. A. (2010). Communication and collective action: Language and the evolution of human cooperation. *Evolution and Human Behavior, 31,* 231–245.
Spence, M. (1973). Job market signaling. *Quarterly Journal of Economics, 87*(3), 355–374.
Spencer, H. (1981 [original 1884]). *The man versus the state.* Indianapolis: Liberty Classics.
Sumner, M. (2015). The social weight of spoken words. *Trends in Cognitive Sciences, 19*(5), 238–239.
Sumner, M., & Samuel, A. G. (2009). The role of experience in the processing of cross-dialectal variation. *Journal of Memory and Language, 60,* 487–501.
van Zanden, J. L. (2009). *The long road to the industrial revolution: The European economy in a global perspective, 1000–1800.* Leiden: Brill.
Wojciszke, B., Bazinska, R., & Jaworski, M. (1998). On the dominance of moral categories in impression formation. *Personality and Social Psychology Bulletin, 24,* 1245–1257.

PART 1

The Linguistic Revolution

Part 1 of this book is dedicated to changes in the linguistic situation across Eurasia during the seventeenth century. The initial chapter sets the stage for the discussion, describing the political, fiscal and military situation in Britain and in each of the three great Asian empires in the year 1600. The three following chapters then present different dimensions of the new communications technologies that were transforming social interaction in Europe during the early modern period, but were not introduced into Asia until the nineteenth century. We begin with the diffusion of the printing press, continue with a description of changes in the degree of literacy and conclude with a study of a critical factor for intra-society cooperation, namely, the degree of language standardization.

CHAPTER 2

1600: The Dynastic Cycle

2.1 The End Is Nigh

It had been a thousand years since Chinese writers first described the dynastic cycle—a recurring pattern in the sequence of hereditary rulers that stretched back into their society's distant past (Chen 2015). The philosopher Mencius (372–289 BCE) had spoken of a cycle that lasted several centuries: "It is a rule that a true royal sovereign should arise in the course of five hundred years, and during that time there should be men illustrious in their generation" (Yang 1954, 341). In the typical cycle, a new ruler with the "Mandate of Heaven" and popular support began a period of prosperity. Over time, however, powerful groups within the society succeeded in minimizing their tax payments and diverting revenues to their own use. As a result, the regime proved unable to respond adequately to natural disasters, outside attack or internal revolt. The dynasty subsequently fell, to be replaced by conquerors from the periphery, and the cycle began anew (Ebrey 1996, 10–12, 214).

In a similar fashion, the fourteenth-century Arab historian, Ibn Khaldun, had noted a dynastic cycle in medieval North African kingdoms. Because of the large number of nomadic potential invaders relative to sedentary farmers in the Maghreb, the cycles in this region were quite short, averaging about a century (Turchin and Nefedov 2009, 34). In India, the sixteenth-century historian `Abd al-Qadir Bada'uni (1898) wrote a critical history of the Muslim dynasties that had ruled northern India from the tenth century up to the later years of the reign of Akbar. Although he did not propose a cyclical theory of history, he was obviously aware of the tendency for the quality of hereditary leadership to decline over time. England too had gone through a series of dynasties in the preceding millennium, although the first systematic study of its rulers, *Anglica Historia*, published in 1534, was not by an Englishman but by an Italian, the humanist scholar Polydor Vergil (Trimble 1950, 35–36).

If we had scanned across the Eurasian landmass in the year 1600, it would have been apparent that the dynastic cycle was well advanced in England and the three great Asian empires. Each dynasty seemed to be nearing the end of its life span. Militarily, all four states faced powerful external threats. In England, the menace came from the Spanish; in China, the Manchus; in India, the Persians; in the Ottoman Empire, the Austrians. At the same time, each regime was fighting to suppress provincial rebels who had rejected central rule. To maintain control over their extended territories, the four states had been forced to make the transition from landholding cavalry and local militia paid in kind to professional soldiers paid in cash.

As a result of this military transformation, over the course of the seventeenth century, each dynasty would face grave fiscal challenges. In Britain, the sovereign would be overthrown by dissident subjects after a civil war fought over the control of military spending. Four decades later, a foreign sovereign would seize the throne by force. Similarly, in China, an alliance of dissident generals and foreign invaders would bring down the bankrupt Ming dynasty. In India, irrepressible regional revolts would prove fatal to the cash flow of the Mughal dynasty early in the eighteenth century. The empire would then dissolve into competing territorial states. As for the Middle East, real power would shift from the Ottoman sovereign to powerful pasha and vizier households and to a corps of soldiers transformed into *rentiers* who were no longer interested in fighting (Quataert 2005, 34). The sultan would henceforth be obliged to reign without ruling, while his territories were gradually whittled away.

By the end of the seventeenth century, the dynastic cycles would have begun once again in Asia, under new rulers. However, in England something unprecedented would have occurred. The state that emerged from civil wars and foreign invasion would have put an end to the dynastic cycle itself. In its stead, England's citizens, or rather a subgroup of them, would create a perpetual *collective* sovereign—an elected assembly.

In the following chapters of Part 1, we shall try to explain why this East-West divergence in the life cycles of dynasties emerged during the seventeenth century. First, however, we must dress a portrait of each of these states in the year 1600, beginning with England, then moving across Eurasia from the Ottoman Empire to India and finally on to China.

2.2 Elizabeth I

In the year 1600, the Tudor dynasty that had reigned over England for over a century was coming to an end. The aged queen, unmarried and childless, had every reason to be anxious. Her Irish possessions were in revolt, relations with Parliament were tense and she had not yet settled the issue of her succession. At age 67 in 1600, Elizabeth I had occupied the English throne for 42 long years. Indeed, she had outlived her most trusted advisers—Leicester, Walsingham and the elder Cecil. Recently the French ambassador, André Hurault, sieur de Maisse, had visited the queen on a delicate diplomatic matter. He had been astonished when she greeted him wearing an unfastened dressing gown, her "bosom" exposed, her hair covered by a red wig. Many of her teeth were missing, and those that remained were yellowed and uneven (see Fig. 2.1). Maisse even had difficulty understanding her speech (Erickson 1983, 384).

When the young Elizabeth, a Protestant, had first come to the throne in 1658 at age 25, there had been strong opposition from powerful Catholic families. However, she had avoided open rebellion by insisting upon the outward forms of loyalty while allowing Catholics to retain their beliefs. The Protestant Reformation was now firmly established in England, although there are still discussions over appropriate rituals. Increasingly, however, the queen found herself at odds with the two houses of the English Parliament. The House of Lords was made up of the hereditary nobility and high clergy, while the House of Commons was composed of elected representatives of the towns and the counties. A property qualification for voting limited the electorate to those of middle and upper incomes. Although parliamentary approval was required for taxation to cover extraordinary expenditures and for passing laws, the sovereign could veto any law. Until recently, Elizabeth's relationship with Parliament had been cordial, although during periods of warfare, it had rarely granted her all the funds she believed necessary.

Elizabeth's greatest successes had come in the area of foreign policy. Thanks to the navy that she had financed largely from the Crown's customary revenues, the country was as secure from invasion as it had ever been.

Fig. 2.1 Queen Elizabeth I in 1595 by Marcus Gheeraerts the Younger. The queen was the fifth and last ruler of the Tudor dynasty (Reproduced from Wikipedia Commons)

In 1588, all of Europe had been astounded by the surprise victory of her ships over the Armada of Philip II of Spain, albeit with considerable help from the weather in the North Sea. Though the Spanish sovereign Philip II had quickly built a new fleet, he had proved reluctant to risk it on a second invasion attempt in the years prior to his death in 1598.

Yet a more objective observer would admit that there was reason to be concerned. Diplomatically, in 1600 Elizabeth found herself isolated. She had lost a trusted ally in 1580, when Spanish *tercios* had invaded Portugal. The only compensation for English merchants was that the Portuguese fleet, now integrated into Spain's military machine, was no longer as powerful as it once had been. Another setback had occurred more recently in 1598, when Elizabeth's French protégé, Henry IV, had abandoned her. Although she had supported Henry in his war with the Catholic League, he had since arranged a separate peace treaty with Spain.

Unlike Portugal and Spain, England still had no overseas possessions. Sir Walter Raleigh's efforts to establish a colony in present-day Virginia in 1587 had proved a lamentable failure. At the end of the first season, the colony's leader had sailed to England to seek supplies. When he returned to America in 1590, the colonists had all disappeared, although their houses were still intact. Since then, England had been obliged to be content with allowing her privateers to raid the Spanish treasure fleets, with a share of the booty going into the royal coffers.

Elizabeth's one piece of empire was the island of Ireland, which the English were gradually reconquering after allowing it to fall into the hands of local lords and clans during the fifteenth century. Predominantly Catholic, the Irish had risen up once again in 1593 against their Protestant overlords. In an alliance of clans under Hugh O'Neill, Earl of Tyrone, they had the financial support of Spain. Elizabeth's most recent commander in Ireland, Robert Devereux, earl of Essex, was presently under house arrest in London after his refusal to remain in the Emerald Isle until it was pacified. Essex's successor, Charles Blount, Baron Mountjoy, now had the difficult task of retaking the territory, aided by a costly army of 18,000 men (Falls 1950, 405).

Indeed, Elizabeth's principal concerns during the last years of her reign were the public finances. After 18 years of war with Spain and some five million pounds of expenditures, the Crown was deeply in debt (Doran 2003, 129). Adding to the Queen's dilemma, an influx of Spanish silver had caused prices to rise, while the tax rates fixed by Parliament had not kept step. The fiscal situation was sufficiently desperate that to satisfy her creditors, the queen had recently agreed to sell the royal family's treasures. The gold whistle and chain of her father, Henry VIII, were auctioned off, along with a number of gold bracelets and jeweled crucifixes. The remaining baubles were dispatched to the mint to be melted into coins (Erickson 1983, 393).

The sale of Crown lands and monopoly rights provided an extra source of income to the government. Since the last parliament, patents had been issued for "currants, iron, powder, cards, ox shin-bones, train oil, oil of blubber, transportation of leather, cloth, ashes, aniseeds, sea-coals, saltpetre, lead, calamine stones, pilchards &c". However, the members of parliament increasingly objected to the resulting increases in prices for the consumers of these products (Black 1936, 192–193).

Petitioning for monopoly patents was not the only type of rent-seeking in Elizabethan England. The English civil service was notoriously corrupt.

In 1586, the surveyor of the ordnance accused three employees of embezzling over £7000 by billing the treasury for quantities of provisions only parts of which were actually received. Five years later, one of the three charged, William Painter, was accused of taking funds for gunpowder and bowstaves that were never delivered. After Painter's death, the steward of the Tower of London estimated that Painter and his son had defrauded the crown of £27,000. Few if any sanctions were imposed in these cases. It was probably realized that the accused were no more guilty than the accusers (Kelly 2004).

Duties on imports should have provided a steady source of income. However, because of endemic collusion between customs officials and importers, the net proceeds had proved disappointing (Peck 1993, 149–150). In 1568, the government had decided to auction the rights to collect customs to private individuals through a system of competitive bidding (Johnson and Koyama 2014, 9). Over the following decades, the farming out of customs collection by auction proved reliable, but there was a major drawback. In times of exceptional spending needs, the possibilities to borrow funds from wealthy merchants who profited from the farms were limited (Johnson and Koyama 2014, 9). In the 1590s, the Elizabethan government therefore abolished tax farming and returned to direct administration of the customs, using the flow of future funds as collateral for loans (Peck 1993, 149).

Economically, the country as a whole was not as well off in 1600 as it had been earlier in Elizabeth's reign. With agriculture still by far the most important sector, the deepening of the Little Ice Age with its cold winters and wet summers was causing considerable hardship. Indeed, four consecutive years of poor harvests during the "Famine Decade" of the 1590s resulted in violent bread riots in the north and west (Erickson 1983, 397). It is estimated that real per-capita income levels fell in the decades after 1570. In 1600, England's income level by this measure was lower than that of Italy and barely two-thirds that of the Netherlands (Maddison 2007, 382).

The structure of England's industrial sector reflected this relative backwardness. The country had a patent system to reward those who wished to produce new products. Although the Crown benefited from the extraparliamentary revenues that these grants brought, the resulting monopolies yielded little in the form of technological improvement. Import substitution rather than innovation was the name of the game. It was said that in 1564 an English apprentice borrowed a pair of worsted wool stockings from an Italian merchant and copied them. Soon there was a thriving stocking industry in southeast England. In 1567, a refugee from Antwerp set up a factory to produce glass, using Venetian workers. In 1574, the firm received a patent. Nevertheless, because of the backwardness of English industry, there was still a strong demand for imports from the Netherlands, France, and Venice. The profits of many London merchants came from selling plain English broadcloth and importing luxury goods and consumer products (Archer 2011, 412–413).

For half a century, England's overseas trade had been dominated by a few powerful syndicates. The Muscovy Company was founded as a joint stock company in 1555. Since the 1570s, however, relations with Russia had cooled. As a result, the merchants of the Company had lost their privileged access to the Russian interior. In 1578, Elizabeth sent an ambassador to the "Porte", the Ottoman Empire, in Constantinople. Under the "capitulations" or trading privileges he negotiated, the English merchants of the Levant Company, formed in 1581, were now trading in the eastern Mediterranean.

One issue that the queen refused to consider in 1600 was her eventual succession. Although childless, never having married, she was still in good health. Unknown to Elizabeth however, her councilor, Robert Cecil, had entered into secret correspondence with James VI of Scotland, the son of her distant cousin Mary, whom she had executed in 1587 (Erickson 1983, 398). While the conditions for the transfer were being negotiated, James continued his polite public correspondence with Elizabeth, who refused to discuss her succession publicly (Doran 2006, 39–40).

Awaiting the death of his royal cousin, James considered the project of uniting England and Scotland—no easy task. Cut off from or abandoned by traditional allies, at war with Europe's most powerful empire, the two kingdoms would have to manage on their own. After almost a century of bitter internal conflict, largely over religious issues, it remained to be seen whether Elizabeth I's English subjects could cooperate sufficiently with one another and with their Scottish neighbors to pursue the ambitious plans of their sovereign's likely successor.

One additional attempt to help finance the English public deficit deserves mention. The decline of Portuguese power in the East, mentioned above, provided a new opportunity for traders from the Netherlands, France and England. On the last day of the year 1600, Elizabeth sold a charter for yet another monopoly—for a trading company, "The Governor and Company of Merchants of London trading into the East Indies" (see Fig. 2.2). Known more simply as the East India Company, the group was given a monopoly

38 2 1600: THE DYNASTIC CYCLE

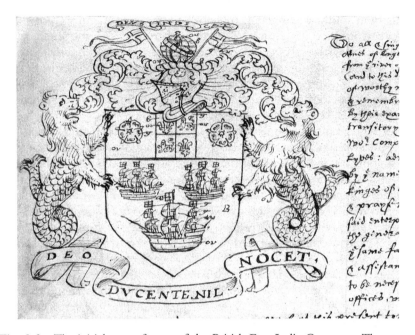

Fig. 2.2 The initial coat of arms of the British East India Company. The motto "Deo ducente nil nocet" may be translated as "If God leads, nothing can harm us." Granted a trading charter in 1600 by Queen Elizabeth I, the commercial firm by 1850 would control territory that accounted for a fifth of the world's population (College of Arms, MS I. 9 f. 84r. Reproduced by permission of the Kings, Heralds and Pursuivants of Arms)

for 15 years over all English trade east of the Cape of Good Hope and west of the Strait of Magellan (MacMillan 2011, 660). The merchants hoped that their venture would be as profitable as those of the Portuguese and Dutch who had preceded them.

2.3 Mehmed III

As the seventeenth century began, the structure of power within the Ottoman Empire was undergoing a major transformation. On 1 April 1600, there was a revolt of cavalry soldiers who objected to being paid with debased coins. It was rumored that the coins had come from the tax farm of Esperanza Malchi, a Jewish woman who served as economic agent or *kira* for the mother of Sultan Mehmed III (r. 1595–1603). The Valide Sultan Safiye herself, secluded within the imperial harem, could not engage in such activities. Ms. Malchi's tax farm or *iltizam* was structured as follows: in return for the right to collect streams of indirect tax revenues from certain territories, she was required to pay a fixed amount annually to the imperial treasury. Such rights were generally sold periodically to the highest bidder by auction (Cizakca 2013, 254). Blaming Ms. Malchi for the effective cut in their wages implied by the reduction in the currency's silver content, the soldiers seized her and one of her sons and stabbed them to death. Her other son saved his life only by suddenly converting from Judaism to Islam and promising to repay the soldiers' debts to the treasury (Tezcan 2010, 188).

Undisciplined troops were not the only problem the Ottoman regime was facing in the year 1600. It had become evident to many that the empire's armed forces were no longer able to dominate the armies of their rivals as easily as they had done in the past. For nine years, the Ottoman army had been fighting the Austrian Habsburgs for control of lands in present-day Rumania, Croatia and Hungary. In 1596, after a series of Austrian victories, the sultan had agreed to command the army personally. On 25 October, he had been present at the Battle of Keresztes in southwestern Hungary. After the first day of fighting, the sultan had seen enough and wished to retire with his army. However, on the second day, having been convinced by his former tutor to stay, Mehmed III witnessed a last-chance push by the Ottoman forces that broke the Austrian attack (Karateke 2012, 120). In the following years, as the war dragged on, the sultan was content to remain in Istanbul. Indeed, it was becoming exceptional for the sultans to campaign with their troops, as most of their illustrious predecessors had done.

As the new century began, the Ottoman regime was also fighting a revolt by irregular troops (*sebkan*) in eastern Anatolia. They had been left with no source of income after the conclusion of a war with Persia ten years earlier. Under an ambitious leader, Karayazici Abdülhalim, the rebels were attempting to set up a separate autonomous kingdom. They were known as *Jelali*, after Celâl, the name of the leader of a similar earlier uprising.

Five years before, in 1595, Ottoman traditions had prevented a possible civil war when on the death of his father, Mehmed III had ascended to the throne at age 28. Crowds outside the gates of the Topkapi Palace in Istanbul had observed the funeral convoy as it left the palace grounds, observing that the late sultan's coffin was followed by those of his 19 other sons. On the orders of the new sultan, all of Mehmed III's brothers and half-brothers had been strangled by the palace's deaf-mute eunuch servants (Inalcik 1973, 60). Some 21 years earlier, Mehmed III's five uncles had all been executed in similar fashion when his father had assumed the throne (Inalcik 1973, 60). This tradition dated back to the reign of the conqueror of Byzantium, Mehmed II (r. 1444–1446, 1451–1481). In order to avoid a war of succession, as soon as he was assured of a male heir, the sultan had ordered that his five surviving brothers be strangled by a silken cord (Dash 2012).

As the seventeenth century began, the institutions of governance of the Ottoman Empire were in a phase of transition. Mehmed III was the last sultan to execute his siblings on accession to the throne. At the insistence of high officials, Mehmed III's son, Ahmed I (r. 1603–1617), would spare his brother Mustafa on becoming sultan (Inalcik 1973, 60). Subsequently, the oldest living male of the imperial lineage would become sultan on his predecessor's death (Goodwin 1998, 168). Mehmed III was also the last ruler to have had children as a prince. Thereafter under the "gilded cage" or *kafes* system, the reigning sultan's siblings and children were kept alive within the palace grounds but were not allowed to have children. Mehmed III was also the last sovereign to have had experience as a prince in governing a province. The children of his successors rarely received any preparation for their royal duties (Quaetert 2005, 92). Indeed, from the seventeenth century on, the sultans rarely initiated policy; rather, they served to legitimize the policies of the grand viziers, their chief ministers (Quaetert 2005, 34).

In the traditional Ottoman military-fiscal system, there were two basic institutions: namely, slavery and the *timar*. The *kul* (slave), the counterpart of the European serf, was the basis of both the Ottoman bureaucracy and its elite infantry, the Janissaries. As under European feudalism, this institution consisted of individuals whose freedom of movement was restricted by custom. In the empire's European territories, however, slavery developed into something quite unique. From the reign of Murad II (r. 1421–1451), boys of 8–18 years of age were recruited by force from the Christian population of Greece and the Balkans. Brought to the capital, the young men were converted to Islam, circumcised and taught Turkish. Each was then trained according to his abilities. The more promising were educated within the royal palace to fill positions of responsibility. Those less cultivated were enrolled in the infantry regiments of Janissaries (Goodwin 1998, 67–68). Under this *devşirme* or boy-slave system, the young men from the periphery were in effect brought to the center for conversion and then sent back out to administer the provinces and extend the state's boundaries—the whole in effect financed by the taxes levied on their families and neighbors.

With the passage from the sixteenth to seventeenth centuries, the Ottoman Empire experienced a shock in the form of accelerated innovation in military technology. Originally, the Janissaries had been armed with composite bows. However, to compete with European soldiers bearing firearms, it now became necessary to equip the Janissaries with muskets. Moreover as the size of opposing European armies increased, it was essential to recruit additional soldiers for the infantry ranks. From 16,905 in 1583, the number of Janissaries on the central treasury accounts increased to 37,627 in 1609 (Tezcan 2010, 177). However, thereafter, instead of expanding the *devşirme* program, the regime began to recruit native Turks. In addition, the state began to hire as irregular infantry young landless villagers who were able to master firearms. After 1590, it was these provincial units rather than the Janissaries who were the most effective foot soldiers in the Ottoman army (Inalcik 1973, 48). Meanwhile, increasing numbers of Janissaries entered into commerce with funds borrowed from their military units (Tezcan 2010, 206).

Change also came to the cavalry. As a feudal military class, the *sipâhîs* considered firearms to be demeaning. However, armed only with bows and arrows and protected by light shields, these traditional horsemen proved vulnerable to European infantry bearing pikes and muskets. Accordingly, the number of *sipâhîs* was reduced, from over 87,000 in the days of Sûleymân the Magnificent (r. 1520–1566) in the middle of the sixteenth century to only 45,000 in 1609 (Inalcik 1973, 48). Instead, irregular cavalry units, *sarica*, bearing firearms were formed (Inalcik 1973, 48).

Although the increase in the size of the army in the last decades of the sixteenth century is usually justified by reference to the needs of warfare, some additional factor is needed to explain the observed troop growth. Only about half of the Janissaries on the payroll of the central army in 1599 can be accounted for on the battle field. Similarly, while the number of *sipâhîs* in active service fell between 1583 and 1609, the number of central cavalry troops on the government registers rose from 8349 to 20,869. As for armorers, their number rose even more rapidly, from 1382 to 5730 over the same period (Tezcan 2010, 177–178).

The most likely explanation for this remarkable expansion of the size of the military at the end of the sixteenth century is rent-seeking on the part of Ottoman bureaucrats (Tezcan 2010, 182). In their rivalries with one another, individual viziers had an incentive to build up a power base of clients while at the same time profiting from the bribes that these men paid for the concessions they received. These appointees and their colleagues became an important interest group in the capital. As we saw earlier, the cavalry soldiers revolted in 1600 over the debasement of the coinage with which they had been paid. Five years earlier, they had rebelled to support a candidate they favored to become grand vizier. If this rent-seeking argument is correct, there was often a strong element of bias in the advice of a vizier in favor of war. The additional spending sanctioned in wartime allowed the viziers to enrich themselves while building up a network of supporters.

The *sipâhîs* were not the only military corps to intervene in the political process. In 1591, the Janissaries had attacked the brother of one of the prominent men in the Ottoman court. Two years later their support was instrumental in securing the appointment of the man who was named grand vizier. In 1595, the Janissaries helped their favorite keep his position by putting down the revolt of the cavalry mentioned earlier in support of another candidate (Tezcan 2010, 184). According to one observer, the cavalrymen who caused the trouble had been appointed because of their political connections rather than their military skills (Tezcan 2010, 183).

The second of the two basic Ottoman institutions mentioned earlier was the *timar*, the approximate equivalent of the fief in medieval Europe (Inalcik 1973, 47). Under Western feudalism, the fief was a certain area of land granted to a noble in exchange for a promise of military service. The Ottoman timar was similar except that the land title remained with the Sultan. The timariot was simply allowed to retain some of the tax revenue that he collected in the Sultan's name. The holder of the timar was generally a *sipâhî*, a cavalry soldier (Goodwin 1998, 67–68).

The *sipâhîs* had played an important role in the Ottoman fiscal system. With no access to cash, the medieval peasant had been obliged to pay his principal tax, the tithe, in kind. Instead of selling the rights to tax collection in a village to a tax farmer in return for cash, the Ottomans had assigned properties to individual *sipâhîs* who received wagonloads of hay, payments in kind, in lieu of a salary (Inalcik 1973, 107). As a resident of the village, the *sipâhî* could assure that taxes were paid while at the same time maintaining his horse easily from the payments he received.

The slave and timar structure could not be expanded without limit. Inevitably, ordinary tax-paying Turkish subjects infiltrated the Janissaries, preferring the career of salaried soldier to that of agricultural laborer

(Inalcik 1973, 48). A similar trend occurred in the central bureaucracy, as Turks were recruited for administrative positions. Monetization of the economy accelerated these changes by making it easier for individuals to capture the rents of the state. A first phase of monetization had come during the fifteenth century when the Ottomans established a single currency, the *akçe*, within their territory in Europe and Anatolia (Tezcan 2010, 89). A second phase began in the late fifteenth century and continued throughout the sixteenth century as tax levies in kind were converted into cash payments (Tezcan 2010, 21). The resulting flow of funds, first from taxpayers to tax collectors and then from the latter to the imperial treasury, constituted a tempting target for the various rent-seeking groups in Ottoman society.

As the Ottoman economy became increasingly monetized during the sixteenth century, it came to be accepted that the rights to a timar be transferable. As a result, it became possible for non-nobles to buy entry into the gentry, the *askeri* class (Tezcan 2010, 186). In the cities and towns, meanwhile, tax farming of indirect taxes continued to be a major source of central-government revenues (Cizakca 2013, 248). By the early seventeenth century, tax farmers included administrative and military personnel, religious functionaries, private entrepreneurs, members of tribal and non-Muslim groups such as the Malchi family, local elites and slaves (Ursinus 2012, 425). Because the regime agreed to "freeze" the nominal annual monetary payments, the yield from these farms was failing to keep up with prices (Cizakca 2013, 254).

Whether primarily because of war or because of rent-seeking, government spending needs were rising rapidly as the seventeenth century began. Inflation caused by an inflow of silver from the Americas was only part of the problem. Over the period from 1575 to 1605, the cost of a basket of goods rose at 1.9 percent per year in terms of silver on average, but at 7.5 percent annually in terms of the *akçe*, due to counterfeiting and clipping of the coinage (Ursinus 2012, 424). As Şevket Pamuk (2000, 131–142) has explained, after 1585 currency debasement was a useful Ottoman policy instrument, especially in periods of war. However, debasement alone was not sufficient to cover the great increase in cash that the Ottoman government required to finance its military arm. Accordingly, the poll tax on non-Muslims, the *cizye*, rose more than fourfold. In addition, the extraordinary taxes, *avariz*, were converted into regular annual cash payments, the amount levied on each taxpayer being increased frequently (Inalcik 1973, 50). In periods of war, Ottoman officials had access to a supplementary source of funds. In normal times, the regime's funds came from the *outer* treasury, made up of receipts from the central provinces plus contributions from the peripheral provinces. However, in times of war, the officials also had access to the sultan's *inner* treasury consisting of revenues from the sultan's personal demesne, namely, Egypt (Tezcan 2010, 182).

In short, as the seventeenth century began, the Ottoman Empire was reaching the limits to the territory it could control with the resources at its disposal. The tax system that had financed the empire's rapid expansion was beginning to buckle under the current strain. However, it will be remembered that the state's predecessor, the Byzantine Empire, centered on the virtually impregnable banks of the Golden Horn, had endured for eight centuries after reaching its peak. Farther east, moreover, another empire seemed to have escaped such fiscal problems—at least for the moment.

2.4 Akbar

The Mughal emperor had long coveted the wealthy Portuguese enclave of Goa on the southwest coast of India (Smith 1917, 262). Lacking a navy capable of challenging the heavily armed Portuguese ships, Akbar (r. 1556–1605) realized that he had to approach the port overland from the interior. To do so, however, he would first have to control the approaches to southern India via the Sultanate of Ahmadnagar. This state in the northwest corner of the Deccan, the triangular plateau that covers most of southern Indian, controlled the main route between the north and the south of the subcontinent. However, in 1596 to the emperor's frustration, the ruler of Ahmadnagar had refused to pay homage to the imperial throne. There was no alternative but to use force.

Akbar, 57 years of age in the spring of the year 1600, was no stranger to the application of military force. He was the grandson of Babur, the Turco-Afghan leader who had invaded northern India from Afghanistan in 1526 in response to a request for help from a local ruler and then decided to stay. It was Babur, a descendant of the Turco-Mongol conqueror Tamerlane, who with the help of recruited Turkish gunners had introduced gunpowder technology to the Indian subcontinent. Babur's son, Humayun (Akbar's father), had managed first to lose then regain this territory before accidentally killing himself in a fall at his palace in Delhi in 1556. At the age of 13, Akbar had suddenly inherited an empire spanning northern India, Pakistan and Afghanistan. He had then spent the following half century expanding his domain to cover all but the southern third of the subcontinent. Like his father and grandfather, Akbar had learned to combine the rapidity of cavalry with the firepower of infantry armed with matchlock muskets and supported by artillery (Keay 2000, 291).

On campaign, Akbar traveled with a force that could number 100,000 men, including 50,000 cavalry, with 500 war elephants and 28 field guns. In order to remain mobile, he did not have a siege train (Richards 1993, 43). Against a force of this size, Bahadur Nizam Shah, the ruler of Ahmadnagar, counted on the safety of his fortress of Asirgarh, 2300 feet (700 m) above sea level and 600 feet (180 m) higher than the surrounding plain. The site was protected by inaccessible cliffs over 80 feet (25 m) high (Smith 1917, 272–273). It was well stocked with food, arms and ammunition and had plentiful supplies of fresh water. Moreover, the rocky terrain prevented an attacker from undermining its walls (Smith 1917, 272–273). When Akbar arrived under the fort in April 1600, he had no alternative but to order his men to dig trenches and begin the long wait for the garrison to surrender. Then in July, with little progress having been made in the siege, Akbar received word that his eldest surviving son, who would reign as Jahangir, had revolted and was moving to attack the imperial capital at Agra.

For the first four years of his reign, Akbar had submitted to the decisions of his father's top general. However, in 1561 he had assumed full power and set about reorganizing his state. Instead of appointing a single chief minister, he divided power among four officials who held responsibility for military, financial, household and religious matters, respectively (Richards 1993, 15). The key to Akbar's power was the strength of his army. He personally commanded 7000 armed cavalrymen or *sowars* and 80,000 gunners and infantrymen. However, the emperor's main military support came from some 200 noble amirs, divided approximately equally among four groups: Shiite Persians, central-Asian Sunni Muslims, Indian Muslims and upper-caste Indian Hindus (Richards 1993, 19–21). Below them in the hierarchy came a new group of regional leaders created by Akbar, namely, some 2000 imperial servants, *mansabdars*, appointed from the dominant castes and rotated periodically. Every amir and high-ranking mansabdar had his own household troop contingent that could number from several hundred to several thousand men (Richards 1993, 80). In addition, each noble was assigned a certain number of cavalrymen, *sowars*, that he was required to supply to the imperial army (Keay 2000, 324). Together the amirs and mansabdars could command from 150,000 to 200,000 cavalrymen. In addition, at the local level, *zamindars* or lineage heads could gather a total of almost five million retainers, most of them infantrymen (Keay 2000, 325).

The glue that held this vast empire together was not religion, language or ethnic group. Rather, it was loyalty to a dynasty (Metcalf and Metcalf 2006, 17). In return for their submission to the Timurids—Akbar's lineage—his officials received generous compensation. As for ordinary subjects, in exchange for their heavy taxes, they at least benefited from long years of peace and political stability. Under the Mughal regime, trade expanded and the population increased, approaching 150 million by the end of the sixteenth century (Richards 1993, 190). Moreover, during Akbar's reign, India's annual per-capita income reached a peak of 682 international dollars of 1990, a level that would not be exceeded before the twentieth-first century (Broadberry et al. 2014, 36).

To provide support for the mansabdars and their households, Akbar assigned to each mansabdar the revenues from a *jagir*, an allotment of land. A jagir might consist of a portion of the lands in a single village or several villages. In a typical village, the yield of a part of the land might be assigned to a noble, another part to the emperor and a third section to a mosque or temple (Keay 2000, 321). However, the grant was only for fiscal rights; ownership remained with the emperor. In order to prevent any long-term attachment of the mansabdars to their land, the finance ministry could transfer them from one region to another as frequently as every two or three years (Richards 1993, 66–67). Consequently, the landholders had little reason to invest in rural infrastructure and every incentive to extract the maximum of the peasants' surplus.

The senior officers of the central administration were either amirs or higher-ranking mansabdars. The same level of officials occupied the positions of provincial governors or senior administrative positions across the empire (Richards 1993, 59). Below them were clerks—accountants recruited from the upper Hindu castes. As the language of the Mughal administration was Persian, written with Perso-Arabic script, the Hindu clerks and secretaries were required to be proficient in this language. Training their young men in Persian terminology and accounting methods, certain families and clans came to monopolize these inferior but highly valued positions (Richards 1993, 71).

The Mughal state itself was an immense fiscal bureaucracy whose main purpose was to finance the military establishment. In streamlining the imperial administration, Akbar's objective was to maximize tax revenues while leaving his subjects with enough food to survive and reproduce. It was therefore essential to retain the support of the majority non-Muslim population. Accordingly, in 1579 he abolished the *jizya*, the special tax on the *dhimmis*, the non-Muslims (Richards 1993, 39). The following year, his finance minister Raja Toda Mal began a five-year period of surveys in order to calculate new assessments for each crop, each region and each soil quality. The result was a great increase in revenues, the reforms enabling the state to seize a third of all grain production and a fifth of other crops (Keay 2000, 325–326).

Of the total imperial revenues of some 100 million silver rupees in 1595–1596, over 80 percent was allocated to the amirs and mansabdars to finance their cavalry and musketeer contingents. A further 10 percent was allocated to the emperor's central military establishment. Less than five percent of the total budget was used to finance the lavish spending of the imperial household. In the last years of Akbar's reign, the state ran an annual surplus of four to five million rupees (Richards 1993, 75).

The revenue system put together by Akbar enabled him to tax his subjects effectively while at the same time paying his soldiers regularly as they pushed the borders of the empire outward. When he died in 1605, he left a treasury with silver and gold valued at over 139 million silver rupees and perhaps the same value of precious stones (Richards 1993, 75). At today's prices, the coinage alone would be worth almost one billion dollars.[1]

As the components of the new military-fiscal structure snapped into place, the emperor used them to augment his territory. For two decades after assuming power, he maneuvered to integrate the Hindu rajput clans that ruled the kingdoms of Rajasthan, the province to the southwest of Delhi, into his empire. In exchange for military support, Akbar granted each raj his ancestral lands as a nontransferable holding (Richards 1993, 21). Next on the emperor's list of targets was Gujarat, the rich agricultural, industrial and commercial kingdom along the northwest coast. By 1573, this region had been annexed and any hostile local rulers pushed out (Richards 1993, 32). The rulers of the eastern provinces of Bihar and Bengal proved more difficult to overcome. Only in 1585, after five years of combat, were the imperial commanders able to chase the last of the rebels from western Bengal (Richards 1993, 40–41). Over the following decade, Akbar sent his armies into the northwest, subduing Kabul, Kashmir, the Sind and Kandahar. Of all the regions in the subcontinent, only the Deccan, the southern triangle, remained to be conquered.

It should be noted that most of the imperial military and fiscal administration was in a sense subcontracted out in decentralized fashion. In order to supply both the soldiers that composed the bulk of the emperor's army and the revenues required to finance his own household and personal troops,

Akbar depended on the compliance of some 2000 individual landholders, each with his own dynastic interests (Keay 2000, 324). The incentives to back the regime were of course not all positive. Should a regional leader decide to withdraw his support for the emperor, punishment was swift and severe.

In the case of Bahadur Nizam Shah, the ruler of the Ahmadnagar Sultanate who had refused to pay homage, the arrival of the emperor and his army in the spring of 1600 signaled that there was a price to be paid. The fortress of the city of Ahmednagar was stormed in August 1600, and 1500 men of the garrison put to the sword (Smith 1917, 272). However, the garrison of the virtually impregnable fortress of Asirgarh had refused to surrender. Meanwhile, as mentioned, the emperor learned that his son, the future emperor Jahangir, had revolted and was threatening to seize the fortifications of the imperial capital of Agra. With more important worries than the siege of an isolated fortress on the edge of his empire, Akbar began negotiations with the garrison. In January of the following year, the fortress surrendered and the garrison was spared. However, the captured ruler and his family would spend the rest of their lives in an imperial prison (Smith 1917, 283).

Meanwhile, to the east, another emperor was also involved in a succession dispute.

2.5 The Wanli Emperor

It was in the year 1600 that the break in governance occurred. For almost two decades, the Wanli Emperor (r. 1572–1620), 37, had dutifully participated in the daily council meetings. Then one morning he refused to attend, instead letting his senior eunuchs represent him. As the weeks and months passed, he rarely met with the officials who governed his vast empire. In previous years, Wanli had usually accepted the recommendations of the senior functionaries who formed his council. Upon occasion, however, he had stubbornly insisted on having his own way, particularly when the subject concerned his favorite concubine. Lady Z was an ambitious young woman who very much desired to have her young son by Wanli come to the throne. The problem was that the emperor already had an older son by his first consort.

Wanli had spent all of his life in the Forbidden City. His father and predecessor, the Longqing Emperor, had died in 1572, when he was nine years old. Over the following decade, a capable official, Zhang Juzheng, who had been his father's chief minister, led the Chinese state. Upon Zhang's death in 1582, Wanli had assumed personal control of the government. During these last years of the sixteenth century, the Ming state was at its peak. Its population—some 160 million people—had grown by over 50 percent over the previous century, although its per-capita income had remained approximately constant (Maddison 2007, 376, 382).

Most Western scholars consider the Ming regime to have been an autocracy (Brook 2013, 87). Power was highly centralized in the imperial capital, where the emperor in theory had the final say. However, in practice there were strong constraints upon Wanli's authority. One such limit was the tradition of succession by the emperor's eldest son. When Wanli's ministers first heard of the emperor's wish to have Lady Zheng's son follow him to the throne, they strongly objected. The emperor, they argued, was "the foundation of the state". Consequently, his legitimacy would be questioned if the correct ritual order were not followed. It was only after years of struggle that the emperor had caved in, agreeing to accept the tradition of having his own first-born son succeed him. Unfortunately, the quarrel left Wanli bitter with the whole process of government. For the last 20 years of his life, he would withdraw into the inner spaces of the Forbidden City, refusing to attend the sessions of court (Brook 2013, 102).

The guiding philosophy of Chinese society in the latter half of the Ming dynasty was the Teaching of the Way, which Western observers refer to as Neo-Confucianism (Brook 2013, 162). The precepts of Confucius, the fifth-century BCE sage, had been repackaged by the thinkers of the Tang and Song dynasties more than a millennium after his death. They had eliminated many of the mystical and superstitious elements that had crept into Confucian thought in order to yield a more rational and secular ethical code. Unlike Christians, Neo-Confucian writers such as Zhu Xi (1130–1200), author of *The Family Rituals*, did not believe in a divine creator. Rather for them, all things result from the interaction of vital force and rational principle. The emphasis was not on an afterlife but on the present life. Accordingly, ancestors were not to be worshiped but rather to be gratefully remembered.

Finally, the basic social unit was not the individual but the family or lineage. Avner Greif and Guido Tabellini (2010) have argued that cooperation in Chinese society was limited largely to such lineages or clans. As Richard von Glahn (2016, 300–301) observed, there was a transition in the nature of such lineages in the late Middle Ages with the formation of localized corporate lineages. As manufacturing and trade expanded, the family unit became too small to supply the necessary capital and personnel. An important step came early in the sixteenth century, when the Ming state allowed lineage trusts to build ancestral halls that became centers of group social life. Nevertheless, in China by the late sixteenth century, the boundaries of the group within which an individual was willing to cooperate were more limited than in the growing towns and cities of contemporary Europe. In the West, it was the urban region rather than the lineage that defined the limits of social interaction.

The most important lineage in China was that of the emperor, for he was the foundation of society, the guarantor of legitimacy. Consequently, Wanli's withdrawal into the inner palace disrupted the governance of the empire. Henceforth, he could be contacted only through the powerful eunuchs who served him personally. Until its twenty-eighth year, the Wanli Emperor's reign had gone reasonably well. He had been able to retain the support of the three principal interest groups in the imperial government without letting any one of them become too powerful. One of these groups was made up of civil servants, men who were rigorously selected from all social classes and all regions under a strict quota system. As explained in Sect. 4.4, candidates had to pass a rigorous set of exams based on knowledge of the classic texts.

Another powerful interest group in Chinese society was made up of eunuchs. For centuries, male servants in the Forbidden City had been castrated in order to prevent any threat to the imperial lineage. The Hongwu Emperor, founder of the Ming dynasty, had specified that eunuchs were not to be taught to read and were not to be allowed to participate in policy-making. However, by the time of Wanli, with these restrictions long forgotten, the eunuchs constituted what was in effect a second bureaucracy. The 10,000 eunuchs in the capital had their own school and were deeply involved in matters of civil and military administration. Another 60,000 eunuchs held positions in the provinces (Ebrey 1996, 194).

Ultimately, however, the positions of the emperor and his officials depended on the capacity of a third interest group—the army—that not only had to protect the borders from hostile invaders but also was responsible for putting down internal revolts. In the fourteenth century, the Hongwu Emperor had set up a structure of self-sufficient military units made up of hereditary farmer-soldiers. Unfortunately, as these soldiers lacked incentives to farm their allotments, many subsequently deserted, selling their lands. With the collapse of this system around 1430, the Ming government had been obliged to form professional volunteer armies and bear the resulting fiscal burden (Dreyer 1988, 105). To do so, under reforms known as the "Single Whip", China in the sixteenth century had gradually converted taxation in kind to monetary payments (Brook 2013, 119–121).

During the first two decades of Wanli's reign, the army had successfully filled its two roles. Between 1593 and 1598, it had been able to block attempted invasions of Korea by the forces of the Japanese regent, Hideyoshi. With this threat removed, Wanli could turn his attention to a revolt of tribesmen under a certain Yang Yinglong on the southwest border. Despite an initial defeat, the imperial forces were eventually successful.

At the turn of the seventeenth century, however, there was a threatening cloud forming on the horizon to the northeast, on the border of present-day Manchuria, homeland of the Jurchen people. Two decades earlier, China's regional general on the northern border, Li Chengliang, had been challenged by an alliance of Jurchens and Mongols that threatened Beijing. Chinese policy had been to form alliances with some Jurchen tribes to offset the power of other more powerful groups. In 1582, while attacking the fort of a Jurchen rebel leader at Mount Gure in southeastern Manchuria, Li Chengliang's forces had killed two Jurchen leaders who had previously been allies of the Chinese.

The two men, Giocangga and Taksi, were the grandfather and father respectfully of a tall, young Jurchen warrior by the name of Nurhaci (Crossley 1997, ch. 3). The following year, with the support of Li Chengliang, Nurhaci had begun a long campaign to unite the Jurchen tribes of Manchuria under his leadership. For administrative and military purposes, he regrouped the clans into companies, *niru*, each composed of some 300 households. These groups were generally families of the same extended lineage or several lineages from the same village. In 1601, these Manchu companies were grouped into four banners or *gusa* symbolized by the colors of the standards under which their warriors fought in battle—yellow, white, red and blue. As new groups joined the Jurchen state, the number of companies and banners was expanded. In 1615, there were already eight Manchu banners, and in 1642 there were 24 banners in all—eight Manchu, eight Mongol and eight Han Chinese (Elliott 2001, 59). The number of companies increased from 201 in 1616 to 419 in 1635 (Elliott 2001, 63).

In 1599, while this reorganization effort was still in progress, Nurhaci directed two of his literate followers to create a writing system for the Jurchen language, adapted from the Mongolian phonetic alphabet (Crossley 1997, ch. 2). United, with their own national written language, the people of Manchuria would offer Wanli's descendants one of the greatest challenges that China's leaders had ever experienced.

It was during Wanli's reign than another potential threat to Chinese civilization appeared—this time in the form of Christian missionaries. In 1582, Matteo Ricci, a 30-year-old Jesuit priest of Italian origin arrived in the Portuguese trading post of Macau in southeastern China (Ebrey 1996, 212). Immediately he began to learn to speak the Chinese language. The following year, Ricci received an invitation from the governor of the city of Zhaoqing, 100 km upstream from Guangzhou (Canton) on the Pearl River. The Chinese elite were impressed by Ricci's skills in mathematics and cartography. In Zhaoqing, he prepared the first Western-style map of the world in Chinese. With a colleague, he also developed a system for transcribing Chinese text into Roman characters. Ricci continued his missionary activity in the south over the next decade and a half, becoming head of the Jesuit mission in China in 1597. However, by 1600, the Christians had still not been officially recognized in Beijing, the Chinese capital.

The original Ming fiscal-military system set up by the Hongwu Emperor in the late fourteenth century was based on taxes in kind and services, along with a largely self-sufficient army of soldier-farmers (Huang 1998, 168). Spending was to be centrally allocated but taxes were to be collected locally (Huang 1998, 107). However, the technologies of transportation and communication of the day were inadequate for such a centralized command society. For example, there was never a complete census of economy's agricultural resources (Huang 1974, 313). Consequently, when the dynasty's third ruler, the Yongle Emperor (r. 1402–1424), moved the capital from Nanjing to Beijing and decided to raise public spending rapidly, it was necessary to graft a set of surcharges and arbitrary requisitions onto the system, while basic tax rates remained unchanged (Huang 1998, 108). Moreover, since soldiers in practice were unable or unwilling to grow their own food, it proved necessary to pay them a salary. In addition, because no provision had been made for adequate salaries for public officials, the latter had to demand "gifts" of money from the citizens that they served in order to survive. Inevitably, tax collectors who were many hundreds of miles (km) distant from the administrators in the capital were able to supplement their incomes at low risk (Huang 1998, 160).

By far the largest part of China's state revenues came from taxes on agricultural production, at rates that were initially set very low and subsequently proved difficult to change. In 1578, the land tax accounted for almost 85 percent of total state revenues (Huang 1974, 177). Cash income from a state monopoly on salt production represented another four percent of public receipts (Huang 1974, 214). However, excise taxes on internal and external trade amounted to only slightly more than one percent of total revenues (Huang 1974, 263). On the whole, then, the tax system was extremely inflexible and difficult to adjust to the needs of financing a large professional army equipped with expensive gunpowder weapons.

With the capital moved to Beijing and the defense forces stationed along the Mongolian and Manchurian borders, it became obvious that northern China would no longer be able to feed itself. Since the state was unable to commandeer sufficient resources to fill this regional food deficit, the private sector would have to play a major role, supplying grain in return for cash payments. Already in the fifteenth century, the state had started collecting some taxes in silver (Huang 1998, 156). In the 1570s, under the Single Whip policy, chief minister Zhang Juzheng, decreed that all tax payments be converted to units of silver (Huang 1998, 163). However, since the regime never did set up a central treasury, it was left to local officials to implement the directive without any central coordination. During the process of converting locally administered labor services into silver payments to the state, there was wide-scale tax avoidance and tax evasion, to the benefit of the local gentry (Huang 1974, 97). However, the conversion was never completed: many payments continued to be specified in units of grain or days of labor service. Meanwhile the imperial government began a program of austerity that reduced the number of soldiers on the northern border (Huang 1998, 162). As a result, by 1587, there were bullion reserves equal to six months of government spending. However, the withdrawal of this amount of cash from circulation caused a depression in the rural economy (Huang 1998, 162–163).

Was the Ming economy over-taxed? Huang (1998, 166) estimated that total taxation of agriculture never exceeded ten percent of production. Moreover, as mentioned, only a small part of total revenues came from taxes on commerce (Huang 1998, 168). The total tax share of income had been much higher under the Song (Huang 1974, 316). Fortunately, for its first two centuries, Ming China was never faced with a serious threat, either external or internal. As a result, there was little pressure to improve the efficiency of the imperial public service, the local tax collection agencies or the armed forces. However, in the 1590s, together, the Japanese invasion of Korea and the Yang Yinglong revolt in the south were sufficient to deplete the empire's reserves. By the early seventeenth century, the state was virtually bankrupt (Huang 1998, 164).

2.6   Whither the Dynastic Cycle?

In the year 1600, we have seen, the symptoms of progressive decline were evident in the autocratic regimes that ruled over England, the Ottoman Empire, India and China. Their problems were not only dynastic but also military and fiscal.

In each state, the customary rule for succession was questioned; in addition, powerful internal interest groups opposed the sovereign's power. The current English sovereign, Elizabeth I, aged 67, was childless. Although negotiations were underway for her distant relative, King James VI of Scotland, to succeed to the English throne, there was no guarantee that the new dynasty would meet popular acceptance. Another threat came from the elected lower house of the legislature, due to its increasing reluctance to approve the Crown's tactics for raising revenue by the grant of monopoly rights. Meanwhile, in the Ottoman Empire, it had become clear that the sultan would henceforth reign rather than rule. Power would be held by those factions within the palace bureaucracy that could command the support of the imperial family and the Janissaries. As for India, although the Mughal dynasty was firmly established under Akbar in the year 1600, the threat of contested successions by the rulers' sons constituted a grave potential weakness. In China in the same year, the Wanli emperor virtually abdicated after a dispute over the naming of his heir, leaving the administration of the empire to his quarreling eunuchs and mandarins.

Militarily, each of these four states had a tenuous hold over its acquired territory, being threatened from both within and without. England had successfully resisted Spanish invasion in 1588. However, the two countries were still at war, and Spain was helping to finance a rebellion in the Tudors' one piece of empire—Ireland. In Eastern Europe, the Ottoman military were beginning to fall behind in the technology race with their Christian rivals. Only by dint of their superior numbers were they able to hold their own in the Long War with Austria while at the same time dealing with a revolt by irregular troops in Anatolia. Meanwhile, the Mughal dynasty that controlled northern India, Pakistan and Afghanistan was experiencing great difficulty in penetrating into the Deccan. In the Far East, Ming armies had managed to block a Japanese invasion of Korea and had put down a revolt in the southwest. However, the recent unification of the Manchurian tribes under a charismatic leader posed a grave threat.

Ultimately, the health of an autocratic state is reflected in the magnitude of its fiscal surplus or deficit. In England, revenues from publicly administered customs, the sale of public lands and the granting of monopoly rights were insufficient to finance military spending. By the last years of Elizabeth's reign, the monarchy was heavily in debt. In the Ottoman Empire, the shift from a feudal force to a professional army had placed great strain on the state treasury. By replacing timars (fiefs granted to cavalrymen) with tax farms while dipping into the sultan's inner treasury, the regime had been able to finance its military campaigns. Nevertheless, revenue from traditional sources was stagnating while, due to rent-seeking, the number of salaried cavalrymen and Janissaries was growing rapidly. In India, a series of fiscal reforms by Akbar's ministers, including a change to monetary tax payments, had allowed the Mughals to accumulate budget surpluses. However, there was a long-term danger: in the process, the emperor had contracted out tax collection and the supply of troops to 2000 noble landholders, each with his own dynastic interests. As for China, the original Ming fiscal system based on taxes in kind and in services could not be adapted to the financing of a professional army in a monetized economy. In the event of a crisis, increasing tax avoidance by the gentry would leave the emperor unable to pay and equip his troops.

Of course, dynasties had come and gone before in England, the Middle East, India and China. However, this time the shock of a new communications technology was disrupting the usual pattern—initially only in the West, but eventually in each of the Asian societies as well.

Note

1. Each coin contained 178 grains of silver.

References

Archer, I. W. (2011). Commerce and consumption. In S. Doran & N. Jones (Eds.), *The Elizabethan world* (pp. 411–426). London: Routledge.

Bada'uni, A.-Q. (1898). *Muntakhabu-t-tawārīkh (Selections from Histories)* (trans: Ranking, G.). Kolkota: Asiatic Society.

Black, J. B. (1936). *The reign of Elizabeth 1558–1603*. Oxford: Clarendon.

Broadberry, S., Guan, H., & Li, D. D. (2014). *China, Europe and the great divergence: A study in historical national accounting, 980–1850*. Retrieved October 17, 2016, from eh.net. http://eh.net/eha/wp-content/uploads/2014/05/Broadberry.pdf

Brook, T. (2013). *The troubled empire: China in the Yuan and Ming dynasties*. Cambridge, MA: Belknap Press.

Chen, Q. (2015). Climate shocks, dynastic cycles and nomadic conquests: Evidence from historical China. *Oxford Economic Papers, 67*, 185–204.

Cizakca, M. (2013). The Ottoman government and economic life: Taxation, public finance and trade controls. In S. N. Faroqhi & K. Fleet (Eds.), *The Cambridge history of Turkey* (Vol. 2, pp. 241–275). Cambridge, UK: Cambridge University Press.

Crossley, P. K. (1997). *The Manchus*. Oxford: Blackwell.

Dash, M. (2012). *The Ottoman Empire's life-or-death race*. Retrieved October 5, 2015, from smithsonian.com. http://www.smithsonianmag.com/history/the-ottoman-empires-life-or-death-race-164064882/?no-ist

Doran, S. (2003). *Queen Elizabeth I*. London: The British Library.

Doran, S. (2006). James VI and the English succession. In R. Houlbrooke (Ed.), *James VI and I: Ideas, authority and government* (pp. 25–42). Aldershot: Ashgate.

Dreyer, E. L. (1988). Military origins of Ming China. In D. Twitchett & F. W. Mote (Eds.), *Cambridge history of China, vol. 7, The Ming Dynasty, 1368–1644, part 1* (pp. 58–106). Cambridge: Cambridge University Press.

Ebrey, P. B. (1996). *The Cambridge illustrated history of China*. Cambridge, UK: Cambridge University Press.

Elliott, M. C. (2001). *The Manchu way: The eight banners and ethnic identity in late imperial China*. Stanford: Stanford University Press.

Erickson, C. (1983). *The first Elizabeth*. London: Macmillan.

Falls, C. (1950). *Elizabeth's Irish Wars*. London: Methuen.

Goodwin, J. (1998). *Lords of the horizons: A history of the Ottoman Empire*. New York: Henry Holt and Company.

Greif, A., & Tabellini, G. (2010). Cultural and institutional bifurcation: China and Europe compared. *American Economic Review, Papers and Proceedings, 100*(2), 135–140.

Huang, R. (1974). *Taxation and governmental finance in sixteenth-century Ming China*. Cambridge, UK: Cambridge University Press.

Huang, R. (1998). The Ming fiscal administration. In D. Twitchett & F. W. Mote (Eds.), *The Cambridge history of China, vol. 8, The Ming Dynasty, 1368–1644, part 2* (pp. 106–171). Cambridge, UK: Cambridge University Press.

Inalcik, H. (1973). *The Ottoman Empire: The classical age 1300–1600*. New York: Praeger.

Johnson, N. D., & Koyama, M. (2014). Tax farming and the origins of state capacity in England and France. *Explorations in Economic History, 51*, 1–20.

Karateke, H. T. (2012). 'On the tranquility and repose of the Sultan': The construction of a topos. In C. Woodhead (Ed.), *The Ottoman world* (pp. 116–129). New York: Routledge.

Keay, J. (2000). *India: A history*. New York: Grove Press.

MacMillan, K. (2011). Exploration, trade and empire. In S. Doran & N. Jones (Eds.), *The Elizabethan world* (pp. 646–662). London: Routledge.

Maddison, A. (2007). *Contours of the world economy, 1-2030 AD: Essays in macroeconomic history*. Oxford: Oxford University Press.
Metcalf, B. D., & Metcalf, T. R. (2006). *A concise history of modern india* (2nd ed.). Cambridge: Cambridge University Press.
Pamuk, Ş. (2000). *A monetary history of the Ottoman Empire*. Cambridge: Cambridge University Press.
Peck, L. L. (1993). *Court patronage and corruption in early Stuart England*. London: Routledge.
Quataert, D. (2005). *The Ottoman Empire 1700–1922* (2nd ed.). Cambridge, UK: Cambridge University Press.
Richards, J. F. (1993). *The Mughal empire*. Cambridge: Cambridge University Press.
Smith, V. A. (1917). *Akbar: The great Mogul 1542–1605*. Oxford: Clarendon.
Tezcan, B. (2010). *The second Ottoman Empire: Political and social transformation in the early modern world*. Cambridge: Cambridge University Press.
Trimble, W. R. (1950). Early Tudor historiography, 1485–1548. *Journal of the History of Ideas, 11*, 30–41.
Turchin, P., & Nefedov, S. A. (2009). *Secular cycles*. Princeton: Princeton University Press.
Ursinus, M. (2012). The transformation of the Ottoman fiscal regime, c. 1600–1850. In C. Woodhead (Ed.), *The Ottoman world* (pp. 423–435). London: Routledge.
von Glahn, R. (2016). *The economic history of China: From antiquity to the nineteenth century*. Cambridge: Cambridge University Press.
Yang, L.-S. (1954). Toward a study of dynastic configurations in Chinese history. *Harvard Journal of Asiatic Studies, 17*, 329–345.

CHAPTER 3

Printing

3.1 Which Was More Important: Paper or the Printing Press?

In 2013, *The Atlantic* magazine assembled a panel of 12 experts to determine the most important inventions since the discovery of the wheel, some 6000 years ago. At the top of the list was the printing press. In sixth place, behind more recently invented electricity, penicillin, the semiconductor and optical lenses, was paper (Fallows 2013). If we look across Eurasia in the year 1600, however, it was unquestionably paper rather than the printing press that had made the greater impact on people's lives.

Paper had allowed block printing to flourish in China. In India and the Ottoman Empire, paper had permitted the wide diffusion of manuscripts in beautiful Perso-Arabic script. Some eight centuries earlier, in 786, Harun al-Rashid came to power at the head of the Abbasid Caliphate in Baghdad. Early in his reign, he had a water-powered paper mill build on the Tigris. Subsequently, all of the Islamic government agencies switched from parchment to paper for their documentation (Kurlansky 2016, 53–54). In India, the surge of new literature in regional languages during the sixteenth and early seventeenth centuries was made possible in part by the diffusion of paper-making technology. Even the cultural explosion of the Italian Renaissance, with the writings of the Dante, Petrarch and Boccaccio, would have certainly been dampened without the wide diffusion on paper.

As for the printing press, prior to the year 1600, it had made virtually no impact outside of Western Europe. Unlike the West, Asia's writing systems were simply too complex to be transcribed cheaply onto the heads of a few dozen metal punches. In the West, it is true, the printing press had facilitated the diffusion of Protestantism. However, as the Latin phrase of the 1555 Peace of Augsburg indicated, "cueius regio, eius religio" (whose realm, his religion), the choice of creed was left in the hands of the ruler rather than those of his subjects. It was only in the late 1500s that more works had begun to be printed in the vernacular dialects than in Latin (Hirsch 1974, 132). In England, the choice of Protestantism over Catholicism had been made for dynastic reasons when the reigning monarch decided that only divorce and remarriage—forbidden by the Catholic Church—would allow him to produce a male heir.

Perhaps the most powerful argument for the importance of paper is that without it, the printing press alone would likely have been a business failure. The number of people willing to pay the price of a Bible printed on parchment would in all probability have been insufficient to justify the decision of Johannes Gutenberg and his partner Johann Fust to pay the high fixed cost of designing, cutting and setting the type.

3.2 Printing in England

It is convenient to break information processing in Europe at the end of the sixteenth century into the three distinct steps, namely, transmission, decoding and storage. A first step was to transmit the information in question to potential recipients. For example, if Queen Elizabeth I wished to inform her courtiers at low cost that she had appointed young Robert Cecil as her Secretary of State, she could do so by addressing them simultaneously orally. A second step was for the recipients to decode the information. Since the queen and most of her household understood the spoken dialect of the London court, the cost of this second step was also low. The third and final step was to store this information. In the example, this stage was also inexpensive, since the courtiers would all have no difficulty in remembering the small amount of information in the queen's message. In short, for a simple message to be transmitted to at most several hundred people at a single location, oral transmission was highly effective.

Suppose, however, that in 1600 the Queen had wished to issue a new set of Articles of Religion to her four million English subjects. How could she reach them all in a short period with the same message? Three hundred years earlier, the task would have been formidable. Because of its complexity, the message would have had to be in written form. The only possibility would have been writing by hand with pen and ink on parchment made from sheepskins. Accordingly, transmission and storage would have been very expensive. Yet an even greater difficulty would have been the decoding of the message. In the fourteenth century, few knew how to read. Moreover, in the absence of a standard vernacular, the message would had to have been written in Latin, which very few apart from the clergy would have been able to understand, even if the message had been read aloud to them.

The high cost of storage was the first difficulty to be attacked. In the twelfth century, the manufacture of paper had been introduced into Europe by the Arabs in southern Spain. Wet rags were pounded and stirred in water. After the resulting paste had been spread onto a flat surface, a massive press was applied to squeeze out the water (Man 2002, 134). The sheet was then spread on a wire rack to dry. By the fourteenth century, there were similar paper factories using this process in Italy, France and Germany.

In the fourteenth and fifteenth centuries, a series of innovations had reduced the cost of transmitting information to large numbers of recipients. First, around 1300 came a form of relief printing known as block printing or xylography, a process that was already widely used in China (Man 2002, 89). The reverse of an image was carved onto a block of wood. Ink was then applied over the parts that had not been cut out and the block pressed onto a sheet of paper. In this way, the original image was reproduced on the paper. In the second quarter of the fifteenth century came a form of intaglio printmaking known as engraving. Using a tool called a burin, the artist cut lines into a sheet of metal. A coating of ink was then applied and wiped off, leaving ink in the indented grooves. When wet paper was pressed onto the plate, the paper absorbed the remaining ink, thereby revealing the image. Block printing and engraving were used frequently for artistic drawings in the West, but for reproducing pages of Roman characters, they were too expensive compared with hand copying.

Although the breakthrough at the top of the list compiled by *The Atlantic* mentioned above is known as the "printing press", its novelty came neither from printing, as we have just seen, nor from pressing. The innovation in Gutenberg's revolutionary technology was movable type: the setting of hundreds of tiny cloned metal castings of letters into a metal frame to which pressure could be applied evenly with a screw press (Man 2002, 134). Gutenberg also developed ink that would adhere to the metal type (Houston 1988, 156). Although it was expensive to set a page of type in this way, each additional printed copy cost only about one three-hundredth of the amount needed to pay a scribe to write the same text (Eisenstein 1979,

46). In other words, there were unprecedented scale economies to be had in the transmission of complex information to many recipients. The alphabetic scripts of the West had a considerable advantage in ease of printing over the characters of other writing systems: the early English printer's box contained fewer than 100 characters (Lagally 1992, 109).

Printing in the Fifteenth and Sixteenth Centuries Gutenberg set up the first printing press in Mainz, Germany, in the early 1450s. Thereafter, the diffusion of this invention was extremely rapid on the Continent, but its adoption was slow in England. It was not until 1476 that William Caxton installed the first printing press in London. The first book published there was *The Dictes and Sayings of the Philosophers* (Bertrand 1969, 27). In 1480, there were 122 towns with printing presses in Western Europe, two-thirds of them in Germany and Italy (Man 2002, 225), but there were only three towns in England other than London that had printing presses in that year. Of the 24,421 "incunables"—that is, books printed up to the year 1500—England accounted for only 474, or less than two percent of the total (Barnard and Bell 1998, 779–780) (Hirsch 1974, 133). Moreover, of all the books published up to 1500, 77 percent were in Latin and only 0.66 percent in the English language. As mentioned, it was not until late in the sixteenth century that the majority of publications in Europe were in the vernacular (Hirsch 1974, 132).

Over the sixteenth century, the number of titles published in England increased steadily—at an annual rate of 2.4 percent (Barnard and Bell 1998, 782–784). Nevertheless, England lagged behind France, Germany and Italy in new titles per million inhabitants until late in the sixteenth century (Baten and van Zanden 2008, 220). One reason for the slow expansion was the limiting of competition. In 1557, the Stationers' Company, the guild of London publishers, was granted a royal charter that gave it a monopoly over book publishing in England. The Company was also given the responsibility of assuring that all books met the standards set by the State and the established Church. Furthermore, once a member of the Company had entered a text in the guild's "entry book of copies", no other member had the right to copy it. This was the origin of the term "copyright". Although in England there seems to have been little interest in domestic news in printed form, there was a strong demand for news from abroad. A report on the sailing of the Spanish Armada in 1588 from Lisbon was originally written in French and then translated into English (Raymond 2011, 506).

In short, until the end of the sixteenth century, English publishers were slower than their Continental in adopting the printing press. Successive English governments, fearing the effects of free circulation of information on royal and church power, tried to restrict the printing and censorship of books to a tightly controlled monopoly. As for the printing of periodicals, because of the censorship of printed matter, news of current events circulated only in hand-written newsletters.

Developments in the Seventeenth Century In England, the year 1603 saw the end of one dynasty and the beginning of another. The childless Elizabeth Tudor was succeeded by her distant cousin, James VI of Scotland, scion of the Stuart family (who became James I of England). For the first time, England, Scotland and Ireland had a single ruler. The technology of printing with movable type had been present in James's three kingdoms for well over a century, but to date the discovery had had little effect on most people's daily lives. Even those able to read and write still had no access to a reliable source of current information about political or economic events. Over the following century, however, the situation of king and subjects would be altered dramatically by the introduction of a new medium of information, even though the technology of printing itself remained essentially unchanged.

For the first four decades of the seventeenth century, the availability of printed information changed very little. Most publishing remained in the hands of the regulated Stationers' Company. The average annual growth rate of new titles of books and pamphlets slowed to somewhat less than two percent. Over 300 titles on average were being published annually at the beginning of the seventeenth century. By the late 1630s, after three more decades of moderate growth, this figure had risen to an annual average of over 600 titles a year (Barnard and Bell 1998, 782–784).

Nevertheless, the industry was changing. One new development in the case of books was the appearance of new capitalist structures in order to take advantage of the scale economies of the printing press. The members of the Stationers' Company had been subjected to increasing competition from bookseller-stationer collaborators toward the end of the sixteenth century (Raven 1998, 568). In the year of James I's coronation, the Company's members reacted by forming a joint-stock company, the English Stock, to allow themselves to profit more easily from the publication of titles in great demand such as almanacs (Raven 1998, 580).

Then in the early 1640s, with the beginning of the English Civil War, the market for printed books and pamphlets suddenly exploded. In the single year of 1642, there were over 3600 titles printed (Barnard and Bell 1998, 782–784). Subsequently, through the 1640s and 1650s, the production of book titles remained at a much higher level than previously observed. Only once after 1640 did production fall to levels approaching those of the 1630s—namely, during the 5 years from 1666 to 1670. The most likely explanation for this temporary decline was the Great Fire of 1666 in London, which caused a severe depression in the book trade (Roberts 1998, 166).

The seventeenth century also witnessed the creation of a market for a completely new printed product—the newspaper. From 1621 to 1640, a series of printed periodicals bringing news from abroad came and went. The first English newspaper appeared in September 1621, in the form of a translation of articles from Dutch and German periodicals. There were seven issues of this *Corante, or newes from Italy, Germany, Hungarie, Spaine and France* (Nelson and Seccombe 1998, 535). Over the following decade, there appeared further periodicals focusing on foreign news that were known as "newsbooks" because they were printed on eight or more small pages in quarto format. However, in 1632, all such publications were banned by the Council of Charles I, after a Spanish duke complained that he had been slandered (Nelson and Seccombe 1998, 537).

In the period between 1641 and 1695, it was not only in the publishing of books and pamphlets that there was a rapid growth: there was an even more remarkable explosion in the production of periodicals. Like the increase in the output of books, the rise in periodical printing began shortly after Charles I called the Long Parliament in November 1640 to request financing for his wars against the Scots. People wanted to be informed about the issues that were shaking the political system. Initially, opposition to the king was expressed in privately published pamphlets. Then in November 1641, a certain John Thomas, probably the nominee of established publishers, produced the first domestic newsbook, entitled *The Heads of Severall Proceedings in This Present Parliament.* The content of this publication was probably pirated from a hand-written daily summary of parliamentary developments (Nelson and Seccombe 1998, 538). Soon the competition was intense. In January 1642, there were 17 newsbook series in print in England. By the end of the year, all had failed, but nine other series were in print. In 1649, less than a decade after the publication of the first newsbook devoted to domestic developments, there were 54 different periodicals being published (see Fig. 3.1) (Nelson and Seccombe 1998, 541).

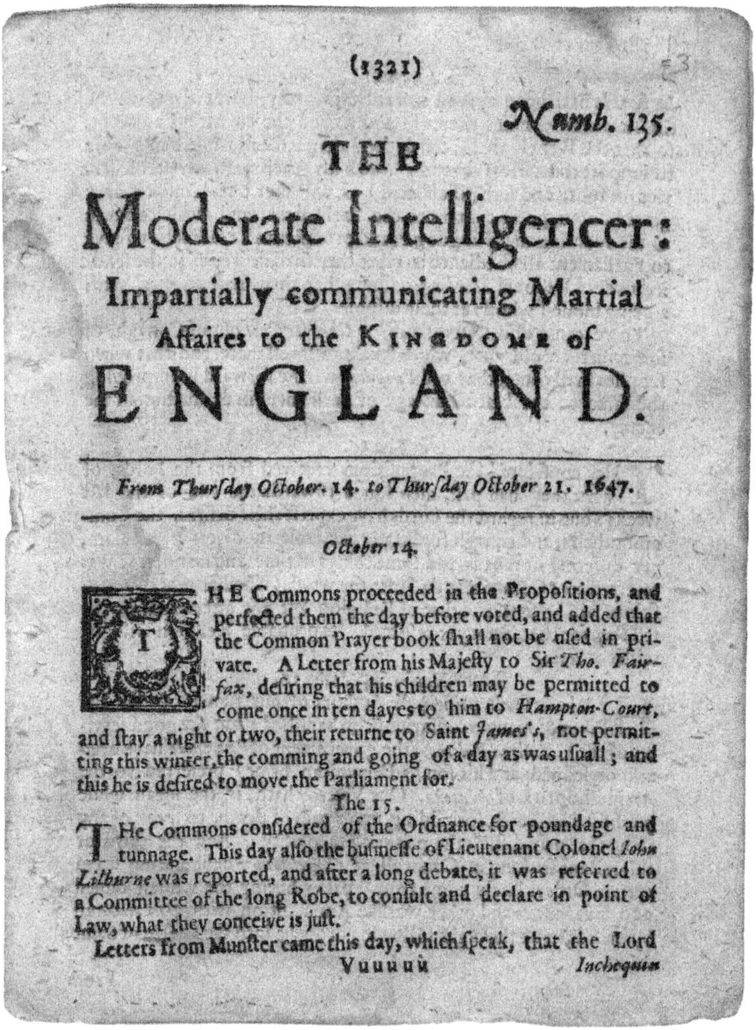

(1321)

Numb. 135.

THE

Moderate Intelligencer:

Impartially communicating Martial Affaires to the KINGDOME of

ENGLAND.

From Thurſday October 14. to Thurſday October 21. 1647.

October 14.

THE Commons proceeded in the Propoſitions, and perfected them the day before voted, and added that the Common Prayer book ſhall not be uſed in private. A Letter from his Majeſty to Sir *Tho. Fairfax*, deſiring that his children may be permitted to come once in ten dayes to him to *Hampton-Court*, and ſtay a night or two, their returne to Saint *James's*, not permitting this winter, the comming and going of a day as was uſuall; and this he is deſired to move the Parliament for.

The 15.

THe Commons conſidered of the Ordnance for poundage and tunnage. This day alſo the buſineſſe of Lieutenant Colonel *John Lilburne* was reported, and after a long debate, it was referred to a Committee of the long Robe, to conſult and declare in point of Law, what they conceive is juſt.

Letters from Munſter came this day, which ſpeak, that the Lord

Vuuuuu *Inchequin*

Fig. 3.1 Copy of a 1647 newsbook, the predecessor of the newspaper. Published in quarto format regularly during the English Civil War, *The Moderate Intelligencer* contained both domestic and foreign news (Reproduced from *Folger Shakespeare Library*)

What were people reading during the seventeenth century? Religion was by far the favorite subject, accounting for almost 30 percent of titles between 1668 and 1699. The top seller was the new edition of the Bible in English translated by a group of scholars at the request of King James I and published initially in 1611 (see Fig. 4.1 in the next chapter). History books were also in great demand, representing some eight percent of the total. It may surprise us to learn that poetry sold very well, accounting for about six percent of all titles sold (Barnard and Bell 1998, 788). Included in this figure, of course, were the popular works of William Shakespeare. In the case of books and pamphlets, then, the middle decades of the seventeenth century saw a large and permanent jump in the demand for a familiar product, an increase that would continue into the following century.

To what extent was the great increase in the number of printed texts after 1640 simply due to looser censorship? In answering this question, it is important to distinguish books, such as the Bible, from periodicals such as the newsbook. Until quite recently, it was argued that the unusually high output of books and pamphlets of the Civil War period was explained by the temporary breakdown of the system of licensing. However, Parliament quickly reinstalled press censorship, which continued in one form or another until the last decade of the century (McKenzie 1998, 560).

In 1662, the restored monarchy appointed as Surveyor of the Press Roger L'Estrange, who was himself an author and publisher and of course a staunch supporter of the new king, Charles II. Under the Press Act of that year, L'Estrange became Licenser of the Press (Dunan-Page and Lynch 2008, 1). However, after reviewing in detail the effect of licensing in the year 1668, D. F. McKenzie concluded that the Crown's constraints were largely ineffective. Fewer than ten percent of the books in that year bore any sort of license (McKenzie 1998, 564). The principal explanation for the weakness of government regulation is that even in the 1660s and 1670s, the task was partly in the hands of the Stationers' Company, whose primary interest was to sell books (Treadwell 1998, 765–766).

In the case of periodicals, licensing clearly had greater success in controlling the volume and content of printed output. As noted above, the royal ban on newsbooks between 1632 and 1640 had been quite effective. By their nature, periodicals have to be published regularly and distributed through known channels, where buyers can find them easily. If the censors had the power of the judiciary behind them, it was not too difficult for them to interrupt the publication of periodicals that they deemed to be threatening.

The result was a cat-and-mouse game between the censors and periodical publishers. In 1655, Cromwell's government suppressed all but two periodicals, both of them under tight government control (Nelson and Seccombe 1998, 543). Between 1662 and the expiration of the Press Act in 1679, Roger L'Estrange was untiring in his attempts to muzzle those who thought that they had "a colourable right, and license, to be meddling with the government" (Nelson and Seccombe 1998, 543). However, he had only mixed success. The principal source of political news after 1665 was the *London Gazette*, printed on both sides of a single half sheet. In 1666, the newsbooks in quarto format ceased publication. However, in 1679, the *Gazette* lost its news monopoly and L'Estrange his position. Although strict controls were reintroduced by James II under the renewed Licensing Act of 1685, these restrictions were relaxed after the Glorious Revolution of 1688 (Nelson and Seccombe 1998, 548). Finally, in 1695, Parliament allowed the Licensing Act to lapse, thereby permitting a virtually unrestricted press.

In short, during the middle decades of the seventeenth century in England, there was a revolution in the information-processing industry. Between the start of the Civil War and the Glorious Revolution, the number of titles of books and periodicals printed in the vernacular virtually exploded. Since printing technology had changed little since the days of Gutenberg, to find an explanation, we must look to the demand side of the market. The next chapter will turn to this subject. First, however, we must examine the impact of printing in the three Asian empires we have been studying.

3.3 Printing in the Ottoman Empire

The decline of the Ottoman Empire that began in the seventeenth century is sometimes explained by that society's delay in adopting the printing press. The explanation relies on a combination of government regulation, opposition from clerics and copyists and a cultural preference for hand-written manuscripts. In 1483, Sultan Bayezid II had issued a decree forbidding the use of printed books by Turks under penalty of death. The ban on the printing of Turkish and Arabic was renewed by his son Selim I in 1515 and continued to be enforced until the eighteenth century (Chambers and Chambers 1848, 44). Without access to the latest technological information, it is argued the Ottoman society gradually fell behind its European rivals (Roper 2010).

Why would such a powerful technology not have spread rapidly from Europe to the Middle East? It has been suggested that Ottoman calligraphers, like their European counterparts, opposed new machinery that would threaten their livelihood. In addition, we are reminded that Muslim societies had long been extremely conservative in their use of symbols. Owing perhaps to the precarious nature of life on the edge of deserts, religious authorities had always played an important role in determining the rituals that governed daily life and in the way that these rules were transmitted from one generation to the next. Although the Quran did not explicitly forbid the representation of humans or animals in drawings, the different schools of Islamic law had long banned the use of such images. Accordingly, there was likely to be strong opposition among scholars and clerics to a radical new technology that allowed simple artisans to break their monopoly over the reproduction of symbolic information.

Block printing had been invented in China during the early centuries of the first millennium CE, at first for printing on cloth and later on paper. By the end of the millennium, under the Song Dynasty (960–1127), the Chinese were printing bound books in volume. In the Muslim Middle East, block printing was used to produce single sheets. However, it was never used to print entire books (Roper 1995, 209).

In the last half of the fifteenth century, printing with movable type spread rapidly across Europe. In the Ottoman Empire too, the printing press was authorized for use by minority religious groups from the 1490s. As early as 1493, Sephardic Jews from Spain published an edition of Jacob ben Aser's *'Arba'ah Tûrîm* (the four orders of the Hebrew code of law) in Hebrew in Istanbul (Offenberg 1969, 96). In 1567, Apkar Tebir printed an Armenian grammar in Istanbul (Sarkiss 1937, 437). The Maronite Christians at the Monastery of Saint Anthony in the Valley of Qozhaya, Lebanon, published a psalter in Syriac in 1585 (Qozhaya 2015).

Printing in Turkish began only in the eighteenth century. Ibrahim Müteferrika (1674–1745) was an Ottoman court official born in Transylvania who had converted to Islam. During a visit to France, he had been impressed by the possibilities of the printing press. In 1726, he wrote a treatise entitled "The Means of Printing" that urged Sultan Ahmed III to support a local printing industry. Some of the ulema and all of the calligraphers expressed their opposition to such a project. Nevertheless, a fatwa and imperial decree of 1727 approved the printing of nonreligious texts. Accordingly, the first Muslim printing press began publishing in that year. Its first book was a Turkish-Arabic dictionary (Watson 1968, 437).

However, there was a limited demand for printed matter in the Ottoman Empire. The printing shop was closed after Ibrahim's death in 1845, although it later reopened. In all, between 1727 and 1838, only 142 books were printed in Turkish (Hanioglu 2008, 38).

Newspapers and political pamphlets also appeared much later in the Ottoman lands than in the West. By 1795, the French community in Istanbul had its own newspaper. Prior to the series of reforms known as the Tanzimat that began in 1839, there was also an official gazette informing the public about government policies, printed in Turkish and French. However, it was not until after 1839 that the first Turkish-language newspaper was published. In 1840, William Churchill, a member of the British mission in Istanbul, published *Ceride-i Havâdis* (Hanioglu 2008, 94). It later was followed by *Ahval* in 1860 and *Tasvir-i Efkâr* in 1862 (Hanioglu 2008, 94). The first privately owned newspaper published by Turkish journalists was *Tercüman-ı Ahvâl* (Interpreter of Events), which appeared in 1860 (Agoston and Masters 2009, 433).

We see, then, that even after the Ottoman regime approved the printing of books, there was very little printed in Turkish or Arabic in the Ottoman Empire before the second half of the nineteenth century—400 years after Gutenberg's invention of the printing press. To explain this long delay, we must compare the costs of manuscript books relative to books produced with block printing or movable type.

Until the Turkish-language reform of 1928, Turkish was written with the Perso-Arabic script, based on the Arabic script but with four additional letters. Arabic and Persian are always written in a cursive script, with rounded letters flowing into one another. The script is referred to as an *abjad*, a writing system in which each symbol usually stands for a consonant. Since the symbols representing short vowels are usually omitted, most of the letters in a given word can be written quickly in a continuous line. As a result, Arabic can be written considerably more rapidly than Roman book scripts, in which the letters are separated.

Consider the cost of handwriting relative to that of block printing for Ottoman Turkish. Printing with wooden blocks, or xylography, was a technique developed by the Chinese and used on a large scale in China from the tenth century on. As explained above, each character of a page of text is cut in relief with a knife or chisel in a single block of wood. Ink is then applied and paper brought into contact with the block. The technique was appropriate for Chinese because each morpheme or basic part of speech is a separate character made up of a series of straight lines. In Arabic, an individual word almost always has two or more characters. Moreover, these characters are generally curved and are joined together by ligatures of different length and height. Diacritics in the form of an apostrophe or sets of points are essential for identifying the individual letters. Although there are no capitals in Arabic, each character has four possible different forms, the use of which depends on the letter's position in a word: initial, intermediate, final or isolated. The task of carving a sufficient number of characters in this demanding script for a whole book must have discouraged any potential commercial printer.

By the seventeenth century, a typical European printer's box contained fewer than 275 different forms of letters, including number, capitals and special characters. To print a single page of Gutenberg's bible, some 5000 characters were required. A European printer had to have 25,000 pieces of type and another 25,000 spaces if he wanted to set more than a single page at a time (Lunde 1981). However, printing in Arabic required roughly 600 different forms (Bloom 1999). The requirements for an equivalent page of Arabic script would have been proportionally greater.

Accordingly, the fixed cost of setting up a printing shop for Turkish or Arabic was considerably higher than for English or French. In addition, the labor required to set a given page of type was higher for the more complex Arabic script than for Roman characters. The first book printed in Arabic was a *Book of Hours* published by Gregorio de Gregorii, a Venetian, in 1514. Readers of Arabic texts tended to be extremely demanding regarding the quality of the calligraphy. As the roughly cut characters were difficult to read, the book did not sell well in its intended market, the Christians of the Levant.

It took the resources of the Vatican to produce an acceptable Arabic typeface. Desiring to unite the Christian churches of Lebanon with the Vatican, Pope Gregory XIII financed the cutting of Arabic type by Robert Granjon, a French designer of type. The first production, under the direction of Cardinal Ferdinando de Medici, was an Arabic edition of the four gospels, which appeared in 1591. However, the publications of the new press did not sell well. The press, type and unsold books were transferred to the Villa Medici in Rome in 1614 and later to Florence. There Napoleon was subsequently able to seize what remained for use in his Egyptian campaign of 1798 (Lunde 1981).

In summary, the hand-copied manuscript remained the principal vehicle for diffusion of scientific and cultural information in the Ottoman Empire prior to the nineteenth century. The long delay in the introduction of printing may be explained in part by the opposition from copyists and religious authorities but also by the high cost of block printing or movable type relative to hand copying for Arabic script. However, the fact that even after printing in Turkish was introduced in the eighteenth century, the *demand* for printed books remained negligible suggests that factors other than the cost of printing were also coming into play.

Further to the east, in the Indian subcontinent, the introduction of printing in the languages of the majority was also long delayed.

3.4 Printing in India

The first printing press in India was installed by Jesuit missionaries in Goa in the mid-sixteenth century, but it was not until the nineteenth century that Indians published in their own languages. João de Bustamante, a Spanish Jesuit, printed the first volume, *Conclusões e outras coisas* (Theses and other things), in Portuguese in 1556 (Naik 2006). In 1580, the Jesuits "presented a polyglot Bible to the Emperor Akbar but did not succeed in arousing much curiosity". The Mughal regime showed little interest in the technology, preferring hand-written manuscripts (Maddison 2005, 65).

The first printing of an Indian language using movable type came in the early eighteenth century. In October 1713, Danish Lutherans at Tranquebar (Tharangambadi) on the southeast coast of India printed the first text in the Tamil language using type cut in Halle, Germany. Reverend Bartholomew Ziegenbalg's *Das Verdammliche allgemeine Heidenthum* (Damnable General Heathenism) was a general refutation of Hinduism (Kesavan 1985, 42).

The printing of what are today known as Urdu and Hindi began only in the last decades of the eighteenth century. In 1782, John Gilchrist, an English surgeon, arrived in Bombay and subsequently took up a position in the Medical Service of the East India Company. Arriving in Calcutta to serve with the Bengal army, he was told that India's principal language was Persian. However, when conversing with the Company's sepoys (Indian infantry soldiers) as he traveled in northern India, he found that few spoke Persian well. Rather, they spoke a lingua franca based on the dialect of Delhi, Khariboli, to which many Persian words had been added. The language was initially known as Hindustani, then later as Urdu. After 1860, a distinction began to be made between two registers of this lingua franca, namely, Urdu printed with Perso-Arabic script and Hindi printed with the Devanagari script. (Devanagari is phonetic writing system in which each letter represents a consonant and an implicit vowel. Other vowels are indicated by accents known as diacritics.)

Gilchrist recommended that Hindustani replace Persian as the administrative language of the Company's growing empire. In 1785, he recruited a team of Indian writers to prepare a dictionary and grammar of this vernacular language for the instruction of the company's British officials. The resulting book, *A Dictionary: English and Hindoostanee*, was published in installments between 1786 and 1790. Its entries were printed in both the Perso-Arabic script and Nagari, the ancestor of the Devanagari script used today to write Hindi. Each entry also had a transliteration in Roman characters and an English translation. The East India Company bought 150 copies of Gilchrist's book. In 1799, the Company established a college to train its employees. Governor Richard Wellesley, the older brother of the future Duke of Wellington, named Gilchrist as the institution's first principal (Begum 1989, 1409).

One of Gilchrist's first appointees to teach in the new college was Lallulal, a Brahman from Agra. In 1802, the Indian scholar published *Premsagar*, a story from the *Bhagavata*, taking care to avoid words of Persian or Arabic origin (Snatak 1989, 2241). It is considered the first work of literature printed in the Hindi language. It was not long before Bengali entrepreneurs began to cater to the demand for books from the growing number of company servants attached to Fort William, the British post in Calcutta. In 1807, a local merchant, Babu Ram, set up a press with Sanskrit characters to print textbooks in Hindustani and Sanskrit for Fort William (Ghosh 2003, 27).

The Bengali language spoken in northeastern India has its own phonetic writing system similar to Devanagari. The earliest printing press equipped with Bengali types was owned by a British bookseller, Andrews of Hooghly. In 1778, he published *A Grammar of the Bengal Language*, a book principally in English, with sections of some Bengali texts for illustration. Over the following two decades, both the East India Company and European publishers printed small numbers of government publications, grammar texts and vocabularies in the Bengali language. In 1800, a British Baptist missionary, William Carey, began publishing large numbers of books in Bengali destined for Indian readers. Since the East India Company had denied him permission to open a mission, these books were printed in the Danish concession of Serampore adjacent to Calcutta. Matthew's Gospel was followed by numerous other books in Bengali (Ghosh 2003, 26).

The first newspaper in India was an English-language weekly, the *Bengal Gazette* or *Calcutta General Advertiser*, launched in January 1780 by James Augustus Hicky. Its content was made up of correspondence from local writers, including gossip from the British community, along with articles from English newspapers and an abundance of advertisements. However, the paper was closed by the government 2 years later, after Hicky insulted the wife of Governor Warren Hastings in print (Natarajan 1962, 14–15). Its place was taken by a more recent rival, the *India Gazette*, with similar content.

In 1818, the Baptist mission in Serampore began printing a weekly newspaper, *Samachar Darpan*, in Bengali. It is considered the first newspaper printed in an Indian language. In 1821, the first Indian-language newspaper published by an Indian, a Bengali weekly, the *Sambad Kaumudi* was launched. It was published by Raja Ram Mohan Roy, a Brahman who had worked as a writer for the East India Company. The following year Mohan Roy, a Bengali scholar, began a weekly in Persian, *Mirat-ul-Akbar*, aimed at readers who were not familiar with English or Bengali. It was not long before a newspaper in the Hindustani language appeared. *Udant Martand* (*The Rising Sun*) was the first Hindi-language newspaper published in India. Started on 30 May 1826 in Calcutta (now Kolkata), the weekly newspaper was published every Tuesday by Pandit Jugal Kishore Shukla (Natarajan 1962, 27).

As in the Ottoman Empire, therefore, we see that printing with movable type was not widely used in India until the nineteenth century, and then only after it had been introduced by Europeans.

3.5 Printing in China

We have seen that after 1450, the use of Gutenberg's press spread quickly across Western Europe. During the sixteenth century, particularly in the Protestant north, printers increasingly emphasized titles in the local vernacular rather than in Latin. Then, in England, from the middle decades of the seventeenth century, there was a remarkable upsurge in the number of book titles printed. Even more astonishing was a simultaneous explosion in the publication of periodicals covering current developments within English and European society. In western and southern Asia, however, the widespread use of printing was delayed by over two centuries.

The history of printing in China differed sharply from that of either the West or the other Asian civilizations, both in the technology used and in its impact on society. The Jesuit missionary Matteo Ricci, who lived in China from 1572 until his death in 1610, was a close contemporary of both England's Queen Elizabeth I and China's Wanli Emperor. Accordingly, he was a reliable observer of the differences between European and Chinese society at the turn of the seventeenth century. Having lived in both the southern provinces of China and in the capital, Beijing, Ricci was struck by the "exceedingly large numbers of books in circulation" and by the "ridiculously low prices" at which they were sold (Ricci 1953, 20–21). However, the printing process by which most Chinese books were printed was quite different from that used in Europe.

Some four centuries before Gutenberg, a Chinese commoner named Pi Sheng invented movable type, using baked-clay pieces set into a metal frame (Temple 2007, 127). However, because the Chinese writing system uses a separate character for each unit of speech or morpheme, a printer required tens of thousands of these small blocks, each individually made. One thirteenth-century Chinese printer used 60,000 wooden characters stored in revolving tables seven feet (2 m) in diameter (Temple 2007, 129). Printing of the Thirteen Confucian Classics would require 6544 *different* characters (Norman 1988, 73). In contrast, as mentioned, an early English printer's box might contain only 100 different forms (Lagally 1992, 109).

Instead of movable type, the Chinese generally used block printing, a method they had developed by the early seventh century (Temple 2007, 123). Matteo Ricci ([1615] 1953, 20–21) described the process as it had evolved by the year 1600. Printers used small tablets of wood, the best of which came from pear or apple trees:

> The text is written in ink, with a brush made of very fine hair, on a sheet of paper, which is inverted and pasted on a wooden tablet. When the paper has become thoroughly dry, its surface is scraped off quickly and with great skill, until nothing but a fine tissue bearing the characters remains on the wooden tablet. Then, with a steel graver, the workman cuts away the surface following the outlines of the characters.

Once the block had been cut, a skilled printer could prepare as many as 1500 copies of a given page in a day. The blocks themselves could be used to print as many as 20,000 copies of a text (Ebrey 1996, 149). However, because Chinese paper, made from the bark of the mulberry tree, was more porous than European paper made from rags, the Chinese could print on only one side of a sheet. Moreover, the sheets were easily torn and subject to wear. Nevertheless, since the wooden blocks could be stored for long periods, a publisher could print on demand, thereby limiting the risk of holding large depreciating inventories of unsold books.

This simple process was put to an astonishing variety of uses. Registration forms, licenses and paper currency were all duplicated in this way, the latter all too frequently by exceedingly competent forgers (Brook 1998, 648). From the earliest days of the Ming Dynasty, the imperial government printed scholarly texts, law books for officials, moralistic texts, monographs praising the regime's accomplishments and guides for acceptable rhymes in poetry (Brook 1998, 650–651). In each region, magistrates published gazetteers that recorded projects in which local officials were involved (Brook 1998, 655). Wealthy member of the gentry also financed new scholarly works or reproductions of their own collections. Buddhist monasteries published religious teachings and prayers (Brook 1998, 637).

The category that accounted for the largest volume of books sold consisted of commercial publications (Brook 1998, 662–664). Scholars were expected to own libraries of classic texts and copies of palace editions. However, the bulk of books sold were inexpensive editions published in large volume. Although classic texts required for the imperial examinations were produced cheaply in this way, by the late Ming period, most commercial printing was made up of publications requiring a more limited vocabulary. Among the popular categories were almanacs, joke books, erotica, novels and accounts of customs in other East-Asian societies. Indeed, in the development of the first novels, the Chinese were a half century or more in advance of the West (Brook 2013, 201).

One type of publication that was missing in mid-sixteenth-century China in comparison to England was the privately printed periodical. As early as 1582, under the late Ming, there were privately published news sheets copied by hand (Brook 1998, 172). However, there was no true newspaper in Chinese until publications such as *Shen Bao*, first published in Shanghai in 1872 (Rowe 2009, 251). Nevertheless, the imperial government did publish an official bulletin that Westerners referred to as the *Peking Gazette*. Printed with changing frequency until the fall of the Qing regime in 1912, the *Gazette* was distributed throughout the administration to inform officials of government actions. In addition to copies of decrees, the publication also related the activities of the emperor and personnel changes, along with military and diplomatic news (Brook 1998, 639). Throughout most of the Ming era, because of the high cost of block printing, the *Gazette* was hand-copied, with a consequently limited diffusion. However, in 1638 the regime began publishing an edition printed with movable type (Brook 1998, 171) Another example of such top-down communication was the gazetteer mentioned earlier, published by magistrates at the county level to inform citizens of projects that their local officials were undertaking (Brook 1998, 655).

As we shall see in the next chapter, it required many years of study to be able to read books in Literary Chinese. However, there was a large market in each region for books written in the local dialect. Readers included women from educated families, merchants and clerks. In Suzhou, the writer Feng Menglong (1574–1645) wrote collections of popular short stories in the vernacular about monks and thieves, kings and courtesans (Ebrey 1996, 202).

The center of the commercial publishing industry was Jiangnan, the wealthy and densely populated lower valley of the Yangtze River. The cities of Suzhou, Hangzhou, Nanjing and Huzhou were home to the principal publishers. Paper made from pounded hemp or mulberry bark had been used in China for writing as early as the first-century CE (Temple 2007, 92). However, by 1600, the principal ingredient in the paper on which inexpensive books were printed was bamboo. Accordingly, the actual printing industry in China was centered south of the Yangtze in the province of Fujian, the location of the country's principal bamboo forests (Brook 1998, 663).

Censorship under the Ming was sporadic and often ineffective. In 1376, the Hongwu Emperor, the founder of the dynasty, had requested that his subjects criticize his regime. Yet when a scholar named Ye Boju wrote that the emperor had imposed unduly harsh sentences for minor crimes, the emperor had him arrested. The prisoner subsequently died of starvation in prison. Several of Hongwu's successors also imprisoned or executed those who dared criticize imperial rule (Ebrey 1996, 212–213). However, in the late sixteenth century, a number of scholars began to use Buddhist and Taoist sources to criticize the use of Confucian texts as required reading for the imperial examinations. In theory, the Board of Rites was supposed to suppress this kind of heterodoxy. Yet despite warnings, publishers found ways to circumvent official sanctions. One author, for example, remarked in his preface that new ideas would be presented only to allow their shortcomings to be exposed. Nevertheless, the reader was left with the possibility of deciding whether or not the novel ideas were valid (Chow 1996, 135).

In early modern China, although printed materials were cheap, there was no sudden increase in the output of books and newspapers comparable to that of England in the mid-seventeenth century. Nor did anything similar occur in India or the Ottoman Empire—at least prior to the nineteenth century. The following chapter will offer an explanation for this difference.

3.6 The Asymmetric Diffusion of Two Macro-inventions

This chapter has compared the impact of two "macro-inventions"—paper and printing—on the circulation of information in England and in the three great Asian empires. Industrial production of paper began in China early in the current era and had diffused widely across the Islamic world by the end of the first millennium. However, paper became common in Northern Europe only in the fourteenth century.

Block printing or xylography was little used for text in the West after the introduction of printing with movable type in the middle of the fifteenth century. Until the end of the sixteenth century, English publishers were slower than their Continental counterparts in adopting the printing press. Then suddenly, in the middle decades of the seventeenth century, there was a great increase in the number of book titles published. In addition, despite government censorship, a new market appeared for newspapers and pamphlets containing news of contemporary developments in England and abroad.

In China, both literary works in Classical or Literary Chinese and popular writings in dialect, printed on bamboo paper with wooden blocks, were inexpensive under the late Ming Dynasty. As for periodicals, the official *Peking Gazette*, hand-copied, informed officials about activities of the central government. Prior to the last decades of the Qing dynasty, there were no privately published printed newspapers! However, nonofficial hand-copied news sheets circulated under the late Ming.

Unlike the Chinese, the Muslim world made little use of block printing, in part because the potential markets were too small to justify the high fixed cost of cutting Perso-Arabic characters into the required wooden blocks. Printing presses with movable type were used by Jewish and Christian minorities within the Ottoman Empire dating from the late fifteenth and sixteenth centuries, respectively. The first Muslim printing press was set up in Istanbul in 1727. However as we saw, only 142 titles were printed before 1838. It was not until the mid-nineteenth century that the first newspapers in Turkish were published.

The first printing presses in India were installed by Jesuit missionaries in Goa in the mid-sixteenth century. However, the Mughal regime showed little interest in print technology, preferring the high quality of hand-written manuscripts for Perso-Arabic script. Danish missionaries were the first to print in an Indian script (Tamil)—in the early eighteenth century. The first books written by Indians in Indian languages were printed only in the first decade of the nineteenth century. The first *newspapers* written by Indians in Indian languages were printed shortly thereafter, in the early 1820s.

In the next chapter, we will examine how this asymmetric diffusion of paper and the printing press across Eurasia influenced people's ability to read and write.

REFERENCES

Agoston, G., & Masters, B. (2009). *Encyclopedia of the Ottoman Empire*. New York: Facts on File.

Barnard, J., & Bell, M. (1998). Statistical tables. In J. Barnard & D. F. McKenzie (Eds.), *The Cambridge history of the book in Britain, vol. IV, 1557–1695* (pp. 779–793). Cambridge, UK: Cambridge University Press.

Baten, J., & van Zanden, J. L. (2008). Book production and the onset of modern economic growth. *Journal of Economic Growth, 13*(3), 217–235.

Begum, F. (1989). John Borthwick Gilchrist. In A. Datta (Ed.), *Encyclopaedia of Indian literature* (Vol. II, pp. 1409–1410). New Delhi: Sahitya Akademi.

Bertrand, C.-J. (1969). *The British press: An historical survey*. Paris: OCDL.

Bloom, J. M. (1999, June). *Revolution by the ream: A history of paper*. Retrieved October 26, 2015, from Aramco World. Vol. 50, Number 3. https://www.saudia ramcoworld.com/issue/199903/revolution.by.the.ream-a.history.of.paper.htm

Brook, T. (1998). *The confusions of pleasure: Commerce and culture in Ming China*. Berkeley: University of California Press.

Brook, T. (2013). *The troubled empire: China in the Yuan and Ming dynasties*. Cambridge, MA: Belknap Press.

Chambers, W., & Chambers, R. (1848). Gleanings in bibliography. *Chambers' Edinburgh Journal, 9–10*(211), 43–45.

Chow, K.-W. (1996). Writing for success: Printing, examinations, and intellectual change in late Ming China. *Late Imperial China, 17*(1), 120–157.

Dunan-Page, A., & Lynch, B. (2008). *Roger L'Estrange and the making of restoration culture*. Aldershot: Ashgate.

Ebrey, P. B. (1996). *The Cambridge illustrated history of China*. Cambridge, UK: Cambridge University Press.

Eisenstein, E. L. (1979). *The printing press as an agent of change*. Cambridge, UK: Cambridge University Press.

Fallows, J. (2013). *The 50 greatest breakthroughs since the wheel*. Retrieved October 19, 2015, from theatlantic.com. http://www.theatlantic.com/magazine/archi ve/2013/11/innovations-list/309536/

Ghosh, A. (2003). An uncertain 'coming of the book': Early print cultures in colonial India. In E. Greenspan & J. Rose (Eds.), *Book history* (Vol. 6, pp. 23–56). University Park: Pennsylvania State University Press.

Hanioglu, M. S. (2008). *A brief history of the late Ottoman Empire*. Princeton: Princeton University Press.

Hirsch, R. (1974). *Printing, selling and reading*. Wiesbaden: Otto Harrassowitz.

Houston, R. A. (1988). *Literacy in early modern Europe: Culture and education 1500–1800*. London: Longman.

Kesavan, B. S. (1985). *History of printing and publishing in India* (Vol. I). New Delhi: National Book Trust, India.

Kurlansky, M. (2016). *Paper: Paging through history*. New York: W. W. Norton.

Lagally, K. (1992). ArabTEX – Typesetting Arabic with vowels and ligatures. *MAPS, 9*, 108–116.

Lunde, P. (1981). *Arabic and the art of printing*. Retrieved October 27, 2015, from aramcoworld.com. http://www.aramcoworld.com/issue/198102/arabic.and.the.art.of.printing-a.special.section.htm

Maddison, A. (2005). *Growth and interaction in the world economy: The roots of modernity*. Washington, DC: AEI Press.

Man, J. (2002). *The Gutenberg revolution: The story of a genius and an invention that changed the world*. London: Review.

McKenzie, D. F. (1998). Printing and publishing 1557–1700: Constraints on the London book trades. In J. Barnard & D. F. McKenzie (Eds.), *The Cambridge history of the book in Britain, vol. IV, 1557–1695* (pp. 553–567). Cambridge, UK: Cambridge University Press.

Naik, P. (2006). *450 years of printing in India*. Retrieved from goanet.org. http://www.mail-archive.com/goanet@lists.goanet.org/msg03166.html

Natarajan, S. (1962). *A history of the press in India*. Bombay: Asia Publishing House.

Nelson, C., & Seccombe, M. (1998). The creation of the periodical press, 1620–1695. In J. Barnard & D. F. McKenzie (Eds.), *The Cambridge history of the book in Britain, vol. IV, 1557–1695* (pp. 533–549). Cambridge, UK: Cambridge University Press.

Norman, J. (1988). *Chinese*. Cambridge, UK: Cambridge University Press.

Offenberg, A. K. (1969). The first printed book produced at constantinople: (Jacob ben Ašer's 'Arba'ah Ṭûrîm, December 13, 1493). *Studia Rosenthaliana, 3*, 96–112.

Qozhaya. (2015). *Short history of the monastery of Saint Anthony, the great valley of Qozhaya*. Retrieved December 16, 2015, from Qozhaya.com. http://www.qozhaya.com/history.html

Raven, J. (1998). The economic context. In J. Barnard & D. F. McKennzie (Eds.), *The Cambridge history of the book in Britain, vol. IV, 1557–1695* (pp. 568–582). Cambridge, UK: Cambridge University Press.

Raymond, J. (2011). News. In S. Doran & N. Jones (Eds.), *The Elizabethan world* (pp. 495–510). London: Routledge.

Ricci, M. (1953 [original 1615]). *China in the sixteenth century: The journals of Matthew Ricci, 1583–1610* (trans: Gallagher, L. J). New York: Random House.

Roberts, J. (1998). The Latin trade. In J. Barnard & D. F. McKenzie (Eds.), *The Cambridge history of the book in Britain, vol. IV, 1557–1695* (pp. 141–173). Cambridge: Cambridge University Press.

Roper, G. (1995). Faris al-Shidyaq and the transition from scribal to print culture in the Middle East. In G. N. Atiyeh (Ed.), *The book in the Islamic world: The written word and communication in the Middle East* (pp. 209–231). Albany: State University of New York Press.

Roper, G. (2010). *Manuscripts and printing in the spread of Muslim science*. Retrieved October 27, 2015, from Muslim Heritage. http://www.muslimheritage.com/article/manuscripts-and-printing-spread-muslim-science

Rowe, W. T. (2009). *China's last empire: The great Qing*. Cambridge, MA: Belknap Press.

Sarkiss, H. J. (1937). The Armenian renaissance, 1500–1863. *Journal of Modern History, 9*(4), 433–448.

Snatak, V. (1989). Lallulal. In A. Datta (Ed.), *Encyclopedia of Indian literature* (pp. 2241–2241). New Delhi: Sahitya Akademi.

Temple, R. (2007). *The genius of China: 3000 years of science, discovery & invention*. Rochester: Inner Traditions.

Treadwell, M. (1998). The stationers and the printing acts at the end of the seventeenth century. In J. Barnard & D. F. McKenzie (Eds.), *The Cambridge history of the book in Britain, vol. IV, 1557–1695* (pp. 755–776). Cambridge: Cambridge University Press.

Watson, W. J. (1968). İbrāhīm Müteferriḳa and Turkish Incunabula. *Journal of the American Oriental Society, 88*(3), 435–441.

CHAPTER 4

Literacy

4.1 Literacy in Britain

Who was reading the great outpouring of material that was printed in England after 1640? Obviously, the readers were the minority of people who were literate. However, there were many shades of literacy. One dimension was the number of words that the individual recognized. Another aspect was whether or not the person also knew how to write. The most commonly used measure of literacy rates for the early modern period is the proportion of brides and grooms able to sign their marriage register. However, it should be realized that although reading and writing were related skills, these signature rates may underestimate the ability to read.

Mastering reading in English took from 1 to 3 years of training. Writing required an additional period of the same length (Houston 1988, 130). However, a child could earn a meaningful wage as a laborer from the age of 7. Accordingly, it was common for a boy or girl to be sent to school until the age of 7 and then put to work, able to read but not to write. As Margaret Spufford (1979, 414) noted, among the children of laborers, the ability to read was therefore more widespread than the ability to write. Consequently, signature ratios may underestimate the percentage of people able to read printed works. Gerald MacLean (1994, 311) pointed out that this measure is particularly biased as an indication of the literate skills of women, since girls were generally allowed fewer years of schooling than boys and accordingly taken out of school before they had learned to write. In one Yarmouth school cited by David Cressy (1980, 34), none of the girls attained the stage of writing, while the boys, who stayed until age 15 or 16, could write reasonably well when they left.

Can changes in literacy levels explain the extraordinary increase in the output of reading material in England in the mid-seventeenth century that we observed in the preceding chapter? In the year 1600, the English were still trying to adjust to the great changes in the education system that had occurred over the preceding century. The population of England and Wales had more than doubled since 1500, increasing from two million to over four million. This demographic growth was felt especially in the capital, London, which quadrupled in population, growing from 50 thousand to 200 thousand, due mainly to migration from the provinces (Bairoch et al. 1988).

As a result of the Reformation, the state had replaced the church as the main promoter of education. By 1538, all churches were required to have a Bible in English (Graff 1991, 151). At the secondary-school level, Henry VIII restructured the Catholic cathedral schools as Protestant grammar schools, with a government-prescribed curriculum (Cressy 1975, 6–7). In addition, there were many new grammar schools founded—at least 136 between 1558 and 1603 (Cressy 1975, 6–7). From the mid-sixteenth century, all teachers were required to be licensed by the Church of England (Cressy 1975, 8). With the break from Rome, there was a new emphasis on teaching the English language. However, the level of instruction depended to a great extent on social class. Sons of privileged families would study under a tutor, while children of less wealthy townsfolk would be sent to the local school. At the elementary level, the public grammar schools taught English to the sons of the professional and middle classes as preparation for Latin. In a number of communities, there were also endowed schools to teach the youngest children the elementary curriculum. These formal institutions were generally financed by charitable foundations or by community subscription (Cressy 1980, 35).

The largest group of pupils was taught where there was no formal school. Provided that there was a competent teacher, a rented room or the parish church would suffice in the place of a schoolhouse. Freelance teachers who moved about from village to village—or in some cases, the parish clergy—might charge three or four pence weekly per child in exchange for teaching reading or grammar (Cressy 1980, 36).

A basic aid to teaching reading was the hornbook, a piece of paper glued to a wooden board and covered with a transparent sheet of horn. On it was written the alphabet along with perhaps a prayer for beginning readers. Also popular were alphabet books with an accompanying religious text. In addition, there were primers for teaching reading, an early example being John Hart's *A Method or comfortable beginning for all unlearned whereby they may be taught to read English in a very short time*, first printed in 1570. Another primer, by Edmund Coote, was printed in 48 editions between 1596 and 1696 (Cressy 1980, 38).

By the year 1600, then, the essential structure of the English educational system had been established. It was a system that favored children of the wealthy over those of the poor, city residents over those in the country, London over the provinces and boys over girls. Nevertheless, access to the printed word was potentially available to most boys and girls for the first time in English history. A hundred years earlier, the literacy rate among men had been around ten percent, among women perhaps two percent. As a result of the expansion of the school system, both formal and informal, almost 30 percent of men and ten percent of women were able to read and write by the end of Elisabeth I's reign (Cressy 1980, 177). An additional but unknown percentage of the population had not learned to write, but were nevertheless able to read. In short, despite extremely rapid population growth, the overall literacy rate had risen from 5 or 6 percent to almost 20 percent by the turn of the seventeenth century.

The challenge for the English was to broaden the percentage of children who had access to this system. Over the course of the seventeenth century, the total population of England and Wales increased by only a quarter (Maddison 2001, 247). For the first four decades of the century, there were no major wars, either external or internal, James I having made peace with Spain in 1603. With a slowing of population growth and the return of peace, it was possible to increase the school attendance rates. Indeed, up until 1640, with sufficient resources available to be channeled into the building of schools and the training of teachers, considerable progress was made, particularly for middle-income social groups (Cressy 1980, 170–171). For example, in the Diocese of Norwich, Cressy's data show that between 1600 and 1640, the literacy rate for trades and craftsmen rose from 50 percent to 70 percent (Graff 1991, 156).

With the outbreak of civil war in the 1640s, the expansion of the school system came to an abrupt stop. University admissions, which had swelled in the 1620s and 1630s, dropped off sharply, thereby reducing the supply of new teachers (Cressy 1980, 172). It was not until the final years of the Protectorate and the beginning of the Restoration in the late 1550s and early 1660s that literacy again became a priority for English society. Then in the 1680s and 1690s, school foundings and university matriculations dropped off once again (Cressy 1980, 173). At the end of the century, the literacy rate for trades and craftsmen in the Diocese of Norwich remained where it had been in 1640 (Graff 1991, 156).

On the whole, over the seventeenth century, the male signature rate rose to only a little over 40 percent. Slightly more than one-quarter of women were able to sign their names. As a result, in 1700 one out of three people in the English population could read and write (Cressy 1980, 177).

This result leaves us with a question. The big change in literacy occurred in the sixteenth century with the Reformation, when the male literacy rate almost tripled, jumping from 10 percent to 29 percent, while the female rate quadrupled, climbing from around two to almost ten percent. Yet during this period, there was only a modest annual increase in the demand for books and virtually no demand at all for periodicals, especially those describing domestic developments. Between 1600 and 1640, the signature rates barely changed, but abruptly from 1641 on, there was nevertheless an explosion of demand for a wide variety of books and pamphlets and, above all, for news.

In short, the explosion in the demand for books and periodicals in the first half of the seventeenth century cannot be explained by the moderate observed increase in literacy rates. What was it, then, that triggered this sudden desire for the most recent information—a craving that quickly became a permanent feature of British society? Chapter 5 will offer an explanation. First, though, for purposes of comparison, we must examine literacy rates in the principal Asian societies.

4.2 Literacy in the Ottoman Empire

The traditional Ottoman society was nomadic, its military success based on a combination of light and heavy cavalry. The constant training for mounted warfare from an early age precluded formal education for men. Similarly, the training of the slave-based infantry units such as the Janissaries was not compatible with learning to read and write. Ottoman society was therefore largely an oral society. Nevertheless, the administration of an empire that stretched from Hungary to the Persian Gulf required literate administrators.

From the late fourteenth to the late seventeenth centuries, as described in Chap. 2, most Ottoman officials were slaves recruited under what was known as the *devşirme* (collecting) system. To break the power of the Turkish nobility, young boys were taken forcibly from Christian families in the Balkans, converted to Islam and trained for military or civil service under the direct command of the sultan. The most promising recruits were trained at the Topkapi Palace to read and write in Ottoman Turkish. Over the course of the seventeenth century, however, this source of administrative personnel gradually became less important than the hiring of sons of the Ottoman elite who had been trained within the households of viziers and pashas (Quataert 2005, 101).

For *Muslim* boys, the principal educational institutions were the traditional Quran schools at the primary level and the *medreses* or Islamic high schools at a higher level. These schools were devoted primarily to religious instruction based on memorization of texts in the Arabic language (Somel 2001, 15–17). A madrasa was generally partly funded by a charitable trust known as a *waqf*. In Istanbul, there were eight higher medreses for advanced studies and eight lower medreses to prepare students for the higher level. The lower institutions gave instruction in writing, Arabic and in the intellectual sciences of logic and dialectics. The higher institutions were devoted to the spiritual sciences, including mathematics, ethics and the study of the Quran. There were similar institutions in the other major cities of the empire (Inalcik 1973, 165–168).

Although the primary objective of the medreses was religious, they did teach the pupils to read and write. On the basis of European travelers' reports, Somel (2001, 19) asserted that in the mid-seventeenth century, at least a quarter of the urban population could read and write in Turkish. However, this figure seems high. Since very few females could read, it would imply a male urban literacy rate of around 50 percent. A more plausible estimate from the early nineteenth century is that the overall Muslim literacy rate was about two percent to three percent (Quataert 2005, 169).

4.3 Literacy in India

To understand the role of literacy in Indian society on the eve of the Industrial Revolution, it is helpful to examine the origins of the society's writing systems. In India prior to 300 BCE, all transmission of literature and culture was oral (Scharfe 2002, 12). Pupils were required to memorize the Vedic hymns and mantras and to be able to recount epics and manuals of behavior. Such education was usually reserved for boys of the highest caste, the Brahmans (Scharfe 2002, 13–15). With the spread of writing from the time of Ashoka (r. 268–232 BCE), education was extended to the Kshatriya (warrior) and Vaishya (commercial) castes, each group receiving training appropriate for its social position (Scharfe 2002, 83). Children of the Shudras, the lowest caste who did menial tasks, were generally excluded from the educational system (Prabhu 2006, 24).

Raids of Muslim Turko-Afghans during the eleventh and twelfth centuries severely disrupted India's traditional educational institutions (Sen 1988, 12). In the first decades of the new millennium, Mahmud of Ghazni sacked numerous cities in northern India, destroying their Hindu temples and sometimes massacring their populations. In 1192, the victory of Mu'izz ad-Din Muhammad (Muhammad of Ghori) against an army of Hindu Rajput nobles at Tarain, 90 miles (150 km) north of Delhi marked the beginning of permanent Muslim conquest in present-day India. By the following year, the invaders had conquered much of the upper valley of the Ganges and its tributaries. The Delhi Sultanate, ruled by a succession of Muslim warriors, lasted as a major power in northern India until the early sixteenth century. The principal interruption to the sultans' rule came in 1398, when a Turko-Mongol army commanded by Timur the Lame (Tamerlane) conquered the Delhi Sultanate and pillaged the city of Delhi, massacring or enslaving all of the non-Muslim population (Keay 2000, 274).

In the sixteenth century, with the establishment of the Mughal Empire, relative peace returned to northern India. The subsequent expansion of industry and trade led to an increased demand for paper. In addition, the system of administration set up under Akbar required great quantities of paper for official documents. The Muslim conquerors placed considerable emphasis on knowledge of the Quran and on the study of other religious documents. The wealthy also had extensive collections of poetry and secular literature. The emperor himself is said to have had a library of 24,000 volumes, although he himself could neither read nor write. Since there were still no printing presses, all books were still copied by hand (Konishi 2013, 49–51).

Paper-making had been introduced into northwest India from Samarkand (in present-day Uzbekistan) in the fifteenth century (Konishi 2013, 98). To meet the growing demand for paper under the Mughals in the sixteenth and seventeenth centuries, hundreds of paper factories and workshops were set up across north and central India (Konishi 2013, 56). However, consumption of paper was not limited to the Muslims. As late as 1800, there were still 100 craftsmen working in Junnar, a short distance north of the capital of the Hindu Maratha Confederacy, Pune, on the Deccan Plateau 90 miles (150 km) east of Mumbai (Konishi 2013, 104).

Akbar greatly expanded the Muslim educational institutions (Kumar 2003, 678). However, he also encouraged the revival of traditional learning in Sanskrit (Yadav 2013). After the destruction of the medieval period, the efforts of Akbar and his successors to support educational institutions in northern India almost certainly raised levels of literacy.

When the British administrators of the East India Company first began to acquire territory in Bombay, Madras and Bengal in the mid-eighteenth century, they discovered well-established education systems at both the elementary and secondary levels. The two levels of schools were organized and financed in quite different ways. Prior to the restructuring of the education system in India by the British in the 1830s, locally financed elementary schools existed in most villages of India. Sir Thomas Munro, a Scottish officer and administrator of the East India Company, estimated that in the Madras presidency in 1822, one boy in six between the ages of 5 and 10 years was attending some form of village school. In the Bombay presidency in the same period, the corresponding figure was one in eight (Jha 2011, 120). In a survey of Bengal and Bihar in the 1830s, William Adams, a British Baptist minister, found that from 2.5 percent to 16 percent of boys between 5 and 14 years of age received some instruction in reading (Scharfe 2002, 84).

At the elementary level, the great majority of pupils in the village schools were Hindus of the upper castes. However, there were also Muslims, Christians and children of other minority religions and castes. Parents often sent their children to study with a teacher of another cast or even another religion (Jha 2011, 128). Instruction was given in the local or regional languages, neither Sanskrit nor Persian being used in elementary education (Jha 2011, 121). The content of elementary education consisted of vernacular writings in the local or regional language. Commercial and agricultural bookkeeping were also taught (Jha 2011, 121). In the towns, every mosque had an attached *maktab* for religious instruction (Kumar 2003, 678). It is interesting to note that in the Indian-language schools, students learned to write the alphabet before they learned to read, whereas in the Muslim schools, the students first learned to read and only later to write (Scharfe 2002, 82).

Post-primary education was reserved for the sons of the upper castes and classes. Schools were divided by religion into two groups. In the Hindu *pathshalas*, teaching was in Sanskrit using classical texts. The Muslim *madrasas* used Persian or Arabic texts. These secondary schools were financed by grants from rulers or wealthy citizens. Not only were there no school fees, but also the schools provided food and lodging to their students (Nurullah and Naik 1964, 21).

The results of these efforts were quite evident to the British, who began colonial rule of Bengal under the auspices of the East India Company in the second half of the eighteenth century. Literacy rates in India in 1800 were quite similar to those in England three centuries earlier. Very few women could read or write. However, men able to sign their names represented about 9 percent of the total male population or perhaps 11–12 percent of adult males (Nurullah and Naik 1964, 18–20). However, after the introduction of school reforms emphasizing the English language under the British in the 1830s, the financing of traditional schools was increasingly neglected. In 1881, in spite of the increasing numbers of pupils educated in English, the literacy rate in India (male and female) was still only 6.3 percent (Aggarwal 2002, 3).

In summary, despite the absence of the printing press, male literacy rates in India were probably rising over the early modern period, first under the Mughals and later under the successor states. Nevertheless, in the 1830s at most one man in ten was able to read (Scharfe 2002, 84).

4.4 Literacy in China

In 1488, a Korean official named Choe Bu was shipwrecked on the coast of China, south of Shanghai. Although he could not speak Chinese, he found that he was able to communicate with the local sailors who found him by drawing characters that Korean scholars had borrowed from the Chinese in devising their own writing system. Subsequently, as he was escorted along the Grand Canal to Beijing, he was astonished to find that not only sailors but also village children and ferrymen were able to read (Brook 1998, 636). At this time in England in contrast, it is unlikely that even one man in ten was able to read (Cressy 1980, 176).

The Ming Dynasty had gradually rebuilt China's education system after the destruction of the civil wars during the last years of the Mongol Yuan dynasty (Hucker 1998, 31). At the lowest level were community schools that taught elementary education in the villages and urban neighborhoods. At the next level was a well-structured hierarchy of local government-financed secondary schools that had no equivalent in Europe. Under the Ming, China was divided administratively into 15 provinces and some 1500 prefectures and counties. The administrative center of each of these regions had its own state school, some of which by the end of the dynasty enrolled up to 2000 students (Lee 2000, 97). The program of study, based on the classics of Chinese literature, was designed to train future government officials. Probably less than one percent of the male population had passed the exams of these county-level colleges that certified their knowledge of the more than 3000 characters required to read Literary Chinese (Heijdra 1998, 561).

Each year, these Confucian schools were required to send their best students to the two national universities, one in Nanjing and the other in Beijing. Under a system of fixed quotas, prefectural schools could send two students a year and county schools one a year (Hucker 1998, 33). Upon graduation from the universities, the scholars could apply for positions in the civil service. However, there was an alternative channel for access to government employment. Parallel to the state school system was a separate network of private academies that also prepared students for official positions under a similar program of classical studies. In addition, these academies hosted scholars who participated in philosophical seminars.

One such institution was the Donglin Academy, in the Yangtze Delta city of Wuxi. The institution had been formed in the twelfth century but had subsequently been allowed to decline. Restored in 1604, it educated many of the imperial officials who were active in the last years of the reign of Wanli. The members of the academy rejected the ideas of the liberal scholar and official Wang Yangming (1462–1529). According to Wang, every person had within him intuitively the knowledge of good and evil. It was through action, rather than through rational reflection, that one could gain further knowledge (Ebrey 1996, 206). The scholars at the restored Donglin Academy argued that instead of allowing each individual to follow his own innate judgment, the society should return to traditional Confucian values. The Academy's graduates were influential in the censorate, the central institution designed to prevent malfeasance and corruption (Ebrey 1996, 213).

With a population approaching 200 million, the Ming Empire required large numbers of trained officials to administer its army, tax system, courts and infrastructure of roads and canals. The Sui and Tang dynasties had made only limited use of state examinations to select promising candidates for civil service positions (Ebrey 1996, 145). Even during the first decades of the Ming Dynasty, most posts were still filled by recommendations from serving officials. After 1440, however, almost all specialized clerical and technical personnel were recruited through the state examination system (Hucker 1998, 35). State schools, universities and private academies were structured in order to prepare students for these empire-wide examinations (Heijdra 1998, 560).

During the Ming Dynasty, the imperial examination system consisted of three levels. The first level of exams was scheduled every 3 years both in the imperial capital and in the capital of each of the 15 provinces. To be able to compete, a candidate had to have completed the program of studies in the state schools or the equivalent in an academy or with a private tutor. In each province, candidates also had to pass an initial test prepared by the education intendant to confirm that their competence justified allowing them to participate in the official examination. Then over a week in the eighth month of the lunar calendar, the candidates would take 3-day-long written examinations based on the Four Books, the Five Classics and the history of China, that is, on the content of the program of study in the Confucian schools. They also had to write an "eight-legged essay" in a prescribed style. The regime fixed a quota for the number of successful candidates in each province. On average, there were in total some 300–400 successful graduates per year at this first level (Hucker 1998, 39–40).

In the second lunar month of the year following the provincial examinations, the second-level exams were held in the imperial capital. All who had ever graduated at the first level were eligible, but by the late sixteenth century, there was a short qualifying test. Of the 1000–2000 candidates, for this "grand competition", on average only 90 were successful. These fortunate few then gathered at the palace at the beginning of the following month for a final brief exam designed to sort the graduates by order of competence (Hucker 1998, 37–38).

There was one other component of the education system that should be mentioned. Since late antiquity, Chinese emperors had employed eunuchs for domestic tasks within the royal household. As mentioned in Sect. 2.5, the founder of the Ming Dynasty, the Hongwu Emperor (1328–1398), had decreed that eunuchs were to remain illiterate in order to prevent them from obtaining power over state policy. However, his successors insisted on having employees who were entirely dependent on their own personal favor. In 1429, the Xuande Emperor (r. 1425–1435) set up a palace school where boy eunuchs were taught to read and write by educated officials (Hucker 1998, 24). Four imperial academy scholars were appointed to educate some 300 castrated boys (Anderson 1990, 223). The inevitable result was a parallel bureaucracy, made up entirely of eunuchs, that competed with the regular civil service.

When the Wanli Emperor died in August 1620, he was succeeded by his first-born son, who was given the reign name Taichang. Less than a month later, however, the new ruler was found dead. In turn, Taichang's oldest son, a boy of 15 years, now mounted the throne as the Tianqi Emperor. The young man had shown little interest in his studies and, although a skilled carpenter, was functionally illiterate. He was content to leave the control of the empire to his nanny, Madame Ke, and her associate, Wei Zhongxian, an illiterate eunuch who was a former butler in the household of the dowager empress, Tianqi's mother. Wei was named chief eunuch and also minister of rites, a position usually reserved for an accomplished scholar. With the emperor's implicit backing, Wei proceeded to replace top officials by men loyal to himself.

In 1622, Wei and his associates arranged to have the Donglin Academy closed. Two years later, in 1624, the emperor received a missive from a leader of the Donglin faction within the administration that accused Wei of 24 great crimes, including murder, forging imperial orders and usurping the power of the Grand Secretariat. After the intervention of Madame Ke and the advisers Wei had appointed, however, the emperor not only forgave Wei but also censored the accuser for false charges. Wei subsequently had the director of the academy and five of its members arrested, tortured and executed. According to one source, in the civil service alone, 365 men were executed, beaten or banished to the empire's borders (Anderson 1990, 252). Meanwhile, Wei built a fortress-like temple for himself 35 miles (55 km) west of Beijing, in which he could take refuge in times of danger (Anderson 1990, 250).

During this period, the Chinese had been paying huge bribes to the Mongols so that they would remain neutral in the empire's conflicts with the Manchu. Fortunately, the imperial armies were still capable of defending China's borders. In 1621, the Chinese had begun to import Portuguese cannon from Macau. Using these weapons, the Chinese inflicted a humiliating defeat on the Manchu, who were attacking Ningyuan (present-day Xingcheng), a coastal town in the Liaoning Peninsula outside the Great Wall, in the northeast. Nurhaci, the Manchu ruler, was wounded by cannon fire and subsequently died of his injuries (Crossley 1997, ch. 1).

In September of the following year, 1627, the carpenter-emperor Tianqi died. His 17-year-old younger brother was put on the throne under the imperial title of the Chongzhen Emperor. As a young prince, the new ruler had always disliked the usurper, Wei Zhongxian. One of Chongzhen's first acts on assuming power, therefore, was to revoke the grants of power given to the eunuch and to banish him to a distant province. While traveling there, Wei learned that he was about to be arrested for his crimes; he thereupon committed suicide, hanging himself from his belt (Anderson 1990, 255). In the meantime, Chongzhen recalled those officials who had managed to survive their banishment or imprisonment at the eunuch's hands. The Ming Empire had gained a brief respite in which to reorganize itself.

4.5 Comparing Literacy Rates

We have seen that in the early nineteenth century, the adult male literacy rate literacy for Muslims in the Ottoman Empire was at best three percent. In India at this same time, the rate was somewhat higher—perhaps ten percent. If we project these rates backward to the early eighteenth century, these estimates should probably be regarded as upper bounds. In the West, literacy in the early modern period is usually measured by the ability to sign one's name on a marriage certificate—an indication that the person was likely able to both read and write. In England in the early 1700s, it is estimated that the male literacy rate by this measure was about 40 percent, and the female rate approximately 25 percent (Cressy 1980, 177). Unfortunately, no comparable information exists for China. However, data from the Chinese Board of Punishment files, which record criminal cases of farmers from the late seventeenth century, suggest that basic literacy among men in China in this period was significantly higher than in Europe (Baten et al. 2010, 353–354).[1]

In comparing literacy between Asia and the West, however, there are three points to consider. The first question is whether literacy means only reading or whether it involves both reading and writing. In England, it was expected that a child who had learned the elements of reading would immediately learn to write. A teaching manual, published in 1588 described how pupils were to be taught not only to pronounce letters, syllables and words with the mouth but also to "write them with the hand" (Cressy 1980, 20).

A second issue in discussing literacy is to examine what people were reading. As already mentioned, in England the rise in literacy over the seventeenth century was accompanied by the diffusion of a version of the Bible in English authorized by King James I in 1611 (see Fig. 4.1). Probate inventories from this period invariably mention the possession of one or more Bibles (Cressy 1980, 50). Of course, not all who owned a Bible were able to read it, but possession of the text may well have been an inducement

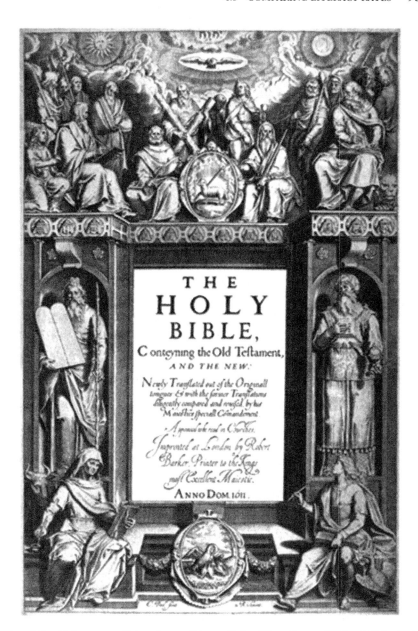

Fig. 4.1 Title page of the first edition of the King James Bible, 1611. This vernacular translation of the Bible has been the best-selling book in English since the seventeenth century (Reproduced from *Wikipedia Commons*)

to literacy. The seventeenth century also saw a great expansion in the publishing of popular literature. An important point to note is that after 1600 in England, almost all books and pamphlets were published in the vernacular.

In the seventeenth century, written Chinese was divided into two quite different registers—a classic case of diglossia. Most texts were written in Literary Chinese, a formal language modeled on the Classical Chinese used by authors such as Confucius in the period from 500 BCE to 200 CE (Dong 2014, ch. 7). Apart from the occasional use of the vernacular, the grammar and vocabulary of this formal language had changed little over the centuries. Literary Chinese was the register on which the state schools and imperial examinations were based.

Over the centuries, the everyday languages or vernaculars in China had drifted further and further from that spoken during the classical period. From the Tang Dynasty onward, some documents were written in a colloquial style based on the spoken language of the period. Buddhist scriptures were written in this style so that they could be more easily understood by the common people. Increasingly, too, there was popular literature composed of fiction, drama and poetry written in the style of the spoken language. This written vernacular was not standardized. In 1956, there were still between 1000 and 1600 "vulgar" forms being used, in addition to the more than 4000 or more characters employed by the educated (Hannas 1997, 20). Note that Standard Chinese or *pǔtōnghuà* today is essentially a standardized version of the vernacular of Beijing (Norman 1988, 136–137).

An important difference between the two registers was the greater use in the vernacular of compound words, that is, words composed of two syllables instead of one. One reason for disyllabification is that over the centuries, as the spoken language became simpler, words that had formerly been pronounced differently became homophones. To avoid confusion, their written forms had to be differentiated. Another reason for this change was the joining together of words that had formerly been separate (Dong 2014, ch. 7). When one speaks of widespread literacy in China in the early modern period, one is referring to literacy in the vernacular rather than in Literary Chinese. Only the relatively few who had qualified to take the first level of imperial examinations could read the Chinese classics (Rawski 1979, 2–3).

A final issue in comparing literacy in the West and Asia is the extent of the vocabulary. With 26 phonetic characters, an English reader had access to some 10,000 common words in the Bible.[2] Because of China's logosyllabic writing system, a passive knowledge of many hundreds of characters was necessary for the comprehension of even the simplest texts. A directive of a 1950 Chinese People's Congress defined literate as the ability to read and use at least 1000 characters. However, it is estimated that even with 1169 characters, one could understand only 91 percent of simple texts (Rawski 1979, 3). Although there were dictionaries for the 50,000 or more characters of Literary Chinese, no dictionary for the vernacular existed before the twentieth century.

In short, on the eve of the Industrial Revolution, despite a widespread ability among the male Chinese population to recognize the several hundred characters or more required in their daily lives, only a small fraction of the male population—perhaps one percent—was fully literate. The situation in the Ottoman Empire and India was similar. However, by 1700 in Britain, one person in three (including women!) was able to read and write, while literacy rates in northern France and America were comparable (Dudley 2016). By this measure, the West had left Asia far behind.

Literacy rates in Germany, Scandinavia and the Netherlands were even higher than in Britain (Reis 2005, 202). Nevertheless, Dudley (2016) found that three-quarters of the major industrial innovations between 1700 and 1850 originated in three narrow bands stretching from London to Manchester in England, from Le Havre through Paris to Lyon in France and from Connecticut to the Potomac River in the United States. Together these three countries contributed 95 percent of the innovations judged important by historians of technology (Dudley 2012, 174). If we wish to explain why before 1850 almost all significant industrial innovation occurred in Britain, France and the United States, rather than elsewhere on the planet, some additional consideration must be found.

Notes

1. This conclusion is based on data that measure age-heaping, the tendency of uneducated people to round off their ages, for example, stating their age as 50 rather than 49 or 51. The authors show that there is a strong negative correlation between age-heaping and literacy.
2. The bible contains 12,143 (http://amazingbibletimeline.com/bible_que stions/q10_bible_facts_statistics/) different words, of which 2600 are proper names (http://en.wikipedia.org/wiki/List_of_biblical_names).

References

Aggarwal, D. D. (2002). *History and development of elementary education in India* (Vol. 1). New Delhi: Sarap and Sons.

Anderson, M. M. (1990). *Hidden power: The palace eunuchs of imperial China*. Buffalo: Prometheus Books.

Bairoch, P., Batou, J., & Chèvre, P. (1988). *The population of European cities, 800–1850*. Geneva: Librairie Droz.

Baten, J., Ma, D., Morgan, S., & Wang, Q. (2010). Evolution of living standards and human capital in China in the 18–20th centuries: Evidences from real wages, age-heaping, and anthropometrics. *Explorations in Economic History, 47*, 347–359.

Brook, T. (1998). *The confusions of pleasure: Commerce and culture in Ming China*. Berkeley: University of California Press.

Cressy, D. (1975). *Education in Tudor and Stuart England*. New York: St. Martin's Press.

Cressy, D. (1980). *Literacy and the social order: Reading and writing in Tudor and Stuart England*. Cambridge, UK: Cambridge University Press.

Crossley, P. K. (1997). *The Manchus*. Oxford: Blackwell.

Dong, H. (2014). *A history of the Chinese language*. London: Routledge.

Dudley, L. (2012). *Mothers of innovation: How expanding social networks gave birth to the industrial revolution*. Newcastle upon Tyne: Cambridge Scholars.

Dudley, L. (2016). Language standardization and the industrial revolution. *Oxford Economic Papers Advance Access*. doi:10.1093/oep/gpw059.

Ebrey, P. B. (1996). *The Cambridge illustrated history of China*. Cambridge, UK: Cambridge University Press.

Graff, H. J. (1991). *The legacies of literacy*. Bloomington: Indiana University Press.

Hannas, W. C. (1997). *Asia's orthographic dilemma*. Honolulu: University of Hawaii Press.

Heijdra, M. (1998). The socio-economic development of rural China during the Ming. In D. Twitchett & F. W. Mote (Eds.), *Cambridge history of China* (Vol. 8, pp. 417–578). Cambridge, UK: Cambridge University Press.

Houston, R. A. (1988). *Literacy in early modern Europe: Culture and education 1500–1800*. London: Longman.

Hucker, C. O. (1998). Ming government. In D. Twitchett & F. W. Mote (Eds.), *The Cambridge history of China* (Vol. 8, pp. 9–105). Cambridge, UK: Cambridge University Press.

Inalcik, H. (1973). *The Ottoman Empire: The classical age 1300–1600*. New York: Praeger.

Jha, H. (2011). Decay of village community and the decline of vernacular education in Bihar and Bengal in the colonial era: A sociological review. *Indian Historical Review, 38*, 119–137.

Keay, J. (2000). *India: A history.* New York: Grove Press.
Konishi, M. (2013). *Hath-Kaghaz: History of handmade paper in South Asia.* New Delhi: Aryan Books International.
Kumar, D. (2003). India. In R. Porter (Ed.), *Cambridge history of science* (Vol. 4, pp. 669–687). Cambridge, UK: Cambridge University Press.
Lee, T. H. (2000). *Education in traditional China: A history.* Leiden: Brill.
MacLean, G. (1994). Literacy, class, and gender in restoration England. *Text, 7,* 307–335.
Maddison, A. (2001). *The world economy: A millennial perspective.* Paris: OECD.
Norman, J. (1988). *Chinese.* Cambridge, UK: Cambridge University Press.
Nurullah, S., & Naik, J. P. (1964). *A students' history of education in India (1806–1965).* Macmillan: Bombay.
Prabhu, J. (2006). Educational institutions and philosophies, traditional and modern. In S. Wolpert (Ed.), *Encyclopedia of India* (Vol. 2, pp. 23–28). Farmington Hills: Thomson Gale.
Quataert, D. (2005). *The Ottoman Empire 1700–1922* (2nd ed.). Cambridge, UK: Cambridge University Press.
Rawski, E. (1979). *Education and popular literacy in Ch'ing China.* Ann Arbor: University of Michigan Press.
Reis, J. (2005). Economic growth, human capital formation, and consumption in western Europe before 1800. In R. C. Allen, T. Bengtsson, & M. Dribe (Eds.), *Living standards in the past: New perspectives on well-being in Asia and Europe* (pp. 195–225). Oxford: Oxford University Press.
Scharfe, H. (2002). *Education in ancient India.* Leiden: Brill.
Sen, S. (1988). Education in ancient and medieval India. *Indian Journal of History of Science, 23,* 1–32.
Somel, S. A. (2001). *The modernization of public education in the Ottoman Empire, 1839–1908: Islamization, autocracy and discipline.* Leiden: Brill.
Spufford, M. (1979). First steps in literacy: The reading and writing experiences of the humblest seventeenth-century spiritual autobiographers. *Social History, 4*(3), 407–435.
Yadav, M. (2013). *Education in Mughal period during Akbar's rule – India.* Retrieved October 20, 2015, from importantindia.com. http://www.importantindia.com/5096/education-in-mughal-period-during-akbar-rule/

CHAPTER 5

Language Standardization

5.1 Language, Nationalism and the Willingness to Pay Taxes

Why are some cultural groups willing to pay a larger percentage of their income in taxes than others? Even among the world's wealthiest countries, there are considerable differences in the public share of total income. In recent decades, the Swiss have generally paid less than a third of their income in taxes, while the Swedes have at times contributed almost two-thirds of their total income to the state (Mueller 2003, 503). To answer this question, we must ask what a typical citizen would lose if he or she were sent into exile or prison, for it is to avoid such a hypothetical fate that one is willing to pay one's membership dues to the state in the form of taxes.

There exists a class of goods characterized by what are known as network externalities. Think of a social network such as *Facebook* of which you are a member. Now suppose that a friend who previously did not belong to the network suddenly decides to join. If so, you receive a benefit—a network externality—since you are now able to communicate with the friend more easily. The firm can charge the advertisers who use its network slightly more to take account of this effect.

Similarly, if the population of a region has learned to read and write using the language of an adjacent region and subsequently has the possibility of merging with that region to form a new state, residents of both regions might be willing to pay more in taxes to avoid being cut off from the benefits of the larger language network. Something very similar happened in 1696 when the

© The Author(s) 2017
L. Dudley, *The Singularity of Western Innovation*,
DOI 10.1057/978-1-137-39822-2_5

Scottish parliament decided to provide a school in every parish to teach reading and writing in Standard English rather than in Scots, a language that had its own literature (Herman 2001, 22). Eleven years later, the Scottish parliament approved the formation of a union with England. From that date, many English and Scots considered themselves to belong to the same nation. As a result, over the following centuries, they were willing to share the enormous cost of defending their joint society's interests.

In short, language standardization can have important fiscal consequences. Let us then examine what was happening across Eurasia during the early modern period to the capacity of people to understand those who were not their immediate neighbors.

5.2 Linguistic Convergence in Britain

Audiences and readers today often have considerable difficulty understanding the plays of Shakespeare.[1] One reason is that the vocabulary, grammar and pronunciation of the English language have evolved considerably since the turn of the seventeenth century. For example, in Act I, Scene 5 of *Hamlet*, first published in 1603, the ghost of the hero's father, who is about to depart as the sky begins to brighten, comments:

> The glow-worm shows the matin to be near
> And 'gins to pale his uneffectual fire.

Today the word "matin" appearing in this quotation may no longer be used as a noun meaning "morning", while "uneffectual" has been replaced by "ineffectual". In addition, the neuter possessive pronoun, which was "his" in Shakespeare's day, has now become "its" (Barber 1993, 186). However, we see that in his later plays such as *Hamlet*, for the third-person singular, Shakespeare was already incorporating the present-day ending "(e)s" instead of the Middle-English "(e)th" in "shows" and "*'gins*".

It was not only vocabulary and grammar that were changing. Since the beginning of the fifteenth century, pronunciation in southern England had been evolving in a process often referred to as the Great Vowel Shift (McMahon 2006, 171). The present-day long vowels in "beet" and "boot" had originally been pronounced as in today's "bate" and "boat". To avoid merging the pronunciation of words already pronounced in this way, this shift had pushed the long vowels in "bite" and "bout" from their late medieval pronunciation as in today's "beet" and "boot" into their current positions as diphthongs (Fennell 2001, 160). In Shakespeare's London, these changes were still in progress (Millward 1988, 219). However, in Northumberland, Cumbria or northern Yorkshire, "long night" would continue to be pronounced "lang neet" well into the nineteenth century (Crystal 2003, 324).

Changes of this kind are known as linguistic drift. They tend to occur in all languages as innovations that originate in one region fail to be adopted in other regions. During the past six millennia, the Indo-European languages and their respective dialects have *diverged* increasingly from one another because of this evolutionary process. As a result of such changes, by the early modern period, the spoken language even in England varied considerably from one region to another. For example, in 1605, Richard Verstegan, an Antwerp publisher who had grown up in London, observed that:

> one would say at London, *I would eat more cheese yf I had it*, the northern man saith, *Ay sud eat more cheese gin ay hadet*, and the western man saith: *Chud eat more cheese an chad it*. (cited in Freeborn 1992, 137)

However, apart from pronunciation, there is another reason why Shakespeare's English is difficult to understand for audiences and readers today. Over the century that followed Shakespeare's death in 1616, there occurred a change in the opposite direction, as the vernacular spoken in different regions of England *converged* toward a standard form. In order to understand this second process, consider another quotation, this one from the *King Lear*, Act IV, Scene 6 (originally published in 1608). Goneril's steward, Oswald, comes across Edgar, a young nobleman disguised as a peasant, in the company of the latter's blind father, Gloucester. Oswald plans to kill the old man in order to receive a reward that has been offered. When Edgar takes his father's arm, he is threatened by the steward. Edgar warns Oswald in a western regional dialect typical of Somerset, Devon or Cornwall:

> Nay, come not near th' old man: keep out che vor'ye, or ice try whither your Costard, or my Ballow be the harder; chill be plain with you. (cited in Freeborn 1992, 138)

Here the words "ice try" mean "I shall try". Shakespeare rarely used dialect in his plays (Freeborn 1992, 137)—probably because regionalisms would not have been understood by many members of his London audience. Grammarian Alexander Gil wrote in 1619 of those speaking regional dialects, "it is easily possible to doubt whether they are speaking English or some foreign language" (Blank 2006, 215).

As Paula Blank (2006, 213) has observed, the English language in the year 1600 was considered to be "confused". Regional heterogeneity was not the only reason for misunderstanding. Another source of confusion was the introduction of thousands of words borrowed from foreign languages. To meet the demand of the middle classes for works in English, it had been necessary to translate classical literature from Latin and Greek. When translators found that the existing treasury of English words was inadequate, they would coin an anglicized variant of the usually Latin original. In this way, words such as *discretion, exaggerate, expect, industrial* and *scheme* entered the English language. Despite being mocked as "inkhorn terms" by scholars who wished to preserve the purity of their tongue, many thousands of these borrowed words have been retained to the present day (Millward 1988, 198–199).

In Shakespeare's play, the actions on stage conveyed the meaning of Edgar's words unambiguously. In other kinds of interaction, such as two inventors working on a joint technical project, comprehension may not have been so easy. Is it possible to quantify the extent to which people from different regions in Shakespeare's day failed to understand one another? We may begin to appreciate their difficulties if we examine *present-day* comprehension of 17 dialects belonging to the Continental Scandinavian language family. A recent study of young Danes from Copenhagen indicated that the average intelligibility of spoken individual words from dialects other than one's own was remarkably low. As the first two lines of Table 5.1 indicate, comprehension ranged from about 50 percent for dialects from neighboring regions to about a third for distant regions within the same language family (Gooskens et al. 2008, 74). The local dialect of Copenhagen—Standard Danish, shown in the third line—was of course well understood.

Table 5.1 Intelligibility of Scandinavian dialects to Danes from Copenhagen

Dialect	*Distance (km)*	*Intelligibility (%)*
Neighboring regions	301	48
Distant regions	956	35
Standard Danish	0	99
Standard Swedish and Norwegian	628	62

Source: Gooskens et al. (2008, 66, 74)

Consider now the bottom line of Table 5.1, which shows the degree of comprehension of Standard Norwegian and Swedish. We see that as a result of exposure to books, newspapers, radio, television and films from the two neighboring countries, young Danes understand on average over 60 percent of these two standardized foreign languages. In the same way, early modern residents of provincial cities who had been exposed frequently to the London dialect, either through their own travel or through hearing visitors from the capital, were probably able to understand this variety of English reasonably well. For communication between two people from different regions, therefore, these London forms would gradually become the preferred medium, since each person could understand the dialect of the capital better than the other's regional dialect.

In the case of English, Milroy (1994, 20) identified two phases of this process of standardization. Between 1400 and about 1600, there was an initial period of supra-local standardization, during which consensus norms emerged spontaneously at the regional level as people from different communities close to one another interacted.

The Pleading in English Act of Edward III in 1362 had specified that all court proceedings must be conducted in English. Yet which English dialect was to be used and how was it to be written? In the 1430s, the Court of Chancery in the London district of Westminster, which dealt with contracts, land law and trusts, ceased preparing documents in French. The Court's clerks began to regularize the usage and spelling of such English words as *can*, *shall* and *should* (Crystal 2003, 41). Thus, when Caxton established his press in Westminster in 1476, he had a model for texts printed in English. This process of triage continued well into the seventeenth century. Despite the Chancery's influence, however, a century after Caxton's first publications, there were still multiple spellings being used; for example, one might find *felow*, *felowe*, *fallow* or *fallowe* (Crystal 2003, 66).

By 1600, the consensual pruning of the language spoken in the capital had about run its course. For the following two centuries, from about 1600 to 1800, language norms would be imposed externally. As Milroy (1994, 20) emphasized, however, the pressure was not overt, as occurred in France through the efforts of the *Académie française*. Rather the constraints were covert, resulting from the publication of written standards in the form of dictionaries and grammar texts. As a result, the variety spoken by a prestige group within London society gradually became the norm for written communication, although regional differences in pronunciation were accepted until more recently (Stein 1994, 4–6).

Before the last decades of the sixteenth century, there had been no need for an English dictionary, since educated male readers would have had little difficulty understanding any new terms that were being introduced into English from Latin or Greek. However, as the number of women who had been educated only in English increased, there was a demand for guidance, not only for reading printed texts but also for expressing oneself in writing (Millward 1988, 206). The first kind of monolingual English dictionary was a compilation of hard words to spell. In 1604, schoolmaster, Robert Cawdrey, published *A Table Alphabeticall*, compiling spellings and definitions for about 2500 difficult words. Over the following decades, increasingly long lists of hard words were published, culminating in 1656 in the 11,000 entries of Thomas Blount's *Glossographia* (Millward 1988, 206).

Two years later, in 1658, Edward Phillips published *The New World of English Words*, a dictionary of the same size, much of it copied word for word from Blount (see Fig. 5.1). Furious to see his own work undercut in this way, Blount took great pains to point out errors in his rival's text. What Blount failed to admit publicly was that he himself had copied 58 percent of the *Glossographia* from two earlier publications and borrowed heavily from a third (Green 1996, 160). In fact, however, Phillips was offering something new. By adding many common words that the hard-word lists had omitted, Phillips published what might be considered the first true monolingual English dictionary. Since his publication sold very well, he was evidently satisfying a demand that earlier word lists had failed to meet. Nathaniel Brooke published a second edition in 1663, and in 1678, a revised edition was published with over 20,000 entries (Millward 1988, 206–207). The 1706 revision of Phillips's dictionary prepared by John Kersey contained some 38,000 headwords. Most of the changes since 1568 were additional general vocabulary rather than the hard words on which Blount and his predecessors had concentrated (Green 1996, 170).

The commercial success of Phillips's dictionary, largely inspired by its immediate predecessor, demonstrated clearly that by the mid-seventeenth century, the English language was becoming standardized—at least in its written form. A publisher could contemplate the expense of setting the type for such a publication only if there were a potential market consisting of tens of thousands of people who wished to follow the same conventions in their reading and writing. During the second half of the century, this potential market even stretched across the Atlantic to New England. In 1666, John Usher, a Boston bookseller, was offering *The New World of English Words* at the London retail price of 10 shillings (Amory 1998, 747).

Fig. 5.1 Title page to *The New World of English Words*, 1658. Though plagiarized in part from an earlier compilation of hard words to spell, Edward Phillips's publication was the first English vernacular dictionary to include common words (Reproduced from *Folger Shakespeare Library*)

Table 5.2 First monolingual vernacular dictionary by country

Country	Year	Author	Publication
England	1658	Edward Phillips	*The New World of English Words*
France (north)	1680	Pierre Richelet	*Dictionnaire français*
Belgium (French)	1680		Same as France (north)
Switzerland (Fr.)	1680		Same as France (north)
Scotland	1707		Year of Union with England
United States	1728	Nathan Bailey	*An Universal Etymological English Dictionary*
Germany	1786	Johann Christoph Adelung	*Grammatisch-kritisches Wörterbuch der hochdeutschen Mundart*
Switzerland (Germ.)	1786		Same as Germany
Ireland	1800		Year of Union with England
France (south)	1815		Standardization delayed[a]
Denmark	1833	Christian Molbech	*Dansk Ordbog*
Belgium (Flem.)	1864		Same as the Netherlands
Netherlands	1864	Marcus and Nathan Solomon Calisch	*Nieuw Woordenboek der Nederlandsche Taal*
Austria	1868	Otto Back et al.	*Österreichisches Wörterbuch*
Italy	1897	Emilio Broglio and Giovanni Battista Giorgini	*Nòvo vocabolario della lingua italiana secondo l'uso di Firenze*
India (Hindi)	1929	Shyamsunder Das et al.	*Hindi shabda sagar*
Turkey	1932	Hamit Zübeyr and Ishak Refet	*Anadilden derlemeler*
China	1937	Zhuyin Fuhao and Gwoyeu Romatzyh	*Guoyu cidian*

Source: Dudley (2016)
Note: Other early dictionaries failed to reflect the existence of a standardized written vernacular. Robert Cawdrey's *Table Alphabeticall* (1604) was a list of hard words to spell. Josua Maaler's *Die Teütsch Spraach* (1561) was devoted to Swiss and Upper German vocabulary. The *Accademia della Crusca*'s dictionary of Italian (1612) was intended to provide a prescriptive norm to which writers were advised to conform. Cornelis Kiliaan's (1599) *Etymologicum* used Latin to explain Dutch words, as did Jean Nicot's (1606) *Trésor de la langue française* for the French language
[a]South of a line from St. Malo to Geneva, standardization occurred through the integrating effects of the revolutionary and Napoleonic Wars (Graff 1991, 193)

The English had been the first to have a monolingual dictionary in the vernacular (see Table 5.2). Shortly after, in 1680, Pierre Richelet published the first true monolingual dictionary of the French language. However it was not until 1786, over a century later, that the German language was sufficiently standardized to merit its own monolingual dictionary, that of Johann Christoph Adelung.

In 1728, John Gay amused London theatergoers with a satiric opera in which characters from the lowest strata of society mocked their middle-class betters. Although readers of the libretto today would note that nouns were still being capitalized, a live audience has no trouble understanding Filch's air describing the female sex.

> 'Tis Woman that seduces all Mankind,
> By her we first were taught the wheedling Arts:
> Her very Eyes can cheat; when most she's kind,
> She tricks us of our Money with our Hearts.
> For her, like Wolves by Night we roam for Prey,
> And practise ev'ry Fraud, to bribe her Charms;
> For suits of Love, like Law, are won by Pay,
> And Beauty must be fee'd into our Arms.

By the 1750s, with the publication of Samuel Johnson's *Dictionary of the English Language*, a standardized vocabulary for written English had emerged (Crystal 2003, 74). Two decades later, John Walker attempted to apply a similar standardization to English pronunciation with his *Pronouncing Dictionary of English* (Crystal 2003, 77). As for standardizing syntax, over 200 English grammar texts were published between 1750 and 1800, the most influential being Bishop Robert Lowth's *Short Introduction to English Grammar* (Crystal 2003, 78). By the end of the century, any deviation from the new norms would be considered an unacceptable mistake in pronunciation, spelling or grammar (Austin 1994, 305).

5.3 Linguistic Divergence in the Ottoman Empire

While in the major states of the West, languages were converging toward standard written and spoken forms, in Asia divergence was the order of the day. The Ottoman Empire in the seventeenth century was divided into three quite distinct regions by language family. Turkic languages were spoken in Anatolia, Semitic in Egypt and the Fertile Crescent and Indo-European in Greece, the Balkans and Kurdish territories. Within each region, there were chains of dialects, the mutual intelligibility of which decreased with the distance that separated them (Kornfilt 1990, 619). Those whose occupations required them to speak with people from different regions communicated in one of three oral lingua franca—vernacular Turkish, Arabic or Greek (Hanioglu 2008, 37).

In the Turkish language itself in the seventeenth century, there were two literary traditions. One current, present since the early fifteenth century, used a written form of the vernacular known as Anatolian Turkish. It was composed of folk tales and mystical stories composed during the previous centuries of strictly oral culture (Kuru 2013, 549). The second and more recent literary tradition took its name from the region where it originated, namely, western Anatolia and Rumeli, the territory in the Balkans administered by the Ottomans. Known as Rum, from the Persian word for the Roman Empire, this tradition had as its center the city of Istanbul. In 1453, following the conquest of the former Byzantine capital by Mehmed II, there had been a wave of immigration of scholars from Damascus, Cairo and from Khorasan, an area encompassing parts of present-day Iran, Afghanistan and Turkmenistan (Kuru 2013, 552). Together these scholars and the imperial bureaucrats developed a new literary style known as the poetry of Rum (Kuru 2013, 549).

Written in the Persian form of Arabic script, the new literature integrated four languages: Anatolian Turkish, Arabic, Persian and Chagatai, the eastern version of Turkish that was spoken in central Asia. The challenge that the poets of Rum, the "suara-yi Rum", set for themselves was to surpass the eloquence of the existing poetry in Persian and Arabic. As a result, there was a vast flow of vocabulary and grammatical structure from these two languages into literary Turkish (Kuru 2013, 557–558).

It was not only poetry that was affected by this movement. By 1600, the imperial bureaucracy itself communicated in writing in the same upper register known as Ottoman Turkish. A mixed language containing many Persian and Arabic components, this register of Turkish had by then replaced Persian as the literary language of the upper classes (Hanioglu 2008, 35). Inevitably, spoken Ottoman gradually became unintelligible for the majority of the Turkish population (Woodhead 2012, 146). However, the second register, Anatolian Turkish, continued to show very little Persian or Arabic influence. A popular literature of folk poetry and mysticism written in this register was aimed at less educated groups in the population. The Republican Turkish spoken in Turkey today—the authorized register since the language reforms of the 1930s—is very close to this simpler variant (Kornfilt 1990, 622).

As the Ottoman bureaucracy grew, the lack of standardization of the official language became a problem for government officials (Hanioglu 2008, 35). Ottoman Turkish developed into one of the most complex languages of Eurasia, with a Turkish syntax but a heterogeneous vocabulary picked up from both its subjects and its neighbors. Initially, Ottoman Turkish was heavily influenced by Persian. With the conquest of Byzantine territories in the fourteenth and fifteenth centuries, many Greek words were added. Expansion into Egypt and the Fertile Crescent in the sixteenth century brought additional borrowings from Arabic. Other influences were Venetian, Spanish and, later, French (Hanioglu 2008, 34–45).

We see, then, that during the seventeenth and eighteenth centuries, while the spoken languages in England and France were converging toward national standards, the Ottoman Empire was experiencing something quite different. In the Turkic areas, the vernacular dialects and the written standard were each going their separate ways. A similar divergence was occurring in the Empire's Arabic regions, where the spoken dialects were diverging from the literary language. The principal difference between the two regions was that Classical Arabic itself remained relatively stable, due largely to the influence of the Quran and the Muslim religion, whereas Ottoman Turkish was continually evolving (Kaye 1990, 666–667). Nevertheless, in both the Turkic and Semitic regions of the Ottoman Empire, the spoken dialects were diverging increasingly from the respective literary languages, Ottoman Turkish and Classical Arabic.

It was with the tardy arrival of the printing press in the Muslim world that this process of divergence finally began to slow. In 1861, James Redhouse, an Englishman who had worked as an interpreter and translator for the Ottoman government, published an English-Turkish dictionary. In 1890, he published a complementary Turkish-English dictionary (Gaam 2002). However, there was no monolingual dictionary of Ottoman Turkish published prior to the twentieth century. Finally in 1901, Semsettin Sami published *Kamus-i-Turki*, printed in Perso-Arabic script (Lewis 2002, 16).

By the late 1920s, due largely to territorial downsizing and migration, the Republic of Turkey had become linguistically much more homogeneous than its predecessor state had been. As part of the language reforms initiated by President Kemal Ataturk, the Turkish language was pruned of many words in Persian and Arabic. In addition, the language was now to be written in a modified Roman script. Finally, in 1932 the first monolingual Turkish vernacular dictionary was published. *Anadilden derlemeler*, by Hamit Zübeyr and Ishak Refet (Lewis 2002, 49) appeared over two and a half centuries after the English and French had begun to speak a standardized language (see Table 5.2).

5.4 Linguistic Divergence in India

India in the year 1600 had a population of 135 million, a level almost twice the 74 million people in Western Europe at that moment (Maddison 2007, 376). Indian society was divided into two major language families: the Indo-Aryan languages spoken by 75 percent of the population and the Dravidian languages by another 20 percent.[2] There were also numerous minor languages that belonged to neither family. To understand the complexity of the language situation, it is necessary to go back to the middle of the second millennium BCE. At that time a nomadic people speaking Indo-Aryan crossed the mountain barriers from central Asia into the northwest of the subcontinent. Over the following centuries, their descendants spread east and south along a wide arc into northern and central India. They transmitted their sacred literature and poetry orally in Sanskrit, the ancestor of today's Indo-Aryan languages. As for the Dravidian languages spoken today in the south of India, it is thought that they are descended from the languages of the subcontinent's original inhabitants (Keay 2000, 118).

By the third century BCE, distinct Indo-Aryan vernacular dialects known as the Prakrits had emerged in a number of regions of northern and central India. Inscriptions written in these dialects may be seen today on rocks and stone pillars that date from the reign of the Mauryan emperor Ashoka, who ruled over most of India from 268 to 232 BCE (Masica 1991, 51). Around the year 1000 CE, after slowly evolving over many centuries, these vernacular dialects underwent a period of rapid change. They emerged as the Indian regional languages, such as Bengali, Marathi, Gujarati and Braj Bhasha, the literary language of the Western Hindi region, including Delhi (Masica 1991, 53).

The early Ashokan Prakrits had been written in a script known as Brahmi, thought by Western scholars to be derived from an early Semitic script (Masica 1991, 133). Brahmi was probably originally an abjad, a phonetic writing system consisting of a series of consonants. Indian traders attached a set of vowel symbols to these consonantal characters to facilitate the pronunciation of the script. Since each such phonetic compound symbol represented a syllable, the type of system is known as an abugida or alphasyllabary. By the modern period, over two dozen Indian languages, both Indo-Aryan and Dravidian, had their own abugida writing systems, all of them variants of the original Brahmi script (Masica 1991, 133). Braj Bhasha (the Delhi region's literary language) and Marathi were written with the same Devanagari script, while Bengali, Gujarati and Punjabi each had their own scripts.

In the twelfth century, Muslim invaders from Afghanistan who spoke a Turkic language overthrew local Hindu rulers, establishing a kingdom in the Punjab and the Ganges valley. Using the Persian language written in a modified Arabic script for official purposes, they established their capital at Delhi on the Yamuna River, a long tributary of the Ganges (Wolpert 1993, 133). Three centuries later, in 1526, the Delhi Sultanate was conquered by Babur, a Turko-Mongol from central Asia. His grandson, Akbar, decided to continue using Persian as the language of administration and law, recruiting his administrative personnel from educated men of the Hindu service castes, the Brahmins, Kayasthas (scribes) and Khatris (traders). Many families trained their young men in official Persian terminology for court positions (Richards 1993, 71).

It is interesting to compare this situation with that of England. In the seventeenth century, under the Stuarts, only the English vernacular was taught in state-regulated schools at the elementary level. In this way, literacy and standardization of the English vernacular reinforced each other. However in India, court patronage from both Muslim and non-Muslim rulers supported not only the imperial standard but also the rival regional Indo-Aryan languages (Richards 1993, 71). For example, Akbar had appointed as court poet laureate Raja Birbal, who specialized in poetry in the Braj Bhasha register of Hindustani (Wolpert 1993, 133).

The late sixteenth and seventeenth centuries also saw an accelerating outpouring of literature in Marathi, Punjabi and other regional languages. Much of the literature was religious in nature. For example, the Bhakti movement was a spiritual current in the Hindu religion that began during the late Middle Ages and continued into the modern period. In this tradition, the Marathi saint Tukaram (1608–1645) was a prominent poet who emphasized the possibility of direct communion with the deity. As for Punjabi literature, it was closely associated with the Sikh movement. Especially popular were the *Janamsakhis*, stories based on the life of Guru Nanak (1469–1539), the founder of Sikhism. The best known of these legends is the Bhai Bala Janamsakhi written in 1592 by Bala Sandhu.[3]

The early Mughal rulers spoke Chagatai, a Turkic language spoken widely in central Asia, but as mentioned, the official language of the empire was Persian. In 1638, Akbar's grandson Shah Jahan (r. 1628–1658) transferred the imperial capital from Agra to Delhi. Over the following decade outside the old town, he built Shahjahanabad, an entirely new city with walls of red sandstone (Keay 2000, 335). Near the citadel—the Red Fort—was a market known as the Urdu Bazar (from the Turkic word for army) that was frequented by his Muslim soldiers. Interaction between native Indians speaking the local Hindustani dialect, Khariboli, and foreigners speaking Persian led to the emergence of a new spoken dialect of north Indian Hindustani, to be known as Urdu, that over the following decades competed with Persian as the lingua franca of the empire. The new register of Hindustani had an Indo-Aryan syntax but borrowed much of its vocabulary from Persian. In its later written form, Urdu used the Perso-Arabic script. By the end of the seventeenth century, Urdu already had a growing literature. For example, Wali Mohammed Wali was using the language to compose *ghazals*, poems similar to European sonnets, in rhyming couplets (Omar 2006, 302). It would take another century, however, before prose came to be written in Urdu (Dua 1994, 4863).

By the late eighteenth century, this emerging local standard was being challenged by a powerful rival—the now-standardized English language promoted by a new wave of invaders. Not until the 1920s was there a monolingual vernacular dictionary for the most widely spoken Indian language, Hindustani, in its Hindi and Urdu registers. The *Hindi shabda sagar* was completed by Shyamsunder Das and his associates in 1929 (see Table 5.2).

5.5 Linguistic Divergence in China

As the modern period began, China was undergoing rapid change, both in the structure of its society and in the means of communication that tied its people together. Timothy Brook has described the first sightings of dragons under the Ming Dynasty. Interpreted as ominous warnings, they occurred during the reign of the Zhengde Emperor (r. 1505–1521), two-thirds of a century prior to the reign of the Wanli Emperor (r. 1572–1620) whom we met in Chap. 2. Zhengde had inherited the throne from his father at the age of thirteen. However, instead of ruling directly, the young emperor initially chose to delegate power to his senior eunuch, Liu Jin. For the next 5 years, the latter took advantage of his position to intimidate the civil service and divert state revenues to his own personal use. Finally, in 1510, when it was rumored that Liu was plotting to seize power, the emperor had him arrested and executed. Two years later, the first sinister omen appeared: a fiery red dragon in the sky in Shandong province to the southeast of Beijing. Fortunately, the dragon's presence does not seem to have been associated with any damage. However, 6 years later, witnesses observed nine black dragons accompanied by an enormous waterspout that destroyed hundreds of homes and sucked dozens of boats into the sky. Then the following year, numerous dragons appeared in a storm that caused tremendous flooding (Brook 2013, 13).

Once the Zhengde Emperor decided to reign on his own, he proved to be as dangerous to the state as his former official had been. On one occasion, the emperor ordered government factories to donate to him over 300,000 pieces of porcelain and 17,000 bolts of silk that he could provide as gifts to his supporters. It is said that in the fall of 1520, he fell out of a boat while drunk. The following spring he died, possibly of complications from this accident, childless despite having spent much time during the preceding 15 years with his consort and concubines (Anderson 1990, 232).

In the middle of the Ming Dynasty, people agreed, something more than the usual downswing in the dynastic cycle was chipping away at the structure of Chinese society. The empire was no longer simply a set of largely autonomous agricultural regions that recognized the authority of a central administration. Nor within each region did individual subjects display the traditional moral integrity and respect for social position (Brook 1998, 579). One dimension of the transformation was a succession of waves of internal migration that accompanied rapid population growth in the central provinces. During the fifteenth century, the province surrounding Beijing had doubled its share of population, passing from three to seven percent, as people moved northeast from Shanxi and Shaanxi provinces. The other principal direction of migration was westward from the densely populated Yangtze Delta region, Jiangnan, toward Jiangxi, Huguang, Sichuan and Yunnan (Brook 2013, 47).

A second transformation under the Ming was an expansion of interregional trade that was weaving the central and northern provinces into a single economic unit. To facilitate the transport of grain needed to feed the armies on the northern frontier without exposing shipping to the dangerous coastal trade routes, the Ming administration directed the restoration of the Grand Canal. Once again, Beijing was connected by river routes with the Yangtze Delta. Another project was in the region of Nanjing, where the construction of the East Dams reduced flooding and improved access to the economically important city of Suzhou. Canal construction to the east of Suzhou further contributed to the economic integration of the Jiangnan (Yangtze Delta) region (Brook 1998, 601).

With merchants traveling from one province to another in search of goods that could be bought cheaply and sold at a profit, it was said that traditional moral values were being replaced by a craving for wealth.

Accompanying these changes in the Chinese economy were disruptions to the country's traditional social structure—a reordering of the ties between people at the local level in the vast empire over which the Ming Dynasty ruled. As the overall literacy rate rose, social status came to depend increasingly on one's education level. In general, women were illiterate, unless their parents had been wealthy enough to afford a private tutor. As for men, since 1440, as we have seen, a necessary condition to be a public servant was to have passed the civil service examinations held once every 3 years.

It would be difficult to overstate the importance of the examination system for late Ming society. At the summit of the social pyramid were the literati who held the highest degree, the *jinshi* or "advanced scholar". Graduates of the highest level of metropolitan exams held in Beijing, they were eligible for the highest offices in the empire, including service in the Grand Secretariat. Only 2000–4000 members of this group—roughly one out of 10,000 men—were alive at any one time (Ebrey 1996, 199).

At the provincial level, not only were successful graduates of the first level of examinations, the *juren* or "recommended men", eligible for public office but also they earned some tax privileges and could wear distinctive clothing. In the empire as a whole, under the late Ming, there were some 12,000 alive at any one time who had managed to pass (only) these provincial exams (Hucker 1998, 39).

Most of these higher degree holders acceded to public positions in urban areas (Heijdra 1998, 555–556). Often they were individuals from families with lower status who had advanced on their own merits. These Mandarins constituted an elite whose career advancement demanded that they place the empire's interest above their own personal considerations (Heijdra 1998, 557). They would generally have mastered to an exceptional degree the Literary Chinese written language, knowing perhaps 4500 or more of the some 7000 characters in current use (Hannas 1997, 131).

During the late Ming period, the Mandarins were less numerous in the capital than the eunuchs with whom they competed for power (Hucker 1998, 21). Poor parents often presented surplus sons to the palace for castration, in the hope that the families would benefit from the favors that the boys would receive later (Hucker 1998, 22). As explained in earlier chapters, these young men were taught to read and write in the palace, but they were not necessarily educated in the values of Confucianism.

Somewhat lower in the social hierarchy than the *juren* or "recommended men" under the late Ming were the 500,000 or so bachelor's degree holders, *shengyuan*, or "student members", who had passed only the college examinations held at the county level (Heijdra 1998, 561). Although these men were required to have studied the same classic texts as the advanced degree holders, their failure to pass the provincial examinations presumably reflected a lower degree of mastery of the characters of Literary Chinese. Relatively few of this second group obtained public employment. However, there were other compensations. All degree holders received partial exemption from taxes and from the corvée labor required to maintain the country's infrastructure (Heijdra 1998, 554, 563). As a result, these men formed the upper level of the local gentry at the county level. However, the gentry also included wealthy merchants and elders (Heijdra 1998, 558).

At the local level, there were other dominant elements in Chinese society. As kinship ties grew more important, certain lineages and families acquired considerable prestige. Landholders as a class also tended to be community leaders, organizing tax collection and corvée duties where these had not been transformed into monetary payments (Heijdra 1998, 558). Finally, as internal security broke down under the late Ming, local strongmen assumed power.

As we have seen, the Chinese had developed wood block printing in the sixth century, using it initially to reproduce Buddhist prayers. Under the Song Dynasty in the tenth century, the technique began to be widely used for commercial printing. Then with the growth of population and expansion of the education system that occurred in the fifteenth and sixteenth centuries, there was a further sharp increase in book production. Because of the large volume, the price of a single copy of an almanac or popular novel in hours of labor was only a half of the price in the West (Angeles 2014, 7–9).

Before the twentieth century, most writing in China was in Literary Chinese, a purely written form of communication based on the language spoken under the Eastern Zhou Dynasty during the Classical period, in the middle third of the first millennium BCE. As the centuries passed, this literary language gradually evolved, but it did so much less rapidly than the increasingly differentiated vernacular dialects (Norman 1988, 108). In the early seventeenth century, there was consequently a standardized (written) form of this literary language. Around 1615, Mei Yingzuo completed his edition of the *Zihui*, a dictionary of over 33,000 entries, with pronunciation indicated by means of homophonous characters (Norman 1988, 172).

Under the late Ming Dynasty, very few people were able to read and write this Literary Chinese. Among men, less than a tenth of one percent had passed the upper-level state examinations held every 3 years at the provincial or metropolitan level. Perhaps another one percent had graduated from the state schools at the county level; they too would be able to read the literary language (Heijdra 1998, 561). If we may assume that half of the remaining urban residents, including eunuchs, had mastered 1000 or more symbols of their written regional vernacular, we have another four percent of men who had acquired basic literacy. As for the rest of the population, there is evidence that half of the other urban and rural men were semi-literate, being able to read the some 400 or more symbols necessary for their daily occupations (Baten et al. 2010).

We see then that while over half of the Chinese male population had some measure of literacy under the late Ming, there were multiple communication networks. Each adult male was in effect on a literary island, mastering the symbols he had been taught in his youth, but able to acquire further vocabulary only at considerable cost. Moreover, with each additional symbol learned, the risk of forgetting a symbol already acquired increased. Missing in seventeenth-century China compared to England were (i) the one-third of the male labor force able to acquire additional information in written form easily, in something close to the spoken language, and (ii) the one-sixth of women able to read well enough to participate actively in the education of their children (Cressy 1980, 177).

While there had long been dictionaries indicating the meaning and (current) pronunciation of Literary Chinese, in the seventeenth century, there were no Chinese equivalents of the vernacular dictionaries of Phillips for the English language or Richelet for French. The explanation for this publishing lapse is less social than technological. As Angeles (2014) has explained, it cost roughly 15 times as much to prepare a page of Chinese text for block printing as to compose an equivalent page of English. Even though each additional page of Chinese could be reproduced cheaply once the blocks had been carved, it would take a very large potential readership to justify the initial preparation. The literate population that spoke the dialect of each regional publishing center was evidently not sufficiently large to justify the high cost of publishing vernacular dictionaries.

Without a written anchor for the vernaculars, these steadily drifted apart, much as the romance languages had done in Europe during the Middle

Ages. In China, the county gazette was an official publication designed to inform local officials of the activities of the regional administration. For example, the 1619 gazette of Hainan Island in the southeast described the manner in which the spoken language differed by region, by social class and by rural-urban residence. The gazetteer distinguished between the *guā nhuà* (language of the officials) or Mandarin spoken in the imperial capital and the version of that koine or lingua franca spoken by the local elite. As for the regional language, the version spoken by gentry was differentiated from that of the lower classes. Moreover, the vernacular spoken in the prefectural capital differed from the patois of the villages. In addition, there was a minority group, the Li, who spoke an entirely different language (Brook 1998, 644–645).

In all, there were seven major groups of Chinese dialects, some of which had their own regional koines (Norman 1988, 246). As different from each other as French, Spanish and Italian, these regional vernaculars were not mutually intelligible (Crystal 1997, 314). It might be thought that members of the elite from different regions could at least communicate in Mandarin, the koine or lingua franca. From the fifteenth to the early nineteenth centuries, this lingua franca was based on the speech of the lower Yangtze (Coblin 2000, 539–540). However, in the 1720s the Yongzheng Emperor, who had been raised in the north, found that he could not understand the speech of his officials from the south. Accordingly, he set up Correct Pronunciation Academies in Fujian and Guangdong in an attempt to standardize the spoken Mandarin. These efforts were apparently not successful, for they were abandoned by his successor (Dong 2014, ch. 9). In part, Yongzheng's problem may have been due to the evolution of Mandarin itself. In the early nineteenth century, Robert Morrison, a British missionary working in Canton, reported that a new koine based on the dialect of Beijing was "rapidly gaining ground" relative to the traditional Nanjing version (Cobrin 2000, 540).

A recent survey gives some indication of the communication problems. The first two lines of Table 5.3 present present-day intelligibility rates of dialects from other regions for residents of the Yangtze Delta city of Suzhou. As one would expect, intelligibility is better for the varieties of Mandarin spoken across the north-Chinese plain than for the less closely related dialects of the mountainous south. Nevertheless, we may infer that conversation between strangers would be difficult. The effect of an informally learned koine is suggested in the third line of the table. The Beijing dialect is close to but not identical to the Standard Chinese to which most of

Table 5.3 Intelligibility of Chinese dialects to rural residents of the Suzhou area

Dialect	Distance (km)	Intelligibility (%)
Northern China	1245	37
Southern China	1001	24
Beijing	1155	64
Suzhou	Approx. 50	65

Source: Chaojua and van Heuven (2009, 719)

the survey's respondents would have been exposed through today's media. The 64 percent intelligibility percentage thus provides some idea of the impact of a koine learned in non-formalized fashion. Finally, the bottom line indicates the impact of the absence of formal teaching of the local vernacular. Rural residents of the Suzhou dialect area understood varieties of their own vernacular little better than that of Beijing.

It is perhaps inaccurate to distinguish sharply between accent on the one hand and intelligibility because of vocabulary differences on the other. In their study of the mutual intelligibility of Chinese regional dialects, Chaojua and van Heuven (2009, 724) found that phonological differences (accent) and lexical differences (vocabulary) are highly correlated, each predicting intelligibility equally well. If one's willingness to trust a stranger decreases with the strength of the other's accent, as argued in Chap. 1, the data in Table 5.3 help explain why China was less capable of developing complex new technologies than Britain and France during the period of the Industrial Revolution.

After 1645, another layer of complexity was added to the linguistic environment of China. The Qing conquerors introduced two new official languages into the Chinese administrative system, namely, Manchu and Mongolian, each written with a script different from that of Chinese. Although in principle all documentation was in the three languages, in practice there were errors, omissions and deliberate censorship of the documents translated into Chinese (Crossley 1997, ch. 1). For military affairs, Manchu was the preferred language of communication as late as the mid-nineteenth century (Crossley 1997, ch. 1).

In short, China on the eve of the Industrial Revolution had completed the first stage in Milroy's (1994) process of language standardization. In each region, there was a supra-local norm for speech or koine for communication between those who came from different areas. The national koine was still the dialect of Nanjing, the cultural center and former capital. However, without a formal printed register of the meanings and pronunciation of the vernaculars, there was little to keep them from drifting further apart. Moreover, even the penetration of the regional koines was limited to the urban gentry, as the lower classes and rural residents were situated at other points on the continuum of dialects.

As the Ming Dynasty aged, the interest groups that dominated Chinese society at the regional level had proved less and less willing to cooperate in the financing of their collective defense. After 1645, the foreign Qing dynasty was able to impose some order of fiscal discipline, but the conquerors were unable or unwilling to prevent further linguistic divergence. The first Chinese dictionary in the vernacular was not published until 1937, a quarter century after the revolution that overthrew the Qing (Dong 2014, 133). In the *Guoyu cidian* (Dictionary of the National Language) by Zhuyin Fuhao and Gwoyeu Romatzyh, pronunciation was now to be based on the Mandarin dialect spoken on the streets of Beijing.

5.6 States of Confusion

At the beginning of the seventeenth century, the English language had been "confused", with considerable differences in pronunciation and vocabulary between regions and many unfamiliar words borrowed from Greek and Latin. In 1658, a rising demand from new readers, particularly from women, for help with the meaning and spelling of words led to the publication of the first monolingual English dictionary that was not just a collection of hard words to spell. A similar French dictionary followed in 1680. By the second half of the following century, Standard English and French had emerged, along with the concept of mistakes in spelling, grammar and pronunciation.

No analogous convergence occurred in the other major civilizations. The Ottoman Empire in the seventeenth century was divided into three distinct linguistic regions: Turkic, Semitic and Indo-European. Within each region, there were multiple dialects and languages. The imperial bureaucracy communicated in Ottoman Turkish, a mixed language written in Perso-Arabic script but containing many Persian and Arabic components. It was not intelligible for the majority of the Turkish population. In addition, there was a non-standardized lingua franca, vernacular Turkish, used for oral communication. It had a written form that served as a medium for transmitting religious texts and folk poetry in Turkic-language regions.

Further east, India in 1600 had a population of 165 million—well over twice that of Western Europe. However, the society was divided among almost two dozen major languages and multiple writing systems. The official language of the Mughal court was Persian, written with Perso-Arabic characters. By the late seventeenth century, however, the lingua franca of the empire was switching from Persian to a new register of north-Indian Hindustani, an Indo-Aryan language spoken in the region of Delhi. The new koine, Urdu, used Indo-Aryan syntax but was written in Perso-Arabic script and had significant borrowings of vocabulary from Persian. In the second half of the eighteenth century, both of these standards were challenged by the penetration of invaders promoting Standard English.

As for China, with a population in 1600 of over 150 million (twice that of Western Europe) who shared the same written language, the society appeared to have a great advantage in communication relative to the rest of Eurasia. However, there were two obstacles to the standardization of the written and spoken language arising from the complexity of the logosyllabic writing system. First, as literacy rates rose under the Ming, the high *variable* cost to the individual of learning additional symbols divided the population into multiple distinct groups. Only a small percentage of the male population could be considered fully literate, that is, able to read and write Literary Chinese. A large portion of the rest of the Chinese men had some basic literacy, but few women were able to read and write. Second, largely because of the high *fixed* cost of preparing a page of text for printing, there was no dictionary in the vernacular to promote convergence of the spoken languages. As a result, the dialects spoken by Chinese society continued to diverge by region, education, social class and rural-urban division.

In short, by the beginning of the eighteenth century, the literate citizens of Britain and northern France were able to communicate in standardized *written* vernaculars. The diffusion of standard *spoken* languages based on the dialects of London and Paris would soon follow. In Asia, however, there was a widening communications gap between a small elite who spoke a vehicular language—whether bureaucratic Mandarin, Persian or Ottoman Turkish—and the great majority who could express themselves only in their local dialects. As new industrial technologies grew in complexity, further innovation increasingly demanded the collaboration of people with different skills. In the following chapters, we will see the technological consequences of this East-West divergence in the degree to which social communications networks were integrated.

Notes

1. This section is based on Dudley (2012, ch. 1).
2. Encyclopedia Britannica, "Indo-Aryan Languages", http://www.britannica.com/topic/Indo-Aryan-languages (5 November 2015).
3. "Bhai Bala Janamsakhi," *Sikhi Wiki*, http://www.sikhiwiki.org/index.php/Bhai_Bala_Janamsakhi (9 November 2015).

References

Amory, H. (1998). British books abroad: The American colonies. In J. Barnard & D. F. McKenzie (Eds.), *The Cambridge history of the book in Britain, vol. IV, 1557–1695* (pp. 744–752). Cambridge, UK: Cambridge University Press.

Anderson, M. M. (1990). *Hidden power: The palace eunuchs of imperial China*. Buffalo: Prometheus Books.

Angeles, L. (2014). *The economics of printing in early modern China*. University of Glasgow.

Austin, F. (1994). The effect of exposure to standard English: The language of William Clift. In D. Stein & I. Tieken-Boon van Ostade (Eds.), *Towards a standard English 1600–1800* (pp. 285–314). Berlin: Mouton de Gruyter.

Barber, C. (1993). *The English language: A historical introduction*. Cambridge, UK: Cambridge University Press.

Baten, J., Ma, D., Morgan, S., & Wang, Q. (2010). Evolution of living standards and human capital in China in the 18–20th centuries: Evidences from real wages, age-heaping, and anthropometrics. *Explorations in Economic History, 47*, 347–359.

Blank, P. (2006). The babel of renaissance English. In L. Mugglestone (Ed.), *The Oxford history of English* (pp. 212–239). Oxford: Oxford University Press.

Brook, T. (1998). *The confusions of pleasure: Commerce and culture in Ming China*. Berkeley: University of California Press.

Brook, T. (2013). *The troubled empire: China in the Yuan and Ming dynasties*. Cambridge, MA: Belknap Press.

Chaojua, T., & van Heuven, V. J. (2009). Mutual intelligibility of Chinese dialects experimentally tested. *Lingua, 119*, 709–732.

Coblin, W. S. (2000). A brief history of Mandarin. *Journal of the American Oriental Society, 120*, 537–552.

Cressy, D. (1980). *Literacy and the social order: Reading and writing in Tudor and Stuart England*. Cambridge, UK: Cambridge University Press.

Crossley, P. K. (1997). *The Manchus*. Oxford: Blackwell.

Crystal, D. (1997). *The Cambridge encyclopedia of language* (2nd ed.). Cambridge, UK: Cambridge University Press.

Crystal, D. (2003). *The Cambridge encyclopedia of the English language*. Cambridge, UK: Cambridge University Press.
Dong, H. (2014). *A history of the Chinese language*. London: Routledge.
Dua, H. R. (1994). Urdu. In R. E. Asher & J. M. Simpson (Eds.), *The encyclopedia of language and linguistics* (pp. 4863–4864). Oxford: Pergamon Press.
Dudley, L. (2012). *Mothers of innovation: How expanding social networks gave birth to the industrial revolution*. Newcastle upon Tyne: Cambridge Scholars.
Dudley, L. (2016). Language standardization and the industrial revolution. *Oxford Economic Papers Advance Access.* doi:10.1093/oep/gpw059
Ebrey, P. B. (1996). *The Cambridge illustrated history of China*. Cambridge, UK: Cambridge University Press.
Fennell, B. A. (2001). *A history of English: A sociolinguistic approach*. Oxford: Blackwell.
Freeborn, D. (1992). *From old English to standard English*. Basingstoke: Macmillan.
Gaam, N. (2002). *The making of a legend – Redhouse*. Retrieved April 24, 2016, from Learning Practical Turkish. http://www.learningpracticalturkish.com/redhouse-dictionary-history.html
Gooskens, C., Heeringa, W., & Beijering, K. (2008). Phonetic and lexical predictors of intelligibility. *International Journal of Humanities and Arts Computing, 2* (1–2), 63–81.
Graff, H. J. (1991). *The legacies of literacy*. Bloomington: Indiana University Press.
Green, J. (1996). *Chasing the sun: Dictionary makers and dictionaries they made*. New York: Henry Holt.
Hanioglu, M. S. (2008). *A brief history of the late Ottoman Empire*. Princeton: Princeton University Press.
Hannas, W. C. (1997). *Asia's orthographic dilemma*. Honolulu: University of Hawaii Press.
Heijdra, M. (1998). The socio-economic development of rural China during the Ming. In D. Twitchett & F. W. Mote (Eds.), *Cambridge history of China* (Vol. 8, pp. 417–578). Cambridge, UK: Cambridge University Press.
Herman, A. (2001). *How the scots invented the modern world*. New York: Three Rivers Press.
Hucker, C. O. (1998). Ming government. In D. Twitchett & F. W. Mote (Eds.), *The Cambridge history of China* (Vol. 8, pp. 9–105). Cambridge, UK: Cambridge University Press.
Kaye, A. S. (1990). Arabic. In B. Comrie (Ed.), *The world's major languages* (pp. 664–685). Oxford: Oxford University Press.
Keay, J. (2000). *India: A history*. New York: Grove Press.
Kornfilt, J. (1990). Turkish and the Turkic languages. In B. Comrie (Ed.), *The world's major languages* (pp. 619–644). Oxford: Oxford University Press.
Kuru, S. S. (2013). The literature of rum: The making of a literary tradition (1450–1600). In S. N. Faroqui & K. Fleet (Eds.), *The Cambridge history of*

Turkey, vol. 2, The Ottoman Empire as a world power, 1453–1603 (pp. 548–592). Cambridge: Cambridge University Press.

Lewis, B. (2002). *What went wrong?: The clash between Islam and modernity in the Middle East*. Oxford: Oxford University Press.

Maddison, A. (2007). *Contours of the world economy, 1-2030 AD: Essays in macroeconomic history*. Oxford: Oxford University Press.

Masica, C. P. (1991). *The Indo-Aryan languages*. Cambridge: Cambridge University Press.

McMahon, A. (2006). Restructuring renaissance English. In L. Mugglestone (Ed.), *The oxford history of English* (pp. 147–177). Oxford: Oxford University Press.

Millward, C. M. (1988). *A biography of the English language*. New York: Harcourt Brace Jovanovich.

Milroy, J. (1994). The notion of 'standard Language' and its applicability to the study of early modern English pronunciation. In D. Stein & I. Tieken-Boon van Ostade (Eds.), *Towards a standard English 1600–1800* (pp. 19–29). Berlin: Mouton de Gruyter.

Mueller, D. C. (2003). *Public choice III*. Cambridge: Cambridge University Press.

Norman, J. (1988). *Chinese*. Cambridge, UK: Cambridge University Press.

Omar, I. A. (2006). Islam. In S. Wolpert (Ed.), *Encyclopedia of India* (Vol. 2, pp. 299–303). Farmington Hills: Charles Scribner's Sons.

Richards, J. F. (1993). *The Mughal empire*. Cambridge: Cambridge University Press.

Stein, D. (1994). Sorting out the variants: Standardization and social factors in the English language 1600–1800. In D. Stein & I. Tieken-Boon van Ostade (Eds.), *Towards a standard English 1600–1800* (pp. 1–17). Berlin: Mouton de Gruyter.

Wolpert, S. (1993). *A new history of India* (4th ed.). Oxford: Oxford University Press.

Woodhead, C. (2012). Ottoman languages. In C. Woodhead (Ed.), *The Ottoman world* (pp. 143–158). London: Routledge.

PART 2

The Industrial Revolution

In Part 2, we move from the seventeenth century on to the eighteenth. An initial chapter compares the degree of success of England, China, India and the Ottoman Empire by the year 1700 in making the fiscal transformations needed to finance a modern army and navy. In England, these changes had been facilitated by increasing language standardization. However, the inability of the three Asian civilizations to apply movable type efficiently to their writing systems had led to increasing coordination difficulties. The analysis then examines the development in the West of three "macro-inventions" conceived initially for civilian purposes, namely, the steam engine, machine tools and interchangeable parts. Lacking a vernacular sufficiently standardized to permit the information flows among strangers that were essential for such innovation, the three Asian societies were increasingly left behind technologically.

CHAPTER 6

1700: Financing the Imperial State

6.1 The Cycles' End

As the seventeenth century progressed, the dynastic cycles across Eurasia appeared to be playing themselves out in typical fashion. In Asia, the period between 1640 and 1700 had seen the beginning of severe decline in two dynasties (Ottoman and Mughal) and complete collapse in another (Ming). In England, after a decade of civil war in the 1640s, the reign of the Tudor and Stuart dynasties, in power since the late Middle Ages, was also nearing its end. With the execution of Charles I and the expulsion of his Catholic son, James II, the English had displayed their opposition to absolutist rule. Because James II's successors, his sisters Mary (with her husband William III) and Anne, were childless, the dynasty would end upon Anne's death in 1714.

Yet there was a difference between East and West. In Asia, the dynastic cycle continued, with new lineages from the periphery taking the place of the preceding lines of rulers. The Qing dynasty from Manchuria took power in China, while the Maratha confederacy from the Deccan extended its territory into northern India. In the Ottoman Empire, the original dynasty continued to reign, but effective political power passed to vizier and pasha households, many of them of provincial slave origin.

In England, however, it was not simply the Tudor and Stuart dynasties but rather the dynastic cycle itself that in effect came to an end. Despite the nominal restoration of the Stuarts, real political power after 1688 passed to an assembly of elected representatives. At the same time, there occurred a radical restructuring of the fiscal state. This chapter first describes the nature of the changes in the English fiscal system and then compares these transformations to contemporary developments in the three Asian empires that we have studied. Our concern will be to discover what it was that allowed the English political system to break out of the dynastic cycle while its Asian counterparts were condemned to repeating the familiar pattern.

Throughout history, the key test of the health of a state has been its ability to collect the taxes necessary to finance the control of its territory. The challenge has been to organize a system that induces taxpayers to yield the required amount of resources while limiting crippling dead-weight losses from the collection and disbursement of such public funds. Let us examine how well the fiscal systems of the four states we are studying met each of these challenges over the course of the seventeenth century.

6.2 England in 1700

To understand the unique situation of England in 1700, it is necessary to go back to the fiscal problems of the state almost a century earlier. By the beginning of the reign of James I in 1603, most of the lands that Henry VIII had confiscated from the monasteries during the Reformation had already been sold. Hence, an alternative reliable source of revenue was needed. Duties on imports should have provided a steady source of income. However, because of endemic collusion between customs officials and importers, the net proceeds had often proved disappointing (Peck 1993, 149–150). In 1568, the government of Elizabeth I had begun to auction the rights to collect customs to private individuals through a system of competitive bidding (Johnson and Koyama 2014, 9). Over the two following decades, the farming out of the customs had provided a reliable revenue source. However, there was an important drawback to this arrangement. In times of exceptional spending needs, the possibilities to borrow emergency funds from the contracting merchant tax farmers had proved limited (Johnson and Koyama 2014, 9). In the 1590s, therefore, direct administration of the customs had been resumed, with the flow of revenue proceeds providing collateral for short-term loans to the Crown (Peck 1993, 149).

Unlike Elizabeth I, James I had both a family to support and a long list of Scottish and English supporters to be rewarded (Brown 2008, 35). In search of more revenue, his officials in 1604 decided to consolidate the collection of customs into the Great Farm, which was then rented out to a syndicate of wealthy men. A royal guarantee of this group's right to the monopoly profits from tax collection then provided security for a series of loans that the Crown demanded to cover its unforeseen spending needs (Johnson and Koyama 2014, 12). Patrick O'Brien (2011) has suggested that this collection of indirect taxes by a "cabal" or monopsony of private agents was the prelude to a series of three path-breaking reforms to the English fiscal system.

The first change was in the manner of financing the military. In 1642, civil war broke out between Parliament and James I's son and successor, Charles I, over the issue of who should control an army recruited to put down a revolt in Ireland. After 3 years of fighting, neither side had been able to gain a decisive advantage, in part because of the reluctance of local militias to serve outside their home territories (Dupuy and Dupuy 1986, 552). The sixteenth century had witnessed the end of small armies armed with bows and arrows, swords and spears (Parker 1996, 1, 17–18). In their place appeared much larger armies equipped with firearms. In the small armies of the medieval period, warriors had received their income in kind from the output of grants of land. However, the soldiers of the much larger armies of the modern period had to be paid in cash. For example, to recruit men for the New Model Army in 1645, Parliament promised each conscripted foot soldier eight pence per day and each cavalryman two shillings (Asquith 1981, 19). It should be noted that these cash contracts between the Long Parliament and individual soldiers of the New Model Army were self-enforcing. If their wages were not paid, the soldiers would refuse to fight and the battle would be lost. Parliament's new policy seems to have been effective in recruiting the services of experienced soldiers. At the decisive parliamentary victory in the Battle of Naseby in June of 1645, Parliament's 13,500 troops outnumbered those of the king by a ratio of two to one (Dupuy and Dupuy 1986, 552).

The second fiscal transformation was in the tax structure. As Parliament attempted to finance the cost of raising a professional army equipped with the latest firearms, it found that traditional direct taxes on property could not be increased enough to generate the needed revenue. As for customs duties, despite the parliamentary expropriation of the previous government's tax farms, receipts from this source amounted to only a fifth of total revenues (He 2013, 53). In 1643, therefore, Parliament imposed for the first time a set of excise taxes applied to domestic production of a variety of consumer goods, such as tobacco, beer and cider (He 2013, 53). By the late 1650s, indirect internal taxes were accounting for over a quarter of government revenues (O'Brien 2011, 429). For the first time, then,

England had a flexible revenue source that could be adjusted quickly to the spending needs of its government.

The third transformation was the centralization of the fiscal structure—a change that would in turn permit increased borrowing. The first steps were taken by the Long Parliament of 1640–1660, during the civil wars. Initially both the customs and excise taxes were to be collected by salaried public employees. However, because the cost of imposing the excise taxes at dispersed points of production was higher than expected, it was decided to farm the excise collection to local business people familiar with conditions in their regions (He 2013, 54). Nevertheless, a state monopoly over customs payments provided a potential stream of income that the state could use as security for borrowing. In the 1650s, the Commonwealth and Protectorate financed their budget deficits by issuing short-term debt instruments—bills of imprest and warrants—backed by future tax revenues (He 2013, 53). However, in 1655, Cromwell's government began a war against Spain in the Caribbean. The English were able to capture Jamaica, but the attacks of Spanish privateers in reprisal temporarily destroyed England's shipping trade. Unable to redeem the government's short-term notes because of the resulting collapse in customs revenues, the navy's victuallers demanded cash payments, thereby bringing the Protectorate government to its knees (He 2013, 55).

Despite this setback, all of the components of the new fiscal state were now in place. Over the following half century, the state and its creditors developed institutions that permitted extending the term of government debt instruments beyond their initial limit of about 1 year. In 1660, following the Restoration of Charles II, England and Spain agreed to end the war between them. Two years later, anxious to have a steady source of income after the recent collapse of its revenues, the Restoration government farmed out customs and excise once again to small groups of financiers (He 2013, 55). However, once the "cabals" of tax farmers had invested in the administrative machinery for efficient centralized collection of these indirect taxes, there was no reason for the state not to take over the whole operation (Johnson and Koyama 2014, 15). As O'Brien (2011, 424) pointed out, the farming out of taxation had not by any means eliminated the opportunities for corruption. However, the government now felt that the resulting revenue losses could be kept within acceptable limits.

In 1667, England had just experienced disastrous defeat in the second Anglo-Dutch War, the Dutch having destroyed the English fleet anchored at Chatham in the Thames estuary. Desperately in need of additional cash,

Charles II appointed a new Treasury Commission to audit the government's revenues and expenditures. The commissioners established a new bookkeeping system to record revenues and departmental spending estimates. After comparing the demands of the customs farm with its costs and the receipts it collected, the commission recommended that the farm not be renewed. Accordingly, in 1671 the collection of customs duties was reassigned to government employees (He 2013, 55). Twelve years later, in 1683, the farming of excise taxes was also canceled, with the central government taking over their collection (Johnson and Koyama 2014, 9). In effect, the state simply took over the organization of dispersed agents that the tax farmers had established. Then over the next 5 years, the officers of the Excise Department standardized the methods of assessing, collecting and registering for England's 886 taxation districts (He 2013, 61).

With the Glorious Revolution of 1688, Parliament, through its now-credible threat of rebellion, acquired complete control of taxation. It now had an effective check on the sovereign's spending power. Yet there was one final step in the development of the modern fiscal state. The arrival of the Dutch stadtholder William III upon the English throne in 1688 immediately plunged England into the heart of a quarter-century power struggle on the Continent—first, the War of the Grand Alliance (1688–1697), then after a pause of barely 3 years, the War of the Spanish Succession (1701–1714). On one side in each conflict was France, seeking to supplement recent gains of territory in the Netherlands and along the Rhine. On the other side were the United Provinces, Spain, the German Empire and now England (after 1707, Great Britain), anxious to restrain French expansion.

Because of the size of the forces involved and the long duration of these two conflicts, there was great pressure on public finances and a consequent need for state borrowing. Even after the sale of short-term notes, tontines, annuities and lottery tickets, there was still a revenue gap to be filled. In 1694, the government therefore granted a charter to a new note-issuing institution, the Bank of England. In return, the Treasury was granted a long-term loan of £1.2 million at a rate of eight percent, payable in newly minted Bank of England notes. In agreeing to hold most of its capital stock in the form of government tally sticks (a type of short-term public debt instrument), the Bank was in effect the agent for the conversion of short- into long-term debt (He 2013, 65).

What had occurred over the course of the seventeenth century that suddenly allowed long-term financing of a state's public debt for the first time in history? For North and Weingast (1989, 817–818), it was the credible threat of parliamentary revolution after 1688 that allowed the English Crown to commit itself to the protection of property rights. At the same time, the king and the judiciary retained sufficient power to provide a check against parliamentary tyranny. It should be noted, however, as O'Brien (2011) and Johnson and Koyama (2014) have pointed out, that the fiscal reform that made possible the commitment to repay long-term debt—the public centralization of tax collection—had already occurred by 1683 under Charles II, that is, *prior* to the Glorious Revolution and its implicit property guarantee.

If not the Glorious Revolution, was it a simple reform in the administration of tax collection that would make possible the expansion of the English/British economy over the following century and a half? As we have already noted, the essential fiscal transformations—cash contracts with individual soldiers (and sailors), the establishment of a system of excise taxes on local production and the issue of transferable debt instruments to finance deficit spending all took place during the civil wars and the Commonwealth—roughly a half century before the first issue of long-term debt. All that was required further to complete the English fiscal state was the development of sufficient mutual trust for individuals to be willing to turn over significant amounts of wealth to the collectivity for long periods on the faith of a written promise.

In *Imagined Communities*, one of the most oft-cited recent publications in the social sciences, Benedict Anderson (2006) offered a plausible explanation for this set of transformations. He argued that millions of people living in England (and later Scotland) suddenly became considerably more willing to trust one another. Across Eurasia over the preceding centuries, people had tended to imagine themselves belonging to distinct communities of individuals whom they would never meet. In the Middle Ages, many Western Europeans saw themselves primarily as members of Christendom, united by a sacred script (Anderson 2006, 15). Then, during the century after the Reformation, many English considered their primary community to be the subjects of the Tudor and Stuart monarchs. With the execution of Charles I in 1649, however, a new identity was required. Gradually, the "imagined community" became the English nation, a geographically limited horizontal brotherhood (Anderson 2006, 21).

This transfer of identities was made possible, Anderson (2006, 37–46) argued, by the combination of the three developments in information technology that we have studied in the preceding chapters. First came movable type, bringing with it the possibility of reproducing at low cost thousands of identical copies of a given message. By 1500, as many as 200 million volumes may have been published (Febvre and Martin 1976, 248–249). Second, over the following century, the Reformation, with its promotion of literacy in the vernacular, generated a remarkable widening of the reading public, including not only merchants but also women. Finally, in each major market for printed material, one dialect gradually attained pre-eminence in the written language, and a standardized grammar and orthography emerged. In England between 1600 and 1700, a written language based on the speech of educated Londoners became the standard for English printers (Borsay 2002, 195). It would take another century, however, before most British citizens were able to speak this standard language. By the year 1800, having acquired the ability to speak the dialect of the capital had become a signal that you could be trusted.

As we have seen, England's first true monolingual vernacular dictionary was published in 1658. Are there any objective measures of an increase in trust in Britain following the appearance of this first sign of standardization of the English language? There were at least three obvious indications of widening social boundaries. First, in the political sphere, there was the coalescence of various interests into two main political groups, Tories and Whigs, who were able to compromise on a formula for sequential sharing of power. Second, in the economic realm, individuals had sufficient faith in the rule of law to be willing to purchase instruments of long-term government debt. Third, as we shall see in subsequent chapters, around the turn of the eighteenth century, British armies and navies began to have unprecedented success against their opponents—and not only because they were being paid regularly.

6.3 The Ottoman Empire in 1700

In the year 1700, the Ottoman Empire was still recovering from a disastrous defeat before the walls of Vienna. Eighteen years earlier, after three centuries of almost uninterrupted Ottoman expansion, the Grand Vizier Kara Mustafa Pasha had decided to complete a task that had been suspended for a century and a half, namely, the capture of the Habsburg capital (Stoye 2007, 23). In the summer of 1683, an Ottoman army of 90,000 was besieging Vienna. However, in September of that year, just as the Ottoman forces were about to storm the beleaguered city, they were attacked and crushed by a coalition army of 68,000 German and Polish warriors (Lynn 1995, 170). Over the following months, the Ottomans lost all of the territory they and their dependents had held in Hungary and Transylvania. Mustafa Pasha retreated to Belgrade. There, on Christmas Day, envoys from the Sultan demanded that the Grand Vizier hand over the symbols of his authority and submit to the executioner with his silken cord (Stoye 2007, 181).

That year, 1683, marked the beginning of a long period of slow decay that would continue until the empire's final dissolution in 1922. Several explanations have been proposed for this decline. One group of observers has argued that there were profound cultural differences between the West and the Islamic world. Eric Jones (1981) explained the Ottoman decline by "obscurantism" that prevented Turkish society from having access to the new scientific ideas that were being developed in Europe. Another set of writers has pointed to an alleged widening gap in military technology. Carlo Cipolla (1966, 95) described an "obsession of the Turks with huge guns", whereas Geoffrey Parker (1996, 127) asserted that the Ottomans never mastered the new complexities of battlefield tactics and siege warfare.

Yet another approach looked at the Ottoman defeat before the walls of Vienna as an accident of history that set off a set of path-dependent changes. For Mesut Uyar and Edward J. Erickson (2009, 98), Mustafa Pasha's error of judgment in not building defensive works to protect his army triggered a series of Ottoman defeats and corresponding victories of its opponents. Instead of being able to complete the modernization of the army, the empire suffered from a series of military rebellions and the politicization of military policy. Thereafter the Ottomans would be on the defensive.

All observers agree that an immediate consequence of the defeats in the Great Turkish War (alternatively, the War of the Holy Alliance) from 1683 to 1699 was a fiscal crisis. As we saw in the preceding section, there were three types of transformation that allowed England to escape from an analogous fiscal crisis in the seventeenth century. First, in military finance, the English made a change from taxation in kind to cash payments. Second, they shifted from direct taxes on property toward indirect taxes levied on importers and domestic producers. Third, the English replaced tax farmers by centrally controlled public officials. Let us now examine to what extent the Ottoman Empire was able to follow the English model.

Consider first the military transformation. We saw earlier that there were two pillars to the traditional Ottoman fiscal system, both involving payments in kind. One was the *timar*, a right to revenue from a certain property that was granted to a cavalryman in lieu of salary. The second basic element was the institution of slave soldiers. The non-Muslim boys recruited under the *devşirme* system were trained to become the sultan's personal infantry troops, the Janissaries. Like the agricultural produce paid in kind by the peasants to the timar-holder, the labor service contributed by these soldiers may be considered a form of taxation in kind.

In the early seventeenth century, because of changes in military technology, both of these pillars were crumbling. As the number of Janissaries peaked, additional infantry soldiers were recruited from the Turkish population of Anatolia (Inalcik 1973, 48). Moreover, the Long War with Austria from 1593 to 1606 saw the completion of the Ottoman army's long conversion from small forces of mounted bowmen to large infantry corps equipped with firearms (Uyar and Erickson 2009, 82). These new professional armies were five times as expensive as the expeditionary armies of the sixteenth century. Most important, their soldiers had to be paid regularly—in cash (Uyar and Erickson 2009, 83). As a result, the Ottoman treasury required massive amounts of silver coin every three months (Darling 2006, 121).

Let us turn next to the structure of the fiscal system. The basic dilemma for the Ottoman treasury during the seventeenth century was to finance the required flow of specie for the armed forces. Because of the overwhelming importance of agriculture in the economy, the opportunities for indirect taxes were limited; nevertheless, new excise taxes were levied on wine and sheep (Darling 2006, 119). However, to raise a significant amount of additional revenue, there was no choice but to increase the receipts of direct taxes paid in cash. Accordingly, allocations of timars to *sipâhî*, the Sultan's household cavalry, ceased. To help meet the imperial treasury's liquidity requirements, vacant timars were now auctioned off as tax farms, *iltizams*, to palace officials and soldiers (Quataert 2005, 30). The largest single revenue source during the seventeenth century was a wealth tax, the *avariz*, which previously had been an occasional tax paid partly in kind. It was now converted into an annual tax collected in cash (Darling 2006, 119).

The direct tax with rates most easily manipulated was the *cizye*, the capitation tax levied on non-Muslims. In 1691, desperate for more revenue after the defeats in the West, the regime raised this tax considerably. The rates of one, two or four gold coins for low-, medium- and high-income subjects, respectively, were now made uniform throughout the empire. In this way income from the *cizye* quadrupled, rising to 40 percent of total receipts (Darling 2006, 125). Inevitably, the base for this tax declined, in part because of the incentive to convert to Islam (Faroqhi 2006, 377).

Despite these changes, additional revenue was still required to finance rising military spending. Therefore, the government in 1695 introduced the *malikane*, a lifetime tax farm applied to certain agricultural lands in Anatolia and the Levant (Darling 2006, 126). Since the annual rate to be paid to the state could not be changed during the lifetime of the tax farmer, these contracts proved extremely profitable for their holders after 1700, when agricultural prices rose (Darling 2006, 125). To complete this list, we should note that in wartime, various extraordinary taxes were also levied, some illegally by unprincipled tax collectors who took advantage of lax supervision in the countryside (Darling 2006, 121).

The final aspect of the fiscal system to be considered is the degree of centralization. To administer the collection procedures and the auditing of the tax collectors' books, it was necessary to increase the size of the central finance bureaucracy. From around 75 members, its personnel rose to about 200 by 1650 (Darling 2006, 121). However, after 1630, the actual collection of taxes was carried out increasingly by agents of the provincial governors. Moreover, the distribution of the proceeds between the central government and the provinces was determined not by a coherent central policy but rather by bargaining between the center and the periphery. In addition, the provinces were allowed to impose their own taxes, labeled as extraordinary levies or as campaign assistance (Darling 2006, 121).

We have seen that after 1600 there was some degree of decentralization as effective power passed from the sultan to the households of viziers and pashas. Nevertheless, there were frequent delays in paying the soldiers. In 1648, there was famine in Istanbul when the Venetians blockaded the Dardanelles. A revolt by the Janissaries led to the overthrow and execution of Sultan Ibrahim I. His six-year-old son, Mehmed IV, was placed on the throne. For most of the next century and a half, executive power resided in the hands of the Grand Vizier, whose position depended on the support of the sultan's family, the ulema and the Janissaries.

Despite these organizational changes, during the last quarter of the seventeenth century, the imperial government was frequently unable to raise the cash needed to pay its large armies and equip them with the latest firearms. The result was a series of mutinies along with shortages of munitions and provisions that together contributed to military defeat (Darling 2006, 124).

It is evident, then, that despite the many modifications to its tax system over the course of the seventeenth century, the Ottoman Empire remained unable to make the transition to the modern fiscal state. With regard to military financing, payment of the troops during the frequent periods of war remained a chronic dilemma throughout the century. As for the tax structure, the Ottoman state was still highly dependent on direct taxation of agriculture and on discriminatory taxes levied on its non-Muslim subjects, a group whose numbers were declining. Moreover, instead of a central taxing authority with collectors who were state employees, the Ottoman regime depended on large numbers of dispersed tax farmers who had little incentive to promote the prosperity of those who paid the taxes. In theory, the lifetime tax farms, the *malikane*, should have alleviated this difficulty. However, in practice, the regime lost any capacity it had previously enjoyed to prevent the tax farmers from over-exploiting the taxpayers (Darling 2006, 126).

Underlying this beginning of imperial decline was a realignment of the boundaries of Benedict Anderson's (2006) "imagined communities" for the Ottoman sultan's subjects. The Turkish literacy rate had undoubtedly risen over the seventeenth century with the ready availability of locally produced paper and the expansion of the education system. However, within the Turkish-speaking community, only a small percentage of men could read Ottoman Turkish. Indeed, with growing divergence of the written from the spoken language, the extent of diglossia had risen. Within the empire as a whole, because of the numerous languages and dialects and many religions and sects, there was as yet no such thing as a Turkish nation. Rather, with the role of the sultan becoming increasingly symbolic, loyalty to a supreme individual was becoming secondary to fidelity to one's clan or ethnic community. Within the Muslim population, each interest group felt justified in doing whatever was necessary to increase its share of the total income even if the empire as a whole suffered as a result.

6.4 India in 1700

Akbar died in 1605, 2 years after Elizabeth I and Mehmed III. However, the basic structure he had established for the Mughal Empire continued to function efficiently for most of the following century. Under his son Jihangir (r. 1605–1627), his grandson Shah Jahan (r. 1627–1658) and his great-grandson Aurangzeb (r. 1659–1707), the economy expanded, population grew and India became integrated into a worldwide trade network. However, the outward territorial expansion of the empire slowed to a virtual halt. Moreover, to the west in Afghanistan, to the east in Assam and to the south in the Deccan, the few new territories that were conquered failed to pay for themselves in additional tax revenue (Keay 2000, 330).

When Aurangzeb died in 1707, it was discovered that his treasury contained gold and silver, some of it coined and some uncoined, amounting to 240 million rupees (Richards 1993, 253). However, a vicious circle of unrest in the countryside that began at about this time prevented zamindars from meeting their fiscal quotas, leading to a precipitous fall in imperial revenues. In 1712, after 5 years of bitter civil war accompanied by Sikh and Maratha revolts, the Mughal state was bankrupt (Richards 1993, 263). In 1719 Farrukhsiyar, the last Mughal emperor to have any real power, was killed by two brothers, the Sayyids, who were former provincial governors (Keay 2000, 366). When they in turn were defeated by an alliance of dissident nobles, the empire broke up into a number of autonomous territorial states (Keay 2000, 326).

Why did the Mughal Empire break apart so suddenly? In a word, it failed to make the transition to a modern fiscal state. Consider first the financing of the army. Most of the troops for the emperor's campaigns continued to be supplied by the nobles and their vassals in feudal fashion. Even the wages of the imperial household troops depended on the arrival of a steady stream of coin from the provincial administrations. Second, the fiscal structure itself remained heavily dependent on skimming off the surplus of agricultural production above the cultivators' subsistence requirements. Roughly 90 percent of revenues came from the land tax and only a tenth from the urban sector (Richards 1993, 186). Finally, although there was a central ministry of finance and revenue (Richards 1993, 56), its role consisted principally of surveying and recording the production and revenue-generating capacity of the land under cultivation. The actual collection of taxes was carried out locally by the zamindars (Metcalf and Metcalf 2006, 20).

As long as the nobility retained their loyalty to the emperor, this system functioned reasonably well. However, on his accession to the throne in 1658, Aurangzeb attempted to engineer what might be termed a restructuring of India's "imagined communities". His great-grandfather, Akbar, who had never learned to read and write, had been a religious eclectic who enjoyed refereeing the disputes between theologians of various persuasions. However, Aurangzeb was a pious Muslim who abstained from alcohol and studied the Quran and treatises on Islamic law (see Fig. 6.1). A religious conservative, Aurangzeb spent considerable energy trying to convert the Mughal Empire into a Muslim state under Sharia law. He ordered a

Fig. 6.1 The emperor Aurangzeb was a pious Muslim who abstained from alcohol and studied the Quran and treatises on Islamic law. However, during his reign, the fiscal regime put in place by Akbar gradually collapsed (Reproduced from *Wikipedia Commons*)

number of Hindu temples to be pulled down and replaced by mosques. To encourage conversions to Islam, Aurangzeb raised tax rates, but in discriminatory fashion. One of his decrees levied taxes on Hindu pilgrims. Another edict set a tax rate for internal customs that was twice as high for non-Muslims as for Muslims. In 1679, he restored the *jizya*, the graduated tax on the property of non-Muslims (Richards 1993, 176).

With Aurangzeb's efforts to promote Islam as the only true religion, it is not surprising that he spent much of his time putting down revolts by his non-Muslim subjects. Among the latter were the adherents of Sikhism, a monotheistic religion that rejected idolatry and the caste system. Akbar's son Jahangir (r. 1605–1627) had begun the Mughals' conflict with the Sikhs by executing Arjun, the fifth Sikh Guru, because he had supported Jahangir's son during a succession conflict in 1605 (Richards 1993, 94–97). In similar fashion, when Jahangir's grandson Aurangzeb heard that Muslims were beginning to convert to Sikhism, he had the ninth Guru, Tegh Bahadur, arrested and executed for blasphemy (Richards 1993, 178). Nevertheless, Sikhism survived in an embryonic territorial state in the foothills of the Punjab (Keay 2000, 345).

The key to the control of northern India was Rajasthan, a semi-arid province lying between Delhi and the Indus basin. In 1678, Aurangzeb intervened in a succession dispute in the Rajasthan state of Marwar to support an unpopular nephew of the late maharaja. This action provoked a revolt by an alliance of Rajput clans against Mughal rule.[1] Although the invading Mughal troops sacked the Rajputs' Hindu temples, the local rulers refused to cede until an honorable peace had been concluded. In 1682 another Hindu kingdom, Ahom on the northeastern frontier in Assam revolted, managing to drive out the Mughal forces permanently (Richards 1993, 247). Moreover, in 1685, the Jats near Agra refused to pay the revenue due to the emperor and began attacking convoys on the road from Agra south to the Deccan (Richards 1993, 250).

The gravest long-term internal threat to the Mughal Timurid dynasty, however, came from the light cavalry forces of the Hindu Maratha in the Deccan. The first signs of danger appeared in 1658 and 1659 while Aurangzeb was waging war on his three brothers over the succession to their father, Shah Jahan. A charismatic Maratha leader, Shivaji, and a group of followers attempted to carve out an autonomous domain in the Western Ghats, a mountain range on the western edge of the Deccan province. Over the next two decades, Shivaji carried out a series of successful raids on Mughal possessions such as the rich west-coast port of Surat. Before he died in 1680, he succeeded several times in escaping from imperial forces ordered to capture him. To his heirs, he left a substantial kingdom stretching almost the whole length of the western peninsula. Two sons and a grandson continued the Maratha resistance in the Deccan, offering protection from Mughal tax collectors in return for payment at 35 percent of the imperial rates (Keay 2000, 357).

The main revenue source for the Mughal emperors was the rich province of Bengal. In 1696–1697, the flow of specie and supplies from the east was cut off by a revolt led by discontented zamindars. The imperial army with light artillery managed to defeat the rebels, but the state's revenues did not recover. In 1701, Aurangzeb sent his chief imperial fiscal officer to investigate. The new diwan soon discovered widespread corruption on the part of imperial officials (Richards 1993, 247–249). Nevertheless, as mentioned above, when Aurangzeb died in 1707, the officials of his third son and eventual heir, Bahadur Shah I, found imperial reserves of 240 million rupees (Richards 1993, 253). However, in 1712, two costly wars of succession later, the imperial government was bankrupt, unable to pay its soldiers (Richards 1993, 263).

What had happened? With the exception of Bengal, the provinces of the empire by this time had stopped sending treasure regularly to the central treasury (Richards 1993, 263). Serious problems had begun during the last decades of the reign of Aurangzeb, when the Sikhs, Rajputs, Jats and Maratha had successfully contested imperial authority. After Aurangzeb's death, the complex tax-collection system organized by Akbar's officials had come undone. In northern and central India, zamindars revolted against the imperial government (Metcalf and Metcalf 2006, 30). Anxious to obtain revenue by whatever means possible, property holders contracted out tax collection to private revenue farmers (Richards 1993, 263). Then in the 1720s, provincial governors in Bengal, Hyderabad and Awadh stopped sending revenue to Delhi. As *nawab*s (viceroys), they ruled over semi-independent states, recognized by an emperor whose de facto territory was gradually melting away (Metcalf and Metcalf 2006, 31). By the middle of the eighteenth century, the Maratha confederacy had replaced the Empire as the dominant power in the subcontinent (Keay 2000, 367).

Metcalf and Metcalf (2006, 25–37) listed several explanations that have been offered for the sudden collapse of the Mughal Empire. Hindu nationalists have emphasized the role of religion. The Maratha, it is argued, were reacting to Aurangzeb's policies aimed at converting the empire into an Islamic state. However, Aurangzeb's sanctions were generally aimed at those he felt had been disloyal to him, whether Muslim or non-Muslim. Moreover, as the empire declined, the Maratha often entered into alliances with Muslim leaders for political gain. For example, in 1719 the Maratha helped the Sayyid brothers to seize power from the reigning emperor, Farrukhsiyar (Wolpert 1993, 170).

Another possible explanation focuses on military technology. While the strong point of the Mughal armies was their heavy cavalry, the Eurasian battlefield was coming to be dominated by disciplined infantry bearing firearms and supported by artillery (Metcalf and Metcalf 2006, 36). However, the decline and breakup of the Mughal Empire between 1660 and 1725 predated the use of European-trained infantry. It was their highly mobile light cavalry that enabled the Maratha to frustrate Aurangzeb's campaign to control the Deccan. Only after 1741 did the rigorous training and equipment of sepoy armies in India begin under the governorship of Joseph-François Dupleix in the French enclave of Pondicherry in southeast India (Wolpert 1993, 176).

Other authors have focused on the great changes in Indian society during the late sixteenth and the seventeenth centuries following the opening of sea routes between Europe and Asia. With the growing monetization of the Indian economy and the expansion of trade, social mobility increased and new commercial and social elites came to the fore (Metcalf and Metcalf

2006, 25–6). Shivaji, the son of a Maratha career soldier who had risen to the rank of general, was one example among several of a leader who through his own talent and charisma was able to create a kingdom and a dynasty.

An important factor that underlies all of these explanations is a change in information technology. The rapid expansion of paper production and the promotion of education under the Mughals had led to rising literacy. However, rather than permitting the predominance of one prestigious dialect as had occurred in England, literacy was accompanied by linguistic divergence. In the case of written languages, the two vehicular tongues, Persian and Sanskrit, were joined by Urdu and the regional Indo-Aryan languages. The result was a breakup of the Mughal Empire into a number of Benedict Anderson's (2006) "imagined communities" as the limits of the group with which each person identified narrowed to the boundaries of the new written languages. By the mid-eighteenth century, the former Mughal provinces had become autonomous states, the centers of which were differentiated by important ethnic identities.

We see then, that growing linguistic divergence was accompanied by internal dissension and breakdown of the fiscal system in both the Ottoman and Mughal Empires. Let us turn next to the third great Asian empire to discover how it was coping with its fiscal challenges.

6.5   China in 1700

To defend its northern border, the Ming administration had relied on frontier guard units, *Weisuo*, and on alliances with local tribes. However, by the early seventeenth century, the *Weisuo*, deprived of resources by the central administration, had declined in effectiveness (Worthing 2007, 16). In addition, the degree of external threat took a turn for the worse in 1616, when the Jurchen leader Nurhaci renounced his loyalty to the Chinese emperor and began attacking Ming territory in the Liaoning peninsula of southern Manchuria. In 1619, local Ming forces equipped with firearms lost a major battle to Manchu cavalrymen armed with bows and arrows at the Sarhu Mountain Pass. The Ming response was to improve their defenses by purchasing Portuguese cannon. These new weapons and other cannon cast with the help of Jesuit missionaries enabled the Ming to fatally wound Nurhaci and defeat the Manchus during their attempted siege of Ningyuan (now Xingcheng), a Liaoning coastal city, in 1626 (Worthing 2007, 19).

Leadership of the Manchu then fell to Nurhaci's son, Hong Taiji, who set about reorganizing his administration on the Chinese model. He greatly increased the size of his army by incorporating new Mongol banners and "Chinese-martial" banners, made up of Han Chinese, into his army.[2] In 1631, to improve the odds of his cavalry armies against Chinese urban defenses, Hong Taiji employed captured Chinese soldiers to produce 40 cannon (Worthing 2007, 21). By the time he died in 1643, he had declared himself the head of a new dynasty, the Qing, and was about to invade China.

Meanwhile, the Ming emperor and his officials were fighting not only foreign enemies from beyond the Great Wall but also armies of their own near-starving subjects who were eager to overthrow the imperial regime. In the northwest, a former army officer, Li Zicheng, led a revolt of a peasant army force that by 1641 may have numbered as many as 400,000 men (Worthing 2007, 22). In April 1644, Li's forces managed to seize the nearly defenseless imperial capital. The last Ming emperor Chongzhen hanged himself from a tree in the garden just north of the Forbidden City. Two months later, Li and his army were driven out of the city and defeated by a Ming general allied with the Manchu regent. The latter then declared the beginning of Qing rule over China (Ebrey 1996, 221).

Among the most plausible explanations for this collapse of the Ming Empire before the Manchu onslaught, Brook (2013) argued, is the Little Ice Age. Between 1300 and 1850, there was a general cooling, particularly in the Northern Hemisphere, with mean temperatures reaching their minima during the seventeenth century. While Europe was wetter than usual, China was abnormally dry (Heijdra 1998, 423). In 1628, for example, there was drought in northwest China in Shaanxi, accompanied by a cold period that continued into the 1640s. Then beginning in 1637, droughts that lasted until 1644 occurred in a number of regions. Simultaneously an epidemic of smallpox struck populations weakened by malnutrition (Brook 2013, 250).

Climate cooling and the resulting crop failures certainly help explain the rural unrest observed in many Chinese regions during the late Ming period. Yet why was the Ming regime fatally weakened, while the reigning Manchu dynasty, which endured equally severe weather conditions (Brook 2013, 243), emerged unscathed—indeed, dominant? To answer this question, it is helpful to consider recent research on the dynastic cycle in China. Chen (2015) studied the determinants of nomadic conquest using dynastic and climate date. He found that a drop in average rainfall significantly increased the probability that pastoral nomads would attack agrarian societies. However, he also showed that the greater the age of the Chinese dynasty relative to that of the nomads, the greater the likelihood that the nomads would be victorious. This result helps explain the victory of the young Aisin Gioro dynasty from Manchuria over that of the Chinese Ming who had ruled for some 276 years.

It might be asked why the ability of a dynasty to defend itself would decrease with the number of years since its founding. John Fairbank and Merle Goldman (2006, 48) offered an explanation in terms of a fiscal base that diminished as the regime aged. At the beginning of a regime, a census of land and population provides a basis for subsequent revenue collection. However, as time passes, powerful groups succeed in removing their lands from taxation or lowering the rates that they pay. Small farmers seeking a means of lowering their own tax payments then attach themselves to large landholders. To finance itself, the regime must then raise tax rates for other landholders, thereby increasing the incentive for the latter to shirk on paying taxes. At the end of this vicious spiral, the existing dynasty is attacked and defeated by a new, more cohesive group.

In applying this paradigm to Ming China, we are again faced with the question of whether the regime in question succeeded in taking the three reforms necessary for founding a modern fiscal state; namely, (i) the transition to cash payments for the military, (ii) the switch from direct to indirect taxation, (iii) the centralization of the tax-collection administration.

With regard to military finance, as we saw earlier, the Single Whip Reform, whereby taxes in kind were replaced by cash payments, was intended to assure regular wages for the armies defending the northern border. In practice, after the withdrawal of the Wanli Emperor from direct administration in 1600 until the Qing conquest in 1644, the Ming state and its army were chronically underfinanced (Huang 1998, 113).

As for tax structure, until its final days, the Ming dynasty depended on the direct taxation of agricultural output in order to finance its household spending and its troops. As we have seen, almost 85 percent of state revenues came from land taxes of one kind or another, while only five percent came from excise taxes, mostly from the profits of the state salt monopoly (Huang 1974, 177, 263). The remaining ten percent of receipts came from a variety of miscellaneous sources. In other word, the transition to efficient indirect taxes for the greater part of state revenues proved unfeasible because of the heavy dependence of the Chinese economy on its agricultural sector.

A large share of the state expenditures in the late Ming period—at least 20–25 percent—was allocated to the emperor's palace compound (Huang 1998, 116). Nevertheless, central control over the reforms to the fiscal system was extremely weak. The government never did set up a central imperial treasury (Huang 1998, 158). Although there was an elaborate four-tiered administrative structure made up of province, prefecture, sub-prefecture and county, in practice, reform depended on the initiative of individual prefects and magistrates. However, these low-level officials generally served terms of only 3 years, often in regions where they did not speak the local dialect (Huang 1974, 96). Moreover, because of the low salaries they were paid, most magistrates expected to receive "gifts" from taxpayers in order to maintain themselves and their families (Huang 1998, 159). It is no surprise that in most jurisdictions, tax assessments and rates were determined not by standard imperial regulations but by bilateral negotiations between local officials and the gentry in their districts (Huang 1974, 96–97).

Why were the late Ming tax reforms unable to generate enough revenue to finance the armies that maintained internal security and assured the empire's borders? Part of the explanation lies in the exceptionally cold dry weather that led to crop failure in many regions. However, the breakdown of the fiscal system also reflects a gradual loss of trust in the imperial government and its officials on the part of landholders distant from the imperial capital. The richest region of China was Jiangnan ("south of the river"), the densely populated triangle of the Yangtze Delta. After the troubled periods of the late Song and Yuan dynasties, Jiangnan was the region that had benefited most from the prosperity that the Ming dynasty had brought to China. However, since the fifteenth century, Jiangnan property owners had been the most flagrant tax evaders in China, piling up arrears that were never paid (Huang 1998, 110). Yet after the fall of Beijing to the Manchu, it was Jiangnan that by supporting Southern Ming pretenders made the greatest sacrifices to protect itself. In 1645 after a long siege, Qing troops pillaged the city of Yangzhou on the north shore of the Yangtze and slaughtered as many as 800,000 of its residents in a 10-day bloodfest (Fairbank and Goldman 2006, 145).

To help explain this high internal cohesion of the provincial gentry but their low willingness to cooperate with imperial officials, it is helpful once again to examine Anderson's (2006) concept of "imagined communities". In the late Ming period, Jiangnan, like Guangdong in the south, had a strong geographic and cultural identity. For centuries one of the rice bowls of China the Yangtze Delta had become the center of a prosperous textile industry, exporting silks and cottons throughout the empire and abroad (Ko 1994, 20). Its cities were also the home of a flourishing upscale publishing industry (Ko 1994, 39). Moreover, it was the dialect of Nanjing, the former imperial capital on the south bank of the Yangtze, rather than that of Beijing which remained the koine, the common spoken language of the empire, during the Ming dynasty (Dong 2014, ch. 10). With the exception of the region around Nanjing, however, the most prestigious spoken dialect in Jiangnan in the late Ming was not the koine but rather one of the Wu dialects of the Lake Tai region south of the Yangtze (Ko 1994, 21).

In conclusion, it may be suggested, that one of the principal reasons for the failure of the Ming dynasty to escape from the excessive rent-seeking and tax evasion typical of a mature dynasty was linguistic. Rising literacy in the sixteenth and early seventeenth centuries had led to a considerable increase in the percentage of men and women able to *read* vernacular publications. However, without a phonetic writing system, the *spoken* vernaculars in the regions drifted ever further apart. Moreover, rather than a single national lingua franca, there was competition between regional koines that were not mutually comprehensible for many speakers. The inevitable result was a decline in the willingness of Chinese elites to trust those from outside their own lineage.

With the passing years, as the local dialects diverged further from one another without a common spoken vernacular, the Chinese from different regions were increasingly reluctant to cooperate with one another. Yet without such cooperation, the Ming regime could not develop the efficient and flexible system of monetary taxation needed to finance its armed forces adequately. Accordingly, it was only a matter of time before an internal crisis coincided with an outside threat from a culturally homogeneous state equipped with the latest military technology. To the north of China, the Manchurian Qing dynasty, ruling over the recently united Manchu clans along with Mongolian and Chinese-martial allies, was only too willing give the dynastic cycle another spin.

6.6 THE FISCAL DILEMMA

We have seen that in the (First) Military Revolution, during the early modern period, gradual improvements in individual firearms, in the defenses against artillery and in the design of warships had created a fiscal dilemma for Eurasian states. Massive walls had to be built around strategic sites. Ever-larger armies and navies had to be equipped with gunpowder weapons. Most important, in a market economy, the soldiers and sailors of permanent armed forces had to be paid regularly in cash. Otherwise, the regime risked being defeated in battle or overthrown by its own troops. At the same time, in the largely agricultural economies of the period, there was a limit to the level of taxes that could be extracted without immiserizing the population.

The English managed to effect the required administrative transformations during the second half of the seventeenth century. There, the gradual standardization of the written and spoken vernacular coincided with a growing feeling of belonging to a single nation. In China, India and the Ottoman Empire, no such linguistic convergence occurred. Nor were the equivalent administrative reforms carried out. The immediate consequence of the resulting fiscal weakness in the Asian states was a gradual undermining of their ruling dynasties' effective power.

Notes

1. The Rajputs were a north-Indian ethnic group known from the sixth century CE for their martial abilities.
2. Crossley (1997, ch. 1) defines the Chinese-martial troops as soldiers from Manchuria and northern China who were fluent in Chinese and had personal associations with the Chinese towns of the Liaodong peninsula.

References

Anderson, B. (2006). *Imagined communities: Reflections on the origin and spread of nationalism* (Revised ed.). London: Verso.

Asquith, S. (1981). *New Model Army 1645–60*. Oxford: Osprey Publishing.

Borsay, P. (2002). The culture of improvement. In P. Langford (Ed.), *The eighteenth century 1688–1815* (pp. 183–212). Oxford: Oxford University Press.

Brook, T. (2013). *The troubled empire: China in the Yuan and Ming dynasties*. Cambridge, MA: Belknap Press.

Brown, K. M. (2008). Monarchy and government in Britain, 1603–1637. In J. Wormald (Ed.), *The seventeenth century* (pp. 13–50). Oxford: Oxford University Press.

Chen, Q. (2015). Climate shocks, dynastic cycles and nomadic conquests: Evidence from historical China. *Oxford Economic Papers, 67*, 185–204.

Cipolla, C. M. (1966). *Guns, sails and empires: Technological innovation and the early phases of European expansion*. New York: Pantheon.

Crossley, P. K. (1997). *The Manchus*. Oxford: Blackwell.

Darling, L. T. (2006). Public finances: The role of the Ottoman centre. In S. N. Faroqhi (Ed.), *The Cambridge history of Turkey, vol. 3, The later Ottoman Empire, 1603–1839* (pp. 118–134). Cambridge: Cambridge University Press.

Dong, H. (2014). *A history of the Chinese language*. London: Routledge.
Dupuy, R. E., & Dupuy, T. (1986). *The encyclopedia of military history from 3500 B.C. to the present*. New York: Harper and Row.
Ebrey, P. B. (1996). *The Cambridge illustrated history of China*. Cambridge, UK: Cambridge University Press.
Fairbank, J. K., & Goldman, M. (2006 [original 1992]). *China: A new history*. (2nd enlarged ed.). Cambridge, MA: Belknap Press.
Faroqhi, S. N. (2006). Rural life. In S. N. Faroqhi (Ed.), *The Cambridge history of Turkey, vol. 3, The later Ottoman Empire, 1603–1839* (pp. 376–392). Cambridge: Cambridge University Press.
Febvre, L., & Martin, H.-J. (1976). *The coming of the book: The impact of printing 1450–1800*. London: NLB.
He, W. (2013). *Paths toward the modern fiscal state: England, Japan, and China*. Cambridge, MA: Harvard University Press.
Heijdra, M. (1998). The socio-economic development of rural China during the Ming. In D. Twitchett & F. W. Mote (Eds.), *Cambridge history of China* (Vol. 8, pp. 417–578). Cambridge, UK: Cambridge University Press.
Huang, R. (1974). *Taxation and governmental finance in sixteenth-century Ming China*. Cambridge, UK: Cambridge University Press.
Huang, R. (1998). The Ming fiscal administration. In D. Twitchett & F. W. Mote (Eds.), *The Cambridge history of China, vol. 8, The Ming Dynasty, 1368–1644, part 2* (pp. 106–171). Cambridge, UK: Cambridge University Press.
Inalcik, H. (1973). *The Ottoman Empire: The classical age 1300–1600*. New York: Praeger.
Johnson, N. D., & Koyama, M. (2014). Tax farming and the origins of state capacity in England and France. *Explorations in Economic History, 51*, 1–20.
Jones, E. L. (1981). *The European miracle*. Cambridge, UK: Cambridge University Press.
Keay, J. (2000). *India: A history*. New York: Grove Press.
Ko, D. (1994). *Teachers of the inner chambers: Women and culture in seventeenth-century China*. Stanford: Stanford University Press.
Lynn, J. A. (1995). States in conflict 1661–1763. In G. Parker (Ed.), *The Cambridge illustrated history of warfare* (pp. 164–185). Cambridge: Cambridge University Paree.
Metcalf, B. D., & Metcalf, T. R. (2006). *A concise history of modern India* (2nd ed.). Cambridge: Cambridge University Press.
North, D. C., & Weingast, B. R. (1989). Constitutions and commitment: The evolution of institutions governing public choice in eighteenth century England. *Journal of Economic History, 49*, 803–832.
O'Brien, P. K. (2011). The nature and historical evolution of an exceptional fiscal state and its possible significance for the precocious commercialization and

industrialization of the British economy from Cromwell to Nelson. *Economic History Review, 64*(2), 408–446.

Parker, G. (1996). *The military revolution: military innovation and the rise of the West, 1500–1800* (2nd ed.). Cambridge, UK: Cambridge University Press.

Peck, L. L. (1993). *Court patronage and corruption in early Stuart England.* London: Routledge.

Quataert, D. (2005). *The Ottoman Empire 1700–1922* (2nd ed.). Cambridge, UK: Cambridge University Press.

Richards, J. F. (1993). *The Mughal empire.* Cambridge: Cambridge University Press.

Stoye, J. (2007). *The Siege of Vienna* (New ed.). Vienna: Birlinn.

Uyar, M., & Erickson, E. J. (2009). *A military history of the Ottomans from Osman to Atatürk.* Santa Barbara: Praeger Security International.

Wolpert, S. (1993). *A new history of India* (4th ed.). Oxford: Oxford University Press.

Worthing, P. (2007). *A military history of modern China: From the Manchu conquest to Tian'anmen Square.* Westport: Praeger.

CHAPTER 7

Steam Makes Waves

7.1 An Innovative Dead End

One day in 1786, a young machinist at a local lead mine was walking with a companion through the Mennock Hass (Pass) in the high moors to the southeast of Glasgow. Suddenly William Symington, 22, realized how he might solve a problem that had been troubling him. He saw that a simple technical change could considerably improve the notoriously wasteful Newcomen atmospheric steam engine being used to pump water from Scottish mines. Taking his walking stick, he drew a diagram on the dirt road, showing his companion how the steam could be cooled efficiently without resorting to an external chamber and pump, as James Watt had done (Harvey and Downs-Rose 1980, 24). Accordingly, there would be little risk of violating Watt's patents. Though practical, Symington's idea would turn out to be a dead end in the development of the steam engine. However, his rough drawing would eventually lead to an important step in the development of transportation technology.

7.2 Who Invented the Steamboat?

Traditionally for French historians, the answer to this question has been the Marquis Claude de Jouffroy d'Abbans (Prost 1889, 312; Daumas 1980, 300). In 1776, the former army officer used a Newcomen-type steam engine to power the mechanical oars of a 13-m boat, the *Palmipède*, on the River Doubs in eastern France. However, when Jouffroy attempted to have the machine row against the current, the blades on the oars collapsed. Several years later, he was able to connect another Newcomen engine to two side paddlewheels in a larger boat, the *Pyroscaphe*. Thousands of spectators gathered to witness his initial trip in 1783 along the Saône in Lyon. However, after 15 minutes, the hull opened and the steam rushed out of the boiler. Subsequently, following the advice of one of Jouffroy's rivals, the French *Académie des sciences* refused to grant the inventor a 15-year monopoly unless he could demonstrate his technology satisfactorily on the Seine. Lacking sufficient financial resources to start anew in Paris, Jouffroy was forced to abandon his project (Flexner 1944, 45).

For American schoolchildren, the name to remember in association with steam navigation is Robert Fulton, the man who developed the first commercially successful steamboat. He and his partner Robert Livingston built the *North River Steamboat*, also known as the *Clermont*, employing a Boulton and Watt engine to turn two side paddlewheels. Beginning in 1807, over three decades after Jouffroy's first efforts, they used the boat to transport passengers on the Hudson River between New York City and Albany (Johnson 2010, 265–266).

For many British historians, however, the crucial developments occurred in England at an intermediate date between the inventions of Jouffroy and Fulton. The first practical steamboat, they argue, was the invention of the young Scot, William Symington. His was the first steam-powered vessel to succeed in doing something useful. Symington's story is interesting because it ties together some of most important phases in the application of steam to industry and transportation.

Prior to the eighteenth century, if people across Europe and Asia wanted to make a machine move, they depended either on muscles—their own and those of their animals—or else on the force of the wind or flowing water. For over two millennia, there had been machines that relied on water power. In the Near East by the third century BCE, waterwheels were used to raise water from a stream for irrigation. In the first century CE, the Romans were making flour with a vertical waterwheel that turned a horizontal millstone by means of interlocking wooden gears (Daumas 1969, 106–108). The Chinese by the sixth century were employing water power to sift and shake flour and to drive the bellows of blast furnaces (Temple 2007, 72–73).

The harnessing of wind power came later, but it too was used for a variety of purposes. In tenth-century China, windmills with adjustable arms were used for drainage or irrigation. Windmills with fixed arms were employed to grind grain in northwestern Europe from the eleventh century (Daumas 1969, 110). The advantage of both wind and water power was that they were renewable. However, a major drawback of each source was the limited number of sites where it could be applied. Moreover, in many locations there were seasonal variations in these natural forces. By the late seventeenth century, therefore, people in the West were beginning to look for a steady source of power that could be used virtually anywhere—even to propel a boat.

Over the seventeenth century, improvements in naval architecture had led to an increase in the size of warships and in the number and caliber of the cannon they carried (Daumas 1980, 371–377). However, apart from their larger size and heavier armament, the British and Dutch ships that defeated the French and Spanish at Vigo Bay in 1702 were not greatly different from those that had attacked the Spanish Armada a century and a quarter earlier. For example, Admiral Rooke's flagship of 1702, the *Somerset*, had 3 decks and 80 guns, whereas Lord Howard's flagship of 1588, the *Ark Royal*, had 2 decks and 32 guns. Moreover, the top speed of sailing ships had changed very little. It is estimated that a frigate running downwind could sail at half the speed of the wind pushing it (Daumas 1980, 394). With a 20-knot tailwind, a speed of 10 knots was possible. However, sailing against that same wind would drastically reduce the boat's speed.

There had been one important change in naval warfare since the Armada. By the beginning of the eighteenth century, oar-propelled ships had been abandoned. Galleys powered by oars, with only a few cannon mounted in the bow, had become incapable of defending themselves against slower sailing ships in which rowers midship had been replaced by multiple decks of cannon (Daumas 1980, 395). Even oar-powered galleasses with an extra deck for 18 cannon could not compete in firepower with ships-of-the-line carrying as many as 80 cannon (Daumas 1980, 390). By the time of the Treaty of Utrecht in 1713, therefore, virtually all of the world's shipping was powered by sail.

Meanwhile the Ottoman Empire continued to dominate the eastern Mediterranean, as well as the Red and Black Seas. After the mid-seventeenth century, the Ottomans too had made the transition from oar-driven galleys and galleasses to sail-driven galleons and frigates (Black 2009, 41). As for the ships of China or India, these were little changed from the medieval period. Compared to Western warships, they were generally smaller and less heavily armed. Consequently, by 1700, Europeans dominated the long-distance trade between southern Asia and the West. Nevertheless, because of their large draft, often over 18 feet (5 m), Western warships could not sail very far inland (Daumas 1980, 377). Accordingly, the interior of the Asian continent was secure from outside attack by sea—at least for the moment.

7.3 Cooperating with Steam

William Symington, the machinist we met earlier in this chapter, was born in 1764 in the village of Leadhills, in the Lowther Hills of south-central Scotland. Because of the arsenic, sulfur and zinc emitted from region's lead smelters, the surrounding countryside was desolate, devoid of trees and shrubs (Pennant 1776, 129). Symington's parents were "respectable but not wealthy". His father was a mechanic and superintendent of the lead mine of the Scots Mine Company at Leadhills (Harvey and Downs-Rose 1980, 3–4). His older brother George worked as an engineer in the lead mines of the Wanlockhead Mining Company in the nearby village of Wanlockhead. There in 1779 George supervised the building of a Boulton and Watt steam engine (Harvey and Downs-Rose 1980, 13). William had learned Latin and some Greek at school as a youth and was intended for the Ministry. However, in his late teens he was to be seen working instead under his brother as a machinist in Wanlockhead (Harvey and Downs-Rose 1980, 5–6).

In the late eighteenth century if you needed a machine to pump the water from your coal or lead mine, you could not simply locate an engine manufacturer and request that he ship you a steam engine. The procedure was more like ordering furniture from IKEA today. In Scotland at that time, an equivalent firm was the Carron Company, an ironworks on the Carron River 45 km (30 miles) west of Edinburgh. The parts of the desired model would be delivered to the mine-head, where the purchaser would have to assemble them (Harvey and Downs-Rose 1980, 6).

For three-quarters of a century, the standard design for machines to pump water from mines had been the atmospheric steam engine, invented by two Devonshire natives, Thomas Newcomen and John Calley, around 1712. Their device made use of a piston in a vertical metal cylinder that was closed at the bottom but open at the top. When a heavy counterweight pulled the engine's piston upward, steam heated from a coal-fired boiler was sucked into the cylinder, where it was then cooled by a jet of water. Atmospheric pressure at the open end of the cylinder forced the piston downward. The piston in turn pulled a chain attached to a swiveling beam. The other end of the beam rose, activating a water pump (Rolt and Allen 1977).

The English were not the only ones to embark upon path-breaking industrial innovation in the first half of the eighteenth century. In Lyon, France during the 1720s, Basile Bouchon and his student, Jean-Baptiste Falcon, developed the first experimental looms for silk textiles in which the selection of colored threads was programmed on perforated paper or punched cards. In effect, these were the first machines to be run by previously coded information (Mokyr 1990, 102). We shall return to possible explanations for this sudden burst of innovation in the West.

The Newcomen technology was simple and effective. Indeed, in the last quarter of the eighteenth century, a number of coalmines in the Edinburgh area still used it (Harvey and Downs-Rose 1980, 13). However, the alternate heating and cooling of the cylinder required so much energy that the engine could be used profitably only near a plentiful supply of coal. There was an alternative, more energy-efficient design of steam engine available, although at a premium. In 1765, James Watt, a Scottish instrument maker employed by the University of Glasgow, had realized that if the steam could be cooled outside the engine's cylinder, it would no longer be necessary to alternatively heat and cool the cylinder. Consequently, much less coal would be required. With venture capital financed by John Roebuck, the founder of the Carron works, Watt obtained an initial patent for a steam engine with an external condenser in 1769. However, before the design could be implemented, Roebuck found himself in financial difficulty and was forced to sell his share in the patent to Matthew Boulton, a wealthy English manufacturer. At Boulton's invitation, Watt in 1774 moved from Glasgow to Birmingham to form a new partnership with Boulton. The following year, with his political connections, Boulton was able to obtain from Parliament an extension of the original patent until 1800 (Marsden 2002). Watt quickly adapted his engine to produce rotary motion, but he treated projects to apply his machines to water transport with great skepticism (Rowland 1970, 22).

Wanlockhead, almost 500 m (1500 feet) above sea level, is the highest village in Scotland. It would seem an unlikely location for the development of the first effective steamboat. However, the village had mines that were frequently flooded by the runoff from winter rains. In the summer months, the rainfall was often not sufficient to turn the mines' water pumps. There was plentiful coal only nine miles (15 km) away at nearby Sanquhar, a mining town on the River Nith, but transporting the coal by wagon up the rough road to Wanlockhead tripled its price. In 1779, the manager of the Wanlockhead Mining Company, Gilbert Meason, had decided to install a Boulton and Watt engine in the company's Margaret Mine. As mentioned, the engine was built on site by William Symington's brother George, almost certainly with the help of William (Harvey and Downs-Rose 1980, 13–14).

Owing to the American Revolutionary War, there had been a strong demand for lead to be cast into balls for muskets. By 1785, Meason realized that the mine needed a newer, larger engine. He had George Symington install a second machine, also ordered from Boulton and Watt (Harvey and Downs-Rose 1980, 15). Although Watt's design burned less coal than the Newcomen engine, it had several disadvantages compared with the older atmospheric engine. Unlike the open-ended cylinder of the Newcomen engine, the Watt cylinder was completely closed at the top. The modification used steam piped in above the piston rather than atmospheric pressure to push the piston down. As a result, there was no feasible way to lubricate the cylinder other than by periodic removal of the cylinder cover and repacking of the piston. In addition, it was necessary to keep the many joints in the engine's piping tight in order to maintain a partial vacuum in the cylinder. Accordingly, unless a skilled and conscientious engine keeper was on site to assure regular maintenance, the machine tended to break down frequently (Harvey and Downs-Rose 1980, 22–23).

William Symington's roadside drawing of a modified atmospheric steam engine lengthened the Newcomen design's cylinder and added a second piston to it. The cylinder was thereby divided into two sections, only one of which would be cooled to condense the steam. The young engineer persuaded manager Meason that his new design would use less energy than the Newcomen machine while also needing less maintenance than Watt's device. Accordingly, Meason allowed Symington to recuperate the cylinder of the firm's first Boulton and Watt engine and have it rebored. By adding a second piston as a false bottom for the cylinder, Symington did away with the need for the air pump required in Watt's design, thereby greatly simplifying the construction and maintenance (Harvey and Downs-Rose 1980, 24). It was a clever idea that Symington was subsequently able to incorporate into over 25 engines (Harvey and Downs-Rose 1980, 24). A comparative test of Symington's rebuilt machine in 1788 revealed that that it operated with a pressure of 12 pounds per square inch, while Wanlockhead's recently installed Watt engine generated only 9½ pounds per square inch (Harvey and Downs-Rose 1980, 30).

Like many other inventors, Symington often had several projects underway at the same time. While he was rebuilding the Watt engine, he built a model of a steam-propelled carriage. The vehicle, pushed by a horizontal steam engine, was taken by Meason to his home in Edinburgh, where it ran on the carpet to the delight of his guests. During the winter of 1786–1787, Meason arranged for his gifted young protégé to attend classes at Edinburgh University. He also paid the cost of a patent application that covered Symington's engine technology (Harvey and Downs-Rose 1980, 28).

One of the visitors who witnessed Symington's little steam carriage in Edinburgh in 1786 was Patrick Miller, a wealthy banker and one of the principal shareholders of the Carron Company. At that moment, Miller may have discussed with Symington the possibility of using a steam engine to power one of the paddlewheel boats he was building. Miller had fitted a trimaran sailboat with paddlewheels turned by hand cranks that would enable it to be maneuvered independently of the wind during combat (Harvey and Downs-Rose 1980, 41–42).

In 1787 James Taylor, the tutor of Miller's two sons, who had attended classes with Symington at Edinburgh University, persuaded his employer to try Symington's engine to power his boat. Miller had recently purchased an estate at Dalswinton in southern Scotland on which there was a small lake. Financed by Miller, Symington built an engine that he installed in Miller's 25-foot double-hulled boat. The vessel, propelled by two inline paddlewheels, was already on the lake's shore. At last, on 14 October 1788, the boat was taken out onto Dalswinton Lock, where it sailed back and forth under steam power before Miller and a number of enthusiastic spectators (Harvey and Downs-Rose 1980, 50). Cooperation among three men of very different backgrounds had yielded a remarkable little machine.

The following spring, Miller agreed to finance a larger boat with a more powerful engine. The second boat was finished at the Carron Company's dock on the River Carron in order that it might be tried on the almost-completed Forth and Clyde Canal linking Edinburgh and Glasgow. However, the boat's first trial in December 1789 with Miller and the management of the Carron Company on board was not a success. When the power of the engine was increased, the pressure proved too great for the arms of the paddlewheels, which broke off one after the other (Harvey and Downs-Rose 1980, 59). Repairs were quickly made, and by December 26, the boat was ready for a second trial. This time all proved satisfactory, the boat reaching a speed of almost seven miles per hour. Yet Miller decided suddenly to abandon the whole project. Symington had little choice but to return to pumping water out of mines using steam engines of his own design (Harvey and Downs-Rose 1980, 65).

The two steamboats that Symington built with Taylor and Miller marked an important step in the development of steam navigation. They demonstrated that a steam-powered paddlewheel boat was feasible and that it could maintain a sufficient speed to be of use on inland rivers, although not yet on the open sea. However, to carry freight or pull barges, it would be necessary to have a larger boat with a much more powerful engine.

It will be remembered that Miller's objective was to use paddlewheel boats armed with cannon in naval warfare. Symington's first boat had originally been built for that purpose. In 1790, Miller sent one of his paddleboats—without a steam engine—to the king of Sweden, asserting that such craft would give that country the mastery of the Baltic Sea (Harvey and Downs-Rose 1980, 62). Might Symington's little boat on Dalswinton Pond be considered the first steam-powered naval vessel?

7.4 Practical Steam Transport

As yet, no steamboat had been able to show that it could turn a profit for its owner by doing something practical. One obvious application as the nineteenth century began was as a tugboat on Britain's growing network of canals. The Forth and Clyde Canal had been started in 1768 and finally completed in 1790. Some 35 miles (56 km) long, it linked the two principal urban centers of Scotland, Glasgow and Edinburgh. However, its owners faced a major problem. Strong winds could delay the passage of boats with sails, forcing them to wait until weather conditions improved. Yet experiments with steam-powered tugs on canals in England had been a failure because of damage to the canals' banks (Harvey and Downs-Rose 1980, 118–119).

Thomas Dundas, Lord Dundas of Kerse and Aske, a Scottish nobleman, was governor of the Forth and Clyde Navigation Company. He was aware of the steam trials of Miller and Symington a decade earlier and knew the reputation of Symington as the inventor behind a number of steam engines installed in England and Scotland. Early in 1800, he seems to have contacted Symington to discuss a possible project with him. In June of that year, the company's directors in London approved a plan to install one of Symington's engines in a boat designed by a Scottish naval officer, Captain John Schank. Accordingly, Symington built a vertical atmospheric steam engine similar to those he had designed for Miller 12 years earlier. The engine propelled two paddlewheels. However, instead of being inline, the paddlewheels were parallel to each other, one on either side of the boat

(Harvey and Downs-Rose 1980, 120). Symington named the boat the *Charlotte Dundas* in honor of Lord Dundas's eldest daughter. In June 1801, Symington made several trials of the boat on the canal and on the Scottish rivers Carron and Forth (Harvey and Downs-Rose 1980, 122). However, the original *Charlotte Dundas* was rejected by the canal company's Committee of Management as not likely to "answer the purpose". Apparently, it was felt that the wash from the boat damaged the canal's banks (Harvey and Downs-Rose 1980, 128).

To overcome the Committee's objections, Symington proposed a new boat that would be powerful enough to tow loaded barges as fast as horses without damaging the canal. Early in 1802, he took a scale model of the new boat to London, where he showed it to Lord Dundas. When the Duke of Bridgewater, a wealthy English entrepreneur, saw the model, he ordered eight boats for the Bridgewater Canal that connected his coalmines to the city of Manchester. Lord Dundas too approved Symington's design for use on the Scottish canal.

As finished, the new vessel was 58-feet (18 m) long, the maximum size allowed by the locks of the Forth and Clyde Canal (Harvey and Downs-Rose 1980, 133). Unlike Symington's earlier engines, the new machine had a single double-acting cylinder and air pump with a condensing chamber. In other words, he used the technology developed by James Watt, for which the patent had now expired (Harvey and Downs-Rose 1980, 133). To minimize damage to the canal banks, Symington placed the single paddlewheel in the middle of the transom under a housing to the rear of the engine. The engine was placed horizontally and acted directly on the paddlewheels, an innovative design that was not to be copied for another two decades (Dickinson 1939, 110).

On 4 January 1803, Symington undertook the first trial of the *Charlotte Dundas II* on the River Clyde in Glasgow, where the offices of the Navigation Company were located (see Fig. 7.1). Although the experiment was a success, the speed of the boat was probably less than Symington had expected. Two and a half months later, after altering the gears, he made another attempt to convince the Committee that his boat could be of use. On a day when adverse winds kept other boats tied up, the Charlotte Dundas II towed two sloops over a distance of 18½ miles. The local newspaper report was favorable, but the average speed, two miles per hour, was no better than with horses (Harvey and Downs-Rose 1980, 134–137).

The local committee had resented Lord Dundas's decision, taken in London, to experiment with steam transport. Refusing to acknowledge

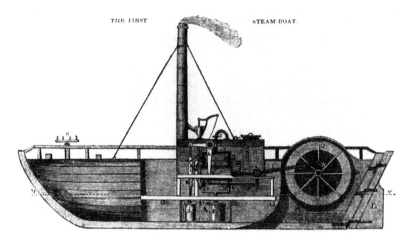

Fig. 7.1 Engraving of the *Charlotte Dundas II* by the son of William Symington. Built in 1802, this boat was the first steam-powered vessel able to perform practical work (Reproduced by permission of *alamy.com*)

the success achieved, they voted to stop all work on the project. Lord Dundas subsequently refused to authorize any further payments or even reply to Symington's messages, leaving the inventor with a stack of unpaid bills (Harvey and Downs-Rose 1980, 137). The excuse given to Symington was that the undulations from the boat's paddlewheel would erode the banks of the canal. However, the wash from the inset paddlewheel of the *Charlotte Dundas II* once underway was unlikely to be greater than that of a boat pulled by horses. A more likely explanation is that there were important local interests involved in supplying the horses to tow the boats along the canal, interests that were threatened by a viable steamboat (Clark 2010, 79–80). In addition, the company's stockholders were likely discouraged by the £1463 that the two boats had already cost (Harvey and Downs-Rose 1980, 138).

There was one more blow to fall. Symington learned that the Duke of Bridgewater had died 2 weeks before the last trial of the *Charlotte Dundas II* and that his heirs were uninterested in pursuing his dream of steam tugboats. Symington died in poverty in London in 1831, aged 67, after many years of fruitless lawsuits. As for the *Charlotte Dundas II*, the boat was abandoned by the side of the canal and later, without its engine, converted into a dredger (Harvey and Downs-Rose 1980, 139).

7.5 Cruising the Hudson

In 1797, the 5-year-long War of the First Coalition between revolutionary France and an alliance that included Britain was drawing to a close. In the spring of that year, David Fulton, an American artist who had established a modest reputation for himself as a portraitist in England, boarded a Channel packet for the short voyage to France. In his letters to his mother back in America, he had written little of the aesthetic aspects of his profession or of any great works of art that he had seen. Instead, he described the business opportunities that were opening up as a result of the canal-building boom in Britain and on the Continent. Indeed, he had not painted a picture in over 2 years (Flexner 1944, 220). In France, he planned to take advantage of the effects of the Revolution in breaking down the barriers between regions. The country would require canals to join its rivers and perhaps steamboats to sail on them (Flexner 1944, 229). Among Fulton's projects was a plan for a long narrow steamboat with a flat bottom (Flexner 1944, 221).

Robert Fulton was not the first American to try to interest the French in steamboats. In the late 1780s, while Symington and Miller were experimenting with their first paddlewheel boats in Scotland, John Fitch, a clockmaker from Connecticut, was building vessels pushed by steam-powered oars on the Delaware River. In the summer of 1790, using a boat of his invention driven by rear duck-foot paddles, he ran a passenger service over 20 miles (32 km) along the Delaware from Burlington, New Jersey, to Philadelphia. However, when he was refused a monopoly patent, his financial backers abandoned him. Fitch gave up and left for France and England, where he was no more successful. He died in 1798 after returning to the United States (Rowland 1970, 32).

In that same year, the War of the Second Coalition broke out, again pitting France against Britain and its allies. Fulton put aside his steamboat plans and began to work on devices for marine warfare that might interest the French government. In the summer of 1801, he tried to attack a British warship anchored in the Channel with a submarine he had invented. When this attempt failed, he made a second effort using a hand-cranked propeller boat loaded with "torpedoes", that is, underwater mines. However, the British frigates that were his target were too closely watched by sailors in rowboats for him to approach them (Flexner 1944, 275).

Back in Paris, Fulton met the new American ambassador to France, Robert R. Livingston. A former New York state official, Livingston, had obtained a monopoly patent for steam transport in that state and was looking for someone able to build a practical steamboat (Flexner 1944, 262, 277). The Scottish engine designer we met earlier, William Symington, later asserted that "Mr. Fulton" had visited him in Scotland in July 1801 and had made drawings of the first *Charlotte Dundas*. He had even been taken onto the canal for a ride (Harvey and Downs-Rose 1980, 139). While there is no evidence to support this claim, it is clear that Fulton was able to profit from the earlier efforts of Jouffroy and Fitch as he worked on a steamboat with the backing of Livingston. In all likelihood, he was also aware of the activities of Symington (Flexner 1944, 288).

Fulton was evidently an excellent salesperson. He managed to convince Napoleon that steamboats would be able to tow the barges of a French invasion fleet across the Channel on an occasion when calm winds prevented British ships from sailing. Fulton's initial steamboat sank at its moorings on the Seine during a violent storm in the summer of 1803 (Flexner 1944, 288). The boat was quickly rebuilt. However, realizing that a Channel crossing with such vessels would be far too risky, Napoleon decided to have nothing more to do with the "adventurer" he described as a "charlatan" (Flexner 1944, 293).

It was then the turn of British Prime Minister William Pitt the Younger to be seduced by Fulton's schemes. With the outbreak of the War of the Third Coalition in 1803, Great Britain too was interested in inexpensive ways to destroy enemy warships. In the spring of 1804, Fulton arrived in London under the assumed name of "Mr. Francis". Experts recruited by the British government kept Fulton waiting for weeks on end while they examined his plan for a submersible boat. Finally rejecting it, they favored an alternative scheme proposed by Fulton that involved partially submerged rafts carrying underwater bombs to blow up surface vessels. After having breakfast with Pitt, Fulton was offered a generous contract to develop this project. In October 1804, however, a British raid on French warships in Boulogne harbor failed when Fulton's mines exploded harmlessly. With Nelson's victory at Trafalgar a year later, any further interest the British might have had in Fulton's inventions disappeared.

In the meantime, Fulton had met Matthew Boulton in Birmingham and ordered a 24-horsepower Boulton and Watt steam engine to be shipped to the United States. When Fulton finally arrived in New York in December 1806, the machine was waiting for him in the customhouse (Flexner 1944, 317–318). Livingston had been busy since his own return to America, arranging a 2-year extension for his steamboat monopoly. All that was now required was to build a hull and linkages connecting the engine to two side paddlewheels. Quickly completed, the *North River Steamboat* made its initial commercial voyage up the Hudson River to Albany with 14 paying passenger on 4–5 September 1807. The trip took 32 hours instead of the 4 days required by a sailing sloop. Despite the obstruction of rival boatmen, the venture was profitable almost from the start. On 2 October, the boat left New York with 90 passengers (Flexner 1944, 327).

During the winter of 1807–1808, Fulton virtually rebuilt the entire boat, keeping the same length but widening it considerably to make it more stable. For the comfort of his passengers, Fulton added three cabins, with berths for 54 people, along with a kitchen and a bar (Flexner 1944, 329). Cruising by steam power had arrived.

7.6 A Steam-Powered Warship

The year 1812 saw the start of a second war between Great Britain and the United States. Two years later, British troops occupied Washington and set fire to many public buildings in retaliation for similar attacks in Upper Canada. Meanwhile, the residents of New York City had realized that they too were at the mercy of the British fleet. Accordingly, they commissioned Robert Fulton to build a steam-powered ship capable of defending their harbor.

The ship, known as the *Demologos*, 167-feet (51 m) long and 56-feet (17 m) wide, was built with a double hull. Wooden walls 5-feet (1.5 m) thick protected a double-action steam engine of 120 horsepower that turned a paddlewheel placed between the two hulls. To deter enemy ships, the *Demologos* was armed with thirty 32-pound cannon capable of firing red-hot shot heated in the boiler's furnace (Rowland 1970, 43).

In 1815, the *Demologos* underwent sea trials, reaching a top speed of over 6 knots (Rowland 1970, 43). However, since by then the War of 1812 was over, the ship never saw active service. It was subsequently retired to the Brooklyn Naval Yard (Flexner 1944, 358). Nevertheless, many naval historians consider Fulton's *Demologos* to be the first steam-powered warship.

7.7 Language Standardization and Innovation

We saw in Chap. 5 that the standardization of the vernacular in England and France in the second half of the seventeenth century was signaled by the publication of the first English and French monolingual dictionaries that were not simply sets of hard words to spell. The invention of the atmospheric steam engine in 1712 came a half century after the English dictionary. The long period of close collaboration between Thomas Newcomen and John Calley during the device's development was unprecedented. As for the French, little is known about Basile Bouchon, who in 1725 invented the first semi-automatic loom, programmed with perforated tape. There was presumably cooperation between him and his assistant, Jean-Baptiste Falcon, who 3 years later developed a loom controlled by punch cards. That their inventions came about a half century after the publication of the equivalent French dictionary is perhaps not coincidental. Thus the timing and cooperative nature of the first technological breakthroughs in the West early in the eighteenth century suggest a link between language standardization and disruptive innovation.[1]

In the Ottoman Empire, India and China, as indicated in the earlier chapter, there was no similar movement toward standardization of the vernacular before the twentieth century. Moreover, between the seventeenth and twentieth centuries, no innovations at all comparable to the steam engine or programmed looms were developed in the three Asian societies. Accordingly, after 1700, the technological gap between East and West became progressively wider. Once again, the absence of both language standardization and progress in industrial technology in Asia is consistent with the argument linking language and technological divergence. In the eighteenth century, the degree of cooperation between people with the specialized skills that was necessary to develop breakthroughs in technology seems to have been unattainable in Asia.

Prior to the nineteenth century, the military impact on the East of the West's growing technological advance was slight. By buying the latest military goods off the shelf, along with the services of Western advisors, the three great Asian societies could manage to repel any attempts by the West to invade their interiors. Meanwhile, in Europe and America, there were no immediate applications of the steam engine in the military domain. In the 1780s, the efforts of Claude Jouffroy d'Abbans to develop the steamboat in France were blocked by rivals. William Symington's *Charlotte Dundas II*, launched in 1803, is today considered to have been the first practical steamboat, but it was judged to be inappropriate for Britain's canals and abandoned.

Nevertheless, in the first decades of the nineteenth century, the approaching storm of Europe's military threat began to form on Asia's western horizon. As we saw, in 1807 Robert Fulton invented the first successful commercial steamboat, the *North River Steamboat*, in New York. Such a vessel could easily carry guns and soldiers into the interior of Asia. Moreover, 9 years later Fulton built the first sea-going steam warship, the *Demologos*. The days of Asian technological innocence were numbered.

Note

1. The hypothesis of a significant effect of the existence of a monolingual dictionary on a region's subsequent capacity to innovate was tested in a study by Dudley (2016). The sample consisted of 117 innovations during the period 1700–1850 and 201 urban regions in Western Europe and the United States. The relationship was found to be particularly strong for cooperative innovations, that is, those with two or more principals.

References

Black, J. (2009). *Naval power: A history of warfare and the sea from 1500.* Basingstoke: Palgrave Macmillan.

Clark, B. E. (2010). *Symington and the steamboat.* Raleigh: Lulu Press.

Daumas, M. (1969). *A history of technology and invention, vol. I, The origins of technical civilization.* London: John Murray.

Daumas, M. (1980). *A history of technology and invention, vol. III, The expansion of mechanization 1725–1860.* London: John Murray.

Dickinson, H. W. (1939). *A short history of the steam engine.* Cambridge, UK: Cambridge University Press.

Dudley, L. (2016). Language standardization and the industrial revolution. *Oxford Economic Papers Advance Access.* doi:10.1093/oep/gpw059.

Flexner, J. T. (1944). *Steamboats come true: American inventors in action.* New York: Viking.

Harvey, W., & Downs-Rose, G. (1980). *William Symington: Inventor and engine builder.* London: Northgate Publishing Co.

Johnson, S. (2010). *Where good ideas come from: The natural history of innovation.* New York: Riverhead Books.

Marsden, B. (2002). *Watt's perfect engine: steam and the age of invention.* New York: Columbia University Press.

Mokyr, J. (1990). *The lever of riches: Technological creativity and economic progress.* Oxford: Oxford University Press.

Prost, J.-C. A. (1889). *Le Marquis de Jouffroy d'Abbans, Inventeur de l'application de la vapeur à la navigation.* Paris: Ernest Leroux.

Rolt, L. T., & Allen, J. S. (1977). *The steam engine of Thomas Newcomen.* Hartington: Moorland Pub. Co.

Rowland, K. T. (1970). *Steam at sea: A history of steam navigation.* Newton Abbot: David & Charles.

Temple, R. (2007). *The genius of China: 3000 years of science, discovery & invention.* Rochester: Inner Traditions.

CHAPTER 8

Machines to Make Machines

8.1 An Uninnovative Invention

In 1774, an English industrialist named John Wilkinson was awarded a patent for a remarkable cannon-boring technology. Five years later, however, the patent was revoked because the technique had been found to be already in use prior to the patent application. It was demonstrated that in 1770, a similar device was already in operation in the royal brass foundry at Woolwich in southeast London (Brown 2008). Nevertheless, the Wilkinson cannon borer is often referred to as the first true machine tool (Singal et al. 2008, 3). Moreover, most accounts of innovation during the Industrial Revolution assign Wilkinson's machine a key role (Rolt 1986, 59). How is it possible that such an important role can be attributed to an invention that was officially declared unoriginal?

8.2 Machines for Making Things

Across Eurasia in the year 1700, there existed no machines capable of cutting precision metal parts. Indeed in Asia, from the shores of the Bosporus to the East China Sea, machine tools had developed very little from the first drills propelled by hand-held bows that are to be seen in sculptures from ancient Egypt (Holtzappfel 1976, 3). By the early eighteenth century, there existed several types of traditional lathes used to turn wood. For example, there was the Indian strap lathe. The worker sat holding a cutting tool with one hand and one foot while an assistant pulled a strap back and forth, spinning the piece of wood to be cut (Holtzappfel 1976, 6). In the Middle East, woodworkers used the Persian bow lathe. The worker knelt, using one hand to hold an adze (a tool with a sharp arched blade attached to the handle). With the other hand, he pulled a bow back and forth, so that the bowstring turned the piece of wood around which it was wrapped. The circular rotation caused the adze to remove wood symmetrically from the piece (Holtzappfel 1976, 9). In China, inventors had developed a treadle lathe that left both hands of the woodworker free to hold the tool (Holtzappfel 1976, 16). Meanwhile, in early modern Europe, the usual device was the pole lathe. In the place of a bow, the worker attached one end of a cord to a treadle, wrapped the cord around the piece to be cut and then tied the cord's other end to a flexible pole above the workbench (Holtzappfel 1976, 19).

A disadvantage of all of these devices was that they used a reciprocal motion. As a result, cutting was limited to the half of the cycle in which the piece was turning toward the worker and his cutting tool (Holtzappfel 1976, 6). By end of the sixteenth century, however, lathes with continuous motion driven by separate flywheels connected to the lathe were being used in the West. The advantage of these devices was that they provided greater and more-uniform power. Yet these lathes were still designed primarily for turning wood. Although there were miniature metal-cutting devices used by clock and instrument makers in the early eighteenth century, there were as yet no machines for precise cutting of larger pieces of metal (Rolt 1986, 28, 44).

A machine tool may be defined as a machine for shaping metal or some other rigid material in which the movement of the workpiece relative to the cutting tool is controlled by the machine itself. As early as 1540, there were water-powered mills for boring cannon (Rolt 1986, 47). The cannon were cast around a clay core that was then removed. To smooth the interior of the barrel, the cannon was mounted on a mobile carriage and penetrated by a rotating horizontal boring bar. As long as the original hole was relatively true, little power or accuracy was needed (Rolt 1986, 48). For the smooth-bore cannon of the period, this technique was quite adequate. Nor was there any major problem when this same principle was used to bore solid cast-iron cylinders for the early English atmospheric steam engines in the middle decades of the eighteenth century. With water-soaked hemp packing on the upper side of the piston, the leakage of air around the piston was limited (Rolt 1986, 55–56).

The problem arose when James Watt had the iron cylinder for his first full-sized steam engine with external condenser bored in this fashion at the Carron works near Falkirk, Scotland, 23 miles (38 km) west of Edinburgh in the 1760s. Because the borer used an unsupported horizontal bar, its heavy boring head caused considerable distortion (Rolt 1986, 57). Although the hole was circular, because the bore was not truly parallel, too much steam leaked around the piston (Rolt 1986, 59). Unlike the Newcomen engine, Watt's cylinder head was closed. Accordingly, he could not use Newcomen's technique of continually moistened hemp to prevent steam from escaping.

The solution was not far off. In 1770, Jan Verbruggen a Dutch gun founder had been fired by the government foundry in The Hague for hiding flaws in cannon he had cast. He was immediately hired as Master Founder by the Royal Arsenal at Woolwich in southeast London (Brown 2008). There he introduced a method of boring cannon from a solid casting by using a water-powered machine to rotate the casting itself around a boring bar (Rolt 1986, 51). Here was the first verified heavy machine tool technology that could produce an acceptable degree of precision (Rolt 1986, 53). John Wilkinson was presumably unaware of Verbruggen's machine, but he may have seen a similar boring mill while traveling on the Continent. In 1774, he applied for and was granted a British patent for the device (Rolt 1986, 60).

It is clear why Wilkinson's copying of the Verbruggen machine did not merit a patent. Might the Wilkinson cannon borer nevertheless have played an important role in the Industrial Revolution?

8.3   John Wilkinson

Between 1767 and 1772, while James Watt was preparing his first experimental steam engine with an external condenser, an English civil engineer named John Smeaton had been busy. Disappointed by the performance of an atmospheric steam engine he had installed, he undertook a systematic study of a number of Newcomen steam engines that had been erected in Cornwall and in northern England (Rolt and Allen 1977, 112). He found that by improving the accuracy of the bores, adjusting the size of the steam pipes and valves and correcting the construction of the boilers, he could double the efficiency of the atmospheric steam engine (Marsden 2002, 101). Thus, despite the external condenser on James Watt's first experimental steam engine, it was little more efficient than Smeaton's improved atmospheric engines.

In Birmingham, Watt and his new partner, Matthew Boulton, belonged to an informal discussion circle, the Lunar Society, to which clergyman and chemist Joseph Priestley, the discoverer of oxygen, also belonged. It was Boulton who in 1774 introduced Watt to Priestley's brother-in-law, John Wilkinson. The manufacturer had just received a patent for the new cannon-boring mill at his factory in Bersham in North Wales (Uglow 2002, 252). There each cannon was cast as a solid block and then rotated by water power around a boring bar using a Verbruggen-type technology. Might Wilkinson's cannon borer possibly produce the tight fit required for Watt's challenging engine specifications?

John Wilkinson was born in 1728 in the village of Little Clifton, Cumbria, 30 miles (50 km) from the Scottish border in northwestern England. The eldest son of Isaac Wilkinson, an iron master who ran a local blast furnace, John was raised as a Presbyterian and sent to a dissenting academy in the nearby town of Kendal. At the age of seventeen, he began an apprenticeship with a merchant in Liverpool, after which he entered into partnership with his father. In 1756, John joined his father to run a furnace in Bersham, north Wales. Then the following year, he set out on his own as manager and partner in a blast furnace at Willey in Shropshire, 40 miles (65 km) northwest of Birmingham. Around 1760, Wilkinson launched another iron works that was to become important in later years, at Bradley in Shropshire, between Willey and Birmingham. By 1766, he had acquired control of both the Bersham and Willey works (Harris 2004).

John Wilkinson left a strong impression on those who met him. He had a heavy frame, a deep voice and a long face marked by the scars of smallpox. Although he had a reputation for being domineering and authoritarian, he was on excellent terms with his business associates (Harris 2004). By the time that he started working with Watt, Wilkinson controlled a vast, vertically integrated iron empire that produced everything from pig iron to finished cannon. His operations included blast furnaces, foundries and rolling mills (Harris 2004). Wilkinson was only too willing to use his new cannon-boring machine to manufacture a steam engine cylinder for Boulton and Watt. In its first test in a colliery at Bloomfield in March 1776, a Boulton and Watt engine with a Wilkinson cylinder managed to drain a pit of 60 feet in under an hour (Uglow 2002, 255). Wilkinson himself ordered one of the engines to operate a bellows for his blast furnace at Willey (Rolt 1986, 62). Thanks to Wilkinson's cooperation, Boulton and

Watt found themselves the owners of arguably the key technology of the Industrial Revolution.

In 1776, Wilkinson devised an improved lathe for boring hollow cast cylinders such as those of the Watt engines that were initially open at both ends. Unlike the earlier cannon borer that he had patented, the rotating cutter of the new machine passed right through the fixed cylinder, the cutting bar being supported at each end. The result was a cylinder bore that for the first time was truly parallel and circular all along its length (Soldon 1998, 109). Wilkinson refrained from patenting the new technology, perhaps believing that his patent of 1774 covered it. It was only after the original patent was canceled that his competitors began to copy his later invention (Rolt 1986, 62). The new cylinders were produced at Bersham with boring rods that were themselves hollow, probably made with the same machine (Rolt 1986, 61).

For a number of years, all cylinders for Boulton and Watt engines were made by Wilkinson. However, by 1794 Boulton and Watt had become aware that Wilkinson was making "pirate" cylinders without declaring these products to them, the patent holders. The manufacturers who bought these cylinders thereby avoided paying Boulton and Watt their fee, which was based on the energy savings obtained compared with the Newcomen technology. In 1796, Boulton and Watt therefore began to produce their own cylinders at the Soho works in Birmingham (Soldon 1998, 230).

Wilkinson was a man of vision who very early saw uses for Watt's steam engines beyond pumping mines, realizing that they could be used for blowing air in blast furnaces, for forging hammers or for operating rolling mills. Wilkinson died a wealthy man in Bradley in 1808. By that year, the cannon-boring device had been joined by a number of other machine tools, the most important of which had been designed by a young London machinist.

8.4   Henry Maudslay

Henry Maudslay, 26 years of age in 1797, had risen rapidly among the workers in the London metalworking shop of Joseph Bramah. Maudslay had married Bramah's attractive housekeeper, Sarah Tindel, who bore him four children (Cantrell 2002, 19). As manager of the shop, with 8 years of service, Maudslay one day dared to ask Bramah for a raise over his meager salary of 30s a week. When Bramah refused the request, the moderate prosperity Maudslay had been counting on for his growing family was suddenly threatened. Yet to resign and set out on his own would entail a considerable risk.

When Maudslay had started for Bramah in 1790, there had been few metalworking tools available for British laborers other than the simple lathe, the hand-drill, the chisel and the file. With Wilkinson's cylinder borer, it had become possible to build efficient steam engines to do work by pumping water, pushing bellows or spinning cotton. Increasingly, however, such machines required accurately made parts. Using the available tools, a skilled craftsman could turn out quality products in wood or brass. However, it was extremely difficult to make two metal parts of precisely the same dimensions. Moreover, the turning of iron on a lathe was an unbelievably laborious task (Rolt 1962, 94). Equally important, years of experience were required to train a skilled metalworker. Might the Industrial Revolution be blocked by a shortage of skilled labor?

The area where the difficulty of producing precision parts caused the most serious problems was in thread cutting. To make a screw or a nut, a machinist had to hold a cutting tool to a cylindrical piece of metal as it was turned by a lathe. As a result, every bolt was different and each had its own nut. Consequently, when a machine was taken apart, every screw had to be identified individually (Rolt 1962, 96). As yet, there was no system for determining the number of threads per inch—the "pitch" of the screw (Smiles, [1863] 1968, ch. XII).

If there was anyone in Britain in the 1790s who could solve this problem, it was Henry Maudslay. Like Wilkinson, he had grown up in the profession in which he would later make his name. Born in 1771, he was the fifth of seven children of Henry Maudslay, a wheelwright in the Royal Engineers at the Royal Arsenal, Woolwich, London. At age 12 he had been set to work in the Arsenal as a "powder-monkey", making musket cartridges and filling them with gunpowder (Smiles, [1863] 1968, ch. 11). When he was 14, he was employed in the carpentry shop with his father. However, it was the work of the blacksmiths in the adjacent forge that fascinated him.

By the time he was 18, young Maudslay's reputation as a skilled metalworker had reached the ears of a manufacturer of plumbing supplies and locks named Joseph Bramah. The successful London machinist was looking for a skilled worker to assist him in manufacturing a new design of lock. The young man who responded to Bramah's summons was a gentle giant, over six feet tall, with blonde hair and a solid build (Rolt 1962, 91). Although Maudslay had not yet served his apprenticeship, his skill in repairing a vice, transforming it into virtually a new machine in a single afternoon, convinced Bramah to hire him on the spot (Roe 1926, 34).

During their years together, Bramah and Maudslay were a remarkably successful team. Maudslay's skill in visualizing how a machine could be designed to do a particular task complemented Bramah's inventiveness in conceiving new products. While working in his new position, Maudslay succeeded in making a set of machines that enabled an unskilled worker to produce precision locks that Bramah had designed. He also aided his employer in the design of the first hydraulic press.

In the mid-1790s, three men—a French mechanic named Senot, an American machinist named David Wilkinson (no relation to John) and Henry Maudslay—were all working independently to improve the basic lathe. Each of the three designed a lathe with a tool-rest and a lead screw to guide the cutting tool (Daumas 1980, 117–118). Senot's remarkable lathe is on display in the *Musée des arts et métiers* in Paris today, but unfortunately little is known of him. Indeed, even his first name has been lost. As for David Wilkinson, his machine, unlike those of Senot and Maudslay, did not have gears to vary the angle and depth of the cut (Rolt 1986, 172). Of the three designs, it was undoubtedly the lathe of Maudslay that made the greatest impact on the machinery industry. His first contribution, in 1794 while collaborating with Bramah, was a lathe with a compound slide rest that allowed a cylindrical metal part to be cut with great precision (see Fig. 8.1).

Would Maudslay be able to succeed on his own without a successful entrepreneur to set his course? Maudslay's first order in his rented shop, just off Oxford Street in central London, was to make a new mechanism for an artist's easel (Cantrell 2002, 19). Soon, because of his good reputation, he was able to attract many of Bramah's customers (Rolt 1962, 94–95). It was only a short time after setting up his own shop that Maudslay made his second important contribution to lathe design. He built a screw-cutting lathe that allowed an unskilled worker to produce a precise screw thread of any desired cut. Although Maudslay's first lead screws for this device were hand cut, the availability of this first-generation machine allowed the cutting of models with ever greater precision (Rolt 1962, 94).

sb -0.01wEach of these two machines—the lathe with a compound slide rest and the screw-cutting machine—constituted a prototype of a work in progress. Over the next decade, Maudslay made continual improvements to both of them (Rolt 1986, 95). Moreover, to assess the accuracy of his metal parts, Maudslay in 1805 invented a micrometer, known in his shop as

Fig. 8.1 James Nasmyth's drawing showing an old lathe and a modern lathe. The machine tools developed by Henry Maudslay and his associates were able to produce metal parts to a tolerance that was without precedent (Reproduced from Robertson Buchanan, *Practical Essays on Mill Work and Other Machinery; Revised into a Third Edition with Additions by George Rennie, Esq., C.E., F.R.S.*, J. Weale, London, 1841, 396)

the "Lord Chancellor", that could measure tolerances of 0.0001 of an inch (0.00254 mm). It was Maudslay who established the principle of standardized threads for the bolts and nuts used by workers in his machine shop. Thanks to a whole generation of British machinists who passed through his workshop as apprentices or employees, Maudslay's standards were transmitted throughout British industry. James Nasmyth, Richard Roberts, Joseph Clement and Joseph Whitworth all worked with him in London for a period before setting up their own workshops (Rolt 1986, 97–98).

It is interesting to note that with the exception of one small lathe, Maudslay did not build machine tools to sell to others (Rolt 1986, 97). Instead, from 1815 on, he specialized in the construction of engines for steamboats. One of his important contributions to this industry was a new design of marine steam engine—the side-lever engine. To save space in a ship's confined engine room, instead of a swiveling beam above the vertical piston as in the designs of Symington and Fulton, he built engines that turned two beams, one on either side of the cylinder. The movement of these side levers propelled the side paddlewheels. As for the production of machine tools for sale to other workshops, Maudslay left this to his younger associates, such as Richard Roberts.

8.5 RICHARD ROBERTS

In 1816, a sign outside the house at No. 15 Deans Gate in central Manchester read, "Turner of plain and eccentric work" (Hills 2002, 15). Richard Roberts had left Maudslay's and London for the booming northern textile city, where there was a rapidly growing demand for those able to design, build and maintain machinery. He set up his lathe in the upstairs bedroom of his rented house, connecting it with a continuous belt to a flywheel in the basement. It is said that Roberts's wife, about whom little is known, turned the crank in the basement that drove the flywheel for her husband's machines upstairs (Hills 2002, 14).

Roberts's first product was the nineteenth-century equivalent of a photocopy machine—a copying press for stationers. Some years earlier, James Watt had invented a process in which an original of a letter or a drawing was written with a special mucilaginous ink on a sheet of paper. When a damp sheet was pressed onto the first sheet, some of the ink would stick to the former. The ink would penetrate this thin second sheet, which could then be read from the "verso" side. The press itself consisted of two smooth plates that when pressed together compressed the sheets of paper. To make the top and bottom faces of the press, Roberts hired a man of considerable strength who chipped and filed them until they were flat. However, the employee, a heavy beer drinker, proved extremely unreliable. Might it be possible to devise a means of replacing him with a machine?, Roberts asked himself (Hills 2002, 84).

Richard Roberts was born in 1789 in Carreghofa in northern Wales, near the border of the English county of Shropshire (Hills 2002, 9). He always considered himself a Welshman and throughout his life spoke English with a Welsh accent (Hills 2002, 52). Roberts's father was a shoemaker who also kept the New Bridge tollgate on a road that ran along the border between Wales and England. As a boy, Roberts attended elementary school in the belfry of the local parish church, where he was taught by the curate. Finding that the young man was more interested in woodworking than in schoolwork, the clergyman, an amateur carpenter, showed Roberts how to use a lathe (Hills 2002, 9).

After his schooling, Roberts found work as a clerk with a firm that carted limestone to the banks of a local canal that had recently been opened. There he met a surveyor for the canal company who taught him to draw. With this new skill, Roberts was able to obtain work as a patternmaker at Bradley Iron Works founded by the late John Wilkinson, where he made drawings of molds for parts to be cast in iron. In 1813, during the Napoleonic Wars, he was working in a similar position at Tipton, near Birmingham, when he learned that his name had been drawn for induction into the militia. To avoid military service, he walked from Manchester to London in the company of two other young engineers (Hills 2002, 10).

After working briefly at one engineering shop, Roberts obtained a position at the new factory in Lambeth Marsh on the south bank of the Thames where Henry Maudslay and his associates were manufacturing steam engines. Roberts worked for 2 years as an iron turner and fitter with Maudslay, where he undoubtedly absorbed his employer's emphasis on accuracy and excellence of finish. Then, after the allied victory at Waterloo in June 1815, the danger of conscription disappeared. Roberts could return to Manchester where the booming cotton industry offered a promising outlet for his inventive talents (Hills 2002, 11–12).

Roberts's first important invention was his planing machine of 1817. Consider the different ways of replacing a skilled metalworker with a machine tool. In the case of Wilkinson's 1776 cannon borer, the cast-metal workpiece was fixed while a rotating drill bit removed metal from the work's interior. With Maudslay's slide-rest lathe, the work itself was rotated as its exterior was reduced by a secure cutting tool. Roberts's challenge was to build a machine that could replace the chisel and a file of his beer-loving employee. His solution was a machine that moved the work in a straight line while bringing it into contact with a secure tool. A chain drive moved the workpiece backward and forward on a sliding table under a cutting tool that removed metal uniformly from the piece's upper surface. Designed to smooth the parts for small copying presses, the machine was long enough to plane the bed of a small lathe. Although Roberts did not have sufficient funds to patent his invention, it nevertheless took another 15 years before planing machines became common in engineering shops (Hills 2002, 83–85). The planing machine was not Roberts's only contribution to the manufacture of machine tools. In 1816, he designed a gear-cutting machine to space accurately the teeth cut into a gear (Hills 2002, 67). Nevertheless, the basic tool in the metalworking shop remained the lathe. At some point between 1817 and 1821, Roberts designed a large metal lathe that could take a workpiece six feet (1.8 m) in length (Hills 2002, 74).

Over the next decade and a half, Roberts used his new machine tools to develop inventions for the textile industry. In 1822, he patented an improved power loom that was soon being modified and improved by other manufacturers (Hills 2002, 128). Eight years later, he obtained the patent for a self-acting spinning mule that incorporated a number of improvements to an unsuccessful machine he had developed earlier (Hills 2002, 146).

Whether driven by water or steam power, a textile mill needed a means of securing the pulleys that propelled each machine to the central drive shaft. As wooden shafts were gradually replaced by those made from wrought iron, it was necessary to cut slots in both the shaft and in the wheel that turned the pulley. In 1824, to avoid the laborious cutting of such slots with chisel and file, Roberts made a special slotting machine for this purpose (Hills 2002, 87).

Richard Roberts was a remarkably inventive engineer but he lacked skill as a businessperson. Fortunately, he met a partner whose judgment and knowledge of the market for machinery were superior to his own. Thomas Sharp III, the son and grandson of Manchester merchants, was active in the iron trade. In 1821, Roberts provided services as a machinist to a textile machinery firm in which Sharp was a partner. Two years later Roberts entered into a formal partnership with Sharp and his associates. In 1826, Thomas and his brother John formed a new partnership with Roberts under the name Sharp, Roberts and Co. to market the machines that Roberts manufactured (Hills 2002, 18). The company and the patents it acquired were commercially highly profitable. However, Roberts left the company in 1843 after the death of Thomas Sharp.

Over the following years, Roberts dissipated the savings from his association with Sharp through a series of unprofitable investments in the shipbuilding industry. The 22 patents filed by Roberts after 1843 were all commercially unsuccessful. In 1860, he moved to London, where he died in poverty 4 years later. As Gillian Cookson (2004) observed, although Roberts was "an outstanding mechanical innovator, his business affairs suffered as invention became an obsession".

8.6 Machines at the Great Exhibition of 1851

On 1 May 1851, the world's first universal exposition opened in London. It was located in Hyde Park, on land that Henry VIII had confiscated from the monasteries in the sixteenth century for use as a hunting ground. Before the Great Exhibition closed on 15 October, six million people had visited the enormous greenhouse over a third of a mile (563 m) long and 150 yards (138 m) wide (Auerbach 1999, 43). They marveled at the fountain and live elm trees in the high transept and some 100,000 different objects exhibited on the ground floor and raised galleries, ranging from sofas and clocks to an artificial silver nose (Auerbach 1999, 110). Yet above all, visitors were attracted to the working machines along the north wall. There were steam-powered printing presses, textile machines for carding, spinning and weaving cotton and an enormous water pump that spewed out two streams of water (Ffrench 1950, 217). These machines were all powered by steam flowing through insulated pipes under the floor boards from an engine house at the northwest corner of the exhibition (Auerbach 1999, 104).

In the two decades that had passed since Maudslay's death in 1831, Britain had become recognized as the "workshop of the world" (Auerbach 1999, 109). The firms founded by Maudslay and his former apprentices and associates dominated the British machinery industry, supplying not only steam engines and textile machinery but also the machine tools with which these machines were built (Rolt 1986, 129). Across the British heartland, from London to Manchester, Maudslay's disciples formed a network trained to design machinery that allowed ordinary workers to produce consumer goods at a price that was within the budget of every household.

However, our story of the development of machine tools is not yet complete. In 1820, thanks to machine tools invented by Wilkinson, Maudslay, Roberts and their colleagues, cylinders could be bored, screws could be cut and metal parts could be planed to a smooth surface. What was still lacking was a means of finishing cast-metal parts so that they would fit together precisely without considerable additional cutting and filing.

References

Auerbach, J. A. (1999). *The great exhibition of 1851: A nation on display.* New Haven: London Yale University Press.

Brown, R. R. (2008). *Verbruggen, Jan (bap. 1712, d. 1781).* Retrieved March 11, 2016, from Oxford Dictionary of National Biography. http://www.oxfo rddnb.com/view/article/47492

Cantrell, J. (2002). Henry Maudslay. In J. Cantrell & G. Cookson (Eds.), *Henry Maudslay & the pioneers of the machine age* (pp. 18–38). Stroud: Tempus Publishing.

Cookson, G. (2004). *Roberts, Richard (1789–1864)*. Retrieved April 15, 2016, from Oxford Dictionary of National Biography, Oxford University Press. http://www.oxforddnb.com/view/article/23770

Daumas, M. (1980). *A history of technology and invention, vol. III, The expansion of mechanization 1725–1860*. London: John Murray.

Ffrench, Y. (1950). *The great exhibition: 1851*. London: Harvill Press.

Harris, J. R. (2004). *Wilkinson, John (1728–1808)*. Retrieved March 14, 2016, from Oxford Dictionary of National Biography, Oxford University Press; online ed. http://www.oxforddnb.com/view/article/29428

Hills, R. D. (2002). *Life and inventions of Richard Roberts, 1769–1864*. Ashbourne: Landmark Publishing.

Holtzapffel, J. J. (1976 [original 1881]). *Hand or simple turning: Principles and practice*. New York: Dover Publications.

Marsden, B. (2002). *Watt's perfect engine: steam and the age of invention*. New York: Columbia University Press.

Roe, J. W. (1926). *English and American tool builders*. New York: McGraw-Hill.

Rolt, L. T. (1962). *Great engineers*. London: Bell.

Rolt, L. (1986). *Tools for the job: A history of machine tools to 1950*. London: Her Majesty's Stationery Office.

Rolt, L. T., & Allen, J. S. (1977). *The steam engine of Thomas Newcomen*. Hartington: Moorland Pub. Co.

Singal, R. K., Singal, M., & Singal, R. (2008). *Fundamentals of machining and machine tools*. New Delhi: I K International Publishing House.

Smiles, S. (1968 [original 1863]). *Industrial biography: Iron-workers and tool-makers*. New York: A. M. Kelley.

Soldon, N. C. (1998). *John Wilkinson, 1728–1808: English ironmaster and inventor*. Lampeter: Edwin Mellen Press.

Uglow, J. (2002). *The lunar men: Five friends whose curiosity changed the world*. New York: Farrar, Straus and Giroux.

CHAPTER 9

Cloning the Industrial Revolution

9.1 Of Muskets and Horse Pistols

In the late eighteenth century, a horse pistol was a large, single-barreled cavalry handgun. The pistols were usually carried in pairs in holsters laid across the horse's back, ahead of the saddle. A musket, in comparison, was a long-barreled gun with a smoothbore firearm, carried by an infantryman. In 1798 during the War of the Second Coalition, the United States and the new French Republic were on the verge of war following France's seizure of American merchant ships accused of trading with Britain. With conflict imminent, the United States War Department decided to order additional stocks of both types of weapon to arm its troops. Accordingly, a contract for the production of 500 horse pistols was issued to Simeon North, a Connecticut maker of agricultural instruments. At the same time, a contract for 10,000 muskets was awarded to Eli Whitney, another New Englander, who was already well known as the inventor of the cotton gin (Hounshell 1984, 28–29). These two arms contracts triggered a chain of developments that would revolutionize the manufacture of all metal products, from rifles to sewing machines and automobiles.

The key component of both the horse pistol and the musket was the firing mechanism, known as the lock. Pulling the trigger caused a piece of flint to generate a spark when it hit the metal firing pan, thereby igniting a charge of gunpowder. At the time, although the iron parts of the locks for pistols or muskets were generally made from standard patterns, considerable cutting and filing was required to assure that the pieces fit together. As a

© The Author(s) 2017
L. Dudley, *The Singularity of Western Innovation*,
DOI 10.1057/978-1-137-39822-2_9

result, each weapon was unique. If one such firearm was damaged in battle, a skilled armorer was required to produce the pieces necessary to repair it. There was thus an incentive to design weapons with parts that were interchangeable so that they could easily be cannibalized for spares as the need arose. Another consideration was that more precise production of parts might also improve the range and accuracy of the weapons themselves.

When fighting broke out between French and American ships in the Caribbean in 1799, the French government quickly made overtures to the Americans. A treaty between First Consul Napoleon and the administration of John Adams brought an end to the undeclared "Quasi-War". However, in their efforts to fulfill the conditions of the two arms contracts, Simeon North and Eli Whitney would set in motion transformations in methods of manufacturing that are still in progress. To understand the nature of these changes, it is necessary to go back more than a half century earlier, to the battlefields of central Europe.

9.2 From Cannon to Clocks

During the eighteenth century, there had been a shift in the nature of warfare, from sieges to open-field battles (MacLennan 2003, 251). As a result, there was a need for more mobile types of artillery that could be maneuvered easily on the battlefield in support of infantry and cavalry. During the War of the Austrian Succession (1740–1745), the introduction of lighter, shorter cannon aided Frederick II to defeat Austria in a number of major battles and seize the Habsburg province of Silesia.

In 1745, Empress Maria Theresa reacted to these defeats by appointing Prince Joseph Wenzel Liechtenstein as director general of Austrian artillery, with a mandate to institute reforms. Beginning in 1749, Liechtenstein conducted 47 experiments and gunnery exercises to compare different types of artillery (MacLennan 2003, 253). The result was a series of reforms to standardize field and siege guns and their transport equipment. One innovation, for example, was to specify that there be two sizes of wheels for artillery transport. The dimensions of these wheels were fixed to within one-quarter inch (0.6 cm) so that they could be interchanged in case of damage (MacLennan 2003, 254). During the Seven Years' War (1756–1763) that followed, the performance of Austrian artillery was considerably improved. Frederick II observed after his defeat at the battle of Kolin in 1757 that "it was not the enemy soldiers but their artillery, over 250 well-positioned cannon", that forced his men to retreat (Kronoskaf 2014).

Serving with distinction under the Habsburgs during the Seven Years' War was a French officer, Jean-Baptiste Vaquette de Gribeauval. Because of this experience, Gribeauval was familiar with the Liechtenstein artillery reforms and their emphasis on standardization. On his return to France in 1763, he was promoted to *Maréchal de camp*, the equivalent of Lieutenant general. The following year, Gribeauval was named Inspector General of the French artillery. He was the strategist behind a 1765 royal decree that introduced what became known as the Gribeauval system for field artillery.

Previously there had been no clear distinction between field pieces and siege and garrison artillery. There were now to be three distinct types of field guns, namely, 4-, 8- and 12-pound guns. Another major change was to establish a method of constructing shorter, lighter, more mobile field guns—an innovation similar to that introduced at about the same time in the British Royal Arsenal at Woolwich. Each cannon was to be cast as a single piece that was then rotated around a drill bit. The result was a lighter, more mobile gun with closer tolerance between the barrel and the cannon ball (Chartrand 2003, 5–7).

In 1774, Gribeauval was appointed First Inspector General of artillery, with the power to introduce his system throughout the French army's artillery corps. The Gribeauval system was based on three principles. The first was *specialization*. As mentioned, there should be different types of cannon for field campaigns, for sieges and for fortifications and coastal defenses. The second principle was *standardization*: the types of guns and their systems of transport should be standardized across the kingdom, not only for field guns but also for siege and fortress artillery. The final and most original requirement was uniformity: the parts for the cannon of a certain type should be interchangeable with those of all other cannon of the same type (Chartrand 2003, 10–12).

As we shall see, through the influence of French officers who served under George Washington during the American Revolution, Gribeauval's principles were transmitted to the officer corps of the new army of the United States. However, there was a second conduit, a civilian channel, by which the notion of interchangeable parts reached American manufacturers in the early nineteenth century.

Eli Terry was born in 1772, 2 years before the start of the American Revolution in a village just outside Hartford, Connecticut. As a young man, he trained with clockmaker Daniel Burnap to be a maker of brass and steel clocks (Muir 2000, 123). He also received instruction from Timothy Cheney who made wooden clocks. In 1793, Terry moved to Plymouth,

25 miles (40 km) southwest of Hartford, where he set himself up as a clockmaker. He used a hand-driven wheel-cutting machine and a small lathe to make the metal parts for the clocks he sold (Hounshell 1984, 51).

Over the following decade, Terry developed a new business plan. Instead of waiting for individual orders for fine clocks with metal movements, he would manufacture cheap clocks with wooden movements by the hundred and market them himself. By 1803, he had acquired his own mill and begun to use waterpower to make wooden wheels for clock mechanisms. At that time, a skilled clockmaker could make six to ten clocks a year (Muir 2000, 120).

To the astonishment of his fellow townsmen, Terry in 1806 signed a contract with a clockmaking entrepreneur, Seth Tomas, whose firm assembled clocks with parts made by others (Netstate 2016). Terry committed himself to making the wooden movements for 4000 clocks in 3 years (Hounshell 1984, 52). In 1807, Terry did not produce a single clock. Instead, he built the machinery that would allow *journeymen* to manufacture parts for clocks with a minimum of intervention from a skilled clockmaker. Then, as promised, over the next 2 years, he produced 4000 wooden clock movements, for which he received four dollars apiece (Hounshell 1984, 52). Note, however, that although machine-made, the pieces of these clocks were not completely interchangeable: they still required some filing by hand to make sure that they fitted together.

Then Terry conceived an idea that would allow him to reduce costs even more while improving the quality of his timepieces. He sold his business and began to build machinery that would allow *unskilled* workers to manufacture what were to all intents and purposes interchangeable wooden parts for clocks. At that time, a clock enclosed in a case sold for $40. Terry in 1816 patented his Pillar and Scroll clock, a device with a retail price of from $15 to $18 (Muir 2000, 120–121). By 1820, Terry had 30 workers under him turning out 2500 clocks a year (Hounshell 1984, 54).

Of course, the wooden clock gears that Terry's machines produced were not perfect replicas of one another. The escapement is a mechanism that allows a clock's pendulum to push its wheels forward by a fixed amount with each swing. Terry's clock was designed so that an expert clockmaker could adjust the escapement easily, thereby assuring that the clock kept good time (Muir 2000, 125). By 1820, then, approximately interchangeable parts had been produced for the wheels of gun carriages, for the barrels of field cannon and for wooden clocks. However, such rough uniformity was inadequate for the locks of small firearms. For a pistol or a rifle to be repaired quickly with parts taken from another weapon, the parts had to be virtually identical.

9.3 ELI WHITNEY

The demonstration took place in Washington, D.C., in January 1801, perhaps in the newly completed Capitol building (Green 1956, 127). Invited were President John Adams, President-elect Thomas Jefferson and selected members of congress and government officials. They witnessed inventor Eli Whitney, using only a screwdriver, fit ten different locks in succession into the same musket (Hounshell 1984, 31). Then, disassembling the locks and placing the mixed parts in a single pile, he proceeded to reassemble them, much to the amazement of his audience (Green 1956, 127).

A similar show had been staged in Paris a decade earlier before a comparable audience of army officers, academicians and politicians. In November 1790, Honoré Blanc, 54, a Parisian gunsmith, had selected metal parts at random from a number of bins. He then assembled them to produce the firing mechanisms of several muskets. Thomas Jefferson, who was in Paris at the time, was sufficiently impressed to write back to US Secretary of Foreign Affairs John Jay, describing what he had witnessed. Indeed, it is quite possible that Eli Whitney's performance was inspired by knowledge of Blanc's exhibition that had been passed on to him by Jefferson (Woodbury 1960, 244). Needless to say, Jefferson was unaware that Blanc's parts had been drop forged and then carefully filed and shaped by hand. Whitney's lock parts were undoubtedly prepared beforehand in the same fashion (Baida 1987).

Eli Whitney, born in 1765, was the son of a prosperous Massachusetts farmer. He had started work at age 14, manufacturing nails in his father's workshop. Having saved enough money for college, he graduated from Yale in 1792 and set off for the southern states for a position as a private tutor. While visiting Mrs. Catherine Greene, the widow of a Revolutionary War hero and owner of a Georgia plantation, he conceived the idea for an engine—a "gin"—that would remove the seeds from cotton. After 6 months of labor, aided by advice from Mrs. Greene, he had developed a simple device that pulled raw cotton through a grill of wires while letting the seeds fall into a box (Green 1956, 47). In March 1794, Whitney received a patent for the cotton gin, an invention that was to reinvigorate slavery in the south, but cause no end of trouble for its inventor. Whitney would spend most of the next decade in fruitless legal efforts to defend his patent (Baida 1987).

It will be remembered that in 1798, 3 years before his demonstration of interchangeable parts, Whitney had obtained a US government contract to supply 10,000 muskets by the end of September 1800. The contract, which provided for an immediate advance of 5000 dollars, was a godsend for Whitney who had exhausted his credit attempting to sue those who had violated his cotton-gin patent. In fact, however, the first of these muskets was not delivered until September 1801, some 8 months after the Washington demonstration. The last of these guns was shipped in 1809. Whitney tried to justify his delays by arguing that the innovations he was introducing to produce uniform parts by machine required time and capital investment (Hounshell 1984, 31). However, in actual production, Whitney's lock parts were not even approximately interchangeable, nor were they in any sense machine-made (Woodbury 1960, 247–249).

Since 1700, the design of pistols and muskets had remained essentially unchanged (Alder 1997, 278). Over the course of the eighteenth century, as the frequency and scale of warfare steadily increased, the armies of Europe, and later the United States, demanded many thousands of such firearms each year. There therefore existed not only a strong incentive to raise productivity but also readily available financing from governments who stood to capture the benefits from any improvements. It was the ideal sector in which to experiment with new techniques of production. Unfortunately, although Blanc and Whitney may have convinced their audiences that standardized parts were a desirable goal, in practice such uniformity still required too much individual adjustment and verification to be feasible (Alder 1997, 308–310). It would take another quarter century before interchangeable parts could be produced efficiently by ordinary workers. First, however, it would be necessary to invent a machine that could remove metal evenly in order to shape a metal part.

9.4 Simeon North

What exactly does interchangeability mean when it comes to the parts for muskets or indeed for any complex product assembled from smaller parts? In evaluating Eli Whitney's contributions, historian of technology Robert Woodbury suggested four criteria that must be met: (1) precision machine tools, (2) precision gauges, (3) uniformly accepted measurement standards and (4) adequately dimensioned drawings. Whitney satisfied none of these criteria, mainly because he had no equipment more sophisticated than a jig (a device to maintain the distance between a piece of work and a tool) to guide a hand-operated file (Woodbury 1960, 247–249).

The most important requirement for producing interchangeable parts was a machine capable of cutting and shaping metal more accurately than a worker with a file. However, the first such milling machine was not produced until 1816—some 15 years after Whitney's Washington performance. Historian of technology Edwin Battison showed that there is no evidence to connect Whitney to the first milling machines (Battison 1966). Credit for inventing this device should be assigned not to Whitney but to Simeon North, a soft-spoken machinist who had set up shop in Middletown, Connecticut.

Simeon North was born in Berlin, Connecticut, 15 miles (24 km) southeast of Hartford, one of six sons of a prosperous farmer. An enterprising young man with an eye for a good business opportunity, North in 1795 bought a sawmill on a stream adjacent to his 66-acre (27 hectare) farm. Adding a forge and trip hammer to the installations, he began to manufacture scythes using imported steel (Muir 2000, 122). In 1798, as mentioned at the beginning of this chapter, he was awarded a contract to produce 900 horse pistols for the United States War Department. Two years later, he received a contract for another 1500 such pistols.

Unlike Whitney, North was able to complete his obligations within the stipulated time period. Indeed, as he progressed in the contracts, North was already innovating. Instead of hiring skilled armorers, each of whom would complete individual weapons, he had each worker make 2000 examples of a single part. As a result of this division of labor, he later reported to the War Department, each part was better made, and he saved a quarter of his labor costs (Hounshell 1984, 28).

In 1813, in the middle of the War of 1812 with Britain, North received a contract from the recently established United States Ordnance Department. It provided an advance of $30,000, stipulating that North was to produce 20,000 pistols. For the first time ever in the United States, and undoubtedly in the world, the contract specified that parts of locks had to be interchangeable (Hounshell 1984, 28). The components were to be fitted such that "any limb or part of one pistol may be fitted to any other pistol of the twenty thousand" (Hounshell 1984, 28).

It should be explained that the ordnance chief, Colonel Decius Wadsworth, had served with a French officer, Major Louis de Tousard, during the American Revolution. Tousard's 1809 book, the *American Artillerist's Companion*, advocated the system of standardization of artillery parts developed by the late French general Jean-Baptiste Gribeauval

Fig. 9.1 Harpers Ferry Armory in 1865, looking downstream. The combined currents of the Shenandoah and Potomac Rivers provided ample power for turning metal-working machinery (Reproduced from *Wikipedia Commons*)

(1715–1789). It became a required textbook for American military cadets. Wadsworth and the young West Point graduates he recruited to serve on his staff played a key role in the development of interchangeable parts. They coordinated the standards of the federal government armories at Springfield, Massachusetts, and at Harpers Ferry, West Virginia (then part of Virginia, see Fig. 9.1), assuring that they were compatible with the methods used by North and other private contractors (Hounshell 1984, 27).

In 1816, North realized that the waterpower in his workshop in Berlin was insufficient for a project of the scale and complexity stipulated in the 1813 government contract. He decided to build a new factory on a more powerful stream, the Coginchaug River, in nearby Middletown, Connecticut (Gordon 1989, 180). However, when he requested $50,000 beyond the initial advance of $30,000 to finance his new installations, the War Department sent the superintendents of the federal armories at Springfield and Harpers Ferry to investigate.

North's milling machine consisted of a table that held the piece to be machined while feeding it into a rotating cutter with multiple teeth (Smith 1973, 576). It enabled a metal piece to be shaped, smoothed or cut out, greatly reducing the hand filing necessary for precise reproduction of a model. In March 1816, the two superintendents of the national armories visited Middleton to inquire whether North was capable of fulfilling the conditions of his contract, particularly those referring to uniformity in the parts of the firing mechanism pistol. They issued a report stating that North had obtained an unprecedented degree of interchangeability in the parts of the lock (Smith 1973, 576). Later in the year, North visited the United States national armory at Harpers Ferry in Virginia to introduce his "uniform plan of work". There he built a second milling machine (Muir 2000, 129).

North had evidently convinced the federal authorities of the usefulness of his milling machine for making certain metal parts with sufficient precision to be interchangeable. However, could interchangeability be applied to all of the steps required to produce a piece of machinery as complex as a rifle?

9.5 John Hall

A single machine tool, however versatile, was not sufficient to assure that all the parts of a complex weapon always fit together, wherever they had been made. In 1818, 2 years after North's visit, another New England gunsmith, John H. Hall, arrived at the Harpers Ferry Armory to begin experimental production of a new breech-loading rifle that he had co-patented.

John Hall was born in 1781 in Portland, Maine, the son of a graduate of the Harvard Divinity School (Muir 2000, 129). As a young man, while serving in the local militia, he had developed an interest in firearms. Hall realized that the principal handicap of a rifle-armed militiaman compared to a professional soldier armed with a musket was the time it took the militiaman to ram powder and ball into the long barrel of a rifle. In 1810, his mother died, leaving him enough money to set up a small carpentry shop. After his day's work in the shop, Hall began to experiment with ways to increase the rate of fire of a rifle (Rose 2008, 74). In 1811, he designed an innovative rifle with a hinged breechblock at the rear of the barrel that enabled the powder and ball to be loaded much more quickly than with a muzzle-loader (Rose 2008, 76).

The next step was to patent the new firearm and begin production. However, Hall's application was turned down by the patent commissioner, Doctor William Thornton, who insisted inaccurately that he himself had already patented the idea. Hall had no choice but to agree to split with Thornton the profits from the sale of patent rights to private armorers, although Thornton graciously allowed Hall to retain the profits from his own production (Rose 2008, 77).

It took another 5 years before Hall could convince the Ordnance Department to offer him a contract to produce an experimental set of 100 rifles at a price of $25 apiece. As the current cost of a musket produced in the federal armories was over $10 lower, there was considerable skepticism that Hall's design could ever be competitive. However, when the initial field test proved favorable, the Ordnance Department in 1818 offered Hall the opportunity to set up his own factory within the federal armory at Harpers Ferry.

Over the following 6 years, Hall set up a production line for this weapon. In doing so, he designed and built three different kinds of cutting machines that improved upon and complemented North's milling machine. He also developed drop forging machines and 63 gauges to measure each machined part with precision. Final filing by skilled machinists enabled Hall to obtain parts that matched to within 0.0006 inches (0.0015 cm). Since Hall's machines were self-acting, they could be operated by young workers without lengthy formal training (Smith 1973, 582).

In 1826, the army conducted 5 months of field tests comparing new smoothbore muskets made at the Springfield armory with the regular rifles made at Harpers Ferry and with the Hall rifles. To test loading speed, ten men each fired their weapons ten times. The exercise took over 6 minutes with the muskets, 17 minutes with the regular rifles but under 4 minutes with the Halls. Then to verify accuracy, 38 men each fired at a target 100 yards (91 m) distant at their own speed for 10 minutes. As expected, the regular rifles were more accurate than the muskets, hitting the target 33 percent of the time against only 25 percent for the muskets. However, 36 percent of the shots of the Hall rifles were on the target. In other words, not only could the Hall rifles be fired more rapidly than smoothbore muskets but also they were more accurate than regular rifles (Rose 2008, 92).

As soon as the report of the field tests became known, the governments of individual states sent orders for the Hall rifles to be delivered to their militias, as stipulated in a federal law of 1808. Because the federal armories were not allowed to build arms for the individual states, the War Department was obliged to supply the state militias by means of a private contractor. Accordingly, in 1828 Simeon North received a contract to produce 5000 Hall rifles at a rate of 1000 per year for which he would be paid $17.50 apiece (Smith 1973, 575). Not only did the parts of these guns have to be interchangeable among others of the same order, but also they had to be interchangeable with those of Hall guns made at Harpers Ferry.

These improvements were transmitted back to Connecticut in 1827 when Simeon North lured Nathaniel French, one of Hall's master machinists, away from Harpers Ferry with an offer of a higher wage (Smith 1973, 586). As a result, North was able to begin producing rifles to Hall's specifications at his Middletown plant by 1828 (Muir 2000, 129). Some 3 years later, in 1831 or 1832 according to historian of technology Merritt Roe Smith, the final step in the development of replaceable parts occurred at this same plant. Under the direction of Simeon North, two of his machinists were able to build a machine in which the cutting blades could be adjusted vertically (Smith 1973, 586–587).

9.6 THE AMERICAN SYSTEM OF PRODUCTION

There remained the question of interchangeability. Because the United States Army Ordnance Department neglected to send Simeon North the pattern pieces for the guns to be made or copies of the gauges that John Hall used to assure uniformity, the first batch of North's guns failed to pass the government's quality tests. However, once this oversight had been corrected, Hall was pleased to report in 1834 that the parts of North's weapons were interchangeable with those of his own production (Smith 1977, 212).

Was this actually the case? Robert Gordon (1989, 183–184) reported the results of his own recent tests of two Hall M1819 rifles in the collection of the Springfield Armory Museum, one of which had been made by Hall at Harpers Ferry and the other by North in Middletown, Connecticut. The results support the evidence in historical documents that the parts of the rifles were indeed interchangeable, although some hand filing had been necessary to finish them after their initial machining.

The most remarkable feature about the development of interchangeable parts was the establishment in the Eastern United States of a *network* for sharing advances in technology. This network included not only the Harpers Ferry Armory and North's Middleton factory but also the federal armory at Springfield, Massachusetts, and a number of private firms. In part, the sharing of information within this network was government-imposed as a condition for obtaining contracts from the US Army. However, as Ross Thomson (2009, 57–58) explained, cooperation was to a great extent voluntary, facilitated by frequent visits by contractors to one another's shops and by the sharing of workers.

What was later to be called the American System of Production had matured. This arrangement, by which complex machinery was manufactured by unskilled labor using self-acting machines, would later be applied successfully to mass-produce typewriters, bicycles, automobiles and many other industrial products.

References

Alder, K. (1997). Innovation and amnesia: Engineering rationality and the fate of interchangeable parts. *Technology and Culture, 38*(2), 273–311.

Baida, P. (1987). Eli Whitney's other talent. *American Heritage, 38*(4), online edition.

Battison, E. A. (1966). Eli Whitney and the milling machine. *Smithsonian Journal of History, 1*(2), 9–34.

Chartrand, R. (2003). *Napoleon's guns 1792–1815 (1)*. Oxford: Osprey Publishing.

Gordon, R. B. (1989). Simeon North, John Hall, and mechanized manufacturing. *Technology and Culture, 30*, 179–188.

Green, C. M. (1956). *Eli Whitney and the birth of American technology*. Boston: Little, Brown and Company.

Hounshell, D. (1984). *From the American system to mass production, 1800–1932: The development of manufacturing technology in the United States*. Baltimore: Johns Hopkins University Press.

Kronoskaf. (2014). *Liechtenstein, Fürst Joseph Wenzel von*. Retrieved October 22, 2016, from Kronoskaf the Virtual Time Machine. http://www.kronoskaf.com/syw/index.php?title=Liechtenstein,_F%C3%BCrst_Joseph_Wenzel_von

MacLennan, K. (2003). Liechtenstein and Gribeauval: 'Artillery revolution' in political and cultural context. *War in History, 10*, 249–264.

Muir, D. (2000). *Reflections in Bullough's Pond: Economy and ecosystem in New England*. Hanover: University Press of New England.

Netstate. (2016). *Eli Terry*. Retrieved April 14, 2016, from Netstate.com. http://www.netstate.com/states/peop/people/ct_et.htm

Rose, A. (2008). *American rifle: A biography*. New York: Delacorte Press.

Smith, M. R. (1973, October). John H. Hall, Simeon North, and the milling machine: The nature of innovation among antebellum arms makers. *Technology and Culture, 14*(4), 573–591.

Smith, M. R. (1977). *Harper's Ferry Armory and the new technology: The challenge of change*. Ithaca: Cornell University Press.

Thomson, R. (2009). *Structures of change in the mechanical age: Technological innovations in the United States, 1790–1865*. Baltimore: The Johns Hopkins University Press.

Woodbury, R. S. (1960). The legend of Eli Whitney and interchangeable parts. *Technology and Culture, 1*(3), 235–253.

PART 3

The (Second) Military Revolution

In Part 3, we continue on into the nineteenth century. We find that the key components of a veritable military revolution—the steam warship, rifled cannon and mass-produced firearms—all had their sources in the West's industrial advances of the previous century. As late as 1793, rulers in China, India and the Ottoman Empire had been confident that the Western powers posed no serious threat to their autonomy. However, by 1860, the three great Asian civilizations had all suffered humiliating defeats at the hands of small numbers of Western troops armed with the military spin-offs of the Industrial Revolution. For the first time in history, one of Eurasia's four great societies had come to dominate the other three.

CHAPTER 10

1793: A Geopolitical Watershed

10.1 An Unstable Equilibrium

In March 1793, Mahadaji Shinde, ruler of the Maratha province of Gwalior celebrated the festival of Rang Panchami together with the Confederacy's peshwa (prime minister), Sawai Madhavrao. With a European-trained army, the Maratha Confederacy was the principal military force in the subcontinent. It was the only Indian state to have inflicted defeat on the British East India Company, a firm now perennially on the verge of bankruptcy. Meanwhile, in Britain, the financially stressed home government, now at war with France, was reluctant to encourage any further Asian conquests beyond the territories that the East India Company already held, principally in the northeast and on the southeastern and western coasts of India.

The year 1793 was one of the last moments at which it might have been said that while there were one or two powerful states in each major area of Eurasia, no region was strong enough to threaten seriously any of the others. In Europe, neither Britain nor revolutionary France—opposed to each other in the newly started War of the First Coalition—had the resources for major expeditions in Asia. China under the venerable emperor Qianlong made it clear that it would not tolerate any further opening of its economy to European traders. In the Middle East, the young Ottoman sultan, Selim III, set up a new treasury to finance the *Nizam-i Djedid* (New Order), a reformed army organized along European lines. There was every indication that this force would henceforth be able to stand up to the armies of the Russian and Austrian Empires.

© The Author(s) 2017
L. Dudley, *The Singularity of Western Innovation*,
DOI 10.1057/978-1-137-39822-2_10

Nevertheless, there were strong cultural and technological forces at work across Eurasia tending to upset this unstable equilibrium. The transformations of the two previous centuries in the West—the Linguistic and Industrial Revolutions—had dealt powerful cards to the Europeans while leaving their Asian neighbors with considerably weaker hands than before. In the absence of similar advances in the major Asian states, any momentary weakness on their part was likely to prove costly.

10.2   Britain in 1793: Gentlemanly Imperialism?

As the year 1793 began, Henry Dundas was busy piloting through Parliament a bill for renewing the charter of the East India Company. Dundas, a prominent Scottish Member of Parliament, was Secretary of State for the Home Department in the Tory government of his friend, William Pitt. For almost two centuries the powerful firm, founded under Queen Elizabeth I in 1600, had possessed a monopoly on trade between Britain and all countries east of the Cape of Good Hope. The Company traditionally exported cotton textiles from India to Europe, paying for its local purchases with a combination of British manufactures and silver. More recently, it had also begun to export to the West silks, tea and porcelain from China. While Dundas pondered whether to weaken this monopoly, he was subjected to pressure from numerous influence groups, each seeking to further its own interests (Webster 2009, 34).

Seventeen years earlier, in 1776, a fellow Scot, the philosopher and economist Adam Smith, had published *The Wealth of Nations*, a treatise advocating free trade and competition. The creation of monopolies, Smith argued in Book I, leads to an undersupply of goods and a price above the "natural" or equilibrium price (Smith [1776] 1977, 41). Although the monopolist may increase his profits thereby, the society as whole is worse off than under competitive markets.[1] In Book IV, Smith was particularly critical of the trade monopoly accorded the East India Company:

> Since the establishment of the English East India company, for example, the other inhabitants of England, over and above being excluded from the trade, must have paid, in the price of the East India goods which they have consumed, not only for all the extraordinary profits which the company may have made upon those goods in consequence of their monopoly, but for all the extraordinary waste which the fraud and abuse inseparable from the management of the affairs of so great a company must necessarily have occasioned. (Smith [1776] 1977, 440–441)

In the debate that surrounded the bill to renew the East India Company's charter, there was indeed considerable opposition to the company's monopoly. However, there was no strong support in Britain for dissolving its charter (Webster 2009, 34). Of course, most of the East India Company's powerful shareholders based in London opposed any concessions to free-trade interests. One group that did want to weaken the monopoly was made up of the private trading companies in London that had agencies in India. Although they could engage in what was known as "country trade" between different Asian ports, they wanted a share of the lucrative European market for Asian goods. A group of Cornish tin-mine owners had a similar position. They wanted to be able to use the Company's ships to export tin and bring back other products on their own account. Other interests desired simply to limit the amount of trade between Britain and India. Manchester and Glasgow textile manufacturers, for example, sought to prohibit both the import of Indian cottons and the export of cotton-producing machinery. Finally, Exeter woolen cloth manufacturers wanted the Company to export fewer long ells of tissue in their unrefined state in order that their own finished products might remain competitive on European markets (Webster 2009, 33–34).[2]

In an influential study, P. J. Cain and A. G. Hopkins (2002) argued that "gentlemanly capitalism" lay at the heart of the British imperial project. As we have just seen, the lobbying concerning the Charter Act of 1793 supports their position. The government minister charged with protecting the public's interest was far from convinced that the Company should be dismantled (Webster 2009, 35). Henry Dundas himself (1742–1811) was the fourth son of a Scottish judge who, like his father, had been trained as a lawyer. A clear speaker and an excellent debater, the young advocate had made a strong impression in London in 1766 when at age 24 he had participated in several appeals before the House of Lords (Matheson 1933, 24). In 1774, he was elected as a Member of Parliament for the Edinburgh seat of Midlothian, joining Lord North's Tories. The next year, following the American Declaration of Independence, Dundas made his first speech in the Commons, opposing any concessions until the Americans recognized British supremacy (Matheson 1933, 35).

In 1773, Parliament nationalized the Indian territory of the East India Company, leasing it back to the firm in return for a payment of £40,000 to the Crown in 2 years. In addition, the India Act specified that the Governor-General would in effect be appointed by the Crown. Since the Company was on the verge of bankruptcy, some way had to be found to increase its revenues. In that year, therefore, the Company obtained a monopoly on trade in opium in Bengal (Windle 2012, 56). It then sold much of the opium to private traders who exported it to China in exchange for payment in silver.

Ten years later, in 1783, with the Company again in financial difficulty, a coalition government in Britain proposed a more radical bill that would transfer control of British India to a parliamentary-appointed council. However, the government subsequently fell when the bill was rejected by the House of Lords (Matheson 1933, 99). With the support of Henry Dundas, William Pitt the Younger, age 24, became prime minister (technically, Chancellor of the Exchequer). Dundas, president of a parliamentary committee relating to India under the outgoing administration, had quickly become recognized as an authority on the subject of India (Furber 1931, 10–11). Pitt therefore assigned him the task of designing a new structure for the Company. "Pitt's India Act" of August 1784, drawn up by Dundas, created a Board of Control composed of two cabinet ministers and four other privy councilors with the power to veto appointments of the principal Indian officials (Matheson 1933, 109). A subsequent bill in 1786 allowed the Governor-General in India also to hold the position of military commander.

By 1793, it was again a question of the Company's charter. Pitt had appointed Dundas interim Secretary of State for the Home Department 2 years earlier. It was in this position that Dundas prepared his proposals for charter renewal. In the revised version of the charter that he presented to Parliament, there was something for almost everyone—provided that the person in question was British. The bill extended the Company's trade monopoly for 20 years and allowed it to increase the dividend to its stockholders. However, the Company had to provide 3000 tons of shipping annually between Britain and India at fixed rates to private traders. Since many of the principals in these private firms were also stockholders in the Company, they had understandably been reluctant to push their individual demands too far (Webster 2009, 36).

The new charter proposals met with general approval. Indeed, they were accepted almost unanimously in the House (Matheson 1933, 179). Surprisingly, given the force of Adam Smith's arguments in favor of free trade, most of the lobbying groups that had participated in the renewal debate wanted simply to maintain the existing charter while making small adjustments to the Company's monopoly (Webster 2009, 35). In effect, the 1793 charter renewal spread the monopoly rents among the most vociferous commercial pressure groups. As yet, as Cain and Hopkins (2002) argued, the British occupation of significant sections of an Asian subcontinent was merely a secondary effect of the pursuit of the profit motive among gentlemen.

Why in 1793 was there no explicit desire in Britain to open the Indian market to all British traders while converting the Company's land holdings into Crown colonies? The simplest answer is that under a private monopoly, it was expected that the Indian possessions could finance themselves, largely through taxes levied in India. The Company had been quite profitable until the middle of the eighteenth century, when the territory it controlled was limited to a few small *comptoirs* along the coast of India. Indeed, by 1744, during the War of the Austrian Succession, the Company had loaned the British state a total of £4.2 million (Webster 2009, 21). However, the subsequent conquests of the Carnatic and Bengal under Robert Clive in the 1750s had saddled the Company with an enormous territory to be defended and administered. In 1773, to avoid the firm's bankruptcy, the government had been compelled to advance the Company a loan of £1.4 million (Webster 2009, 23). Moreover, it was becoming increasingly difficult for the Company to finance its "Investment"; that is, the funds that were raised in India to purchase Indian commodities for sale in Britain. By 1793, the Company's debts to Europeans and local residents in India amounted to £9 million (Webster 2009, 41).

In effect, by 1793 the British East India Company had become a regulated utility. As in the later examples of railroad or telephone companies that had built up transport or communication networks, state intervention prevented the excessive exploitation of the (British) public while at the same time allowing smaller competitors to use its costly infrastructure at a fair price. At the same time, there was considerable reluctance on the part of the government to subsidize further territorial expansion. In 1795, Lord Cornwallis was sent to India for a second term as Governor-General with firm instructions from Dundas to cut expenses—if necessary, by giving back some of the territory that the Company had conquered previously (Wickwire and Wickwire 1980, 263).

10.3 THE OTTOMAN EMPIRE IN 1793: A NEW ORDER

As the year 1793 began, there was a new mood of openness in Istanbul, the capital of the Ottoman Empire. French Jacobins favorable to the Revolution that was shaking their own country dared to plant an *Arbre de la liberté* on a terrace that could be seen easily from the palace of the Sultan. After centuries of isolation, the Turkish and foreign residents of the great city were beginning to enter into social contact with one another. In all strata of Ottoman society, there was a new fascination with European architecture, furniture, clothing and music. The young Sultan, Selim III himself, was reported to have arranged performances of European plays in his palace (see Fig. 10.1). He was even observed, in disguise, attending parties held at European embassies and individual homes (Shaw 1971, 194–195).

Born in 1762, Selim III was the son of Sultan Mustafa III (r. 1757–1774) who had been succeeded by Selim's paternal uncle, Abdul Hamid I (r. 1774–1789). Selim III's ascent to the throne in April of 1789 at the age of 27 on his uncle's death had coincided with the dawn of the new revolutionary era in Europe. Fortunately, both his father and his uncle had taken care to assure that Selim was rigorously educated and well prepared for the responsibilities of a ruler. However, the initial years of his reign had

Fig. 10.1 In 1793, the young sultan Selim III introduced new army units, the *Nizam-i Djedid*, intended to bring the Ottoman army up to European standards (Reproduced from *Wikipedia Commons*)

been marked by the last years of the disastrous Russo-Turkish War of 1787–1792.

Abdul Hamid I had declared war on Russia in 1787 in an attempt to retake lands lost during the previous Russo-Turkish War of 1768–1774. He had especially hoped to regain control of the strategic Crimean peninsula. Instead, the Ottomans had been defeated on both land and sea by Austria and Russia. The critical event in the war had been the siege of Ochakov, on the Black Sea in the southern Ukraine. A Russian army under Prince Grigori Potemkin had invested the Ottoman city-fortress in June of 1788, successfully repelling a sortie by the Janissaries the following month. Meanwhile, the Russian navy's control of the Black Sea had prevented the arrival of supplies for the Ottoman troops. Finally, in December of that year, the Russians had crossed a frozen marsh, stormed the walls and proceeded to massacre some 20,000 of the city's inhabitants (Jacques 2007, 746). Indeed, the disastrous fall of Ochakov is said to have precipitated the death of Sultan Abdul Hamid I 4 months later. By the Treaty of Jassy of 1792, the Ottoman Empire had lost additional territory on the Black Sea coast to Russia and had been obliged to recognize Russia's possession of the Crimea.

With peace restored, Selim III could proceed with a major reorganization of the Ottoman armed forces that he had been considering. Soon after his accession to the throne, Selim had begun to meet with a number of young men interested in reforms that would avoid a continuation of the military defeats of the most recent decades. The group was composed of about 20 men, including two foreigners. Most were lower officials, friends and slaves with whom the sultan had grown up. There were also some older men who hoped that they could strengthen the regime by imitating the West (Shaw 1971, 86). At the sultan's request, the group's members had presented him a series of written proposals for reform. Virtually all of the reports criticized the military's system of command and control. Instead of auctioning leading positions to the highest bidder regardless of experience or qualification, they argued, the government should reorganize the recruitment and training of officers (Shaw 1971, 99).

One of the most perceptive sets of suggestions came from Ebubekir Ratib Efendi, an official who had just returned from a posting as ambassador to the Habsburg court in Vienna. Ratib explained the recent military successes of the Europeans by three factors: first, the organization and discipline of their soldiers; second, by the efficiency of the treasuries that financed military spending; and third by the integrity, competence and ability to cooperate of European officials (Shaw 1971, 97). He advocated the establishment of a military academy for officer training.

On the basis of these reports and recommendations, the sultan issued a series of decrees designed to bring the Ottoman army up to European standards. The reforms of the conventional units announced in 1793 focused on the Kapikulu Corps, the sultan's personal troops, made up of *sipâhís*, the feudal cavalry and the Janissaries, the light infantry. The *sipâhís* would no longer automatically be allowed to return to their landholdings during the winter months. In addition, palace officials would henceforth be unable to charge for confirming officers' appointments (Shaw 1971, 118). As for the Janissaries, they would be rearmed with up-to-date firearms and provided with new barracks. The size of the corps, currently 50,000, would be reduced by a half through the dismissal of members who held positions as merchants or artisans (Shaw 1971, 119–120). Reforms to the artillery corps would introduce new cannon and would merge traditional units with new formations organized by French advisors (Shaw 1971, 122).

Using these modest changes to traditional formations as a cover, the reformers decided to establish a completely new infantry corps, the *Nizam-i Djedid* (New Order), trained and equipped according to the European model. A new fiscal organization, the Treasury of the New Revenue was organized to support the new units financially (Shaw 1971, 127). During the most recent war, the grand vizier, Koca Yusuf Pasha, had formed a company of German and Russian deserters. Afterward they were stationed at some distance outside Istanbul to avoid their discovery by conservative elements (Uyar and Erickson 2009, 122). Additional soldiers were recruited from the Istanbul urban unemployed, with renegade Germans and Russians appointed as their officers and drill trainers (Shaw 1971, 127–128).

The Ottoman Empire held a vital strategic position at the intersection of a principal waterway between northern and southern Europe and a main overland land route between Europe and Asia. If carried out effectively, the reforms instituted by Selim III and those who supported him promised to restore the empire's power and prestige. The Ottoman Empire might thereby avoid becoming the "sick man of Europe".[3]

To the east, the Maratha had been more successful than the Ottomans in adopting European military technology, owing to their willingness to hire foreign advisors and purchase foreign equipment. However, the financing of the resulting increase in military expenditures posed no less a problem for the Maratha than it had for the Ottomans.

10.4 India in 1793: The Apogee of a Hegemon

Rang Panchami is a festival held by the Hindus of the west-central province of Maharashtra every year, 5 days after Holi, the spring festival of sharing love. During the festivities, people celebrate by splashing one another with a red fragrant powder and colored water. On 13 March 1793, the two most important rulers in the Maratha Confederacy celebrated Rang Panchami together in Pune, their capital city, on the Deccan Plateau 90 miles (150 km) southeast of present-day Mumbai. Over the eighteenth century, as Maratha power grew, their capital, Pune, had become the political center of the Indian subcontinent.

One of the pair was Sawai Madhavrao, the peshwa or prime minister, the hereditary head of state of the Maratha Confederacy. The Maratha were the Hindu warriors who had brought down the powerful Mughal Empire earlier in the century. More recently, during the First Anglo-Maratha War, from 1775 to 1782, the Maratha had fought the armies of the East India Company to a draw. The two parties had signed the Treaty of Salbai in 1782.

The other man was Mahadaji Shinde, the ruler of Gwalior, a state in north-central India. Born around 1730, Mahadaji was the youngest of five sons of an officer in the peshwa's army (Rathod 1994, 2). Because of his skills on the battlefield, he had risen steadily in standing among the Maratha commanders. It was Mahadaji who had inflicted a decisive defeat on a British army in 1781, forcing the East India Company to negotiate a peace treaty. The Gwalior ruler was now the most powerful of the peshwa's vassals. In 1792, the people of Pune had therefore been both surprised and relieved when Mahadaji had arrived in the Maratha capital. Before his own retinue and that of the court, Mahadaji had rested his head on the feet of the peshwa in a gesture of respect.

Mahadaji's military success against the British and subsequently against the Maratha's Indian opponents had been due in part to his recruitment of 260 European officers. Following the East India Company's example, these mercenaries had trained their Indian troops by Western standards, arranging that they be equipped with up-to-date artillery and firearms (Roy 2007, 10). However, the cost of their salaries and the new equipment they had introduced had placed a heavy burden on the Gwalior state finances. One of the main reasons for Mahadaji's visit to Pune was to persuade the peshwa and his principal adviser, Nana Phadnis, to pay an appropriate share of these costs (Rathod 1994, 162–163). Besides Gwalior, there were four other

Fig. 10.2 A memorial near Pune, India, commemorating Mahadaji Shinde, ruler of the Maratha state of Gwalior in central India (Reproduced from Wikipedia Commons)

prominent states within the Maratha Confederacy. Mahadaji also wished to make sure that the peshwa did not unduly favor one of the other regional Maratha rulers (Fig. 10.2).

By 1793, the only possible serious rival to the Maratha in India was the British East India Company. However, during the most recent Indian conflict, the Third Anglo-Mysore War of 1790–1792, the two parties had been allies in a campaign that defeated Tipu Sultan, the ruler of the south-Indian state of Mysore. The Governor-General of the East India Company territories was Charles Cornwallis, the eldest son of an aristocratic family with estates in Kent. Born in 1738, Cornwallis had served with distinction on the Continent during the Seven Years' War. However, he had been the losing commander at the Battle of Yorktown of 1781 that had brought the American War of Independence to a conclusion.

Cornwallis was nevertheless Dundas's first choice to succeed the controversial Warren Hastings as Governor-General in India in 1786.[4] Cornwallis had insisted that Dundas allow him also to hold the position of commander in chief, in order to avoid the divided responsibility that had crippled Britain's American campaign (Wickwire and Wickwire 1980, 17). Accordingly, with supreme power over Britain's resources in India, Cornwallis had been able to carry out the campaign against Tipu successfully, despite lukewarm support from the Maratha (Wickwire and Wickwire 1980, 152).

In Bengal, Cornwallis had reformed the system of tax collection that provided the bulk of Company revenues. The zamindars, the traditional tax collectors, were given title to the land they administered in return for the obligation to pay a fixed amount annually to the Company, based on the productivity of their holdings (Wickwire and Wickwire 1980, 65). However, the extra revenues that the new scheme generated were insufficient to cover the high cost of the war against Tipu (Wickwire and Wickwire 1980, 175). Consequently, when Cornwallis set sail for his return to England in October 1793, the financial situation of the Company was worse than it had ever been. Without the implicit guarantee of its debt by the government, the Company would have been insolvent, unable to pay its troops.

In short, in the year 1793 it appeared that the Maratha, with their access to foreign military expertise and technology, were in a strong enough position to defend their extensive territories not only from local rivals but also from an East India Company perpetually on the verge of bankruptcy. Fortunately for the Company, there were other options. To revive its fortunes, it was counting on an expansion of the lucrative opium trade with China.

10.5   China in 1793: A Delicate Mission

The emperor was late. George Macartney and his delegation had been waiting for an hour before they finally heard the drums and music announcing the sovereign's approach. As the Qianlong Emperor passed on a palanquin carried by 16 bearers, the assembled Chinese fell to their knees and touched their foreheads to the ground. However, the British, following their ambassador's lead, simply knelt on one knee, as they would have done before their own king. Then, after the emperor had ascended his throne inside a vast circular tent, the visitors walked to the entrance for a formal presentation.

The date was 14 September 1793. The meeting was taking place outside the imperial summer palace at Chengde, 140 miles (225 km) to the northeast of Beijing, in the shadow of the Great Wall. The British ambassador, George Macartney, 56, was no simple civil servant. In recognition of his contributions as colonial administrator and diplomat, he had recently been created Earl Macartney of the Irish peerage. Earlier in his career, he had negotiated peace treaties with Catherine the Great of Russia and with the Maratha of India. In addition, he had served as governor of the West Indies and of the Madras Presidency, as well as a member of the British parliament.

He had spent most of the preceding year aboard a 64-gun British man-of-war, the *Lion*, sailing from England to Tianjin, the port of Beijing.

Sent by Britain's secretary of state Henry Dundas, Macartney had instructions to request trade concessions from the Qing-dynasty rulers of China. The British were anxious to be allowed to trade at ports other than Guangzhou (Canton) in the south, to which they and other Western merchants had been restricted. They also wished to have a permanent representative and trade warehouse in the capital, Beijing. Unlike the leaders of previous foreign delegations, however, Macartney had refused to perform the ritual kowtow, the touching of one's forehead to the floor in recognition of the emperor's greatness. The difficulty, Macartney realized, was that, "Such are the avowed and affected notions here of superiority and independence of the Empire, no transaction is to be admitted with foreign nations on the ground of reciprocal benefit, but as grace and condescension from the former to the latter." It is only after protracted negotiations that the British had been allowed to abbreviate the ceremony by kneeling on one knee (Fig. 10.3).[5]

Sitting erect on his throne scrutinizing Macartney was his host, the "healthy and vigorous" ruler over a third of the planet's population. The Qianlong emperor, who was about to celebrate his 83rd birthday, was not a Han Chinese. He was rather a direct descendant of Nurhaci, the Manchu chieftain who had united the tribes of his semi-nomadic people on China's northeastern frontier late in the sixteenth century. Nurhaci had begun his campaign against the powerful armies of the Ming dynasty in 1618. It would take another 63 years before his great-grandson, the Kangxi Emperor (the Qianlong emperor's grandfather), finally conquered the last Ming general.[6]

Macartney climbed the steps to the throne and presented Qianlong a golden box encrusted with diamonds that contained a somewhat patronizing letter from George III. The message stated that the British were not sending ships for the sake of conquest but "for communication of the arts and comforts of life to those parts where they were hitherto little known". The king had closed with a prayer for the emperor: "May the Almighty have you in his holy protection."[7] As personal gifts, Macartney then gave the emperor two precious enameled watches set with diamonds. Macartney's secretary, Sir George Staunton, came forward at this point to present Qianlong two elegant air guns—rifles charged with a pump, used to hunt big game (Robbins [1908] 2010, 304).

10.5 CHINA IN 1793: A DELICATE MISSION 207

Fig. 10.3 Caricature of the reception of British delegate Lord Macartney by the Chinese emperor Qianlong in 1793 (Reproduced from the National Portrait Gallery)

The British were eager to expand their trading rights in China, with which they ran a large trade deficit. Europeans had developed a strong preference for Chinese teas, silks and porcelains, but had considerable difficulty persuading the Chinese to purchase Western products. In addition to personal gifts for the emperor, Macartney had brought to Beijing a number of scientific instruments and examples of British industry and art to donate to the Chinese.[8] There were muskets, pistols, swords and cannon, woolen cloth, fine chinaware and pottery produced in modern kilns, as well as tapestries, carpets, saddles and two carriages. In addition, there was a mechanical planetarium, along with telescopes and measuring devices (Hevia 1995, 77).

However, the foreign product most in demand in China, apart from the silver that Britain acquired through its own trade surplus with other states, was opium. The East India Company produced this narcotic drug at its holdings in Bengal, selling it to European traders who exported it illegally to China.[9] Since 1757, under the "Canton system", Western merchants had been restricted to the port of Guangzhou (Canton) in the south. There, each arriving vessel had to be overseen by one of the local Chinese merchant firms. The "barbarian" traders themselves were allowed to remain in China only during the trading months and were forbidden to bring their wives and dependents.[10] Accordingly, Macartney had been instructed to request the right to trade at three other important Chinese ports, along with the permission to open a warehouse in the capital, Beijing.[11]

For the moment, the two powers were evenly matched. Great Britain's trade expansion was the irresistible force, as that country's merchants sought profitable opportunities for arbitrage, taking advantage of price differences around the globe. Indeed Macartney's entire mission had been financed by the British East India Company.[12] The immovable object in southeast Asia was the Qing administration. It had banned the practice of Christian proselytizing early in the eighteenth century (Rowe 2009, 141). Beginning in 1757, the Qianlong Emperor had formalized earlier restrictions on European traders. As mentioned, under the "Canton system", they were allowed to trade only in the southern port of Guangzhou (Canton).

The success of the mission depended on how the Chinese reacted to the display of the latest technologies that the British had offered in their "presents" to the emperor. If the emperor and his advisors were impressed, they would likely be willing to come to terms; if not, they would be unlikely to grant special concessions to the British. On the day following the formal presentation, Macartney and his aides were offered a tour of the royal gardens at Jehol in the company of the First Minister, Heshen. A magnificent yacht transported the group along the shores of a vast lake, where they visited some 40 different palaces. Each castle contained fine furnishings of Asian manufacture along with numerous European clocks, musical automatons and gold jewels. In the words of Macartney, "our presents must shrink from the comparison and *hide their diminished heads*" (Robbins [1908] 2010, 309).

Macartney was a keen observer who took copious notes of all that he saw. He was careful to mention not only economic conditions but also the state of the Chinese army and navy. He was astonished by the gap in military techniques between his own nation and the Chinese. While anchored off Macao early in his visit, he had remarked that the *Lion* attracted great curiosity from the Chinese pilot and his men, for they had never seen a ship of that size or construction (Robbins [1908] 2010, 245). Later, on the route from Tianjin to Beijing, Macartney observed soldiers armed only with sabers. As for the cavalry, each member of the attending troops carried a bow and a quiver of arrows, but no firearms (Robbins [1908] 2010, 256). Toward the end of his stay in China, as he approached the heavily defended city of Guangzhou (Canton), Macartney could not help noticing the awkwardness of the poorly disciplined Chinese soldiers armed with obsolete matchlock muskets, bows and arrows and swords (Robbins [1908] 2010, 376).

It came as no great surprise, then, that as a diplomatic venture designed to resolve trade disputes, the Macartney mission turned out to be a failure. In his reply to the letter of George III, the emperor explained his reasons for continuing to impose the trade restrictions:

> Our Celestial Empire possesses all things in prolific abundance and lacks no product within its own borders. There was therefore no need to import the manufactures of outside barbarians in exchange for our own produce. But as the tea, silk, and porcelain which the Celestial Empire produces are absolute necessities to European nations and to yourselves, we have permitted, as a signal mark of favor, that foreign hongs (Chinese business associations) should be established at Canton, so that your wants might be supplied and your country thus participate in our beneficence. (Qianlong 1793).

The stage was thus set for an eventual confrontation between China and Britain over trading rights. For the moment, however, Britain's concerns were directed elsewhere. In February 1793, while Macartney had been crossing the Indian Ocean en route to China, France had declared war on Britain. For more than two decades, Britain would be organizing coalitions to counter the expansionist moves of the French. Only when that conflict was finally resolved, in 1815, could British leaders turn their attention once more to China. Readers of Macartney's journal would have had no trouble predicting the outcome of that confrontation. When the smoke over Guangzhou and Shanghai cleared, a half century after the Irish lord's mission, the balance of power between Britain and China would have changed dramatically.

10.6 THE SHIFTING BORDERS OF IMAGINED COMMUNITIES

Despite the apparent territorial equilibrium of the major Eurasian civilizations at the end of eighteenth century, powerful linguistic forces were causing shifts in the boundaries of Benedict Anderson's (2006) "imagined communities". In Britain, under the impact of "print-capitalism", there was convergence of the written and spoken language toward a national standard. However, in the three major Asian societies, where the nature of the writing system delayed the diffusion of movable type, linguistic divergence was undermining the legitimacy of the ruling dynasties.

By the year 1800, in Great Britain, a society of over ten million people, male literacy in Standard English was over 60 percent while female literacy was approaching 40 percent (Cressy 1980, 177). Not only were more and more people able to read and write but also they were increasingly communicating using a standardized medium. The publication in 1755 of Samuel Johnson's *Dictionary of the English Language* with 40,000 well-researched definitions demonstrated that after several centuries of rapid change, the vocabulary of the English language had finally become stabilized (Crystal 2003, 74). Moreover, after 1750, there were a growing number of publications purporting to show people how to write and speak. In the second half of the eighteenth century, over 200 different works on English grammar and rhetoric were printed (Crystal 2003, 78).

Parallel to this linguistic development, individuals in both Britain and America were developing a remarkable ability to collaborate with their fellow citizens. One indication was that each society had developed a system of representative government with stable political parties willing to accept a change in regime after electoral defeat. Another sign was the evidence of cooperation to innovate. In Scotland, Symington and his partners were developing the first practical steamboat, while in England, Maudslay was building a network of machine-tool builders. In the United States, under the leadership of the War Department, Simeon North and John Hall were on their way to mass-producing standardized firearms.

In China, by the reign of Qianlong's son, the Jiaqing Emperor (r. 1796–1820), the majority of officials of the Manchu regime that had ruled over Chinese society for a century and a half could no longer speak or write Manchu (Rhoades 2000, 51). Nevertheless, the regime continued to use Manchu and Mongol as well as Chinese for its documentation. Moreover, within the Han elite, there were two competing standards for the Mandarin koine, one based on the vernacular of Nanjing and the other on the everyday language of Beijing (Kaske 2008, 66–67).

In India, Persian had been the official language for two centuries. However, British officials noticed that it was competing increasingly with the Hindustani koine, a blend of languages that had developed around the Mughal army bases in northern India.

Meanwhile, in the Middle East, the Ottoman language used by the official class could no longer be understood by ordinary Turks. In the empire's Arabic-speaking territories, the vernaculars were diverging increasingly from one another and from the Classical Arabic that was used on formal occasions.

As the three Asian societies became linguistically less homogeneous, their autocratic regimes had increasing difficulty in controlling their territories. In the year 1800, the Chinese Jiaqing Emperor was having problems in trying to put down the White Lotus Rebellion in a mountainous region of west-central China. At the same time in India, the stability of the Maratha confederacy was threatened by quarrels between the peshwa or prime minister and the powerful Shinde and Holkar clans. The situation was no calmer in the Ottoman Empire where Napoleon's brief invasion of Egypt in 1798 had been followed by the collapse of imperial power in both Egypt and the Balkans.

Fortunately for the Asian dynasties, the attention of governments in Europe and America was for the moment directed elsewhere. As mentioned, on 1 February 1793, revolutionary France had declared war on Great Britain and the Netherlands. Austria and Prussia had already been fighting French armies since the preceding year. Soon Spain, Portugal, Naples and Tuscany also joined the First Coalition against France. For the following 12 years, the major Western powers would generally be too busy fighting among themselves to be able to divert large amounts of scarce resources to overseas conquest.

By 1815, with steamboats in regular service on the rivers of Europe and North America, it would only be a question of time, before someone in Britain, France or the United States mounted cannon on a steam-powered vessel and used it to tip the balance of power in Eurasia. Yet when change came, it was not through the navies of the Western Great Powers but at the initiative of a single private citizen fighting for a country that did not yet exist.

Notes

1. For an analysis of Smith's critique of monopoly, see Salvadori and Signorino (2014).
2. An ell was a measure of length used for tissues, about 45 inches (115 cm) long.

3. Howard Temperley (1936, 272) quoted Czar Nicholas I of Russia as saying in 1853 that the Ottoman Empire was "a sick man—a very sick man", a "man" who "has fallen into a state of decrepitude".
4. Hastings was impeached in the House of Commons for alleged crimes during his tenure in India. However, he was subsequently acquitted by the House of Lords.
5. Hevia, 1995, 101–102.
6. Crossley (1997, 95).
7. Rowe (2009, 146).
8. Hevia (1995, 102).
9. Rowe (2009, 148).
10. Rowe (2009, 142).
11. Rowe (2009, 145).
12. Hevia (1995, 82).

References

Anderson, B. (2006). *Imagined communities: Reflections on the origin and spread of nationalism* (Revised ed.). London: Verso.

Cain, P. J., & Hopkins, A. G. (2002). *British imperialism: 1688–2000*. London: Routledge.

Cressy, D. (1980). *Literacy and the social order: Reading and writing in Tudor and Stuart England*. Cambridge, UK: Cambridge University Press.

Crossley, P. K. (1997). *The Manchus*. Oxford: Blackwell.

Crystal, D. (2003). *The Cambridge encyclopedia of the English language*. Cambridge, UK: Cambridge University Press.

Furber, H. (1931). *Henry Dundas, first Viscount Melville, 1742–1811*. Oxford: Oxford University Press.

Hevia, J. L. (1995). *Cherishing men from afar: Qing guest ritual and the Macartney Embassy of 1793*. Durham: Duke University Press.

Jacques, T. (2007). *Dictionary of battles and sieges: A guide to 8500 battles from antiquity through the twenty-first century* (Vol. 2). Westport: Greenwood Press.

Kaske, E. (2008). *The politics of language in Chinese education, 1895–1919*. Leiden: Brill.

Matheson, C. (1933). *The life of Henry Dundas – First Viscount Melville*. London: Constable & Co.

Qianlong, "Letter to George III, 1793," *Modern history sourcebook*. Fordham University. https://sourcebooks.fordham.edu/mod/1793qianlong.asp. 10 Sept 2014.

Rathod, N. G. (1994). *The great Maratha Mahadji Scindia*. New Delhi: Sarup & Sons.

Rhoads, E. J. (2000). *Manchus and Han: Ethnic relations and political power in late Qing and early republican China, 1861–1928*. Seattle: Washington University Press.

Robbins, H. H. (2010 [original 1908]). *Our first ambassador to China: An account of the life of George, Earl of Macartney*. Cambridge: Cambridge University Press.

Rowe, W. T. (2009). *China's last empire: The great Qing*. Cambridge, MA: Belknap Press.

Roy, K. (2007). The armed expansion of the English East India Company: 1740s–1849. In D. P. Marston & C. S. Sundaram (Eds.), *A military history of India and South Asia* (pp. 1–15). Bloomington: Indiana University Press.

Salvadori, N., & Signorino, R. (2014). Adam Smith On monopoly theory. Making good a lacuna. *Scottish Journal of Political Economy, 61*, 178–195.

Shaw, S. J. (1971). *Between old and new: The Ottoman Empire under Sultan Selim III, 1789–1807*. Cambridge, MA: Harvard University Press.

Smith, M. R. (1977). *Harper's Ferry Armory and the new technology: The challenge of change*. Ithaca: Cornell University Press.

Temperley, H. (1936). *England and the near East: Crimea*. London: Longmans, Green and Co.

Uyar, M., & Erickson, E. J. (2009). *A military history of the Ottomans from Osman to Atatürk*. Santa Barbara: Praeger Security International.

Webster, A. (2009). *The twilight of the East India company: The evolution of Anglo-Asian commerce and politics, 1790–1860*. Rochester: Boydell Press.

Wickwire, F., & Wickwire, M. (1980). *Cornwallis – The imperial years*. Chapel Hill: University of North Carolina Press.

Windle, J. (2012). Insights for contemporary drug policy: A historical account of opium control in India and Pakistan. *Asian Criminology, 7*, 55–74.

CHAPTER 11

Steamships

11.1 Steam at Sea

For 3000 years, warships had been propelled by either oars or sails. Then, in the early nineteenth century, the technology that had been pumping water from coal mines for a century began to be applied to commercial shipping. By 1819, there was regular passenger service by steamboat on the rivers of the United States, Britain and the Continent (Rowland 1970, 50). In that same year, an American ship, the *Savannah*, made the crossing from Savannah to Liverpool, using its steam-powered paddlewheels to supplement its sails when the winds were calm (Rowland 1970, 57). If maritime transport by steam could find applications in the civilian sphere, could it not also do so in the military domain? Who would be the first to realize the advantages of mounting guns on a vessel capable of sailing for considerable distances against a strong wind or when there was no wind at all? Surprisingly, the answer to this question is neither the British navy nor that of the French. The innovation occurred in the navy of a state that did not yet exist—Greece. Initially, the impact of the steamship was felt only in the westernmost outposts of the Asian civilizations, in southwestern Europe. However, it would not be long before the people of the Asian continent itself began to suffer militarily from their civilizations' lag in industrial technology.

11.2 Steam Versus the Ottoman Empire

Amfissa, or Salona as it had been known since the Middle Ages, was a town eight miles (13 km) inland from the north shore of the Gulf of Corinth, some 130 miles (200 km) to the northwest of Athens. On 29 September 1827, a Turkish squadron of ten ships was anchored at the adjacent port of Itea on Salona Bay, providing support for Turkish forces that for 5 years had been attempting to suppress an uprising of Greek nationalists. Sent to oppose the Ottoman ships was a small Greek squadron financed largely by Western European philhellenes. The Greek fleet was commanded by Frank Hastings, an English volunteer. It consisted of his flagship, the *Karteria*, an English-built sloop powered by steam, and 500 yards (450 m) back, the *Sauveur*, a conventional brig,[1] along with two small gunboats. Daylight revealed the Ottoman fleet that the Greek patriots were seeking, consisting of three schooners, three brigs and a gunboat, accompanied by three transports with 500 soldiers, all well protected by shore batteries.[2]

As the *Karteria* approached, the Ottoman forces held their fire, confident of the superiority of their firepower. At a distance of about 500 yards (450 m) from the Turkish boats, Hastings ordered his little fleet to drop anchor (Finlay 1861, 176). As soon as the *Karteria* fired an initial ranging shot, all of the Turkish guns began to fire, concentrating their shots on the steamship. In reply, the *Karteria*'s carronades shot red-hot grape to disable the Turkish crews and destroy their ships' rigging, while the Greek ship's guns opened fire with explosive shells at a low angle. By noon, the battle was to all purposes over. Three of the larger Ottoman warships had been destroyed and the others disabled. The three Austrian troop ships hired by the Ottoman regime had been captured intact.

The Battle of Itea of 1827 marked the first occasion on which a steam-powered warship was used in naval combat. The vessel that inflicted this devastation, the *Karteria*, was a wooden-hulled sloop-of-war 126 feet (38 m) long with three masts—and two steam-driven side paddlewheels (see Fig. 11.1). She had been built the previous year at Deptford, on the Thames in southeast London and was propelled by two small steam engines manufactured, not without considerable delay, by Alexander Galloway of West Smithfield in central London (Abney-Hastings 2011, ch. 7). The armaments that had caused so much destruction were of two types. Four conventional 68-pound short cannon—carronades—fired red-hot shot heated by the ship's engines. In addition, there were four longer, heavier

11.2 STEAM VERSUS THE OTTOMAN EMPIRE

Fig. 11.1 The *Karteria*, the first steam-powered vessel to be used in combat. In the Battle of Itea in September 1827, the Hellenic Navy ship's explosive shells penetrated the wooden hulls of the opposing Ottoman fleet, setting the ships on fire (Reproduced from *Wikipedia Commons*)

guns designed by Frank Hastings to fire not solid projectiles, as was customary, but explosive shells.

Hastings had good reason to be satisfied with the performance of the steamship and armaments that he had designed. However, apart from its new technology, the little fleet had had an additional advantage over the Ottoman squadron that it had destroyed. The captain had been trained in the British navy, his officers were experienced British seamen and most of the crew were Europeans who would have been able to speak English. Hasting had spent long hours over the previous months training them for the new type of combat that he had conceived (Abney-Hastings 2011, ch. 7). In other words, communication in standardized English had produced a team with a level of skill and cohesion that the Ottoman forces could not match.

Frank Abney Hastings, born in 1794, was descended from two wealthy English families. He was the younger son of a British general who had sent him to sea at the age of 11 as a volunteer in Nelson's fleet. Six months later, on board the sloop *Neptune*, the young boy had seen his first action in the Battle of Trafalgar. By age 25, as a capable leader and knowledgeable artillery specialist, he had risen to the command of a brig. However, when a superior officer aboard another ship criticized him publicly for a slight error—letting his anchor cable overlay that of the other ship—Hastings took the comment as a slur upon his honor. He challenged the other captain to a duel and quickly found himself dismissed from the Navy for insubordination.

Seeking an output for his energy, Hastings had sailed to Greece in 1822 to take part in the War of Independence. The following year he wrote a memorandum to Lord Byron who was an associate of the leader of one of the Greek factions. Hastings proposed what in effect was a revolutionary new strategy of naval warfare that made use of explosive shells fired at a low angle. It was essentially the same technique that, as we shall see, Henri-Joseph Paixhans was proposing to the French Navy at about the same time.[3] "My object", he wrote, "would be, to arrange it so as to make the shell stick in the ship's side and explode there". Explosive shells fired at a high trajectory from short-barreled mortars had long been in terrestrial combat. In naval warfare, however, the firing of explosive shells was considered too dangerous, because of the possibility that the shell might lose its fuse and explode before leaving the barrel. However, Hastings proposed attaching a wooden support or *sabot* to the shell to keep it from rolling while still in the gun (Abney-Hastings 2011, ch. 6). The response of Byron and his advisors was unenthusiastic.

Meanwhile the Ottoman sultan, Mahmud II, had appealed to his Egyptian vassal, Muhammad Ali, for help in suppressing the Greek revolt. Accordingly, in July 1824 the Khedive's son, Ibrahim Pasha, sailed from Alexandria with 25 warships, 100 transports and 10,000 men to aid the Ottoman forces. Ibrahim established a base on Crete to conduct a war of pacification on the Greek mainland. Faced with a full-scale invasion by the combined Ottoman and Egyptian forces, the Greek leaders agreed to purchase two steamships. Hastings offered to pay £5000 from his personal funds toward the purchase of one of these ships. In August 1824, Hastings returned to London with representatives of the Greek government for negotiations with the London Greek Committee, a private group formed to raise funds for Greek Independence. Because of numerous delays, it was not until 2 years later that the steamship he had proposed was ready to sail. On 14 September 1826, the sloop, named the *Perseverance*, finally steamed into the port of Nafplio, on the northeastern coast of the Peloponnese, the seat of the provisional Greek government. Two days later, the ship's initial English name was removed and *Karteria*, the Greek translation, was painted on the ship. In December, the ship's American-built cannon arrived and were installed.

During the winter of 1826–1827, Ibrahim was in the process of brutally pacifying the Peloponnese using a scorched-earth policy. By the summer of 1827, he controlled large sections of the peninsula, including the main coastal forts such as Navarino, on a large bay on the western coast. When he learned of Hastings's victory at Salona Bay in late September, Ibrahim vowed to take revenge, using his large fleet to destroy the *Karteria* (Finlay 1861, 178). However, bad weather and harassment by British navy ships forced the Egyptian leader and his fleet to take refuge in the port of Navarino.

The bay of Navarino is some two miles (3.2 km) wide and three miles (4.8 km) long, with an opening to the sea only three-quarters of a mile (1.2 km) wide. On the morning of 20 October 1827, Ibrahim's Ottoman fleet of 82 ships protected by shore batteries was anchored in a long crescent facing outward toward the entrance to the bay. Confident of their superiority in numbers, the Ottoman gunners held their fire as a combined British, French and Russian force of 27 ships entered the bay one after the other. Before the allied ships could reach their stations, the Turks opened fire. From this point onward, it was a question of accuracy of fire and the weight of the shot fired by each side. On both scores, the allies had an advantage: Ibrahim's outgunned fleet was virtually annihilated. By the next morning, only 29 of the Ottoman ships remained afloat. Although some of the allied ships had suffered extensive damage, none was lost (Finlay 1861, 181–182).

In June of the following year, Frank Abney Hastings was badly wounded in an attack on the Turkish-held town of Aitoliko in Western Greece and died shortly thereafter. However, the Greek Independence campaign was a success. The landing of a French expeditionary force in the southern Peloponnese in August 1828 obliged Ibrahim Pasha to withdraw his forces from Greece. In 1832, after suffering yet another military defeat at the hands of Russia, and under pressure from Britain and France, the Ottoman sultan finally accepted an independent Greek state.

It would take another quarter century before the world's navies realized the full implications of the Battle of Itea. With the invention of ever more powerful cannon firing explosive shells rather than solid shot, the days of the wooden sailing warship were numbered. The French and the British began to equip their ships with shell-firing guns as part of their armament in the late 1830s (Black 2009, 124–125). In 1853, as we shall see in the next chapter, Russian ships armed with shell-firing cannon had a decisive encounter with a conventionally armed Turkish sailing fleet in the Battle of Sinop.

The *Karteria*, with its ability to maneuver easily and to sail against the wind, had demonstrated that in coastal waters a steamship armed with cannon that fired explosive shells could perform very effectively against wooden sailing ships. However, with its single-layered wooden hull, it was not the ideal vessel for the long, often-shallow rivers of the Asian and African continents. A grounding or collision with a rock could easily prove fatal to such a ship in combat conditions. For the moment, therefore, the continental interiors of Asia were still secure from European naval invasion.

11.3 Steam Versus the Qing Dynasty

We have seen that a steam-powered European warship had invaded the waters of the Ottoman Empire in 1827. It was only a matter of time before the new technology penetrated farther east. In 1830, a wooden-hulled passenger steamship built in India, the *Hugh Lindsay*, began service between Bombay and Suez at the head of the Red Sea (Headrick 1981, 23). Because of the fuel requirements of the ship's engines, on the first lag to Aden, coal was piled in the saloon and even in the passenger cabins (Blythe 2004, 73). Upon their arrival in Suez, the travelers faced a 50-mile (80-km) ride by horse-drawn wagon across the desert to Cairo.

Because the East India Company objected to this intrusion into its transport monopoly, a select committee of the House of Commons on Steam Navigation to India began hearings in 1834 (Headrick 1981, 24). One testimony that aroused great interest was that of Macgregor Laird, an expert on steamboats who had just returned from a visit to explore the Niger River in West Africa. Laird was able to compare the performance of two steamboats he had taken on this expedition, the *QuorraI* made of wood and the *Alburkah* of iron. The latter had been the first iron ship to dare to embark on a long voyage on the open sea (Headrick 1981, 27–28). According to Laird, there were numerous advantages to the use of iron: it was easier to keep clean, lighter, allowed greater speed with the same fuel, was less vulnerable to puncture from grounding and allowed the possibility of watertight bulkheads.

This testimony was not lost on another prominent witness, Thomas Love Peacock, a novelist and poet, who since 1819 had been an administrator of the East India Company at India House in London. Peacock had prepared a memorandum for the committee on possible routes of steam transport between India and Britain, recommending the Euphrates or the Red Sea rather than the Cape of Good Hope (Headrick 1981, 24). Peacock noted that the *Alburkah* had been built by the iron works of Laird's father and brother, William Laird and Son, at Birkenhead, across the Mersey from Liverpool.

Four years later, Peacock, now one of the highest officers of the East India Company, placed an order with the Lairds' firm for four steam-powered iron gunboats. One of these, launched in 1840, was the heavily armed *Nemesis*, the largest iron ship built to date. The ship was 184 feet (56 m) long, with two 60-horsepower engines to power its side paddlewheels. Its armament included two 32-pound swivel guns, one fore and one aft, that could fire either shot or shell (Hall and Bernard 1845, 6). In addition, there were 15 smaller guns and a rocket launcher. The ship had a flat bottom and a two-piece removable keel (Hall and Bernard 1845, 3). According to rumors, the *Nemesis* was to be used in the eastern seas (Headrick 1981, 26). In April 1840, the ship set sail for Macao via the Cape of Good Hope. The voyage took almost 7 months, interrupted by rough weather in the Indian Ocean that caused the hull to split open. Fortunately, the ship had been designed with a double hull and an interior divided into seven watertight compartments.

The arrival of the *Nemesis* on the Chinese coast was followed by a dramatic escalation in an ongoing conflict between British merchants and the Qing authorities. In 1834, the British government had finally ended the East India Company's monopoly on (legitimate) trade between Britain and China. Previously, the Company had auctioned opium that it grew in Bengal to private traders who smuggled it into China in return for payment in silver. Now, in exchange for Indian opium, private British companies such as Jardine Matheson & Co. could purchase Chinese silks and teas that they could sell directly on the European market (Fairbank and Goldman 2006, 199). From 1000 chests of opium in 1767, imports into China had risen to 40,000 chests in 1839 (Worthing 2007, 43).

Alarmed by the resulting surge in opium addiction, the Beijing regime appointed Imperial Commissioner Lin Zexu, with full powers to put a stop to opium smuggling. Lin seized the drug stocks of Guangzhou (Canton) traders and demanded that foreign nations sign a bond promising not to trade in opium. Pressured by private interests, the British government decided instead upon a military response (Fairbank and Goldman 2006, 199–200).

The Boca Tigris is the mouth of the main channel of the Pearl River in southeastern China, providing access to the port of Guangzhou (Canton) some 50 miles (80 km) upstream. On 7 January 1841, an approaching British fleet observed that the entrance to the river was defended by forts on the islands of Chuenpi on the east and Tycocktow on the west (Hall and Bernard 1845, 109). While British troops landed on shore and approached the islands' fortifications from the rear, the *Nemesis* joined the navy's men-of-war in blasting the forts with solid shot and shell. Several miles further up, the river was defended by a fleet of Chinese war junks armed with small cannons. With the forts about to fall, the *Nemesis* then sailed upriver to deal with the Chinese fleet. Approaching the junks, the *Nemesis* began to fire her guns and rockets. The first Congreve rocket hit one of the largest junks, igniting a powder magazine and blowing the ship apart. The remaining Chinese ships were then abandoned by most of their crew, leaving them to be destroyed or captured by the British. Faced with the fall of the Pearl River defenses, the Chinese were willing to negotiate. However, a preliminary treaty between the Qing commander and the British consul to end the dispute was subsequently rejected by both governments (Worthing 2007, 38–39).

With a draft of only five feet (1.5 m) in battle trim, the *Nemesis* could sail in shallow water where ocean-going sailing ships could not pass (Headrick 1981, 50). Accordingly, in late February 1841, after the breakdown of negotiations, the *Nemesis* led a small fleet of steamers upriver, destroying any obstacles on its path toward Guangzhou (Canton). Upon arrival at the approaches to the great Chinese port, the British fleet quickly chased off defending junks, captured the principal fort and destroyed the *Cambridge*, a former British sailing warship that had been taken over by Chinese defenders (Hall and Bernard 1845, 165–169). Three months later, the British seized the remaining defenses of Canton. Yet despite further successive defeats along the southern coast and the Yangtze Delta, the Qing regime refused to submit.

The decisive blow came only in July 1842, when a British fleet led by the *Nemesis* captured the vital city of Zhenjiang at the intersection of the Grand Canal and the Yangtze River (Headrick 1981, 53). The resulting threat to the food supply of northern China forced the regime to come to terms. Under the conditions of the September 1842 "unequal" Treaty of Nanjing, the Qing government opened Canton and four other ports to international trade. It also agreed to grant most-favored-nation rights to all countries under a modest tariff. In addition, the Chinese agreed to pay stiff reparations and ceded Hong Kong to Britain in perpetuity (Fairbank and Goldman 2006, 202).

Beginning in 1850, the Qing regime faced a massive insurrection that spread from the underdeveloped southwest into the prosperous Yangtze valley. The revolt began as a religious movement under Hong Xiuquan, a village schoolteacher introduced to Christianity who believed himself to be the younger brother of Christ (Rowe 2009, 187). By the mid-1850s, the Taiping Rebellion had seized much of the middle and lower Yangtze valley, including the early Ming capital of Nanjing.

The Western powers had been seeking a pretext by which they could profit from the resulting weakness of the Qing regime. In 1856, the Chinese authorities in Guangzhou had arrested the crew of a Chinese-owned ship, the *Arrow*, that had been registered by the British in Hong Kong. Reportedly, the Chinese had pulled down the ship's Union Jack in the process (Worthing 2007, 42). The Chinese accused the crew of importing opium, which despite British insistence was still a crime in China (Rowe 2009, 191).

When the Chinese refused to apologize for the insult to Britain, the British consul ordered his navy's ships to bombard Guangzhou (Worthing 2007, 43). The next year the Whigs were returned to power with a large majority. Foreign secretary Lord Palmerston sent an expeditionary force to retaliate for the insult to his country's flag. A French force joined the mission, their government having accused China of unjustly executing a French missionary. In June 1858, the joint force attacked the Taku Forts on the Hai River,[4] the water route for access to Beijing. When the poorly aimed Chinese guns were unable block the allied fleet's advance, the Chinese were forced to sign yet another "unequal" accord (Hanes and Sanello 2002, 212). The Treaty of Tianjin granted Britain, France, Russia and the United States representation in Beijing. In addition, the agreement legalized the opium trade, opened ten further ports to foreign commerce and imposed a heavy indemnity on the Chinese.

In June 1859, representatives of Britain and France returned with a powerful fleet to implement the treaty. However, they found that the Chinese had rearmed the Taku Forts and blocked the Hai River leading to Beijing with three thick bamboo booms (Hanes and Sanello 2002, 231). When his gunboats proved unable to break through the barrier, the British commander unwisely ordered a frontal attack on the forts at low tide. This time the Chinese artillerymen were better prepared than they had been in the first battle. Their well-aimed guns heavily damaged the gunboats and decimated attacking troops caught in the mud on the river shore (Porter 1889, 509). Having suffered 400 casualties, the British were forced to withdraw (Worthing 2007, 44).

Evidently, if the Asian opposition had access to the same armaments as the attackers, the advantage of steam transport was not always sufficient to guarantee Western dominance. As we shall see in the next two chapters, it would take a series of innovations in artillery and individual firearms to assure victory over the Chinese. First, however, we should take note of perhaps the most important advantage of nineteenth-century Western armies over their opponents in Asia and Africa.

11.4 The Imagined Community Adopts Steam Technology

Meerut, a town 45 miles (72 km) northeast of Delhi, was the site of the second-largest cantonment of the East India Company's army. On 24 April 1857, the soldiers in a unit of the Company's Native Infantry were ordered to load their new Enfield rifles by biting the end of greased paper cartridges and ramming them down the barrels. Rumors about the cartridges had been circulating among the troops for several weeks. As explained in the next chapter, the Muslim soldiers believed that the tallow on the cartridges contained pig fat, while the Hindus thought that the lubricant was made from cow fat. When 85 soldiers refused the order, they were arrested and imprisoned. Two weeks later, on 10 May, their comrades released the prisoners, setting off a rebellion that quickly spread across northern India (Metcalf and Metcalf 2006, 101).

It was not until 11 July, 2 months later, that news of the uprising at Meerut finally reached London. On the following day came the dramatic news that Delhi too had fallen to the rebels. Immediately a telegram was sent to the Second Dragoon Guards, known as the Queen's Bays, a unit first formed under James II in 1685. The cavalry regiment was to make its way to Liverpool and thence to Canterbury for embarkation at Gravesend, on the south bank of the Thames, some 25 miles (40 km) east of London (Griffin 2015).

On 25 July 1857, the regiment's 28 officers, 47 sergeants and 635 other ranks boarded two iron-hulled paddle steamships bound for Calcutta by the Cape of Good Hope. Both ships had been built in Scotland, on the banks of the River Clyde, the *Monarch* in 1846 in West Renfrew and the *Blenheim* 2 years later in Glasgow. Like almost all ocean-going steamships until the last decades of the nineteenth century, they were built with masts, in order to save fuel by the use of sails when winds were favorable. Four months later, on 25 and 27 November, the two ships and their passengers reached Calcutta. In January 1858, the unit was ordered to join the cavalry units of Sir Colin Campbell's force at Allahabad on the Ganges some 500 miles (800 km) inland. Accordingly, in March 1858, as we shall see in Chapter 13, the regiment participated in the retaking of Lucknow, which had been held by the rebels since May of the previous year (Griffin 2015).

The example of the Queen's Bays shows that within a few months (six in the case of India), the resources of the Empire, mobilized by telegraph and steamship, could be deployed virtually anywhere on the planet. Yet in the mid-nineteenth century, the population of the United Kingdom was only 25 million, while that of India was approaching 250 million (Maddison 2007, 376). In India itself, 40,000 British troops commanded 250,000 sepoys (Wolpert 1993, 233–234). Even reinforced with extra troops from outside the subcontinent, how could so few British hope to control so many Indians? A true sea story provides an explanation.

The *Sarah Sands* was built on the Mersey in Liverpool in 1846, at about the same time that the *Monarch* and *Blenheim* were being constructed further north on the Clyde. Unlike the Scottish paddle ships, however, the British vessel had a revolutionary new screw propeller. After service on the North Atlantic, it had been conscripted as a troop ship during the Crimean War in 1855. In the summer of 1857, after the Indian Mutiny outbreak, the ship was again called into public service, to help transport the 54th Regiment of Foot to India. The British infantry unit had previously served in India between 1824 and 1840 (Griffin 2015).

The tale is told by Rudyard Kipling ([1865] 2009). Two ships had already left England with other sections of the regiment. The remaining 354 rank and 14 officers along with a dozen women boarded the *Sarah Sands* at Plymouth for the voyage to Calcutta. The ship also carried a load of munitions divided between two of its magazines. In mid-October, the ship docked at Cape Town for 5 days to replenish its supply of coal and then set out again for the east. Then 3 weeks later, on the afternoon of 11 November, during a storm in the middle of the Indian Ocean, fire broke out in the engine room. The ship's boats were immediately lowered over the side and the women put into them. At this point, a group of mutinous engineers, firemen and other hands, knowing full well the danger of explosion, lowered the long-boat and rowed away from the ship.

The troops on board behaved in a more disciplined fashion, following their officers' orders. At great risk to their own lives, they began emptying the barrels of munitions in the two magazines threatened by the fire and proceeded to dump them overboard. They had almost finished this task when in succession the remaining cartridges and the ship's signaling powder exploded, completely destroying the saloon and the cabins in the aft part of the ship. With the vessel illuminating the night sky, one wag among the troops called, "Lights out!" Fortunately, because the *Sarah Sands* had been built of iron with watertight compartments, the ship remained afloat. Finally, by noon the next day, the fire had been extinguished. However, three of the four original masts had been lost. Nevertheless, with the boats recovered and one sail rigged on the remaining mast, the *Sarah Sands* was able to reach Mauritius 2 weeks later.

There the troops were packed into another ship and after a further 5 weeks arrived at the Hooghly River, the arm of the Ganges that gives access to Calcutta. The soldiers' greatest complaint by this time was that they had run out of tobacco. Luckily, on the way upriver, they met an American trading ship, the *Hamlet*. When he heard their tale, the ship's captain contributed "four hundred pounds of the best Cavendish and one thousand Manila cigars for the officers", refusing to accept any payment in return (Kipling [1865] 2009, 108).

This example of extraordinary cooperation among people from diverse backgrounds speaking the same standardized language under the most trying of circumstances illustrates an important advantage of the British over the Indian rebels. While the British were greatly outnumbered by their opponents, they were able to cooperate sufficiently among themselves to coordinate their efforts under extreme conditions. The question was whether the Indian rebels could cooperate sufficiently among themselves to overcome this remarkable cohesion of the Europeans.

11.5 The Industrial Revolution Goes to War

During the Industrial Revolution of the eighteenth century, England, France and the United States had developed a number of breakthrough technologies that relieved bottlenecks threatening to impede economic growth. However, prior to the second quarter of the nineteenth century, these innovations had little impact on warfare. The first military application of the new technologies, in the second quarter of the nineteenth century, was the use of the steam engine to propel an ocean-going warship. Able to maneuver rapidly in constrained quarters, such a vessel equipped with explosive shells was able to wreak havoc on traditional sailing ships. When subsequently installed on shallow-draft boats with metal hulls, steam engines allowed Western forces to penetrate into the interior of the Asian continent. Moreover, by the mid-nineteenth century, Western troops had another important advantage over their Asian counterparts. With high rates of effective literacy and a common spoken vernacular, large groups of men from diverse backgrounds were able to exhibit extraordinary cohesion under stress.

To date, however, European forces whether at sea or on land were still using missile technologies little advanced from the smoothbore cannon and arquebus developed at the end of the Middle Ages. Only in the 1850s would the machine tools recently developed in the West begin to have a significant impact on the artillery and firearms used in Eurasian warfare and then solely in the hands of Western troops.

Notes

1. A brig was a small, maneuverable two-masted ship, while a sloop-of-war was larger, with three masts.
2. This account of the Battle of Itea is based on Abney-Hastings (2011, ch. 10).
3. See Sect. 12.1.
4. Westerners also called the Hai River the Bei He.

References

Abney-Hastings, M. (2011). *Commander of the Karteria: Honoured in Greece. Unknown at home.* Bloomington: AuthorHouse.

Black, J. (2009). *Naval power: A history of warfare and the sea from 1500.* Basingstoke: Palgrave Macmillan.

Blythe, R. J. (2004). Aden, British India and the development of steam power in the Red Sea, 1825–1839. In D. Killingray, M. Lincoln, & N. Rigby (Eds.), *Maritime empires: British imperial maritime trade in the nineteenth century* (pp. 68–83). Woodbridge: Boydell Press.

Fairbank, J. K., & Goldman, M. (2006 [original 1992]). *China: A new history.* (2nd enlarged ed.). Cambridge, MA: Belknap Press.

Griffin, C. (2015). *The Queen's Bays (2nd Dragoon Guards).* Retrieved November 2, 2015, from The British Empire. http://www.britishempire.co.uk/forces/armyunits/britishcavalry/queensbays.htm

Hanes, W. T., & Sanello, F. (2002). *Opium wars: The addiction of one empire and the corruption of another*. Naperville: Sourcebooks.

Headrick, D. R. (1981). *The tools of empire: Technology and European imperialism in the nineteenth century*. Oxford: Oxford University Press.

Kipling, R. (2009 [original 1865]). The burning of the "Sarah Sands". In R. Kipling (Ed.), *Land and sea tales for scouts and guides* (pp. 100–108). Kelly Bray: Stratus Books.

Maddison, A. (2007). *Contours of the world economy, 1-2030 AD: Essays in macro-economic history*. Oxford: Oxford University Press.

Metcalf, B. D., & Metcalf, T. R. (2006). *A concise history of modern India* (2nd ed.). Cambridge: Cambridge University Press.

Rowe, W. T. (2009). *China's last empire: The great Qing*. Cambridge, MA: Belknap Press.

Rowland, K. T. (1970). *Steam at sea: A history of steam navigation*. Newton Abbot: David & Charles.

Wolpert, S. (1993). *A new history of India* (4th ed.). Oxford: Oxford University Press.

Worthing, P. (2007). *A military history of modern China: From the Manchu conquest to Tian'anmen Square*. Westport: Praeger.

CHAPTER 12

Rifled Artillery

12.1 From Bows and Arrows to Nuts and Bolts

It is quite astounding that in the four centuries between the end of the Hundred Years' War and the Crimean War, there was little change in the heavy arms used by Western armies and navies. Whether in massed artillery corps on land or in lumbering men-of-war at sea, cannoneers used muzzle-loading cannon with smoothbores cast from iron or bronze that fired solid-metal spherical projectiles. The maximum effective range of such weapons in Napoleon's day was from 800 to 1000 m (Chartrand 2003, 8), or less than twice the equivalent distance for the composite bow and arrow invented 4000 years earlier (see Lhagvasuren). Since the Middle Ages, the problem for manufacturers of armaments had been the difficulty of shaping large metal parts with precision. However as we saw in Chap. 7, from the end of the eighteenth century, the invention of modern machine tools—the boring machine, the lathe with compound tool rest, the screw-cutting machine, the planing machine and the milling machine—finally made possible the accurate shaping of metal components. If these machine tools could make the intricate parts for automatic spinning and weaving machines, could they not also fabricate more precise weapons? It was only a matter of time before the West was able to apply to warfare the technologies it used to manufacture nuts and bolts.

12.2　The Ottoman Empire: The End of the Wooden Warship

It is ironic that the man most responsible for bringing an end to the age of wooden sailing warships was an *army* officer. Henri-Joseph Paixhans was a French artillery commander, a graduate of the *École Polytechnique*, who had served during the Napoleonic Wars. Placed on reserve in 1815, he had ample time to consider the implications of French defeats, particularly those at sea. In 1823, he designed a shell-firing gun that was shorter and lighter than guns of the same caliber that used solid shot (Potter 1981, 118). The shell itself was a hollow metal sphere fitted into a wooden support or *sabot* in order to minimize jamming during loading. A delay fuse prevented the shell from exploding before it hit the target (Hogg 1970, 165).

Paixhans proposed that the guns be used to fire shells at high velocity with a flat trajectory against the wooden hulls of enemy ships (Potter 1981, 118). The following year, two series of tests at Brest against the old ship-of-the-line *Pacificateur* showed that the shells penetrated into the wooden planks, causing extensive damage when they exploded (Taillemite 2005). In 1825, Paixhans was finally reintegrated into the army as a lieutenant colonel. As we saw in the preceding chapter, Frank Abney Hastings employed shell-firing guns of his own design in a battle against Ottoman warships in 1827. However, it was not until 1835, over a decade after Paixhans's first tests, that the French navy began installing shell-firing guns as auxiliary armament on its ships (Taillemite 2005). In that same year, tests conducted by the British Navy with the wooden battleship *Prince George* also demonstrated that when such shells exploded as intended, they caused great damage. However, little attention was paid to these results before the surprising effects of the Paixhans-type guns used by the Russian navy during the Crimean War.

In May 1853, Tsar Nicholas I decided to take advantage of the Ottoman Empire's chronic weakness by threatening war unless Russia were named the protector of the Empire's Orthodox subjects. Supported by Britain and France, the Sultan rejected the Russian ultimatum. Accordingly, in July 1853, Russian armies occupied the Ottoman provinces of Moldavia and Wallachia in modern Romania. After Western intervention to find a compromise failed, Sultan Abdülmecid I declared war on Russia on 18 October (Small 2011, ch. 2).

In early November 1853, the Ottomans sent a fleet of 10 ships under Vice Admiral Osman Pasha to protect shipping along the western coast of

Anatolia. However, because of a sudden storm, the admiral was forced to take refuge in the harbor of Sinop, a port 400 miles (640 km) east of Istanbul on the southern coast of the Black Sea (Özcan 2012, 50). On 17 November, one of his ships, the *Pervaz-i Bahri*, an Egyptian steam frigate, was sailing to the Black Sea port of Eregli 250 miles (400 km) west of Sinop to take on coal. The ship was spotted by a small Russian squadron commanded by Admiral Vladimir Kornilov on his flagship, the steamship *Vladimir*. During the battle that followed, the Russian guns severely damaged the Ottoman ship. The Ottoman crew lost 22 men against only one for the Russians. The *Pervaz-i Bahri* was seized and taken to Sevastopol where it was renamed the *Kornilov* (Badem 2010, 118).

This naval engagement was the first in history between steamships (Badem 2010, 119). It is not clear whether the *Vladimir* was equipped with Paixhans guns and if so, whether they played a role in the battle. However, such a situation seems quite possible since her sister ships used shell-firing guns to deadly effect two weeks later during a historic battle farther east.

A Russian squadron under Admiral Pavel Nakhimov had discovered Osman Pasha's fleet in the harbor of Sinop. Despite the protection the harbor offered, the Ottoman commander must have been dismayed on 29 November to see two Russian squadrons under Admiral Nakhimov in the process of assembling before Sinop. Since the Russian fleet included six ships-of-the-line with 68-pound guns, whereas the largest Turkish ships were frigates with 24-pounders, the Ottoman ships were heavily outgunned, although they were protected by shore batteries (Badem 2010, 120). However, Osman Pasha was presumably unaware that the Russian navy had developed its own version of the Paixhans gun, with greater capacity and range than earlier French models. The Russian ships carried 38 of these powerful cannon (Badem 2010, 120).

On the morning of 30 November, the Russian fleet entered the bay and Nakhimov demanded that the Turks surrender. While the Russian ships were anchoring at a distance of 1000 yards (900 m) from their opponents, the Ottoman cannon opened fire.[1] At first, the Ottoman gunners had the advantage, but before long, the Paixhans's guns began to turn the tide of battle in favor of the Russians. Their shells penetrated the Ottoman wooden hulls and exploded, setting the ships ablaze. Only one Ottoman ship, the steamer *Taif*, escaped, outracing two pursing Russian ships (Badem 2010, 120–121). Some 3000 Turks were killed in the battle, but just 37 Russian lives were lost (Clodfelter 2008, 195). Calling the event a "massacre", the

British press insisted that their government intervene on the Ottoman side (Small 2011, ch. 2). Finally, in February 1854, with Lord Palmerston installed as foreign secretary, Britain and France declared war on Russia (Small 2011, ch. 2).

The strategy used by Admiral Nakhimov, anchoring his ships close to the enemy and firing high-velocity shells in a flat trajectory at short range, was effective against smaller ships at anchor. However, against larger ships-of-the-line at sea in a running battle, the long-range solid shot of the enemy heavy guns would have prevented such a close approach. Moreover, at a longer range, Paixhans guns with shells were considerably less accurate than long guns firing solid shot (Brown 1995, 210). For the near term, therefore, the Paixhans could only be considered as special-purpose weapons. As mentioned, both the British and French navies had adopted the guns as auxiliary armaments for their ships in the late 1830s (Potter 1981, 118). At Sinop, the Russian gunners had held a technological advantage over their Ottoman opponents. What would happen if both Europeans and Asians had exactly the same artillery hardware and training?

12.3 India: Redcoat Against Redcoat

In the preceding chapter, we observed how from the second quarter of the nineteenth century, ships powered by steam allowed European military assets to be transported reliably into the distant river valleys of Asia. During the same period, European machine tools permitted the manufacture of powerful shell-firing guns that could destroy the fleets of wooden sailing warships used by Asian powers to defend their coasts. However, what would happen when non-Europeans too acquired these advanced weapons along with the skills necessary to use them?

As described in the last chapter, following the revolt of sepoys in Meerut in northern India in early May of 1857, it took over 6 months for troops from Britain sent around the Cape of Good Hope to arrive in India. Meanwhile in northern India, for most of the intervening period, a small force of Europeans was opposed by a much larger force of Indian soldiers whom the British had trained. Moreover, most of the military hardware of the rebels was identical to that of the Europeans. Accordingly, at least until British reinforcements arrived, the outcome of the struggle would be decided largely by the willingness of those within each group to cooperate with one another.

As we saw, on 10 May 1857, two Native Infantry and one Native Cavalry regiment of the East India Company rebelled at Meerut, 40 miles (64 km) northeast of Delhi. They killed some of their officers and British families and released their comrades who had been imprisoned. The following day, they arrived in Delhi, where they rallied three other sepoy regiments and seized the city, whereupon they killed any Europeans they could find (Callahan 2007, 26). The Company had allowed the last sovereign of the Mughal dynasty, 81-year-old Bahadur Shah II, to hold the title, King of Delhi, although his nominal territory was limited to the city of Delhi. However, on 13 May, the rebels proclaimed him the new Mughal emperor of the whole of India.

The previous day, 12 May 1857, Lord Charles Canning, the British Governor-General at Calcutta, had learned by telegraph of the catastrophic situation at Meerut and Delhi. Canning's first priority was to retake the fortress city of Delhi, the former Mughal capital. Delhi was now the center of the revolt and the seat of the "emperor" who represented its legitimacy in the eyes of its supporters. In theory, Canning had three armies at his disposal, namely, the 140,000 men of the Bengal Army in the north and smaller forces based in Bombay and Madras (Callahan 2007, 19). However, although most of the soldiers in the Bombay and Madras Armies remained loyal, 96 of the 123 units of the Bengal Army mutinied wholly or in part (Fremont-Barnes 2014, ch. 2). The only forces in the north on which the British administration could really count were the 40,000 British soldiers in India, most of whom were in the far northwest.

The closest British units to the crisis were the 3000 soldiers stationed at Ambala, 130 miles (209 km) north of Delhi under Major General Sir Henry Barnard, an officer who had commanded troops during the Crimean War. On 25 May, 2 weeks after the outbreak, a column of infantry and cavalry under Barnard set out for the march to Delhi (Spilsbury 2007, ch. 5). They were joined on 7 June at Alipur, 20 miles (30 km) north of Delhi, by what was left of the garrison from Meerut under Colonel Archdale Wilson, a career officer in the Indian Army.

Barnard learned that the rebels had set up a strong defensive position to block his advance at Badli-ki-Serai, a cluster of walled houses and gardens, formerly residences of Mughal court officials, six miles (10 km) northwest of the former Mughal capital. On a low ridge, the rebels had installed four heavy guns along with a number of lighter field guns and a troop of horse-drawn artillery (Spilsbury 2007, ch. 5). Barnard sent a troop of cavalry and mobile artillery to attack the rebels' left flank and another cavalry unit to attack their right. Outnumbered and outgunned, he then had little choice but to order a frontal assault on foot on the rebels' artillery position. Attacked simultaneously from three sides, the rebels' defenses collapsed. They withdrew toward Delhi leaving a thousand dead and abandoning 13 pieces of artillery (Spilsbury 2007, ch. 5).

Upon their arrival before Delhi, the British forces and their Indian employees seized a long ridge two miles (3 km) northwest of the city. Some forty feet (12 m) above the plain, it overlooked three of the ten bastions protecting the city gates, which were over 1100 yards (1 km) away at the closest point (Spilsbury 2007, ch. 5). The city was surrounded by a thick wall 24 feet (7 m) high and by a deep ditch on the sides away from the Yamuna River—a tributary of the Ganges (Fremont-Barnes 2014, ch. 4). Within the walls, the rebels initially had a force of 20,000 sepoys and 114 guns, most of them heavy 24-pounders (Spilsbury 2007, ch. 5). Against them, Barnard had 22 light field guns, 3000 British troops and one battalion of Gurkhas (Spilsbury 2007, ch. 5). For the moment, storming the city walls was out of the question.

For the next 2 months, British reinforcements continued to trickle in, but they barely made up for losses due to frequent rebel attacks and to illness. Meanwhile the rebels were continually being reinforced by units that had mutinied in outlying bases and then marched to reinforce the occupying force at Delhi. The loyalty of the newly arrived rebel troops would invariably be tested immediately by having them attack the British on the Ridge (Spilsbury 2007, ch. 5). As early as 20 June, there was a massive attack by sepoy infantry, cavalry and artillery, all wearing their British uniforms while their bands played "God Save the Queen" (Spilsbury 2007, ch. 5). On 2 July, a brigade of Indian troops arrived from Bareilly, 170 miles (272 km) east of Delhi, under Bakht Khan, 60, a noncommissioned officer with 40 years of experience in the Bengal Horse Artillery. "Emperor" Bahadur Shah II thereupon named Khan commander of the rebel army (Spilsbury 2007, ch. 5). In their second attack on 9 July, the new troops from Bareilly almost overran the Ridge before the British could regroup.

On 1 August, the Festival of the Sacrifice for Muslims, the rebels prepared again for a major assault. Frederick Roberts, an officer of the Bengal Horse Artillery, described the day's events:

> All the morning of the 1st August mosques and Hindu temples were crowded with worshippers offering up prayers for the success of the great attempt. ... Time after time they rallied and hurled themselves against our breastworks. All

that night and well into the next day the fight continued, and it was past noon before the devoted fanatics became convinced that their gods had deserted them, that victory was not for them, and that no effort, however heroic on their part could drive us from the Ridge. (Spilsbury 2007, ch. 5)

General Barnard had died of cholera on 5 July. He was succeeded as commander by Archdale Wilson who received the temporary rank of major general. Then on 14 August, just as the situation on the Ridge was becoming desperate, the British received an important reinforcement. A column of 4000 soldiers under Brigadier General John Nicholson, who had been active in combat on the northwest frontier over the previous 15 years, arrived from the Punjab (Fremont-Barnes 2014, ch. 4). Nicholson immediately took over command of the siege.

Shortly afterward, word reached the rebels that the British siege train from the Punjab was approaching with its heavy guns. On 25 August, therefore, a rebel force of 6000 under Bakht Khan, an experienced cavalry soldier, as we saw earlier, set out from Delhi to prepare to intercept the British convoy. At the serai (a walled enclosure) of Najafgarh, about 16 miles (26 km) from Delhi, the sepoy army prepared a site with 13 guns while occupying the villages to the left, right and rear.

Upon observing their departure, Nicholson too set out—with 2500 soldiers and 16 field guns, aiming to overtake the rebels. Having approached the mutineers from the rear, he led a sudden cavalry charge into the center of their defenses. The sepoy troops fled, leaving 800 dead and abandoning all of their artillery (Fremont-Barnes 2014, ch. 4).

Finally, on 4 September, the first elements of the British siege train from the Punjab began to reach the Ridge. Eight miles (13 km) long, the convoy contained 32 pieces of ordnance pulled by elephants. There were 24- and 18-pound guns along with 10- and 8- inch howitzers and mortars (Spilsbury 2007, ch. 9). The next day, the British heavy siege guns began to pound the masonry walls of the fortress city. There were soon breaches that the defenders were unable to repair despite their frenzied overnight efforts. With the rebels continually being reinforced but with little more help to be expected by the British in the short term, there could be no more favorable moment to storm the city's defenses.

Early on the morning of 14 September, five columns of British and Indian troops with ladders attacked the breaches and succeeded in entering the city. They had been given orders to take no prisoners (Fremont-Barnes 2014, ch. 4). There followed almost a week of deadly street fighting before the last rebel pockets were eliminated. On 21 September, the king, Bahadur Khan II, was forced to surrender. Enemy fire during the long siege had cost the lives of 1000 of the attacking soldiers. About half of them were British, including General John Nicholson. In addition, many others, like General Henry Barnard, had died from cholera, dysentery and heat stroke (Fremont-Barnes 2014, ch. 4). There is no accurate estimate of the total number of civilians and rebel troops who lost their lives during the siege.

The siege of Delhi was the key event during the Indian Rebellion. Once Delhi had fallen, British troops could be released to retake the other centers that been seized by the rebels. Meanwhile, as we saw in the last chapter, the Empire was concentrating its forces to assure that once defeated, the rebels would be incapable of rising again.

Why did the rebellion fail? At Delhi, the rebels had numerous advantages over the besiegers. They had a well-supplied base, many more trained soldiers and considerably more of the best weapons that the technology of the day had to offer. Nevertheless, the insurgents lost the key field battles at Badli-ki-Serai and Najafgarh. Moreover, despite their greater numbers and heavier weapons, they were unable to overcome the defenses on the Ridge during the hot summer months before the British siege train's arrival.

The consensus among military historians is that the rebels suffered primarily from problems of command and control (Callahan 2007, 27). The sepoys were accustomed to following the orders of their trained British officers. It was not simply a question of knowledge of battlefield tactics. With their access to the telegraph for communication and their monopoly of shipping, the British could operate on external lines, bringing whatever force was necessary to defeat a given concentration of rebels.

There was, however, another factor that may well have been pertinent in explaining the outcome of the Delhi siege, namely, language standardization and its effect on people's willingness to cooperate with one another. It is striking that even under the most desperate conditions of the siege, the morale of the British held up, while in one example after another, once the sepoys saw the tide turning against them, they preferred to withdraw. One element of the language question is literacy. While the British officers and most of the British soldiers were literate, the male literacy rate in India in the mid-nineteenth century was probably under ten percent (Aggarwal 2002, 3). If literacy enables people better to empathize with one another as Pinker (2011, ch. 4) has argued, it alone would encourage cooperation. Accordingly, the British soldiers at Delhi would have been more willing to collaborate with one another than the north-Indian sepoys of the Bengal Army opposite them.

A second consideration is language standardization. The British troops communicated orally among themselves in an English vernacular that was now standardized. Under the extreme conditions that they experienced on the Ridge, the British troops undoubtedly felt that they belonged to the same community and were willing to cooperate fully with one another. In contrast, the sepoys of northern India lived a diglossic society. As children, all had learned the dialects of their villages. However, in order to speak with their fellow soldiers who came from other areas, they were obliged to speak "military Hindustani", the camp language of Indian military bases since the late Mughal Empire (Green 2012, 143). As a result, in the terminology of Benedict Anderson (2006), it is quite likely that many rebels considered sepoys from other regions as coming from beyond the boundaries of their "imagined community" and not fully trustworthy.

As we shall see in the next chapter, there was still another factor that contributed to the eventual defeat of the sepoys, namely, their choice of infantry small arms. First, however, we must return to China during the final year of the Second Opium War. We have seen that the Paixhans gun was effective as an auxiliary naval weapon against ships with wooden hulls. However, against the ironclad ships that began to be introduced in the late 1850s, it was much less effective. As yet, there was no replacement for the smoothbore muzzle-loaded cannon.

12.4 China: If at First You Don't Succeed

When war broke out between Russia and the Ottoman Empire in October 1853, Western armies were still using artillery weapons that dated from the Napoleonic Wars. It would take a major military setback to stimulate research into new ways to fire heavy projectiles through the air. As the second year of the Crimean War began in the fall of 1854, French and British forces were attempting to aid the Ottoman Empire against its traditional Russian enemy in territory on the eastern shores of the Black Sea. Their objective was the Russian port of Sevastopol on the western Crimean Peninsula. At the Battle of Inkerman on 5 November 1854, a British army was advancing through the hills of the Crimea toward Sevastopol when it suddenly found itself under a surprise Russian attack. Lacking horses, some 150 British soldiers labored for 3 hours to haul two heavy guns through thick mud into position. During the operation, inadequately protected from Russian artillery, the British force suffered 2500 casualties (Heald 2012, 84).

As we have seen, the technology for field guns had developed little since the reforms of Liechtenstein and Gribeauval that had standardized Austrian and French gun and munition sizes over a half century earlier. Indeed armies across Eurasia were still using muzzle-loading smoothbore cannon cast from bronze or iron that fired spherical solid shot, just as the French had done 400 years earlier, during the last years of the Hundred Years' War. The disadvantages of the existing technology were well known. To achieve any degree of accuracy, the cannon had to be fired at close range—under a kilometer. Moreover loading from the muzzle was both slow and dangerous for the gun crew.

Artillery weapons were particularly primitive when compared to small arms. With the improved machine tools of recent decades, rifling had been introduced for muskets, as we shall see in the next chapter. Grooves in the barrels caused the conoidal or cylindrical bullets to spin on leaving the barrel, thereby stabilizing their flight and increasing their range. However, these individual firearms were still loaded from the muzzle and consequently had a low rate of fire. There existed breech-loading small arms such as the 1819 Hall rifle that had a more rapid rate of fire, but these suffered from the problem of obturation—the leakage of gas around the breech that reduced the rifle's range and power. As yet, the lack of precision of large machine tools had prevented the application of either rifling or breech loading to artillery.

William Armstrong, 43, was a Newcastle lawyer and amateur engineer who had set up a successful engineering firm to build bridges and hydraulic cranes. Upon learning of the debacle of British artillery at Inkerman, Armstrong sat down with his friend James Rendel, a native of Devonshire and chief civil engineer of the Royal Navy, to design a lighter, more mobile field gun. Ideally, it would offer the desirable rapid-firing features of a breech-loading rifle. To reduce the weight and permit the use of rifling, the gun would be made of wrought iron and would fire cylindrical shells (Heald 2012, 85).

In pitching his concept to the British War Department, Armstrong emphasized that because of its rifling the gun would be more accurate and would have a longer range than current artillery pieces of the same caliber. The gun would have a steel core, enveloped in wrought iron cylinders that were successively shrunk one over the other to strengthen the cylinder. The shell and propellant would be loaded into the rear of the barrel, which would then be closed by a sliding breech. The breech itself would be locked into place by the turning of a screw cover.

In order to keep the project secret, the precision machine rifling of the prototype's core was done at night with only Armstrong and a skilled machinist present. The first trials in the summer of 1856 demonstrated that a version of the gun firing a 5-pound bullet had unprecedented range, accuracy and destructive force (Heald 2012, 89). Two years later, an 18-pound version of the gun that fired cylindrical explosive shells was tested against a conventional cannon that fired 32-pound solid shot. Two targets were set at distances of 2000 and 3000 yards (1800 and 2700 m), respectively. The cast-iron gun was unable to hit either of the targets. However, in 22 rounds, the Armstrong gun made 397 holes in the target at 2000 yards, and in ten rounds, it made 180 holes in the target at 3000 yards (Heald 2012, 91). Upon the recommendation of the committee that had carried out these tests, the British War Office ordered 100 of the guns, to be built at Armstrong's Newcastle factory. Armstrong was appointed to a new position as Engineer of Rifled Ordinance. In return, he ceded his patents for the gun to the government (Heald 2012, 102).

It will be remembered from Chap. 11 that in 1859, a modest Anglo-French force attempting to implement the Treaty of Tianjin of the preceding year had been unable to overcome the defenses of the Taku Forts that blocked river access to Beijing. As a result of this humiliation, the fragile minority Conservative government of Lord Derby had fallen and was replaced by a much more militant Liberal government headed by Lord Palmerston (Hanes and Sanello 2002, 234). By the following year, the military situation in India after the Rebellion of 1857–1858 had been sufficiently stabilized to allow British troops there to be released for a third attempt to reach the Chinese capital.

Accordingly, a force of 41 warships carrying 18,000 British and French troops under the joint command of Sir Hope Grant and his French counterpart, Charles Cousin-Montauban, set out for the Far East. In August 1860, they arrived at the mouth of the Hai River, the body of water connecting Beijing and Tianjin to the Yellow Sea (Worthing 2007, 44). The expedition had been joined by a diplomatic mission under Lord Elgin, the former Governor-General of Canada, who in 1857 had been appointed High Commissioner and Plenipotentiary in China and the Far East. Instead of trying to force the river passage past the Taku Forts, the allies landed troops on the shore, ten miles to the north (Porter 1889, 511). The British and French forces then advanced on foot toward the river and proceeded to set up five artillery batteries in range of the larger of the two northern forts. Four of the batteries consisted of conventional muzzle-loading smoothbore

Fig. 12.1 Interior of the Taku North Fort immediately after its capture, 1860. The explosive shells fired by British 12-pound Armstrong guns proved deadly for the fort's Chinese defenders (Reproduced from Wikipedia Commons)

guns, while the fifth comprised six deadly 12-pound Armstrong rifled breechloaders (Porter 1889, 512).

After 4 hours of British and French bombardment on the morning of 21 August, the artillery in the Chinese fort was finally silenced. The French and British assault columns then approached the fort with ladders to scale the walls. After fierce struggles with the defenders, the attacking forces reached the parapets and overcame the last opposition. Pastor Robert M'Gee described the scene inside the fort when the British observers arrived (see Fig. 12.1):

> Inside the work was a scene no pen can describe; fifteen corpses lay stretched in every variety of ghastly attitude round one gun; the men had clearly been working the gun by threes and by threes that fearful Armstrong gun sent them

to their account; it was indeed an awful sight; limbs blown away, bodies literally burst asunder, one black and lived (sic) mass of blood and wounds;... the same scene was repeated at every gun. (M'Ghee 1862, 114)

The other three forts then surrendered without resistance. In subsequent negotiations, the Chinese yielded the defensive posts on the river, along with the town of Tianjin (Porter 1889, 513). The way was clear for the allied force to advance toward Beijing, where a Chinese army three times their size was awaiting their arrival.

12.5   From Conquest to Control

By the end of the Crimean War in 1856, Britain and France had assumed joint custody of the crumbling Ottoman Empire. Two years later, Britain had added all of present-day India, Pakistan and Bangladesh to its territory when it converted the East India Company's territory into a crown colony. As for China, in August 1860 the two divisions of a European expedition had been able to overcome the local units defending the Taku Forts blocking access by water to Beijing. However, how could such a small force hope to defeat the field armies of a state with a population of over 350 million (Maddison 2007, 376)? More generally, how could some 60 million British and French possibly ever permanently dominate three Asian empires that together outnumbered them by 10–1?

As the American army learned in Vietnam, control of territory inevitably involves soldiers on the ground fighting other soldiers on the ground. The question then becomes one of the relative killing power of the weapons in the hands of the troops on each side. In their favor, the Europeans by 1860 had the advantage of individual firearms of unprecedented range and rapidity of fire. Moreover, these rifles were the first modern industrial products, mass-produced with interchangeable parts.

Note

1. Note that the distance separating the two lines of ships was over three times that at the Battle of Salona Bay, where Hastings had used a similar strategy, also firing shells with a flat trajectory.

References

Aggarwal, D. D. (2002). *History and development of elementary education in India* (Vol. 1). New Delhi: Sarap and Sons.

Anderson, B. (2006). *Imagined communities: Reflections on the origin and spread of nationalism* (Revised ed.). London: Verso.

Badem, C. (2010). *The Ottoman Crimean War: (1853–1856)*. Boston: Brill.

Brown, D. K. (1995). Wood, sails and cannonballs to steel, steam and shells. In J. R. Hill & B. Ranft (Eds.), *The Oxford illustrated history of the Royal Navy* (pp. 200–226). Oxford: Oxford University Press.

Callahan, R. (2007). The great sepoy mutiny. In D. P. Marston & C. S. Sundaram (Eds.), *A military history of India and South Asia from the East India Company to the nuclear era* (pp. 16–33). Bloomington: Indiana University Press.

Chartrand, R. (2003). *Napoleon's guns 1792–1815 (1)*. Oxford: Osprey Publishing.

Clodfelter, M. (2008). *Warfare and armed conflicts: A statistical reference to casualty and other figures, 1500–2000.* Jefferson: McFarland.

Fremont-Barnes, G. (2014). *Osprey guide to the Indian mutiny 1857–58.* Oxford: Osprey Publishing.

Green, N. (2012). *Islam and the army in colonial India: Sepoy religion in the service of empire.* Cambridge, UK: Cambridge University Press.

Hanes, W. T., & Sanello, F. (2002). *Opium wars: The addiction of one empire and the corruption of another.* Naperville: Sourcebooks.

Heald, H. (2012). *William Armstrong: Magician of the North.* Alnwick: McNidder and Grace.

Hogg, O. F. (1970). *Artillery: Its origin, heyday and decline.* Hamden: Archon Books.

M'Ghee, R. (1862). *How we got to Pekin: A narrative of the campaign in China of 1860.* London: Richard Bentley.

Maddison, A. (2007). *Contours of the world economy, 1-2030 AD: Essays in macro-economic history.* Oxford: Oxford University Press.

Özcan, B. (2012). 1853–1856 Ottoman-Russian war and Egypt state. *Ekev Akademi Dergisi, 16*(51), 45–59.

Pinker, S. (2011). *The better angels of our nature: Why violence has declined.* New York: Viking Penguin.

Potter, E. B. (1981). *Sea power: A naval history.* Annapolis: Naval Institute Press.

Small, H. (2011). *The Crimean War: Victoria's war with the Russian Tsars.* Slough: Tempus Publishing.

Spilsbury, J. (2007). *The Indian mutiny.* London: Weidenfeld & Nicolson.

Taillemite, É. (2005). *Henri-Joseph Paixhans et sa nouvelle force maritime.* Retrieved June 17, 2014, from Institut de stratégie comparée. http://www.institut-strategie.fr/PN4_TAILLEMITE.html

Worthing, P. (2007). *A military history of modern China: From the Manchu conquest to Tian'anmen Square.* Westport: Praeger.

CHAPTER 13

Mass-Produced Firearms

13.1 The Marginal Cost of Victory

By the mid-nineteenth century, Western armies were generally able to defeat those of Asia, whether the forces of the Ottoman Empire, those of the independent Indian states or those of the Qing dynasty. However, the increasing cost of doing so was threatening the economic advantages of empire. It was true that ocean-going steamships could transport European soldiers to the far coasts of Asia, while shallow-draft steamboats could carry them upriver into the interior of the continent. Moreover, the artillery defenses of the Asian opponents, whether on ships or on land were no match for the latest rifled cannon developed in the West. Nevertheless, could small European expeditionary forces hope to defeat the huge field armies that the Asian empires could muster at a cost that was acceptable to their governments back home? If the technology of the West's individual firearms failed to improve, it was only a question of time until the Asians, properly equipped and trained, could win by weight of numbers.

For two centuries prior to the end of the Napoleonic Wars in 1815, the powder in an infantryman's flintlock musket had been ignited by a spark generated when a piece of flint hit the iron of the gun's firing pan. The main disadvantage of this mechanism was that if the flint were dull or the powder in the firing pan wet, the gun would not fire. However, with the new machine tools available in the second quarter of the nineteenth century, it became possible to improve the common flintlock. By the 1840s, the latest muskets were fired by a percussion cap inserted into the breech of the gun.

© The Author(s) 2017
L. Dudley, *The Singularity of Western Innovation*,
DOI 10.1057/978-1-137-39822-2_13

Pulling the trigger released a metal hammer that struck the metal cap. The blow caused the primer in the cap, a compound such as fulminate of mercury, to explode and ignite the gunpowder that had been rammed down the barrel, thereby expelling an accompanying spherical metal projectile (Smithurst 2011, ch. 1). As a result, muzzle-loading muskets could now be fired reliably even in wet weather.

Yet the principal shortcoming of the muzzle-loading smoothbore musket remained. Even as close as 100 yards, infantrymen using such a weapon could hit a target 10 feet by 10 feet (3 m by 3 m) on average with fewer than 45 percent of their shots. In contrast, a rifle at 100 yards had a rate of accuracy of over 95 percent (Fuller 1958, 53 ff). The explanation is that the spinning caused by the rifling stabilized the bullet, preventing the friction due to tumbling and causing the projectile to travel farther and more accurately. However, the elongated lead rifle bullet had to be of a diameter only slightly smaller than the barrel. Because of the resulting difficulty of ramming the shot down the barrel, a conventional rifle's rate of fire was considerably less than that of a smoothbore.

The challenge was to devise a projectile that would engage the spiraled grooves of the rifle but could be loaded quickly from the muzzle. In 1844, Captain Claude Étienne Minié of the French Chasseurs designed a projectile that could easily be pushed down a rifle barrel. When the gun was fired, the explosion caused the base of the bullet to expand, fitting into the rifling grooves (Smithurst 2011, ch. 1). In 1851, the British Army decided to replace its smoothbore "Brown Bess" musket by a Minié rifle with a large bore of 0.702 inch (18 mm). The new rifle used the original Minié bullet—a cone with an indentation in its base. However when fired, the conoidal projectile generally left the barrel canted to one side (Smithurst 2011, ch. 2). Consequently, the heavy Minié rifle was less accurate and had a shorter range than lighter traditional rifles, although it could be fired more rapidly (Williams and Johnson 2001, 323).

In 1852, the British Army carried out tests of a new set of rifles submitted by private gunmakers. The goal was to find an effective rifle that would allow the soldier to carry 60 rounds of ammunition without fatigue (Williams and Johnson 2001, 323). The result of the selection process was the Pattern 1853 Enfield, which had a 0.577 inch (15 mm) bore, rather than the larger diameter of the Minié and weighed 12 percent less (Smithurst 2011, ch. 2). For the new Enfield rifle, London gunmaker Robert Pritchett designed a cylindro-conoidal bullet—that is, a cylinder with a rounded nose (Smithurst 2011, ch. 2). Like the Minié bullet, Pritchett's design had a hollow base that expanded upon firing so that it fitted into the rifling grooves. However, since the axis of the bullet was identical to that of the barrel, the new rifle was more accurate than the Minié or, of course, the smoothbore "Brown Bess" that it replaced. Equally important was the new weapon's greater range. The smoothbore was ineffective at a distance of over 300 yards, whereas the Enfield (like the Minié) could kill a man at a distance of 600 yards (550 m) (Small 2011, ch. 4).

13.2 The Crimean War

With the new developments in firearms, it became essential that infantry officers and their troops be willing to adapt readily to new tactics and procedures. However, in the Ottoman army of the mid-1820s, the Janissaries had become little more than a powerful group of rentiers living off the regime's fiscal surplus and unwilling to change their ways. Of some 140,000 on the government payroll, only about 10,000 were on duty in Istanbul (Aksan 2007, 303). On the battlefield in Greece, the sultan's "rag-tag army" formed a marked contrast to the disciplined troops of his Egyptian viceroy, Muhammad Ali (Aksan 2007, 299). Moreover, within Istanbul society, the Janissaries were a disruptive force, an obstacle to any attempt at political or military reform.

The current Ottoman ruler, Mahmud II (r. 1808–1839) was a cousin of Selim III, the reformist sultan who had been assassinated during the Janissary revolt of 1808. Selim's immediate successor was another cousin, Mustafa IV, who with the support of the Janissaries had ordered the execution of both Selim III and Mahmud II, who was his own younger half-brother. However, Mahmud II's mother had hidden him until loyalist troops could arrive and overthrow Mustafa IV.

By 1826, Mahmud II was well aware of the need for military reform. For several years, he had carefully placed officials loyal to himself in key positions (Aksan 2007, 298). Then in late May, he took advantage of an initial set of Ottoman victories over Greek rebels to propose a modest reform of the Janissary Corps. Chosen soldiers from existing units would be grouped into 51 new companies to be trained by European methods. In what is known as the Auspicious Incident, dissident Janissaries then revolted, as the government expected. The Sultan reacted vigorously, using loyal artillery, armorer and other specialized corps for a bloody suppression of all resistance. The Janissaries and affiliated units were completely disbanded, the rebel leaders executed and loyal soldiers incorporated into new units (Neumann 2006, 60).

Additional infantry troops were recruited by conscription from the urban unemployed and grouped into new regiments structured on the European model. Yet Ottoman officers continued to train troops using pre-Napoleonic methods (Uyar and Erickson 2009, 49). In addition, much Ottoman equipment was by now inferior to that of the major European nations. Since the fifteenth century, there had been within the Ottoman army a corps of armorers (Cebecis) whose main responsibility was to manufacture and repair weapons, including both artillery and muskets. Until the eighteenth century, Ottoman artisans had generally been able to keep up with the slow evolution of smoothbore musket and artillery technology. However, by the nineteenth century, the Ottoman arms industry had fallen far behind technologically. In 1826, Mahmud II was obliged to import 50,000 Belgian muskets to equip his new infantry units (Aksan 2007, 299). These technological shortcomings became glaringly evident during the Russo-Turkish War that followed, in 1828–1829.

In retaliation for Russian participation in the disastrous—for the Ottoman navy—Battle of Navarino, Mahmud II in late 1827 decided to close the Dardanelles to shipping and declare war on Russia. During the campaign of 1828, the Turkish defenses were successful in blocking Russian attacks. However, in the following year, Russian armies in the Balkans and the Caucasus inflicted a series of humiliating defeats on Ottoman forces. One of the keys to Russian success was the "devastating superiority" of its field artillery (Uyar and Erickson 2009, 137–139). The War of 1828–1829 also demonstrated the weakness of the Ottoman officer corps. For example, at the outset of the Balkan campaign, the Ottoman commanders in the West made no attempt to prevent the Russians from crossing the Danube River barrier (Uyar and Erickson 2009, 136). The Treaty of Adrianople (Edirne) of 1829 confirmed Russian territorial gains in the Balkans and the Caucasus and also granted autonomy to Serbia and Greece.

In the last years of his reign, Mahmud II realized the need to integrate better the various groups within Ottoman society. Although he himself died from tuberculosis in July 1839, his son and successor Abdülmecid I (r. 1839–1861) continued his reforms. Under the Edict of Gülhane that the new sultan issued in November 1839, tax farming was to be ended, conscription reorganized and the basic rights of all citizens guaranteed regardless of religion (Aksan 2007, 386). Though unrealizable in 1839, the decree marked the beginning of a period of reform known as the

Tanzimat (Reorganization) that would continue until the issue of the first Ottoman constitution in 1876.

One of the principal results of these reforms was the beginning of modern education, both civilian and military, in Turkey. In 1834 Mahmud II had established the Turkish Military Academy, an institution for training army officers modeled on the École Spéciale Militaire de Saint-Cyr founded by Napoleon in 1802 (Uyar and Erickson 2009, 147–148). Military preparatory schools were now set up at each of the Ottoman army's regional headquarters to educate pupils for enrolment in the Istanbul academy—a modest beginning of secular education (Aksan 2007, 396). In 1846, the regime also enacted a new conscription law that called for 30,000 young men to be chosen annually by random draw for a 5-year term of service (Aksan 2007, 394).

By 1853, the Empire had an army of almost a half million men, made up of 123,000 Nizamiye (regular soldiers), the rest being reservists (Redif), that is, irregular troops along with units from North Africa. Despite the education reforms, however, there were not enough trained officers for the Nizam units. Even worse, there were virtually no educated commanders for the Redif sections. Nevertheless, the Ottoman regime was able to field 12 elite Nizam battalions (Şişhaneci) equipped with Minié-type rifles (Uyar and Erickson 2009, 160).

The first major test of the new type of warfare with rifled firearms came with the Crimean War of 1853–1856. In the spring of 1853, as we saw in Chap. 12, Tsar Nicholas I threatened the Ottoman sultan with invasion if he did not accept a new treaty extending the rights of the Orthodox Church in Ottoman territory. When Abdülmecid I rejected Russia's demands, Russian troops were duly sent to occupy Wallachia and Moldavia (modern Rumania). Russia's subsequent refusal to withdraw its troops from these provinces led the Ottoman government to declare war in October 1853.

The Ottoman strategy in the war that followed was to defend its territories south of the Danube valley, while attacking aggressively on the Caucasian front to the east (Uyar and Erickson 2009, 160). Nevertheless, the Sultan and his advisors assigned the best imperial guard divisions to the West, where they were surprisingly successful in blocking the major Russian offensives. However, in the east, the bulk of the Ottoman army was made up of Başıbozuk (irregular cavalry) and tribal levies. Russian armies rolled over this weak Ottoman opposition. One bright note for the Ottomans on the eastern front during the summer and fall of 1855 was the success of their troops defending the east-Anatolian fortress city of Kars. Using their Minié rifles, these units were able to repel repeated Russian attacks (Uyar and Erickson 2009, 160). Nevertheless, when relief attempts failed, the decimated garrison was finally obliged to surrender on 27 November (Badem 2010, 255).

The primary interest of the Ottoman regime's allies, Britain and France, in entering the war was to weaken the Russian naval presence in the Black Sea. Accordingly, their key objective was the heavily fortified naval base of Sevastopol on the southwest coast of the Crimean peninsula. After declaring war on Russia, the Western allies landed troops at the port of Eupatoria (Yevpatoria) some 70 miles (115 km) north of the Russian fortress on 14 September 1854 and began to advance toward the south.

The approach to Sebastopol was defended by 36,000 Russians in a heavily fortified position atop a steep hill overlooking the Alma River, half way between Eupatoria and Sevastopol (Smithurst 2011, ch. 3). On the morning of 20 September, the Russian artillery thus had the advantage of height over the guns of the Allies along with a precipitous incline to protect it from British and French cavalry. As for the infantry threat, in battles over the three previous centuries, artillery had had little to fear from soldiers on foot. Cannon firing grapeshot consisting of small metal balls packed into a canvas bag—the artillery equivalent of a shotgun shell—could easily break up an infantry attack. Although the range of grapeshot was only a few hundred yards, this distance was beyond the range of the smoothbore muskets used by foot soldiers (Small 2011, ch. 4).

Using solid shot and grapeshot, the Russian artillery decimated the first wave of charging British attackers. However, the second British wave hesitated and began firing their Enfield rifles at long range, disregarding their commander who had ordered, "Don't pull a trigger till you're within a yard of the Russians." The effect of this distant rifle fire on Russian infantry and artillery was deadly, forcing the defenders to withdraw. In all, the Russians lost 1800 soldiers, compared to only 500 for the British and French (Small 2011, ch. 4).

The road to Sevastopol was open. However, because of a delay in following up the victory at the Alma, the Allies were forced to settle in for a long siege. Over the following months, climate and sanitary conditions would claim many more lives than did enemy shells and bullets. Moreover, the Russians were by no means ready to accept defeat. On 25 October, a large Russian force attacked the principal British supply port at Balaclava on a bay 11 miles (17 km) south of Sevastopol. The Ottoman regime had been obliged to contribute one division to the Allies' Crimean campaign.

Ottoman soldiers in redoubts around the Balaclava base armed only with Minié rifles held off the Russian artillery and infantry until British reinforcements could arrive from the site of the siege (Badem 2010, 272). A Russian cavalry charge was then met by the 93rd (Sutherland) Highlanders in line formation, two deep, rather than in a square. At distances of 600 and 150 yards, successive British rifle volleys by the "Thin Red Line", were able to break the Russian attack (Small 2011, ch. 5). The Russian cavalry was obliged to withdraw after heavy losses.

The Siege of Sevastopol itself lasted for another 10 months, until the main bastion of the fortress finally fell to a French assault in August 1855. With heavy ongoing costs and little chance that a clear winner would emerge, all parties finally agreed to stop the carnage. By the Treaty of Paris of March 1856, conquered territories were returned to their original possessors. However, Russia was forbidden, at least for the time being, to establish a naval presence in the Black Sea.

Nevertheless, the Crimean War marked a watershed in the history of the Ottoman Empire. For first time in three centuries, the Ottoman military, now reorganized along Western lines, had been able to inflict numerous defeats on a modern European army. However, virtually every piece of military equipment used by the Ottoman forces—including percussion muskets and Minié rifles from Belgium and France—had been imported (Uyar and Erickson 2009, 170). In addition, it was the fall of Sevastopol to the British and French rather than defeat at the hand of Ottoman armies that had forced the Russians to come to terms. For the final decades of its long life, the Ottoman Empire would depend for its survival not only on the valor of its troops but also on the self-interest of the Great Powers in preserving a nominally autonomous presence on the Bosporus.

One of the consequences of Ottoman territorial losses in the earlier Russo-Turkish Wars and in the War of Greek Independence, combined with Egypt's obtaining virtual autonomy, had been a de facto ethnic cleansing of the Ottoman Empire. Migration after the resulting treaties accentuated this process. By 1850, the relative importance of speakers of Turkish dialects within the empire had risen considerably compared to the situation a century earlier. Since Christians and Jews had always been exempted from military service in exchange for payment of the cizye, the army now reflected better the ethnic composition of the empire as a whole. The establishment of the Military Academy and a system of conscription for the Muslim population also increased the homogeneity of the Ottoman army, reducing its dependence on provincial irregular units. It is not surprising that, at least on the Balkan front, the empire's regular army units for the first time in a century had been able to compete successfully with European troops.

13.3 The Indian Rebellion of 1857

We have seen that the Pattern 1853 Enfield with its rifled barrel and cylindrical-conoidal bullets formed part of a revolution in the technology of infantry warfare. Equally as interesting as the story of the design of this weapon is the history of its manufacture.

The first orders for the different components of the Pattern 1853 Enfield were placed with private gunsmiths in Birmingham in 1853. The parts were then sent to London in order to be shipped to a second group of contractors for assembly (Smithurst 2011, ch. 4). However by 1854, under this traditional "workshop system", the Board of Ordnance was having difficulty in obtaining sufficient quantities of the new rifle for the thousands of soldiers being sent to fight in the Crimea. The Board therefore searched for ways to step up the rate of production (Hounshell 1984, 17). One solution was to enter into agreements with foreign arms-makers. Accordingly, during the Crimean conflict, contracts were awarded to firms in the United States, Belgium and France (Williams 2014, 41).

An alternative way of speeding up the production process had been suggested by an exhibit at the World's Fair held at the Crystal Palace in London, in 1851. An American manufacturer named Samuel Colt had displayed a number of different revolvers that had been made by machine at his factory in Hartford, Connecticut. He had then proceeded to build a second small-arms factory in London on the Thames that began production in 1853. In its 1854 report, the British Board of Ordnance noted that Colt employed the same machine-based manufacturing procedures that were used by the United States federal armories at Springfield and Harpers Ferry, each of which produced 30,000 muskets a year. In order to manufacture muskets cheaply and rapidly in Britain, the Board recommended that the government establish a state-owned small-arms factory modeled on the two American armories (Hounshell 1984, 18).

Later in the year of 1854, a select committee of the British Parliament held hearings to consider the Board of Ordnance report. It heard evidence from Colt along with testimony from British engineers who had visited the American arms factories. It soon became clear to the committee that at the heart of what was to become known as the "American System of Production" were two principles. First, each operation was assigned to a separate machine. As a result, there was no need continually to reset a single machine to make different parts. Second, a set of gauges was used to verify the size and shape of the manufactured parts. In this way, skilled artisans who had undergone a long and costly apprenticeship could be replaced by specialized machines operated by semi-skilled workers with a minimum of training. At the committee's recommendation, the Royal Small Arms Factory at Enfield in North London was enlarged and equipped with machinery imported from the United States. The first British rifles with interchangeable parts were produced there, beginning in 1857 (Smithurst 2011, ch. 4).

In early 1857, the Bengal Army of the East India Company was beginning to train its sepoy troops for the Enfield rifles that were arriving from Britain. It will be remembered that the Enfield used a paper cartridge that contained both gunpowder and a cylindrical-conoidal projectile. The soldier was instructed to bite the cartridge open, pour the powder into the barrel and then, using a ramrod, push the rest of the cartridge down the barrel. To ease its entry into the barrel, the cartridge was coated with tallow. In February, although no cartridges had yet been issued, a rumor circulated among the sepoys of the Bengal Army that the lubricant contained fat from both cows and pigs, the former an abomination to Hindus and the latter unacceptable to Muslims (Callahan 2007, 24).

Lieutenant Colonel George Carmichael-Smyth was the commander of the Third Bengal Light Cavalry, a unit with a large number of Hindus, stationed at Meerut, 45 miles (72 km) north of Delhi. The previous year, the surrounding province of Oudh had been integrated into the Company's territory. As a result, there was discontent among the sepoys, since they and their families no longer had exclusive access to the British justice system, formerly a source of power and prestige in the local society (Spilsbury 2007, ch. 1). On 24 April 1857, in order to demonstrate how to load the new rifles that were to be issued to them, Carmichael-Smyth ordered 90 of his men to tear with their fingers, rather than bite, cartridges for their old smoothbore weapons. All but five men refused. For disobeying an order, the 85 men were court-martialed and sentenced to 10 years of prison. Two weeks after the incident, on Saturday 9 May under a blistering sun, Carmichael-Smyth had them stripped of their uniforms and shackled before the entire garrison (Callahan 2007, 26).

The next day was Sunday. While a British infantry battalion was assembling for the evening church parade, a rumor circulated among the sepoys that the units of Indian troops were going to be attacked and disbanded. The Third Cavalry Regiment and two Native Infantry regiments rose up, shooting their officers, releasing the prisoners, setting their huts on fire and killing any Europeans they could find. Some 50 European men, women and children lost their lives. In addition, many Indian Christians and other Indians viewed as having profited from the British presence were slaughtered (Spilsbury 2007, ch. 2). However, most of the British residents were able to find safety in the protection of a British infantry regiment, the 60th Rifles, and the European-recruited Bengal Horse Artillery (Spilsbury 2007, ch. 2). It should be noted that many British officers, especially those most popular with their troops, were spared, and that some British women and their children were escorted to the European lines by their Indian servants (Spilsbury 2007, ch. 2).

During the night, the mutinous sepoys marched off to the protection of the walls of Delhi, where no British troops were stationed. Meanwhile, the British commander back in Meerut, General William Hewitt, 67 years of age, overweight and well past his prime, refused to allow his cavalry units to overtake the rebels, arguing that they would likely disperse to their homes (Spilsbury 2007, ch. 2). However, the revolt spread rapidly across northern India. Garrison commanders who waited too long before disarming their sepoys suffered the same fate as Hewitt, seeing their local troops rise up, murder Europeans and pillage the towns under their protection. In the preceding chapter, we saw how the British with great difficulty managed to retake Delhi.

One of the other centers touched by the rebellion was Lucknow, located 310 miles (500 km) southeast of Delhi on the west bank of the River Gomti, a tributary of the Ganges. The city was the capital of the province of Oudh, a region that the British had seized from its nawab a year earlier. The new foreign rulers had disbanded the nawab's 200,000 soldiers and forbidden all private armies. There were thus tens of thousands of unemployed warriors in the city and its environs who blamed the British for their fate. At Lucknow on 3 May, a week before the uprising at Meerut, Chief Commissioner Sir Henry Lawrence had disbanded a unit of discontented sepoy irregulars (Spilsbury 2007, ch. 8). When news of the revolt reached him on 16 May, he began to fortify the Residency, a short distance from the river bank, and to stock provisions (Fremont-Barnes 2014, ch. 4). A week later, he gathered the city's Europeans within the Residency walls. Meanwhile across the province, the rebels were capturing outlying British outposts one after the other and killing their European populations.

There was a single British regiment, the 32nd Foot, stationed in Lucknow (Fremont-Barnes 2014, ch. 4). In all, Lawrence had at his command a garrison of 1000 British, 700 Indians and 150 volunteers. In addition, he had 1300 noncombatants to take care of (Fremont-Barnes 2014, ch. 4). On 30 May he used his British troops to drive from the city one Indian cavalry regiment, three Indian infantry regiments and a battery of artillery who, he learned, were about to mutiny (Fremont-Barnes 2014, ch. 4). Over the next month, the situation in Lucknow remained relatively calm. However on 27 June, rebels under Nana Sahib, son of the last Marathi peshwa, captured the British base at nearby Cawnpore on the Ganges and massacred its garrison, despite having granted it a safe-conduct. The European women and children seized in Cawnpore were later slaughtered before a British relief force could arrive to retake the city.

On 29 June, learning that the rebels were assembling north of Lucknow, Lawrence made the error of leaving the relative safety of the residency with a small force before determining the enemy's strength. He found himself outnumbered 10–1 by mutineer units who were dressed identically to his own troops. In the ensuing battle, Lawrence lost almost half of his men and his guns before retreating to the Residency. There followed several days of pillaging of the city.

The siege of the Residency began in earnest on 1 July. For the following two and one-half months, there was almost continuous bombardment by the rebel artillerists who, taught by the British, showed considerable skill (Spilsbury 2007, ch. 8). On 2 July, Lawrence himself was fatally wounded by an exploding shell. Military command then passed to Lieutenant Colonel John Inglis, commander of the 32nd Foot, who had served in Lower Canada during the 1837 rebellion.

The Pattern 1853 Enfield had been the factor that triggered the 1857 rebellion. It now played a not inconsiderable role in its conclusion. The rifles of Inglis's outnumbered troops enabled them to repel the first major attack on the compound on 20 July. L. E. R. Rees wrote:

> They were mowed down by our grape in scores; and as their leaders advanced, shouting and encouraging their men, they were picked off by our rifles and muskets ... I saw the men still advancing, but evidently not so boldly as before. I picked off a few of them, and then a strange feeling of joy came over me. I no longer thought of myself, but only of the numbers I could kill. (Spilsbury 2007, ch. 8)

Although the defenders were able to repel subsequent attempts to storm their walls, conditions deteriorated within the compound. By the siege's end, as many people had died from dysentery, cholera and smallpox as from enemy fire (Fremont-Barnes 2014, ch. 4).

At last, on 19 September, a relief force of over 3000 under Sir Henry Havelock and Sir James Outram set out from Cawnpore, 55 miles (90 km) southwest of Lucknow on the Ganges. It managed to reach the Residency, but it had suffered over 500 casualties. Outram decided that, slowed by women and children, his force was not strong enough to fight its way back. His troops therefore reinforced the garrison and set about enlarging its perimeter while awaiting a second relief column (Spilsbury 2007, ch. 8).

It took a month and a half to assemble a new relief force of sufficient strength to break through to Lucknow. On 9 November, Colin Campbell, the new Commander-in-Chief in India, left Cawnpore and headed for Lucknow with a force of 4500 men. He decided to approach the Residency by blasting his way through the maze of the city's streets, rather than proceeding along the river, as Havelock and Outram had done and as the rebels undoubtedly expected him to do (Fremont-Barnes 2014, ch. 4).

One of the most dangerous obstacles on Campbell's route through the city was Sikandar Bagh (Alexander's Palace) a two-story mansion surrounded by gardens and a masonry wall with loopholes for muskets. It was defended by 2000 sepoys. While the British 18-pound guns were pounding a hole at one place in the wall, the infantry soldiers were forcing open a gate that the defenders had delayed in closing. There was now no way for the sepoys to escape. Once again, the powerful Enfield rifles provided an advantage to the British (see Fig. 13.1). Lieutenant Arthur Lang described what followed:

> Such a distracting row of thousands of rifles firing without intermission I never heard, and such a sight of slaughter I never saw. In the open rooms right and left of the archway Pandies (Sepoys) were shot down and bayoneted in heaps, three or four feet deep; in the centre Bara Dari they made but little stand, but at the house in the middle of the rear wall and in the semicircular court beyond it they shut the many thin doors and thousands of bullets were poured in. ... The mass of bodies were set fire to, and to hear the living as they caught fire calling out in agony to be shot was horrible even in that scene where all men's worst passions were excited. (Blomfield 1992, 139)

Finally, on 17 November Campbell's forces broke through to join those of the Residency. Two days later began the evacuation of the civilians and the garrison (Fremont-Barnes 2014, ch. 4). On the night of 22–23 November,

Fig. 13.1 The 93rd Highlanders at the storming of the Sikandar Bagh. During the second relief of Lucknow in November 1857, the powerful Enfield rifle provided a significant firepower advantage to British troops (Reproduced from Wikipedia Commons)

there was some hesitation as the final officers were about to leave the compound. Both Outram and Inglis wished to have the honor of being the last to depart. Outram then diplomatically suggested that they both leave together. The two officers shook hands and descended at the same time (Spilsbury 2007, ch. 11).

With Delhi once again in British hands and the siege of Lucknow finally lifted, it was just a matter of time before the rebellion was extinguished. British units had been summoned from Persia, Burma, and Ceylon, while troops en route to China had been diverted to North India. Eventually other troops arrived from Australia, Southern Africa and Britain. By the middle of 1858, almost two-thirds of the British army would be serving in India (Fremont-Barnes 2014, ch. 2).

On 21 February 1858, Lieutenant Arthur Lang was part of an army of 20,000 under Sir Colin Campbell en route from Cawnpore to retake Lucknow, where Campbell had left a small force behind under Outram.

Lang's unit was defending an old fort at Jalalabad on the outskirts of Lucknow when the rebels attacked:

> Masses of infantry with scaling ladders came on against Jalalabad, but they could not stand the penetration of our bullets, which would kill two men, one behind the other. Those 'Minies' and 'Lancasters' do give us a wonderful advantage over Pandy, and he finds it very disagreeable to find the conical bullets dropping in at 1500 yards into his columns. He can hardly ever get the pluck up to venture within range of his own muskets. He must now mourn his folly in rejecting these same cartridges, which play such mischief with him. (Blomfield 1992, 158)

The new siege of Lucknow began on March 8, with Campbell's army facing some 120,000 defenders. Neighborhood by neighborhood over the following weeks, the city was recaptured. By 21 April, the whole of Lucknow was once more under British control (Fremont-Barnes 2014, ch. 4). It took another 8 months, but by the end of 1858, the last of the rebels in the Oudh had been defeated.

In summary, during the Indian Rebellion of 1857, the insurgent troops greatly outnumbered the British, Sikhs, Gurkhas and Afghans who fought against them. Moreover, the rebels had the same military training, artillery pieces, and ammunition as the British troops on the other side. Against them, however, were the command and control problems mentioned in the last chapter due to the absence of a standardized vernacular. Most of the sepoys were illiterate, and they lacked a common mother tongue, although they shared the Hindustani koine of the north-India military camps as a second language. Also against them was a disparity in small-arms technology. As Lieutenant Lang put it so clearly, in rejecting the new Enfield rifled muskets in favor of the "Brown Bess" smoothbores, the rebels deliberately forsook the one technology that might have provided them with the margin of victory.

An Act of Parliament passed on 2 August 1858 disestablished the rule of the East India Company over India. Henceforth the subcontinent would be governed directly as a colony of the British Crown. At the same time, the subcontinent's three armies were restructured. In the new Indian forces, there would no longer be an artillery service, except in a few special units (Spilsbury 2007, ch. 14). Moreover, in future, Indian soldiers would bear only smoothbore weapons, the deadly rifled arms being reserved for Europeans (Hunting 2014). Finally, in 1859, the British decided to use beeswax instead of tallow as a lubricant for the Enfield's ammunition. The official explanation for the change was to avoid possible corrosion of the bullet casing caused by tallow (Smithurst 2011, ch. 3).

13.4 Lances Versus Rifles

The introduction of the accurate, light-weight, long-range Pattern 1853 Enfield rifle in 1854 during the Crimean War had marked a revolution in warfare, giving the European foot soldier an unprecedented capacity to fight against artillery and cavalry. In essence, anyone the infantryman could see he could kill. However, for the first 3 years of production in England under the traditional "workshop system", the parts of the Pattern 1853 were not interchangeable.

In 1850, Birmingham was the principal center for the manufacture of small arms in Britain. There was no single firm that dominated the industry. Instead, there were many small masters skilled at producing individual parts. Although the Birmingham gunmakers used machinery for boring the gun barrels, the manufacture of the locks and other small metal parts was carried out by lock filers. The cast parts were then fitted together by "rough stockers and setters up" equipped with hand tools. In short, guns were "fitted rather than assembled" (Williams and Johnson 2001, 325).

The undesirable consequences of this production system were clearly evident to a soldier in a Massachusetts infantry regiment that received a shipment of weapons produced in this way in 1861:

> The Enfield received would not compare favorably with the Springfield musket, new pattern. The workmanship was rough and they were poorly rifled, and the parts would not interchange like the American gun. It was necessary to keep an armorer with the Regiment, to fit such parts of the musket as were accidentally broken in service. (Newell 1875, 30)

In contrast, the advantages of American rifles manufactured by machine, the British Select Committee on Small Arms of 1854 had noted, were: "cheapness in manufacture, an exact similarity in the several parts so that they may be readily interchanged and replaced, and above all, the facility of rapidly producing muskets" (Hounshell 1984, 18).

Of course, machine-made parts were not necessarily always interchangeable. Although Colt's revolvers appeared visually identical, their individual parts could not be replaced without fitting by a specialist (Smithurst 2011, ch. 2). From a manufacturing standpoint, the revolutionary development came with the first production from the London Enfield factory in 1857.[1] The tolerances demanded from the British armory were unprecedented—0.001 inch (0.025 mm) rather than 0.0038 inch (0.097 mm) at the Arsenal of Vienna or 0.0025 inch (0.064 mm) at the US armories (Williams and Johnson 2001, 320). By 1858, the factory at Enfield was producing 2000 virtually identical rifles per week (Williams and Johnson 2001, 326).

Once this rate of production of interchangeable rifles had been reached, it was relatively straightforward to convert large numbers of raw recruits into armies that could destroy any opposing force in Asia. In 1854, Britain had established the School of Musketry in the former barracks of the Royal Staff Corps in Kent. Through drill and practice, it trained officers and noncommissioned officers who could then serve as instructors in their home regiments. Trainees were taught to fire at targets at distances of from 100 to 1000 yards (90–900 m) by increments of 50 yards (45 m) (Smithurst 2011, ch. 4). Any opposing foot soldiers, cavalrymen or artillerists who were equipped with previous generations of weapons technologies could now be killed from a distance with unprecedented efficiency.

It will be remembered that Tianjin is a port on the Hai River, 40 miles (64 km) inland from the Yellow Sea, with connections by the Grand Canal to the Yellow and Yangtze Rivers. Much of the food and other provisions necessary to supply the Chinese capital 90 miles (140 km) to the northwest passed through this city. Its seizure by the British and French after the surrender of the Taku Forts in August 1860 therefore obliged the Qing regime to offer to begin serious negotiations (Hanes and Sanello 2002, 256). However, with Beijing within their grasp, the British and French now demanded concessions considerably stiffer than those of the Treaty of Tianjin 2 years earlier. The amount of reparations to be paid had doubled; the Allies would now continue to hold Tianjin; the Chinese would have to apologize for the British killed a year earlier (Hanes and Sanello 2002, 257).

Despite initial hesitation by the emperor's delegates, the Chinese had little choice but to accept the British ultimatum—at least on paper. The British negotiator, Harry Parkes, 32, had lived in China since childhood and was fluent in Chinese. On 17 September, accompanied by Lord Elgin's private secretary, Henry Loch, and Times journalist Thomas Bowlby, along with a small guard of British dragoons and Sikhs, he rode ahead of the allied army to the Beijing suburb of Tongzhou. Parkes intended to finalize an agreement he had arranged with Chinese negotiators 4 days earlier. Instead, he and his party were arrested. When Parkes refused to kowtow before the Mongol Prince Sengge Rinchen, his captors smashed his head numerous times against the marble floor of the reception room (Hanes and Sanello 2002, 263).

After the British delegation failed to return, the allied commanders on 18 September decided to continue their advance toward Beijing. The 2500 British and 1000 French troops found their route blocked by 20,000 Mongol cavalry on a three-mile front outside the town of Zhangjiawan (Hanes and Sanello 2002, 263). In the ensuing battle, the lance-bearing Chinese cavalry were decimated by the Allies' rifles and Armstrong guns. Meanwhile the Chinese infantry, armed with bows and arrows along with a few firelock muskets, proved to be no match for the British and French troops with their Enfield and Minié rifles. There were 1500 Chinese casualties against only 35 suffered by the Allies (Hanes and Sanello 2002, 266).

Three days later, on 21 September, the allied armies reached a canal at Palikao on the outskirts of the capital. Defending the access to a bridge across the canal was a Chinese army 50,000 strong consisting mostly of cavalry (Chief of Staff 1911, 435). In the opposing allied army, the British were on the left and the French on the right. Once again, access to rifled weapons gave the allies a great advantage. The antiquated Chinese artillery was not effective and its infantry proved unable to face the massed Enfield and Minié rifles. British field guns and rifles again proved deadly against Chinese cavalry units that attacked the allied left, while the French infantry squares held off a cavalry attack on the right. When the Chinese cavalry on the allied right withdrew to check the British advance, the French elite columns were able to advance toward the bridge. The Chinese commander was forced to withdraw his forces over the bridge to avoid being trapped on the wrong side of the canal. In the battle, the Chinese lost at least 1200 men while only five British and French were killed (Siggurdsson 2013).

There proved to be no further contact between the two opposing armies; the Chinese forces gradually withdrew from Beijing. With their departure, the capital was protected only by its walls, some 40 feet (12 m) high and 60 feet (18 m) thick. The British commander, General Hope Grant, a veteran of the First Opium War and the Anglo-Sikh Wars, decided to wait for the arrival of heavy artillery from Tianjin. Meanwhile, the Allies refused to negotiate until the prisoners were released. It was not until 5 October that the siege guns finally arrived (Hanes and Sanello 2002, 271). The British and French commanders then decided to march their forces in opposite directions around the city in order to threaten the emperor's residence, 12 miles (19 km) to the northwest.

Yuanmingyuan was known to Europeans as the Summer Palace, although the emperor in fact lived there most of the year. It was a vast estate covering three square kilometers, with lakes, gardens and many temples, pagodas, audience halls and other buildings. While the British infantry set up camp in a forest at some distance from the palace, the French troops along with the British cavalry reached the walls of the compound on the evening of 6 October (Ringmar 2013, 69).

Early the following morning the French commander, General Charles Montauban, entered the palace accompanied by his senior officers. As the site had been abandoned by all except a group of unarmed eunuchs, Montauban placed armed guards at the different gates, specifying that only those with a laissez-passer could enter the palace grounds. Before returning to his camp for breakfast, he suggested that his officers each pick a souvenir from the jewelry, watches and other fine objects in the vast imperial collection. It appears that this was the signal for which the French soldiers had been waiting. A few hours later, when the general returned, even the guards were looting the emperor's riches. By late afternoon, the imperial warehouses had been forced open and clothing, hats and rolls of tissue were being carried back to the French camp (Ringmar 2013, 70).

Prince Gong, the emperor's half-brother, had been left to negotiate with the Europeans. On the day of the Summer Palace looting, he received orders from the emperor, who was at Rehe beyond the Great Wall, to release the prisoners immediately. Parkes and Loch were released outside the city gates. Later there arrived a counter-order to execute the prisoners in retribution for the looting of the Summer Palace (Hanes and Sanello 2002, 282). Nevertheless, over the next few days the other captives were surrendered (Ringmar 2013, 78).

The prisoners described the ill-treatment they had been forced to endure. They had been beaten and kicked, had gone for days without food and been left outside under a blazing sun. Their captors had tied the prisoners' hands behind their backs and poured water on the rope to cause it to shrink and bite into the men's skin. The wrists of several captives had turned black and become infested with maggots. Of the 39 original prisoners only 18, including Parkes and Loch, survived. The reporter for the Times, Harry Bowlby, had died in great pain (Ringmar 2013, 78).

On 10 October, the Allies sent an ultimatum to the Chinese: if the Anting gate were not opened within 3 days, they would begin firing their

Armstrong guns. Two days later, the Chinese sent word that they would yield. Shortly before noon on 13 October, the Anting gate swung open, allowing Lord Elgin and his troops to enter the city (Ringmar 2013, 146).

Elgin now faced a personal dilemma: how to punish the Chinese for their treatment of the Allied hostages. Should the Chinese be forced to turn over the men responsible for the mistreatment, or should they perhaps pay an indemnity? Finally, Elgin proposed to the other commanders that to punish the emperor and at the same time send a powerful signal to the Chinese people, the Summer Palace should be destroyed. Baron Jean-Baptiste Louis Gros, his French counterpart, strongly objected, refusing to offer French support for the destruction of the palace complex. General Montauban concurred with his colleague. However, the British officers supported Elgin, observing to the French that the proposed punishment would simply be completing the work that they, the French, had begun (Ringmar 2013, 79). Thus it passed that on 18 and 19 October 1860, all of the many buildings at Yuanmingyuan and what was left of their contents were set afire. The cedar burned easily, creating dense columns of smoke that gradually spread over the city of Beijing (Ringmar 2013, 80).

On 24 October, the British delegation led by Lord Elgin and the Chinese under Prince Gong met in the Hall of Ceremonies in central Beijing. The two parties signed the Treaty of Tianjin and the new Beijing Convention. The following day the same ceremonies were repeated by the French and Chinese (Ringmar 2013, 163). The Allies were now free to leave Beijing, which they were anxious to do before the arrival of winter.

13.5 THE TOOLBOX FOR EMPIRE

The military byproducts of three civilian "macro-inventions" of the eighteenth century—the steam engine, machine tools and interchangeable parts—constituted the West's toolbox for empire in the nineteenth. With ocean-going steamships, European soldiers and their armaments could be transported quickly to any point on the planet. Smaller shallow-draft steamboats with iron hulls could convey troops upriver to put down any local rebellions inland. At sea, guns built to fire explosive shells with flat trajectories could easily destroy the wooden sailing ships used by Asian navies. On the battlefield, long-range rifled cannon firing similar explosive shells could decimate enemy cavalry fortifications. In individual combat against massed infantry, Western soldiers given rudimentary training and equipped with mass-produced rifles now had the capacity to kill anyone they could see.

The key to success in the Darwinian competition unleashed by the Industrial Revolution lay in the prior creation of networks of literate citizens able to communicate in a standardized vernacular. As long as Europe and its offshoots were the only societies able to apply movable type cheaply to their writing systems and then impose a common vocabulary, syntax and pronunciation on their citizens, the latter would display a willingness to cooperate that had no equal in the East. Until Asia too raised its literacy rates and standardized its vernaculars, the technological gap between East and West could only grow wider.

Note

1. Robbins and Lawrence of Windsor, Vermont, were already making rifles with interchangeable parts in 1851, although not with the tolerance demanded at Enfield (Smithurst 2011, ch. 2).

References

Aksan, V. H. (2007). *Ottoman wars, 1700–1870: An empire besieged*. Harlow: Longman.
Badem, C. (2010). *The Ottoman Crimean War: (1853–1856)*. Boston: Brill.
Blomfield, D. (1992). *Lahore to Lucknow: The Indian mutiny journal of Arthur Moffat Lang*. London: Leo Cooper.
Callahan, R. (2007). The great sepoy mutiny. In D. P. Marston & C. S. Sundaram (Eds.), *A military history of India and South Asia from the East India Company to the nuclear era* (pp. 16–33). Bloomington: Indiana University Press.
Chief of Staff, A. H. (1911). *Frontier and overseas expeditions from India* (Vol. 6). Calcutta: Superintendent Government Printing.
Fremont-Barnes, G. (2014). *Osprey guide to the Indian mutiny 1857–58*. Oxford: Osprey Publishing.
Fuller, C. E. (1958). *The rifled musket*. New York: Bonanza Books.
Hanes, W. T., & Sanello, F. (2002). *Opium wars: The addiction of one empire and the corruption of another*. Naperville: Sourcebooks.
Hounshell, D. (1984). *From the American system to mass production, 1800–1932: The development of manufacturing technology in the United States*. Baltimore: Johns Hopkins University Press.
Hunting, M. (2014, Summer). Musket smooth bore pattern of 1858 and 1859. *Black Powder*, p. 27.
Neumann, C. K. (2006). Political and diplomatic developments. In S. N. Faroqhi (Ed.), *Cambridge history of Turkey, vol. 3, The later Ottoman Empire, 1603–1839* (pp. 44–64). Cambridge, UK: Cambridge University Press.

Newell, J. K. (1875). *Ours. Annals of 10th regiment.* Springfield: Nichols & Co.
Ringmar, E. (2013). *Liberal barbarism: The European destruction of the palace of the emperor of China.* New York: Palgrave Macmillan.
Siggurdsson. (2013). *Battle of Palikao (Baliqiao), Anglo-French force defeats Chinese army, clearing way to Peking.* Retrieved 2016, from The American Legion's Burn-Pit. http://www.burnpit.us/2013/09/battle-palikao-anglo-french-force-defeats-chinese-army-clearing-way-peking
Small, H. (2011). *The Crimean War: Victoria's war with the Russian Tsars.* Slough: Tempus Publishing.
Smithurst, P. (2011). *The pattern 1853 enfield rifle.* Botley: Osprey Publishing.
Spilsbury, J. (2007). *The Indian mutiny.* London: Weidenfeld and Nicolson.
Uyar, M., & Erickson, E. J. (2009). *A military history of the Ottomans from Osman to Atatürk.* Santa Barbara: Praeger Security International.
Williams, D. (2014). A St-Étienne Made Pattern 1853 Rifle Musket. *Arms & Armour, 11,* 40–43.
Williams, D. J., & Johnson, W. (2001). Schön's view of rifled infantry arms in the mid 19th century. *International Journal of Impact Engineering, 25,* 315–330.

CHAPTER 14

Conclusion

14.1 THE GREAT GAME

The "Great Game" was a term used in the nineteenth century to describe the rivalry between Great Britain and Russia for the control of central Asia and access to the Mediterranean Sea. However, the term might equally well be applied to the competition between students of history in recent decades to explain most convincingly why the West was the victor in its conflicts with the great Asian civilizations during the modern period. Over a half century ago, William A. McNeill rebutted predictions of Western decline by Oswald Spengler and Arnold Toynbee with his brilliant synthesis of world history, *The Rise of the West*. McNeill observed that although at one period or another during the past 5000 years, one or the other of the Eurasian civilizations rose temporarily above the others, the complete dominance of the West from the mid-nineteenth century onward was unprecedented.

In his study, McNeill (1963, 730–744) hesitated to single out one factor that accounted for the lead of Europe and the United States over Asia. He suggested that pluralistic institutions, access to natural resources, population growth and industrialization with inanimate power were all important. However, to explain the sudden change in relative positions of East and West during the half century after the Congress of Vienna in 1815, he assigned a prominent role to military technologies that were unique to the West, namely, new weapons and new means of transport and communication. He extended this argument in detail in his seminal 1982 study, *The Pursuit of Power: Technology, Armed Force, and Society Since A.D. 1000*. In the middle decades of the nineteenth century, he argued there was an acceleration in the development of armaments technology in the West that coincided with the "industrialization of war" (McNeill 1982, 223). No such acceleration occurred in Asia (McNeill 1982, 256). However, McNeill made no attempt to evaluate the relative importance of the influences that underlay the resulting nineteenth-century divergence in military capabilities.

The preceding chapters of the present study have been devoted to possible explanations for the economic and military divergence between the East and West over the eighteenth and nineteenth centuries. The discussion has focused on three types of activity, namely, language, the use of code to communicate; innovation, the creation of novelty; and warfare, violent intergroup conflict. Together, these three types of behavior—language, innovation and warfare—are perhaps the activities that most distinguish humans from other species. Although humans' claim to exclusivity in these three domains is continually being challenged by ongoing research, it is difficult to imagine how human society could have evolved without a complex system of communication, or in the absence of the ability to create new tools and articles of consumption, or without institutions that rewarded successful organized violence.

Among these three variables—language, innovation and warfare—there are six possible binary causal relationships. As we shall see, three of these relationships emphasize cooperation *within* groups, while the other three focus on competition *between* groups. The language-standardization hypothesis proposed in the present study emphasizes the three links that depend on cooperation within social groups. The model posits a causal chain running from warfare to language, then onward from language to innovation and finally from innovation back to warfare.

In contrast, most studies in the "Great Game" over the last few decades have followed McNeill directly, focusing on the effects of competition *between* states. In the resulting *tournament model*, the causal chain runs from warfare to innovation, then from innovation onward to language and nationalism and then back to warfare.

It might be helpful, then, to situate the analysis of Parts 1, 2 and 3 with respect to the alternative position presented in several previous studies. Let us begin with the tournament model.

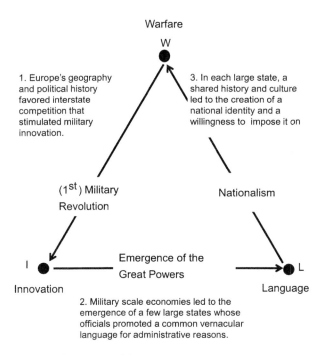

Fig. 14.1 The tournament model

14.2 THE TOURNAMENT MODEL

In the tournament model, the state itself is modeled as a predator, using its monopoly of the means of violence to extort taxes from its citizens (Tilly 1990, 67–76). Figure 14.1 presents schematically this view of society. The arrows in the diagram represent three possible binary causal relations between language, innovation and warfare, links that are neglected in the language-standardization hypothesis presented in the preceding chapters. In the tournament model, warfare leads to innovation which generates changes in language and culture that in turn feed back in a third step to warfare.

Let us start at the point W at the top of the triangle. Eric Jones (1981, 90, 104–108) and Jared Diamond (1997, 413–415) suggested that Europe's central mountain ranges and long indented coastline with numerous bays prevented any one state from dominating the region. However, for Hoffman (2015, 17), it is rather Europe's divided political history after the fall of the Roman Empire that explains the endemic interstate warfare of the later Middle Ages. In the fourteenth and fifteenth centuries, the city-states of Northern Italy challenged one another for control of the trade routes between the eastern Mediterranean and Northern Europe. Meanwhile, further north, the Hundred Years' War was being fought over the feudal rights of the English king with respect to the territories that he held as fiefs from the king of France.

The first arrow, linking warfare to innovation, WI in Fig. 14.1, captures the effect of this perpetual tournament on military technology. As Philip T. Hoffman (2015, 38–48) explained, each state had a strong incentive to develop a technology that was marginally superior to that of its rivals. For example, in the first half of the fifteenth century, improvements to artillery under the Valois dynasty allowed the French to drive the English archers from their territory. Beginning in the late fifteenth century, a continuing series of innovations changed the nature of warfare. Geoffrey Parker (1996, 43) identified three transformations in the early modern period that were sufficiently important to be termed a Military Revolution. These developments were first, the use of massed firepower; second, the *trace italienne* or bastion fortifications; and third, an increase in the size of armies. Ian Morris (2010, 403–404) too dated the beginning of the West's catching up to the East to the fifteenth century, when competition drove change in military technology.

Tonio Andrade (2016, 3–5) explained the absence of Chinese innovation since the late Middle Ages by long periods in which China faced no external threats. However, if we put aside a brief period of copying of Western cannon and muskets from the mid-sixteenth to the mid-seventeenth centuries, we are faced with over a half millennium of Chinese technological stagnation, from the mid-fifteenth to the late twentieth centuries. During this long interval, China was continually challenged militarily—by pirates on its coasts, by Japanese invasion, by the Mongols and Manchu, by internal revolts and by the West. Hoffman (2015, 69–71) argued that firearms were of little use against the nomads who constituted China's principal enemies. However as we saw in the preceding chapter, during the Second Opium War, the West's mobile artillery and rifled firearms proved deadly against cavalry armies. Accordingly, some additional influence is required to explain the widening East-West technological gap.

Turn now to the second arrow, running from I to L in Fig. 14.1 and representing the impact of military innovation on language. In the West, the scale economies implicit in the (First) Military Revolution allowed the larger states to seize the territory of their smaller rivals. This continued competition therefore led to the emergence of a few large states (Kennedy 1987, 70–72). In order to finance their armies, the officials of these states had an incentive to develop more efficient methods to raise tax revenues. In the seventeenth century, those who had political power had an interest in promoting the use of standard vernacular languages for purely administrative reasons. In the case of France, James C. Scott (1998, 72) has argued the imposition of Standard French was a form of overt "domestic colonization" designed to subdue "foreign provinces". In England, according to James Milroy (1994, 20–25), the process was more covert, through the codification of a standard language in dictionaries and manuals of grammar and pronunciation.

The third arrow in Fig. 14.1, LW, stands for the impact of language standardization in the West on its military aggression in other regions of the world. In the principal European states, a shared language and culture led to the creation of a national identity (Kennedy 1987, 70) and a collective willingness to impose it on other societies (Seton-Watson 1977, 277–281). By the middle decades of the nineteenth century, European elites were eager to spread the influence of their cultures to other parts of the world (Hoffman 2015, 202). The British colonial administrator Thomas Babington Macaulay, writing in 1835, could envisage an Indian elite who were "English in taste, in opinions, in morals, and in intellect" (Ferguson 2004, 158). Thus, there was a demand for empire and a willingness to finance colonial expansion by military means.

With its emphasis on competition, the tournament hypothesis fits the overall picture of the West's gradual dominance of the Asian civilizations during the modern period. By the early sixteenth century, after long years of interstate warfare, Europe had developed a set of military technologies—the caravel, cast-metal cannon and individual firearms—that had no equal in Asia. The West's technological lead continued to widen over the following centuries (Hoffman 2015, 94–100). The emergence of a small number of powerful states with centralized finances would enable the West to project its military force into the farthest corners of the planet.

However, the thesis fails to answer the following questions.

First, why were Britain, its American offshoot and France the first societies to have large networks of people who spoke standardized vernacular languages?

Second, why were the key technological breakthroughs of the Industrial Revolution—such as the steam engine, machine tools and interchangeable parts—all developed through collaboration between specialists with different skills, often from different regions, within these same three countries?

Third, why after 1800 were the Asian civilizations no longer able to defend themselves by buying or copying the latest Western technologies, as they had done previously?

Consider, then, an alternative approach that emphasizes cooperation.

14.3 THE LANGUAGE-STANDARDIZATION HYPOTHESIS

If the tournament model highlights competition between states, the language-standardization hypothesis in contrast emphasizes cooperation within the language networks of each society. To illustrate the principal ideas of this alternative approach, consider the triangle WLI in Fig. 14.2. The arrows represent the other three directions of causality between Warfare, Language and Innovation. The arrows thus stand for the three transformations that marked the seventeenth, eighteenth and nineteenth centuries, namely, the Linguistic, Industrial and (Second) Military Revolutions, respectively.

Let us begin with the arrow WL running from warfare to language. Both England and France were protected from outside attack by their geography—England by the Channel and France by a sequence of water and mountain barriers. In each case, therefore, the diffusion of gunpowder weapons led to the creation of a large centralizing state. Power was concentrated in one city that soon had several times the population of the next largest center. Even before the diffusion of the printing press, the dialects of the two capitals had attained special status.

A necessary condition for top-down language standardization, then, was the centralization of power. The insular geography of England and the hexagonal bounded space of France enabled a single center in each state to acquire control over its periphery. With the population of London and Paris consequently growing much more rapidly than that of the country as a whole, their dialects gradually acquired precedence.[1] In 1362, under Edward III, the English parliament passed the Pleading in English Act. The legislation stipulated that all pleading and judgments in courts should be in the English tongue rather than in Norman French (Bragg 2003, 66). Henry V, who reigned from 1413 until his death in 1422, wrote in English in his dispatches while on campaign in France (Bragg 2003, 95). Moreover, it was during his reign that the Chancery, the seat of government in London, began to standardize the English used in court documents (Bragg 2003, 98).

A similar process occurred in France. The precedence of the sovereign's mother tongue—*francien*, the dialect of the Ile de France—over Latin and regional dialects in the French administration dated from the reigns of Charles VII and Louis XI during the fifteenth century (Martel 2002, 98). In 1539, François I's Ordinance of Villers-Cotterêts declared that all legal acts, contracts and official legislation in France should be in *langage maternal francoys* (Harris 1990, 211). Because standardization of the vernacular allowed the authorities better to supervise their agents and communicate with their subjects, it was encouraged by both France and England from the late medieval period (Bragg 2003, 98). This promotion of a standard vernacular in the two most centralized states of the West accelerated with the wide diffusion of printed documents and a resulting rise in rates of literacy. As Benedict Anderson (2006, 37–46) suggested, linguistic standardization led to a redefining of community boundaries in Britain and France. Vague borders of religion or personal loyalty were replaced by much more sharply defined linguistic boundaries.

In China, over the centuries, an initially logosyllabic writing system became increasingly removed in pronunciation, vocabulary and syntax from the variants of the spoken language. Since the cost of imposing a standardized vernacular with the existing communications technology would have been prohibitive, neither the Ming nor the Qing dynasty made a sustained effort to bring together the written and spoken languages (Norman 1988, 187–190). We saw in Part 1 that the relative cost of printing with movable type was higher for the Chinese and Perso-Arabic scripts than for Europe's alphabetic characters. During the seventeenth century, the book markets of Britain and France were flooded with hundreds of new titles in the vernacular languages every year, the great majority published in the national capitals or in neighboring foreign centers such as Geneva and Amsterdam. In the three main Asian civilizations, however, publishing was limited to a much smaller number of titles, whether block-printed or hand-copied, most of them written in vehicular languages that were inaccessible for the majority of the population (Burlinge and van Zanden 2009, 437). While effective literacy rates rose in the West after 1600, they stagnated in the East.

In Europe by the 1550s, after over a century of gunpowder warfare, there were three patterns of linguistic and political boundaries. First, in settings where the centripetal forces of military scale economies were greater than the centrifugal forces of transport and communication costs, there were large empires that encompassed several language communities. Accordingly, the Habsburg and Ottoman regimes promoted vehicular languages—Latin and Ottoman Turkish, respectively—at the expense of vernacular dialects. Second, in regions where state boundaries were smaller than those of a family of dialects—notably in Germany (including the Netherlands) and Italy—there were multiple printing centers. As a result, the local dialects of these centers—Dutch, Low German, High German, Venetian and Florentine—survived as independent languages, but with an insufficient number of speakers to become important centers of innovation. Finally, in a third group—England and France—state boundaries were approximately equal to those of a dialect family. Consequently, over the following century, printing led to early standardization, with the dialects of the two capitals becoming the national standards (Dudley 1991, 145).

During the seventeenth century, an accelerated outpouring of printed materials and a continued rise in literacy led to the standardization of *written* English and French beyond the central administrations of each country. Standardization of the *spoken* language of educated English and French citizens then followed. Elsewhere in the West, where power was more dispersed geographically, the persistence of regional dialects limited the penetration of national linguistic standards until the nineteenth century.

In Fig. 14.2, a second arrow of causality (LI) runs from language to innovation. By the early eighteenth century, the standardization of French and English began to encourage cooperation among potential innovators, thereby stimulating several remarkable technological breakthroughs (Dudley 2012, 2016). As explained in Part 2, in the year 1700, there were several obstacles that had prevented the production of goods beyond the artisanal stage whereby each product was made by an individual worker with simple tools. One problem was the frequent lack of alternative energy sources. Wind, water and animal power were all of limited availability or of high cost. Another was the difficulty of shaping metal parts. Considerable hand filing was required to produce metal parts that were smooth and of a desired measurement. The third challenge was the absence of interchangeability of manufactured parts. If a component of a mechanical device broke, since each piece was unique, it required the services of a skilled metalworker to fashion and fit a replacement part.

Overcoming each of these obstacles was sufficiently complex to require the talents of two or more individuals with different skills. As Margaret Jacob (1997, 106) has made clear, the typical eighteenth-century innovation required the talents of an entrepreneur familiar with the market and its needs and a technician able to bring together the required mechanical knowledge and skills. It is not surprising, then, that the countries that were the first to have standardized languages were subsequently those in

14.3 THE LANGUAGE-STANDARDIZATION HYPOTHESIS

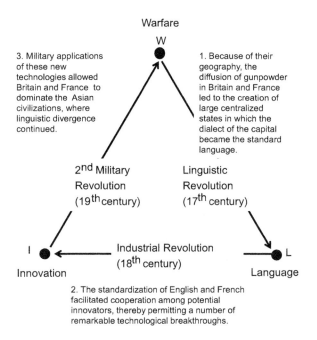

Fig. 14.2 The language-standardization hypothesis

which cooperation among innovators generated important contributions to manufacturing technology. The standardization of the written and spoken language widened the set of trustworthy people beyond the boundaries of family, neighbors and friends. In effect, use of the standardized national language was a signal that one could have confidence in the other person.[2] In the words of the nineteenth-century German philosopher and sociologist Ferdinand Tönnies ([1887] 2001), one's social network expanded from the local *Gemeinschaft* (community) to the broader *Gesellschaft* (civil society). Accordingly, by Metcalfe's Law the number of potential pairings of collaborators expanded with the *square* of the number of individuals in the network.[3]

Britain, its American offshoot and northern France experienced language standardization roughly a century or more before the rest of Europe. Because of the resulting facility of communication, potential innovators with different skill sets in these countries became more willing to cooperate with one another. For the century and a half that followed, between 1700 and 1850, small regions centered in these countries' largest cities contributed three-quarters of the world's important industrial innovations (Dudley 2016).

We first examined a set of three path-breaking civilian "macro-inventions"—the steam engine, machine tools and interchangeable parts—all requiring cooperation between specialists with different skills for their development. Working together, three teams of British and American innovators developed the macro-inventions that overcame the obstacles just mentioned. Thomas Newcomen and John Calley invented the first functioning steam engine. Joseph Bramah and Henry Maudslay combined to invent some of the first precision machine tools. Finally, New England clockmakers Eli Terry and Seth Thomas were the first to realize the goal of producing manufactured products with virtually interchangeable parts.

We then studied three downstream military innovations, also cooperative, to which these macro-inventions gave rise, namely, the steamship, rifled artillery and mass-produced firearms. The first practical steamship in 1789 was the result of the efforts of three Scots, merchant Patrick Miller, educator James Taylor and engineer William Symington (Rowland 1970, 34). The initial successful shell-firing rifled cannon was conceived by Newcastle manufacturer William Armstrong and Devonshire engineer James Rendel (Heald 2012, 85). Finally, the perfection of the technology to develop the truly interchangeable Pattern 1853 Enfield rifle was the product of collaboration between employees of the Royal Small Arms Factory at Enfield and American machinery firms (Smith 1977, 302, 312). In short, the technologies underlying the (Second) Military Revolution in the nineteenth century resulted from collaboration between British and Americans who spoke a common vernacular.

Finally in Fig. 14.2, there is the arrow IW running from innovation to warfare. By 1860, military applications of the steamship, machine tools and interchangeable parts had given the West unprecedented dominance over the major Asian civilizations. As explained in Part 3, during the half century after 1815, the asymmetric diffusion of the steam-powered warship, shell-firing cannon and mass-produced firearms allowed Britain and France virtually to dictate the conditions of treaties that brought to an end the pre-modern empires of the Chinese, Indians and Ottomans. Unlike earlier military developments between the fifteenth and eighteenth centuries—often described as the (First) Military Revolution—the transformations to which these later technologies gave rise were sufficiently rapid to be termed a revolution. The accelerated speed of innovation allowed insufficient time for the Asian societies to defend themselves.

There was a second channel by which language standardization contributed to the dominance of Britain and France over their Asian opponents in the nineteenth century. Close cooperation among European officers and soldiers who all spoke the same mother tongue appears to have considerably increased the relative effectiveness of Western armies, even though they were often greatly outnumbered in combat with Asian forces. For example, we saw that this linguistic advantage was particularly important during the first key phase of the Indian Rebellion of 1857, when both sides had the same military technologies.

In short, the language nexus helps explain the singularity of Western innovation in the century and a half after 1700, along with the realignment of power structures in Eurasia that accompanied it.

14.4 Competition or Cooperation?

How and to what extent are we influenced by the actions of others? Is it competition from strangers that spurs us to action, or are we motivated primarily by the positive influence of those with whom we associate within our own culture? These are the questions behind our efforts to assess the tournament model relative to the language-standardization hypothesis. Which approach explains better the rise of the West economically and militarily relative to Asia?

As we have seen, if we examine the overall economic and military dominance of the West over the civilizations of Asia in the modern period, the tournament model fits the observed facts well. In the West, geography favored competition, which in turn created an incentive for military innovation. In the resulting large, centralized states, one requirement for an efficient administration that could extract a large and steady flow of revenue and spend it effectively was a standard vernacular. The rise of nationalism that accompanied the diffusion of this common language gradually instilled in the citizens of the Western states a willingness to sacrifice in order to extend their national power and increase their collective wealth.

The Invisible Hand Indeed, we might consider the tournament model to be an extension into the geopolitical domain of Adam Smith's metaphor of the invisible hand. In his 1776 classic study *The Wealth of Nations*, Smith, then aged 53, argued that under competitive markets, each person in seeking to maximize his own income enhances the production that the economy as a whole can produce from given resources.

> As every individual, therefore, endeavours as much as he can, both to employ his capital in the support of domestic industry, and so to direct that industry that its produce maybe of the greatest value; every individual necessarily labours to render the annual revenue of the society as great as he can. He generally, indeed, neither intends to promote the public interest, nor knows how much he is promoting it. By preferring the support of domestic to that of foreign industry, he intends only his own security; and by directing that industry in such a manner as its produce may be of the greatest value, he intends only his own gain; and he is in this, as in many other cases, led by an invisible hand to promote an end which was no part of his intention. (Smith et al. [1776] 1977, 313)

In the same way, the competitive states of the West improved their collective position relative to the monopolistic regimes in each of Asia's principal regions.

However, there are certain features of the rise of the West that are not well explained by the tournament model, particularly during the century and a half after 1700. The competitive approach does not explain why all of the most important innovations in civilian technology, the so-called General Purpose Technologies, were developed in narrow territorial bands around the largest cities in just three Western states, Britain, France and the United States.[4] Nor does the competitive approach explain why each of these breakthroughs involved nonmarket cooperation between two or more individuals. These same three states were responsible for the crucial military innovations that gave the West its great advantage—in each case the fruit of a collaborative effort. In short, if the issue is the economic and military rise of the Britain, France and the United States in the period between 1700 and 1860, something is missing in the tournament model.

Moral Sentiment In 1759, some 17 years before the appearance of *The Wealth of Nations*, Adam Smith, then 36, published *The Theory of Moral Sentiments*, a book that provided the behavioral underpinnings for his later theories of economic activity. Smith realized that the very market institutions that make possible efficient competition were in reality the product of trust and cooperation between large numbers of people. His fellow citizens were not purely selfish individuals, he believed. To the contrary, they were able to sympathize with the emotions of others and were influenced by others' attitudes toward themselves.

> How selfish soever man may be supposed, there are evidently some principles in his nature, which interest him in the fortune of others, and render their happiness necessary to him, though he derives nothing from it except the pleasure of seeing it. (Smith 1759, 3)

This sensitivity to others explained much observed social behavior.

> Our uncertainty concerning our own merit, and our anxiety to think favourably of it, should together naturally enough make us desirous to know the opinion of other people concerning it; to be more than ordinarily elevated when that opinion is favourable, and to be more than ordinarily mortified when it is otherwise. (Smith 1759, 132–133)

It is in this way that social norms emerged. Some of these norms, particularly those of the judicial system, were enforced by the state.

> The wisdom of every state or commonwealth endeavours, as well as it can, to employ the force of the society to restrain those who are subject to its authority, from hurting or disturbing the happiness of one another. (Smith 1759, 231)

Other values were maintained only by the influence that individuals have on one another.

> Our concern in the happiness or misery of those who are the objects of what we call our affections; our desire to promote the one, and to prevent the other; are either the actual feeling of that habitual sympathy, or the necessary consequences of that feeling. (Smith 1759, 233)

Smith also considered the question of whose feelings one should consider, that is, with whom one should cooperate. He observed that people should often behave charitably even with associates who are not family members.

> Among well-disposed people, the necessity or conveniency of mutual accommodation, very frequently produces a friendship not unlike that which takes place among those who are born to live in the same family. (Smith 1759, 237)

However, cooperation with others generally stopped at the national borders. Although Smith did not mention language standardization explicitly, the concept was implicit in the territorial boundaries he set for such sentiments.

> The state or sovereignty in which we have been born and educated, and under the protection of which we continue to live, is, in ordinary cases, the greatest society upon whose happiness or misery, our good or bad conduct can have much influence. (Smith 1759, 242)

In short, as Smith argued, since people were sensitive to the emotions of others, they were strongly influenced by the people with whom they associated, whether family, neighbors, colleagues or others of their fellow citizens. In seeking praise and avoiding criticism, they came to share their values and develop a willingness to cooperate with them. Just as they traded goods and services through economic markets, so they exchanged mutual support in their social relations.

The important point to notice here is that in both works, Smith was describing British society in the second half of the eighteenth century. His two essays portrayed the market and nonmarket behavior that enabled his nation and its American offspring, along with their French neighbor, to dominate the rest of the world during most of the century after his death in 1790.

14.5   Six Arrows of Geopolitical Change

We may perhaps conclude, agreeing with Adam Smith, that both competing with rivals and cooperating to win the approval of our family and friends help explain human behavior. If so, all six of the arrows linking language, innovation and warfare in Figs. 14.1 and 14.2 have played a role in the historical dramas we have been discussing. As previous participants in the Great Game of explaining the rise of the West have argued, the tournament model, with its three competitive links from war through innovation to language surely explains part of the observed divergence between the East and West, particularly in the early modern period. However, the cooperative chain in the opposite direction, from war through language to innovation and then back to war, as suggested by the language-standardization hypothesis, seems to have been equally important, especially from the seventeenth to the nineteenth centuries.

Over the two centuries between 1660 and 1860, the rise of the West was in many ways the rise of three particular Western societies—those of Britain, France and the United States. To explain how these states came to dominate other European and Asian societies it is important, this study has argued, to consider the effects of three revolutions, each corresponding roughly to a separate century. In the 1600s came the Linguistic Revolution leading subsequently to the standardization of the written and spoken vernaculars in England and France. In the 1700s, there was the Industrial Revolution, the development of innovations that made possible inanimate power, precision machining and mass replication. Finally, in the nineteenth century, there occurred the (Second) Military Revolution, the extension of Western mechanical violence into the remote corners of the world.

14.6 Persistence

We saw in Part 2 that three Western states—Britain, France and the Unites States—dominated the wave of mechanical innovations in the century and a half between 1700 and 1849. It is important now to say something about what happened during the century and a half that followed, between 1850 and 1999. Were the West's initial technological lead and the tight geographic limits to its new-found capacity to innovate a temporary shock that soon dissipated? Or did the pattern tend to persist?

Chapter 3 reported that a panel of experts chosen by *The Atlantic* magazine recently selected the printing press and paper as two of the greatest technological breakthroughs since the wheel (see Fallows 2013). To examine the question of persistence, it is interesting to break down by period all 50 of the innovations suggested by the experts. In addition, with the resources of *Wikipedia*, it is possible to attribute each discovery to an individual country.

In Table 14.1 we begin by examining the almost five millennia from 3000 BCE to 1699 CE. The 15 breakthroughs of this long period are ordered by country and year. It is no surprise to see that China accounted for a third of the total, with the abacus, paper, gunpowder, paper money and the compass heading the list. Note that the latter three inventions came during the brief flourishing of the Song Dynasty. However, if we define the West as the territory stretching from Greece to Scotland, we find that 7 of the 15 technologies were invented there. It should be noted that the origin of the printing press is debatable. The technology of printing with movable characters was invented in China early in the second millennium. Gutenberg's discovery of

Table 14.1 Great breakthroughs by country, 3000 BCE–1699 CE

Year	Country	Invention
−500	China	Abacus
100	China	Paper
900	China	Gunpowder
1000	China	Paper money
1111	China	Compass
−3000	Egypt	Sailboat
−3000	Egypt	Nail
−2500	Egypt	Lever
1450	Germany	Printing press
−700	Greece	Alphabetization
−300	Greece	Archimedes screw
100	Italy	Cement
1250	Italy	Optical lenses
1582	Italy	Gregorian calendar
1300	UK	Mechanized clock

Source: Fallows (2013), *Wikipedia*

the printing press three centuries later appears to have been independent. As indicated in Chap. 3, Sect. 3.5, because of the nonalphabetic structure of Chinese writing with its many thousands of characters, the original invention had little impact in China before the late nineteenth century, when Western printing techniques were adapted to Chinese script (Reed 2004). As for the three remaining innovations in the table, the first records of their appearance come from early in Egyptian antiquity.

Let us now turn to the following period, the century and a half of the West's industrial revolution and imperial extension between 1700 and 1849. The key innovations of the period are presented in Table 14.2. The steam engine, studied in Part 2 of this book, is one of the five breakthroughs attributed to Britain in the table. However, the experts recruited by *The Atlantic* failed to select machine tools or interchangeable parts, the two innovations in production techniques that we studied in detail in preceding chapters. The effects of these production technologies were felt only indirectly—downstream—through their effect on subsequent inventions such as the combine harvester that depended on precision manufacturing. Indeed, almost all of the great inventions of the following century and a half, such as the automobile, the airplane and semiconductor electronics, would have been unthinkable without the capacity of machines to produce virtually identical metal parts. Instead, the emphasis in the 2013 *Atlantic* article was on innovations that had a direct social impact.

Table 14.2 Great breakthroughs by country, 1700–1849

Year	Country	Invention
1830	France	Photography
1846	Russia	Oil drilling
1712	UK	Steam engine
1730	UK	Moldboard plow
1757	UK	Sextant
1796	UK	Vaccination
1837	UK	Telegraph
1793	USA	Cotton gin
1834	USA	Combine harvester
1846	USA	Anesthesia

Sources: See Table 14.1

What does stand out in this second table, as in the discussion of preceding chapters, is the concentration of innovation in just three countries—Britain, France and the United States. These states accounted for all but one of the ten breakthroughs in the table. Thus the societies that were first to standardize their vernacular, in the seventeenth century, were the most fertile innovators over the century and a half that followed.

The question in our minds as we turn to the final period, the 150 years from 1850 to 2000, is whether or not this geographic clustering of innovation persisted. In Table 14.3, we find that this pattern did indeed continue into the contemporary period. All but 4 of the 15 inventions chosen here were developed in France, the United Kingdom and the United States, the first three states to have a standardized vernacular. In Table 5.2, we saw that Germany lagged behind Britain and France by over a century, becoming in 1786 the third society to have a monolingual vernacular dictionary. It is interesting then that this country supplied three of the more recent innovations, namely, the internal combustion engine, the automobile and nitrogen fixation, a process used to manufacture fertilizer, explosives and other products.

Over the course of the twentieth century, each of the three Asian civilizations we have studied deliberately attempted to reduce its dependence on technology imported from the West. In varying degrees, each raised its literacy rate, took steps to standardize the written and spoken language and mastered the new media of mass communication. While Turkey switched from a Perso-Arabic script, China kept its logosyllabic system, using phonetic Romanized script, to teach standard pronunciation. India established Hindi, written with the phonetic Devanagari script, as its

Table 14.3 Great breakthroughs by country, 1850–2000

Year	Country	Invention
1859	France	Refrigeration
1863	France	Pasteurization
1890	Germany	Internal combustion engine
1890	Germany	Automobile
1918	Germany	Nitrogen fixation
1850	UK	Oil refining
1856	UK	Bessemer process for steel
1870	UK	Sewage treatment
1884	UK	Steam turbine
1928	UK	Penicillin
1876	USA	Telephone
1890	USA	Electricity
1902	USA	Air-conditioning
1903	USA	Airplane
1906	USA	Radio
1913	USA	Assembly line
1920	USA	Scientific plant breeding
1926	USA	Rocketry
1927	USA	Television
1939	USA	Nuclear fission
1950	USA	Semiconductor electronics
1950	USA	Green revolution
1960	USA	Birth-control pill
1965	USA	Internet

Sources: See Table 14.1

first official language. However, India has continued to use English as a nationwide second official language.

Are the findings of a positive relationship between language standardization and rates of innovation during the Industrial Revolution still relevant today? One of the costs of high ethnic diversity in a society, Alberto Alesina and Eliana La Ferrara (2005, 764) have argued, may be a lower supply of public goods. If each ethnic group has different preferences for public goods such as primary education and transportation infrastructure, a higher degree of diversity may result in a suboptimal level of public goods and lower welfare. They found empirical support for this proposition: across countries, greater diversity tends to be associated with slower growth. However, they also found that the negative effect of ethnic diversity tends to diminish at higher levels of per-capita income. A possible explanation, they suggested, is that wealthier societies may have developed institutions to resolve the conflicts associated with higher diversity. Indeed, examples of such institutions might be educational and legal systems that promote knowledge of a common language.

In a more recent study covering 173 countries, Alesina et al. (2016, 478) found that ethnic diversity has a significant negative effect on real income (measured by nighttime light intensity) only when it is accompanied by differences in geographic endowments such as arable land, temperature, rainfall and distance from the sea. Once one controls for these geographic variables, ethnolinguistic fragmentation is no longer a significant determinant of per-capita GDP.

A possible contributing factor that might explain why the negative effect of ethnolinguistic diversity on income levels is less important in richer countries, and why such diversity has no significant impact if endowment disparities are absent, is the effect of a standard tongue. To the extent that language standardization permits greater geographic and sectoral factor mobility, individuals are less constrained by the geographic heritage of their ethnic group. However, the choice of which language should be the standard vernacular, taught in schools and authorized for public institutions, is often a sensitive political question. If the Canadian province of Québec may be cited as an example, a promising strategy is to promote a standard language close to the vernacular of the majority, supplemented by a vehicular language such as English to assure effective communication with the rest of the planet.

An important issue currently is the extent to which state efforts to standardize communication are breaking down internal barriers to cooperation within *non*-Western countries. In recent decades in the Asian societies that we have been studying, government efforts to promote language standardization have tended to coincide with accelerated innovation. Firms in China and India have been particularly successful in adapting Western technology to create affordable good-enough products such as small, no-frills washing machines and automobiles (Zeschky et al. 2011). As for Turkey, multinational corporations are attracted to this country because of its young and well-educated population. For example, General Electric has established one of its nine centers for aviation research in Turkey (Kömürcüler 2016).

Whether or not the next breakthrough technologies will come from these emerging societies remains to be seen. If the analysis of this book is correct, much depends on the extent to which their governments are successful in imposing the dialect of the capital as the standard vernacular tongue. At issue also is the role, if any, to be assigned to an international tongue such as English as a vehicular language to be used for contact with the outside world. If such policies succeed in promoting cooperation between potential innovators in these populous societies while giving them access to progress elsewhere, the rise of the West in the late second millennium may well prove to have been no more permanent than the brief flourishing of the Song Dynasty in China almost a thousand years earlier.

Notes

1. In 1400, the population of Paris was 275,000, while that of Rouen, the next largest city was 35,000; the English equivalents were London, 45,000, and York, 12,000 (Bairoch et al. 1988).
2. Implicitly, following the signaling theory of Spence (1973), people assumed that acquisition of the standardized language had a cost to the individual that decreased with the competence and reliability of the person.
3. The simplest version of Metcalfe's law states that the value of a communications network is proportional to the square of the number of users connected of the system (Briscoe et al. 2006).
4. As indicated in the introduction, a General Purpose Technology is one that may be adapted for use in a variety of applications in a number of industries.

References

Alesina, A., & La Ferrara, E. (2005). Ethnic diversity and economic performance. *Journal of Economic Literature, 43*, 762–800.

Alesina, A., Michalopoulos, S., & Papaioannou, E. (2016). Ethnic inequality. *Journal of Political Economy, 124*, 428–488.

Anderson, B. (2006). *Imagined communities: Reflections on the origin and spread of nationalism* (Revised ed.). London: Verso.

Andrade, T. (2016). *The gunpowder age: China, military innovation, and the rise of the West in world history.* Princeton: Princeton University Press.

Bairoch, P., Jean, B., & Pierre, C. (1988). *The population of European cities. Data bank and short summary of results: 800–1850.* Geneva: Librairie Droz.

Bragg, M. (2003). *The adventure of English.* London: Hodder and Stoughton.

Briscoe, B., Odlyzko, A., & Tilly, B. (2006). *Metcalfe's law is wrong.* Retrieved January 15, 2015, from IEEE Spectrum. http://spectrum.ieee.org/computing/networks/metcalfes-law-is-wrong

Diamond, J. (1997). *Guns, germs, and steel: The fates of human societies.* New York: W.W. Norton & Co.

Dudley, L. (1991). *The word and the sword: How techniques of information and violence have shaped our world.* Oxford: Basil Blackwell.

Dudley, L. (2012). *Mothers of innovation: How expanding social networks gave birth to the industrial revolution*. Newcastle upon Tyne: Cambridge Scholars.

Dudley, L. (2016). Language standardization and the industrial revolution. *Oxford Economic Papers Advance Access*. doi:10.1093/oep/gpw059

Fallows, J. (2013). *The 50 greatest breakthroughs since the wheel*. Retrieved October 19, 2015, from theatlantic.com. http://www.theatlantic.com/magazine/archive/2013/11/innovations-list/309536/

Ferguson, N. (2004). *Empire: The rise and demise of the British world order and the lessons for global power*. New York: Basic Books.

Harris, M. (1990). French. In B. Comrie (Ed.), *The world's major languages* (pp. 210–235). Oxford: Oxford University Press.

Heald, H. (2012). *William Armstrong: Magician of the North*. Alnwick: McNidder and Grace.

Hoffman, P. T. (2015). *Why did Europe conquer the world?* Princeton: Princeton University Press.

Jacob, M. C. (1997). *Scientific culture and the making of the industrial West*. Oxford: Oxford University Press.

Jones, E. L. (1981). *The European miracle*. Cambridge, UK: Cambridge University Press.

Kennedy, P. (1987). *The rise and fall of the great powers*. New York: Random House.

Kömürcüler, G. (2016). *Turkey among most innovation-ready nations in region, says general electric report*. Retrieved November 18, 2016, from Hürriyet Daily News. http://www.hurriyetdailynews.com/turkey-among-most-innovation-ready-nations-in-region-says-general-electric-report-.aspx?pageID=238&nID=74129&NewsCatID=344

Martel, P. (2002). Occitan, français et construction de l'État en France. In D. Lacorne & T. Judt (Eds.), *La politique de Babel: du monolinguisme d'État au plurilinguisme des peuples* (pp. 87–116). Paris: Editions Karthala.

McNeill, W. H. (1963). *The rise of the West*. Chicago: University of Chicago Press.

McNeill, W. H. (1982). *The pursuit of power: Technology, armed force, and society since A.D. 1000*. Chicago: University of Chicago Press.

Milroy, J. (1994). The notion of 'standard Language' and its applicability to the study of early modern English pronunciation. In D. Stein & I. Tieken-Boon van Ostade (Eds.), *Towards a standard English 1600–1800* (pp. 19–29). Berlin: Mouton de Gruyter.

Morris, I. (2010). *Why the West rules – For now: The patterns of history, and what they reveal about the future*. New York: Farrar, Straus and Giroux.

Norman, J. (1988). *Chinese*. Cambridge, UK: Cambridge University Press.

Parker, G. (1996). *The military revolution: military innovation and the rise of the West, 1500–1800* (2nd ed.). Cambridge, UK: Cambridge University Press.

Reed, C. A. (2004). *Gutenberg in Shanghai: Chinese print capitalism, 1876–1937*. Vancouver: UBC Press.

Rowland, K. T. (1970). *Steam at sea: A history of steam navigation.* Newton Abbot: David & Charles.
Scott, J. C. (1998). *Seeing like a state: How certain schemes to improve the human condition have failed.* New Haven: Yale University Press.
Seton-Watson, H. (1977). *Nations and states: An inquiry into the origins of nations and the politics of nationalism.* London: Methuen.
Smith, M. R. (1977). *Harper's Ferry Armory and the new technology: The challenge of change.* Ithaca: Cornell University Press.
Smith, A., Cannan, E., & Stigler, G. J. (1977 [original 1776]). *An inquiry into the nature and causes of the wealth of nations.* Chicago: University of Chicago Press.
Spence, M. (1973). Job market signaling. *Quarterly Journal of Economics, 87*(3), 355–374.
Tilly, C. (1990). *Coercion, capital and European states.* Oxford: Blackwell.
Tönnies, F. (2001 [original 1887]). *Community and civil society.* Cambridge: Cambridge University Press.
van Zanden, J. L. (2009). *The long road to the industrial revolution: The European economy in a global perspective, 1000–1800.* Leiden: Brill.
Zeschky, M., Widenmayer, B., & Gassmann, O. (2011). Frugal innovation in emerging markets. *Research-Technology Management, 54*(4), 38–45.

REFERENCES

Abney-Hastings, M. (2011). *Commander of the Karteria: Honoured in Greece. Unknown at home*. Bloomington: AuthorHouse.
Acemoglu, D., & Robinson, J. A. (2012). *Why nations fail: The origins of power, prosperity and poverty*. London: Profile Books.
Aggarwal, D. D. (2002). *History and development of elementary education in India* (Vol. 1). New Delhi: Sarap and Sons.
Agoston, G., & Masters, B. (2009). *Encyclopedia of the Ottoman Empire*. New York: Facts on File.
Aksan, V. H. (2007). *Ottoman wars, 1700–1870: An empire besieged*. Harlow: Longman.
Alder, K. (1997). Innovation and amnesia: Engineering rationality and the fate of interchangeable parts. *Technology and Culture, 38*(2), 273–311.
Alesina, A., & La Ferrara, E. (2005). Ethnic diversity and economic performance. *Journal of Economic Literature, 43*, 762–800.
Alesina, A., Michalopoulos, S., & Papaioannou, E. (2016). Ethnic inequality. *Journal of Political Economy, 124*, 428–488.
Allen, R. C. (2009). *The British industrial revolution in global perspective*. Cambridge, UK: Cambridge University Press.
Amory, H. (1998). British books abroad: The American colonies. In J. Barnard & D. F. McKenzie (Eds.), *The Cambridge history of the book in Britain, vol. IV, 1557–1695* (pp. 744–752). Cambridge, UK: Cambridge University Press.
Anderson, M. M. (1990). *Hidden power: The palace eunuchs of imperial China*. Buffalo: Prometheus Books.
Anderson, B. (2006). *Imagined communities: Reflections on the origin and spread of nationalism* (Revised ed.). London: Verso.

Andrade, T. (2016). *The gunpowder age: China, military innovation, and the rise of the West in world history*. Princeton: Princeton University Press.

Angeles, L. (2014). *The economics of printing in early modern China* (Working paper). Adam Smith Business School, University of Glasgow.

Archer, I. W. (2011). Commerce and consumption. In S. Doran & N. Jones (Eds.), *The Elizabethan world* (pp. 411–426). London: Routledge.

Asquith, S. (1981). *New Model Army 1645–60*. Oxford: Osprey Publishing.

Auerbach, J. A. (1999). *The great exhibition of 1851: A nation on display*. New Haven: London Yale University Press.

Austin, F. (1994). The effect of exposure to standard English: The language of William Clift. In D. Stein & I. Tieken-Boon van Ostade (Eds.), *Towards a standard English 1600–1800* (pp. 285–314). Berlin: Mouton de Gruyter.

Bada'uni, A.-Q. (1898). *Muntakhabu-t-tawārīkh (Selections from Histories)* (trans: Ranking, G.). Kolkata: Asiatic Society.

Badem, C. (2010). *The Ottoman Crimean War: (1853–1856)*. Boston: Brill.

Baida, P. (1987). Eli Whitney's other talent. *American Heritage, 38*(4), online edition.

Bairoch, P., Batou, J., & Chèvre, P. (1988). *The population of European cities, 800–1850*. Geneva: Librairie Droz.

Barber, C. (1993). *The English language: A historical introduction*. Cambridge, UK: Cambridge University Press.

Barnard, J., & Bell, M. (1998). Statistical tables. In J. Barnard & D. F. McKenzie (Eds.), *The Cambridge history of the book in Britain, vol. IV, 1557–1695* (pp. 779–793). Cambridge, UK: Cambridge University Press.

Baten, J., & van Zanden, J. L. (2008). Book production and the onset of modern economic growth. *Journal of Economic Growth, 13*(3), 217–235.

Baten, J., Ma, D., Morgan, S., & Wang, Q. (2010). Evolution of living standards and human capital in China in the 18–20th centuries: Evidences from real wages, age-heaping, and anthropometrics. *Explorations in Economic History, 47*, 347–359.

Battison, E. A. (1966). Eli Whitney and the milling machine. *Smithsonian Journal of History, 1*(2), 9–34.

Begum, F. (1989). John Borthwick Gilchrist. In A. Datta (Ed.), *Encyclopaedia of Indian literature* (Vol. II, pp. 1409–1410). New Delhi: Sahitya Akademi.

Bertrand, C.-J. (1969). *The British press: An historical survey*. Paris: OCDL.

Black, J. B. (1936). *The reign of Elizabeth 1558–1603*. Oxford: Clarendon.

Black, J. (1991). *A military revolution? Military change and European society 1550–1800*. London: Macmillan.

Black, J. (2009). *Naval power: A history of warfare and the sea from 1500*. Basingstoke: Palgrave Macmillan.

Blank, P. (2006). The babel of renaissance English. In L. Mugglestone (Ed.), *The Oxford history of English* (pp. 212–239). Oxford: Oxford University Press.

Blomfield, D. (1992). *Lahore to Lucknow: The Indian mutiny journal of Arthur Moffat Lang*. London: Leo Cooper.

Bloom, J. M. (1999, June). *Revolution by the ream: A history of paper*. Retrieved October 26, 2015, from Aramco World. Vol. 50, Number 3. https://www.saudiaramcoworld.com/issue/199903/revolution.by.the.ream-a.history.of.paper.htm

Blythe, R. J. (2004). Aden, British India and the development of steam power in the Red Sea, 1825–1839. In D. Killingray, M. Lincoln, & N. Rigby (Eds.), *Maritime empires: British imperial maritime trade in the nineteenth century* (pp. 68–83). Woodbridge: Boydell Press.

Borsay, P. (2002). The culture of improvement. In P. Langford (Ed.), *The eighteenth century 1688–1815* (pp. 183–212). Oxford: Oxford University Press.

Bowman, J. S. (2000). *Columbia chronologies of Asian history and culture*. New York: Columbia University Press.

Boyd, R., & Richerson, P. J. (2009). Culture and the evolution of human cooperation. *Philosophical Transactions of the Royal Society B, 364*, 3281–3288.

Bragg, M. (2003). *The adventure of English*. London: Hodder and Stoughton.

Bresnahan, T. F., & Trajtenberg, M. (1995). General purpose technologies: 'engines of growth'? *Journal of Econometrics, 65*, 83–108.

Briscoe, B., Odlyzko, A., & Tilly, B. (2006). *Metcalfe's law is wrong*. Retrieved January 15, 2015, from IEEE Spectrum. http://spectrum.ieee.org/computing/networks/metcalfes-law-is-wrong

Broadberry, S., & Gupta, B. (2009). Lancashire, India, and shifting competitive advantage in cotton textiles, 1700–1850: The neglected role of factor prices. *Economic History Review, 62*, 279–305.

Broadberry, S., Guan, H., & Li, D. D. (2014). *China, Europe and the great divergence: A study in historical national accounting, 980–1850*. Retrieved October 17, 2016, from eh.net. http://eh.net/eha/wp-content/uploads/2014/05/Broadberry.pdf

Brook, T. (1998). *The confusions of pleasure: Commerce and culture in Ming China*. Berkeley: University of California Press.

Brook, T. (2013). *The troubled empire: China in the Yuan and Ming dynasties*. Cambridge, MA: Belknap Press.

Brown, D. K. (1995). Wood, sails and cannonballs to steel, steam and shells. In J. R. Hill & B. Ranft (Eds.), *The Oxford illustrated history of the Royal Navy* (pp. 200–226). Oxford: Oxford University Press.

Brown, K. M. (2008a). Monarchy and government in Britain, 1603–1637. In J. Wormald (Ed.), *The seventeenth century* (pp. 13–50). Oxford: Oxford University Press.

Brown, R. R. (2008b). *Verbruggen, Jan (bap. 1712, d. 1781)*. Retrieved March 11, 2016, from Oxford Dictionary of National Biography. http://www.oxforddnb.com/view/article/47492

Bullinger, A. C., Neyer, A.-K., Rass, M., & Moeslein, K. M. (2010). Community-based innovation contests: Where competition meets cooperation. *Creativity and Innovation Management, 19*, 290–303.

Buringh, E., & Van Zanden, J. L. (2009). Charting the "rise of the west": Manuscripts and printed books in Europe, a long-term perspective from the sixth through eighteenth centuries. *Journal of Economic History, 69*, 409–445.

Cain, P. J., & Hopkins, A. G. (2002). *British imperialism: 1688–2000*. London: Routledge.

Callahan, R. (2007). The great sepoy mutiny. In D. P. Marston & C. S. Sundaram (Eds.), *A military history of India and South Asia from the East India Company to the nuclear era* (pp. 16–33). Bloomington: Indiana University Press.

Cantrell, J. (2002). Henry Maudslay. In J. Cantrell & G. Cookson (Eds.), *Henry Maudslay & the pioneers of the machine age* (pp. 18–38). Stroud: Tempus Publishing.

Cardwell, D. S. (1991). *Turning points in western technology*. Canton: Science History Publications.

Chambers, W., & Chambers, R. (1848). Gleanings in bibliography. *Chambers' Edinburgh Journal, 9–10*(211), 43–45.

Chaojua, T., & van Heuven, V. J. (2009). Mutual intelligibility of Chinese dialects experimentally tested. *Lingua, 119*, 709–732.

Chartrand, R. (2003). *Napoleon's guns 1792–1815 (1)*. Oxford: Osprey Publishing.

Chen, Q. (2015). Climate shocks, dynastic cycles and nomadic conquests: Evidence from historical China. *Oxford Economic Papers, 67*, 185–204.

Chief of Staff, A. H. (1911). *Frontier and overseas expeditions from India* (Vol. 6). Calcutta: Superintendent Government Printing.

Chow, K.-W. (1996). Writing for success: Printing, examinations, and intellectual change in late Ming China. *Late Imperial China, 17*(1), 120–157.

Cipolla, C. M. (1966). *Guns, sails and empires: Technological innovation and the early phases of European expansion*. New York: Pantheon.

Cizakca, M. (2013). The Ottoman government and economic life: Taxation, public finance and trade controls. In S. N. Faroqhi & K. Fleet (Eds.), *The Cambridge history of Turkey* (Vol. 2, pp. 241–275). Cambridge, UK: Cambridge University Press.

Clark, B. E. (2010). *Symington and the steamboat*. Raleigh: Lulu Press.

Clodfelter, M. (2008). *Warfare and armed conflicts: A statistical reference to casualty and other figures, 1500–2000*. Jefferson: McFarland.

Coblin, W. S. (2000). A brief history of Mandarin. *Journal of the American Oriental Society, 120*, 537–552.

Cookson, G. (2004). *Roberts, Richard (1789–1864)*. Retrieved April 15, 2016, from Oxford Dictionary of National Biography, Oxford University Press. http://www.oxforddnb.com/view/article/23770

Cressy, D. (1975). *Education in Tudor and Stuart England*. New York: St. Martin's Press.
Cressy, D. (1980). *Literacy and the social order: Reading and writing in Tudor and Stuart England*. Cambridge, UK: Cambridge University Press.
Crossley, P. K. (1997). *The Manchus*. Oxford: Blackwell.
Crystal, D. (1997). *The Cambridge encyclopedia of language* (2nd ed.). Cambridge, UK: Cambridge University Press.
Crystal, D. (2003). *The Cambridge encyclopedia of the English language*. Cambridge, UK: Cambridge University Press.
Darling, L. T. (2006). Public finances: The role of the Ottoman centre. In S. N. Faroqhi (Ed.), *The Cambridge history of Turkey, vol. 3, The later Ottoman Empire, 1603–1839* (pp. 118–134). Cambridge: Cambridge University Press.
Dash, M. (2012). *The Ottoman Empire's life-or-death race*. Retrieved October 5, 2015, from smithsonian.com. http://www.smithsonianmag.com/history/the-ottoman-empires-life-or-death-race-164064882/?no-ist
Daumas, M. (1969). *A history of technology and invention, vol. I, The origins of technical civilization*. London: John Murray.
Daumas, M. (1979). *A history of technology and invention, vol. II, The first stages of mechanization, 1450–1725*. New York: Crown Publishers.
Daumas, M. (1980). *A history of technology and invention, vol. III, The expansion of mechanization 1725–1860*. London: John Murray.
de Vries, J., & van der Woude, A. (1997). *The first modern economy: Success, failure and perseverance of the Dutch economy, 1500–1815*. Cambridge: Cambridge University Press.
Diamond, J. (1997). *Guns, germs, and steel: The fates of human societies*. New York: W.W. Norton & Co.
Dickinson, H. W. (1939). *A short history of the steam engine*. Cambridge, UK: Cambridge University Press.
Dong, H. (2014). *A history of the Chinese language*. London: Routledge.
Doran, S. (2003). *Queen Elizabeth I*. London: The British Library.
Doran, S. (2006). James VI and the English succession. In R. Houlbrooke (Ed.), *James VI and I: Ideas, authority and government* (pp. 25–42). Aldershot: Ashgate.
Dreyer, E. L. (1988). Military origins of Ming China. In D. Twitchett & F. W. Mote (Eds.), *Cambridge history of China, vol. 7, The Ming Dynasty, 1368–1644, part 1* (pp. 58–106). Cambridge: Cambridge University Press.
Dua, H. R. (1994). Urdu. In R. E. Asher & J. M. Simpson (Eds.), *The encyclopedia of language and linguistics* (pp. 4863–4864). Oxford: Pergamon Press.
Duchesme, R. (2011). *The uniqueness of western civilization*. Leiden: Brill.
Dudley, L. (1991). *The word and the sword: How techniques of information and violence have shaped our world*. Oxford: Basil Blackwell.

Dudley, L. (2012). *Mothers of innovation: How expanding social networks gave birth to the industrial revolution.* Newcastle upon Tyne: Cambridge Scholars.

Dudley, L. (2016). Language standardization and the industrial revolution. *Oxford Economic Papers Advance Access.* doi:10.1093/oep/gpw059

Dunan-Page, A., & Lynch, B. (2008). *Roger L'Estrange and the making of restoration culture.* Aldershot: Ashgate.

Dupuy, R. E., & Dupuy, T. (1986). *The encyclopedia of military history from 3500 B.C. to the present.* New York: Harper and Row.

Ebrey, P. B. (1996). *The Cambridge illustrated history of China.* Cambridge, UK: Cambridge University Press.

Eisenstein, E. L. (1979). *The printing press as an agent of change.* Cambridge, UK: Cambridge University Press.

Elliott, M. C. (2001). *The Manchu way: The eight banners and ethnic identity in late imperial China.* Stanford: Stanford University Press.

Erickson, C. (1983). *The first Elizabeth.* London: Macmillan.

Fairbank, J. K., & Goldman, M. (2006 [original 1992]). *China: A new history.* (2nd enlarged ed.). Cambridge, MA: Belknap Press.

Fallows, J. (2013). *The 50 greatest breakthroughs since the wheel.* Retrieved October 19, 2015, from theatlantic.com. http://www.theatlantic.com/magazine/archive/2013/11/innovations-list/309536/

Falls, C. (1950). *Elizabeth's Irish Wars.* London: Methuen.

Faroqhi, S. N. (2006). Rural life. In S. N. Faroqhi (Ed.), *The Cambridge history of Turkey, vol. 3, The later Ottoman Empire, 1603–1839* (pp. 376–392). Cambridge: Cambridge University Press.

Farrell, J., & Rabin, M. (1996). Cheap talk. *Journal of Economic Perspectives, 10*(3), 103–118.

Fauconnier, G., & Turner, M. (2002). *The way we think: Conceptual blending and the mind's hidden complexities.* New York: Basic Books.

Febvre, L., & Martin, H.-J. (1976). *The coming of the book: The impact of printing 1450–1800.* London: NLB.

Fennell, B. A. (2001). *A history of English: A sociolinguistic approach.* Oxford: Blackwell.

Ferguson, N. (2004). *Empire: The rise and demise of the British world order and the lessons for global power.* New York: Basic Books.

French, Y. (1950). *The great exhibition: 1851.* London: Harvill Press.

Fiske, S. T., Cuddy, A. J., & Glick, P. (2007). Universal dimensions of social cognition: warmth and competence. *Trends in Cognitive Sciences, 11*, 77–83.

Flexner, J. T. (1944). *Steamboats come true: American inventors in action.* New York: Viking.

Fordham University. (2014). *Letter from Qianlong emperor to George III, 1793.* Retrieved September 30, 2014, from Fordham University Modern History Sourcebook. http://sourcebooks.fordham.edu/mod/1793qianlong.asp

Frank, A. G. (2001). Review of the great divergence: Europe, China, and the making of the modern world economy by Kenneth Pomeranz. *Journal of Asian Studies, 60*, 180–182.

Freeborn, D. (1992). *From old English to standard English*. Basingstoke: Macmillan.

Fremont-Barnes, G. (2014). *Osprey guide to the Indian mutiny 1857–58*. Oxford: Osprey Publishing.

Fukuyama, F. (1995). *Trust: The social virtues and the creation of prosperity*. New York: Free Press.

Fuller, C. E. (1958). *The rifled musket*. New York: Bonanza Books.

Furber, H. (1931). *Henry Dundas, first Viscount Melville, 1742–1811*. Oxford: Oxford University Press.

Gaam, N. (2002). *The making of a legend – Redhouse*. Retrieved April 24, 2016, from Learning Practical Turkish. http://www.learningpracticalturkish.com/redhouse-dictionary-history.html

Ghosh, A. (2003). An uncertain 'coming of the book': Early print cultures in colonial India. In E. Greenspan & J. Rose (Eds.), *Book history* (Vol. 6, pp. 23–56). University Park: Pennsylvania State University Press.

Goodwin, J. (1998). *Lords of the horizons: A history of the Ottoman Empire*. New York: Henry Holt and Company.

Gooskens, C., Heeringa, W., & Beijering, K. (2008). Phonetic and lexical predictors of intelligibility. *International Journal of Humanities and Arts Computing, 2*(1–2), 63–81.

Gordon, R. B. (1989). Simeon North, John Hall, and mechanized manufacturing. *Technology and Culture, 30*, 179–188.

Graff, H. J. (1991). *The legacies of literacy*. Bloomington: Indiana University Press.

Green, C. M. (1956). *Eli Whitney and the birth of American technology*. Boston: Little, Brown and Company.

Green, J. (1996). *Chasing the sun: Dictionary makers and dictionaries they made*. New York: Henry Holt.

Green, N. (2012). *Islam and the army in colonial India: Sepoy religion in the service of empire*. Cambridge, UK: Cambridge University Press.

Greif, A., & Tabellini, G. (2010). Cultural and institutional bifurcation: China and Europe compared. *American Economic Review, Papers and Proceedings, 100*(2), 135–140.

Griffin, C. (2015). *The Queen's Bays (2nd Dragoon Guards)*. Retrieved November 2, 2015, from The British Empire. http://www.britishempire.co.uk/forces/armyunits/britishcavalry/queensbays.htm

Hanes, W. T., & Sanello, F. (2002). *Opium wars: The addiction of one empire and the corruption of another*. Naperville: Sourcebooks.

Hanioglu, M. S. (2008). *A brief history of the late Ottoman Empire*. Princeton: Princeton University Press.

Hannas, W. C. (1997). *Asia's orthographic dilemma*. Honolulu: University of Hawaii Press.
Harris, M. (1990). French. In B. Comrie (Ed.), *The world's major languages* (pp. 210–235). Oxford: Oxford University Press.
Harris, J. R. (2004). *Wilkinson, John (1728–1808)*. Retrieved March 14, 2016, from Oxford Dictionary of National Biography, Oxford University Press; online ed. http://www.oxforddnb.com/view/article/29428
Harvey, W., & Downs-Rose, G. (1980). *William Symington: Inventor and engine builder*. London: Northgate Publishing Co.
He, W. (2013). *Paths toward the modern fiscal state: England, Japan, and China*. Cambridge, MA: Harvard University Press.
Headrick, D. R. (1981). *The tools of empire: Technology and European imperialism in the nineteenth century*. Oxford: Oxford University Press.
Headrick, D. R. (2010). *Power over peoples: Technology, environments, and western imperialism, 1400 to the present*. Princeton: Princeton University Press.
Heald, H. (2012). *William Armstrong: Magician of the North*. Alnwick: McNidder and Grace.
Heblich, S., Lameli, A., & Riener, G. (2015). The effect of perceived regional accents on individual economic behavior: A lab experiment on linguistic performance, cognitive ratings and economic decisions. *PLoS One, 10*, 1–16.
Heijdra, M. (1998). The socio-economic development of rural China during the Ming. In D. Twitchett & F. W. Mote (Eds.), *Cambridge history of China* (Vol. 8, pp. 417–578). Cambridge, UK: Cambridge University Press.
Herman, A. (2001). *How the scots invented the modern world*. New York: Three Rivers Press.
Hevia, J. L. (1995). *Cherishing men from afar: Qing guest ritual and the Macartney Embassy of 1793*. Durham: Duke University Press.
Hills, R. D. (2002). *Life and inventions of Richard Roberts, 1769–1864*. Ashbourne: Landmark Publishing.
Hirsch, R. (1974). *Printing, selling and reading*. Wiesbaden: Otto Harrassowitz.
Hoffman, P. T. (2011). Prices, the military revolution, and western Europe's comparative advantage in violence. *Economic History Review, 64*, 39–59.
Hoffman, P. T. (2015). *Why did Europe conquer the world?* Princeton: Princeton University Press.
Hogg, O. F. (1970). *Artillery: Its origin, heyday and decline*. Hamden: Archon Books.
Holtzapffel, J. J. (1976 [original 1881]). *Hand or simple turning: Principles and practice*. New York: Dover Publications.
Hounshell, D. (1984). *From the American system to mass production, 1800–1932: The development of manufacturing technology in the United States*. Baltimore: Johns Hopkins University Press.

Houston, R. A. (1988). *Literacy in early modern Europe: Culture and education 1500–1800*. London: Longman.
Huang, R. (1974). *Taxation and governmental finance in sixteenth-century Ming China*. Cambridge, UK: Cambridge University Press.
Huang, R. (1998). The Ming fiscal administration. In D. Twitchett & F. W. Mote (Eds.), *The Cambridge history of China, vol. 8, The Ming Dynasty, 1368–1644, part 2* (pp. 106–171). Cambridge, UK: Cambridge University Press.
Hucker, C. O. (1998). Ming government. In D. Twitchett & F. W. Mote (Eds.), *The Cambridge history of China* (Vol. 8, pp. 9–105). Cambridge, UK: Cambridge University Press.
Hunting, M. (2014). Musket smooth bore pattern of 1858 and 1859. *Black Powder*, p. 27.
Inalcik, H. (1973). *The Ottoman Empire: The classical age 1300–1600*. New York: Praeger.
Jacob, M. C. (1997). *Scientific culture and the making of the industrial West*. Oxford: Oxford University Press.
Jacques, T. (2007). *Dictionary of battles and sieges: A guide to 8500 battles from antiquity through the twenty-first century* (Vol. 2). Westport: Greenwood Press.
Jevons, S. (1865). *The coal question: An inquiry concerning the progress of the nation and the probable exhaustion of our coal-mines*. London: Macmillan.
Jha, H. (2011). Decay of village community and the decline of vernacular education in Bihar and Bengal in the colonial era: A sociological review. *Indian Historical Review, 38*, 119–137.
Johnson, S. (2010). *Where good ideas come from: The natural history of innovation*. New York: Riverhead Books.
Johnson, N. D., & Koyama, M. (2014). Tax farming and the origins of state capacity in England and France. *Explorations in Economic History, 51*, 1–20.
Jones, E. L. (1981). *The European miracle*. Cambridge, UK: Cambridge University Press.
Jones, E. L. (2010). *Locating the industrial revolution: Inducement and response*. Singapore: World Scientific.
Karateke, H. T. (2012). 'On the tranquility and repose of the Sultan': The construction of a topos. In C. Woodhead (Ed.), *The Ottoman world* (pp. 116–129). New York: Routledge.
Kaske, E. (2008). *The politics of language in Chinese education, 1895–1919*. Leiden: Brill.
Kaye, A. S. (1990). Arabic. In B. Comrie (Ed.), *The world's major languages* (pp. 664–685). Oxford: Oxford University Press.
Keay, J. (2000). *India: A history*. New York: Grove Press.
Kelly, L. G. (2004). *Painter, William (1540?–1595)*. Retrieved October 12, 2015, from Oxford Dictionary of National Biography, online ed. http://www.oxfordnb.com/view/article/21135
Kennedy, P. (1987). *The rise and fall of the great powers*. New York: Random House.

Kesavan, B. S. (1985). *History of printing and publishing in India* (Vol. I). New Delhi: National Book Trust, India.

Kipling, R. (2009 [original 1865]). The burning of the "Sarah Sands". In R. Kipling (Ed.), *Land and sea tales for scouts and guides* (pp. 100–108). Kelly Bray: Stratus Books.

Ko, D. (1994). *Teachers of the inner chambers: Women and culture in seventeenth-century China*. Stanford: Stanford University Press.

Kömürcüler, G. (2016). *Turkey among most innovation-ready nations in region, says general electric report*. Retrieved November 18, 2016, from Hürriyet Daily News. http://www.hurriyetdailynews.com/turkey-among-most-innovation-ready-nations-in-region-says-general-electric-report-.aspx?pageID=238&nID=74129&NewsCatID=344

Konishi, M. (2013). *Hath-Kaghaz: History of handmade paper in South Asia*. New Delhi: Aryan Books International.

Kornfilt, J. (1990). Turkish and the Turkic languages. In B. Comrie (Ed.), *The world's major languages* (pp. 619–644). Oxford: Oxford University Press.

Kronoskaf. (2014). *Liechtenstein, Fürst Joseph Wenzel von*. Retrieved October 22, 2016, from Kronoskaf the Virtual Time Machine. http://www.kronoskaf.com/syw/index.php?title=Liechtenstein,_F%C3%BCrst_Joseph_Wenzel_von

Kumar, D. (2003). India. In R. Porter (Ed.), *Cambridge history of science* (Vol. 4, pp. 669–687). Cambridge, UK: Cambridge University Press.

Kurlansky, M. (2016). *Paper: Paging through history*. New York: W. W. Norton.

Kuru, S. S. (2013). The literature of rum: The making of a literary tradition (1450–1600). In S. N. Faroqi & K. Fleet (Eds.), *The Cambridge history of Turkey, vol. 2, The Ottoman Empire as a world power, 1453–1603* (pp. 548–592). Cambridge: Cambridge University Press.

Lagally, K. (1992). ArabTEX – Typesetting Arabic with vowels and ligatures. *MAPS, 9*, 108–116.

Lee, T. H. (2000). *Education in traditional China: A history*. Leiden: Brill.

Lev-Ari, S., & Keysar, B. (2010). Why don't we believe non-native speakers? The influence of accent on credibility. *Journal of Experimental Social Psychology, 11*(2), 77–83.

Lewis, B. (2002). *What went wrong?: The clash between Islam and modernity in the Middle East*. Oxford: Oxford University Press.

Lunde, P. (1981). *Arabic and the art of printing*. Retrieved October 27, 2015, from aramcoworld.com. http://www.aramcoworld.com/issue/198102/arabic.and.the.art.of.printing-a.special.section.htm

Lynn, J. A. (1995). States in conflict 1661–1763. In G. Parker (Ed.), *The Cambridge illustrated history of warfare* (pp. 164–185). Cambridge: Cambridge University Paree.

M'Ghee, R. (1862). *How we got to Pekin: A narrative of the campaign in China of 1860*. London: Richard Bentley.

MacLean, G. (1994). Literacy, class, and gender in restoration England. *Text, 7,* 307–335.
MacLennan, K. (2003). Liechtenstein and Gribeauval: 'Artillery revolution' in political and cultural context. *War in History, 10,* 249–264.
MacMillan, K. (2011). Exploration, trade and empire. In S. Doran & N. Jones (Eds.), *The Elizabethan world* (pp. 646–662). London: Routledge.
Maddison, A. (2001). *The world economy: A millennial perspective.* Paris: OECD.
Maddison, A. (2005). *Growth and interaction in the world economy: The roots of modernity.* Washington, DC: AEI Press.
Maddison, A. (2007). *Contours of the world economy, 1-2030 AD: Essays in macroeconomic history.* Oxford: Oxford University Press.
Man, J. (2002). *The Gutenberg revolution: The story of a genius and an invention that changed the world.* London: Review.
Marks, S. G. (2016). *The information nexus: global capitalism from the renaissance to the present.* Cambridge: Cambridge University Press.
Marsden, B. (2002). *Watt's perfect engine: steam and the age of invention.* New York: Columbia University Press.
Martel, P. (2002). Occitan, français et construction de l'État en France. In D. Lacorne & T. Judt (Eds.), *La politique de Babel: du monolinguisme d'État au plurilinguisme des peuples* (pp. 87–116). Paris: Editions Karthala.
Marx, K. (1990 [original 1867]). *Capital: A critique of political economy* (Vol. 1). London: Penguin.
Masica, C. P. (1991). *The Indo-Aryan languages.* Cambridge: Cambridge University Press.
Matheson, C. (1933). *The life of Henry Dundas – First Viscount Melville.* London: Constable & Co.
McKenzie, D. F. (1998). Printing and publishing 1557–1700: Constraints on the London book trades. In J. Barnard & D. F. McKenzie (Eds.), *The Cambridge history of the book in Britain, vol. IV, 1557–1695* (pp. 553–567). Cambridge, UK: Cambridge University Press.
McMahon, A. (2006). Restructuring renaissance English. In L. Mugglestone (Ed.), *The oxford history of English* (pp. 147–177). Oxford: Oxford University Press.
McNeill, W. H. (1963). *The rise of the West.* Chicago: University of Chicago Press.
McNeill, W. H. (1982). *The pursuit of power: Technology, armed force, and society since A.D. 1000.* Chicago: University of Chicago Press.
Metcalf, B. D., & Metcalf, T. R. (2006). *A concise history of modern India* (2nd ed.). Cambridge: Cambridge University Press.
Millward, C. M. (1988). *A biography of the English language.* New York: Harcourt Brace Jovanovich.
Milroy, J. (1994). The notion of 'standard Language' and its applicability to the study of early modern English pronunciation. In D. Stein & I. Tieken-Boon van

Ostade (Eds.), *Towards a standard English 1600–1800* (pp. 19–29). Berlin: Mouton de Gruyter.

Mokyr, J. (1990). *The lever of riches: Technological creativity and economic progress.* Oxford: Oxford University Press.

Mokyr, J. (2002). *The gifts of Athena: historical origins of the knowledge economy.* Princeton: Princeton University Press.

Mokyr, J. (2009). *The enlightened economy: An economic history of Britain 1700–1850.* New Haven: Yale University Press.

Morris, I. (2010). *Why the West rules – For now: The patterns of history, and what they reveal about the future.* New York: Farrar, Straus and Giroux.

Mueller, D. C. (2003). *Public choice III.* Cambridge: Cambridge University Press.

Muir, D. (2000). *Reflections in Bullough's Pond: Economy and ecosystem in New England.* Hanover: University Press of New England.

Naik, P. (2006). *450 years of printing in India.* Retrieved from goanet.org. http://www.mail-archive.com/goanet@lists.goanet.org/msg03166.html

Natarajan, S. (1962). *A history of the press in India.* Bombay: Asia Publishing House.

National Army Museum. (2014, July 7). *54th (West Norfolk) regiment of foot.* Retrieved May 30, 2016, from Famour Units. http://www.nam.ac.uk/research/famous-units/54th-west-norfolk-regiment-foot

Needham, J. (1965). *Science and civilisation in China, vol. 4, physics and physical technology, part II, mechanical engineering.* Cambridge, UK: Cambridge University Press.

Needham, J. (1969). *The grand titration.* Toronto: University of Toronto Press.

Nelson, C., & Seccombe, M. (1998). The creation of the periodical press, 1620–1695. In J. Barnard & D. F. McKenzie (Eds.), *The Cambridge history of the book in Britain, vol. IV, 1557–1695* (pp. 533–549). Cambridge, UK: Cambridge University Press.

Netstate. (2016). *Eli Terry.* Retrieved April 14, 2016, from Netstate.com. http://www.netstate.com/states/peop/people/ct_et.htm

Neumann, C. K. (2006). Political and diplomatic developments. In S. N. Faroqhi (Ed.), *Cambridge history of Turkey, vol. 3, The later Ottoman Empire, 1603–1839* (pp. 44–64). Cambridge, UK: Cambridge University Press.

Newell, J. K. (1875). *Ours. Annals of 10th regiment.* Springfield: Nichols & Co.

Nicholas, T. (2010). The role of independent invention in U.S. technological development, 1880–1930. *Journal of Economic History, 70,* 57–82.

Norman, J. (1988). *Chinese.* Cambridge, UK: Cambridge University Press.

North, D. C. (1981). *Structure and change in economic history.* New York: Norton.

North, D. C., & Weingast, B. R. (1989). Constitutions and commitment: The evolution of institutions governing public choice in eighteenth century England. *Journal of Economic History, 49,* 803–832.

Nurullah, S., & Naik, J. P. (1964). *A students' history of education in India (1806–1965).* Macmillan: Bombay.

Nuvolari, A., & Vasta, M. (1913). *Independent invention in Italy during the liberal age, 1861–1913*. Pisa: Sant'Anna School of Advanced Studies.

O'Brien, P. K. (2011). The nature and historical evolution of an exceptional fiscal state and its possible significance for the precocious commercialization and industrialization of the British economy from Cromwell to Nelson. *Economic History Review, 64*(2), 408–446.

Offenberg, A. K. (1969). The first printed book produced at constantinople: (Jacob ben Ašer's 'Arba'ah Ṭûrîm, December 13, 1493). *Studia Rosenthaliana, 3,* 96–112.

Omar, I. A. (2006). Islam. In S. Wolpert (Ed.), *Encyclopedia of India* (Vol. 2, pp. 299–303). Farmington Hills: Charles Scribner's Sons.

Özcan, B. (2012). 1853–1856 Ottoman-Russian war and Egypt state. *Ekev Akademi Dergisi, 16*(51), 45–59.

Pamuk, Ş. (2000). *A monetary history of the Ottoman Empire*. Cambridge: Cambridge University Press.

Parker, G. (1996). *The military revolution: military innovation and the rise of the West, 1500–1800* (2nd ed.). Cambridge, UK: Cambridge University Press.

Peck, L. L. (1993). *Court patronage and corruption in early Stuart England*. London: Routledge.

Percy, J. (1864). *Metallurgy: Iron and steel*. London: John Murray.

Peterson, W. (1998). Confucian learning in late ming thought. In D. Twitchett & F. W. Mote (Eds.), *The Cambridge history of China, vol. 8, The Ming dynasty, 1368–1644, part 2* (pp. 708–788). Cambridge: Cambridge University Press.

Pincus, S. (2009). *1688: The first modern revolution*. New Haven: Yale University Press.

Pinker, S. (2011). *The better angels of our nature: Why violence has declined*. New York: Viking Penguin.

Pomeranz, K. (2000). *The great divergence: China, Europe, and the making of the modern world economy*. Princeton: Princeton University Press.

Potter, E. B. (1981). *Sea power: A naval history*. Annapolis: Naval Institute Press.

Powell, B. B. (2009). *Writing: Theory and history of the technology of civilization*. Chichester: Wiley-Blackwell.

Powell, W. W., Koput, K. W., & Smith-Doerr, L. (1996). Interorganizational collaboration and the locus of innovation: Networks of learning in biotechnology. *Administrative Science Quarterly, 41,* 116–145.

Prabhu, J. (2006). Educational institutions and philosophies, traditional and modern. In S. Wolpert (Ed.), *Encyclopedia of India* (Vol. 2, pp. 23–28). Farmington Hills: Thomson Gale.

Prost, J.-C. A. (1889). *Le Marquis de Jouffroy d'Abbans, Inventeur de l'application de la vapeur à la navigation*. Paris: Ernest Leroux.

Qozhaya. (2015). *Short history of the monastery of Saint Anthony, the great valley of Qozhaya*. Retrieved December 16, 2015, from Qozhaya.com. http://www.qozhaya.com/history.html

Quataert, D. (2005). *The Ottoman Empire 1700–1922* (2nd ed.). Cambridge, UK: Cambridge University Press.

Rathod, N. G. (1994). *The great Maratha Mahadji Scindia*. New Delhi: Sarup & Sons.

Raven, J. (1998). The economic context. In J. Barnard & D. F. McKennzie (Eds.), *The Cambridge history of the book in Britain, vol. IV, 1557–1695* (pp. 568–582). Cambridge, UK: Cambridge University Press.

Rawski, E. (1979). *Education and popular literacy in Ch'ing China*. Ann Arbor: University of Michigan Press.

Raymond, J. (2011). News. In S. Doran & N. Jones (Eds.), *The Elizabethan world* (pp. 495–510). London: Routledge.

Reed, C. A. (2004). *Gutenberg in Shanghai: Chinese print capitalism, 1876–1937*. Vancouver: UBC Press.

Reis, J. (2005). Economic growth, human capital formation, and consumption in western Europe before 1800. In R. C. Allen, T. Bengtsson, & M. Dribe (Eds.), *Living standards in the past: New perspectives on well-being in Asia and Europe* (pp. 195–225). Oxford: Oxford University Press.

Rhoads, E. J. (2000). *Manchus and Han: Ethnic relations and political power in late Qing and early republican China, 1861–1928*. Seattle: Washington University Press.

Ricci, M. (1953 [original 1615]). *China in the sixteenth century: The journals of Matthew Ricci, 1583–1610* (trans: Gallagher, L. J.). New York: Random House.

Richards, J. F. (1993). *The Mughal empire*. Cambridge: Cambridge University Press.

Ringmar, E. (2013). *Liberal barbarism: The European destruction of the palace of the emperor of China*. New York: Palgrave Macmillan.

Robbins, H. H. (2010 [original 1908]). *Our first ambassador to China: An account of the life of George, Earl of Macartney*. Cambridge: Cambridge University Press.

Roberts, M. (1956). *The military revolution, 1560–1660*. Belfast: M. Boyd.

Roberts, J. (1998). The Latin trade. In J. Barnard & D. F. McKenzie (Eds.), *The Cambridge history of the book in Britain, vol. IV, 1557–1695* (pp. 141–173). Cambridge: Cambridge University Press.

Roe, J. W. (1926). *English and American tool builders*. New York: McGraw-Hill.

Rolt, L. T. (1962). *Great engineers*. London: Bell.

Rolt, L. (1986). *Tools for the job: A history of machine tools to 1950*. London: Her Majesty's Stationery Office.

Rolt, L. T., & Allen, J. S. (1977). *The steam engine of Thomas Newcomen*. Hartington: Moorland Pub. Co.

Roper, G. (1995). Faris al-Shidyaq and the transition from scribal to print culture in the Middle East. In G. N. Atiyeh (Ed.), *The book in the Islamic world: The written*

word and communication in the Middle East (pp. 209–231). Albany: State University of New York Press.
Roper, G. (2010). *Manuscripts and printing in the spread of Muslim science.* Retrieved October 27, 2015, from Muslim Heritage. http://www.muslimheritage.com/article/manuscripts-and-printing-spread-muslim-science
Rose, A. (2008). *American rifle: A biography.* New York: Delacorte Press.
Rowe, W. T. (2009). *China's last empire: The great Qing.* Cambridge, MA: Belknap Press.
Rowland, K. T. (1970). *Steam at sea: A history of steam navigation.* Newton Abbot: David & Charles.
Roy, K. (2007). The armed expansion of the English East India Company: 1740s–1849. In D. P. Marston & C. S. Sundaram (Eds.), *A military history of India and South Asia* (pp. 1–15). Bloomington: Indiana University Press.
Salvadori, N., & Signorino, R. (2014). Adam Smith On monopoly theory. Making good a lacuna. *Scottish Journal of Political Economy, 61,* 178–195.
Sarkiss, H. J. (1937). The Armenian renaissance, 1500–1863. *Journal of Modern History, 9*(4), 433–448.
Scharfe, H. (2002). *Education in ancient India.* Leiden: Brill.
Schumpeter, J. A. (2008 [original 1942]). *Capitalism, socialism and democracy.* New York: HarperCollins.
Scott, J. C. (1998). *Seeing like a state: How certain schemes to improve the human condition have failed.* New Haven: Yale University Press.
Sen, S. (1988). Education in ancient and medieval India. *Indian Journal of History of Science, 23,* 1–32.
Seton-Watson, H. (1977). *Nations and states: An inquiry into the origins of nations and the politics of nationalism.* London: Methuen.
Shaw, S. J. (1971). *Between old and new: The Ottoman Empire under Sultan Selim III, 1789–1807.* Cambridge, MA: Harvard University Press.
Siggurdsson. (2013). *Battle of Palikao (Baliqiao), Anglo-French force defeats Chinese army, clearing way to Peking.* Retrieved 2016, from The American Legion's Burn-Pit. http://www.burnpit.us/2013/09/battle-palikao-anglo-french-force-defeats-chinese-army-clearing-way-peking
Singal, R. K., Singal, M., & Singal, R. (2008). *Fundamentals of machining and machine tools.* New Delhi: I K International Publishing House.
Small, H. (2011). *The Crimean War: Victoria's war with the Russian Tsars.* Slough: Tempus Publishing.
Smiles, S. (1968 [original 1863]). *Industrial biography: Iron-workers and tool-makers.* New York: A. M. Kelley.
Smith, V. A. (1917). *Akbar: The great Mogul 1542–1605.* Oxford: Clarendon.
Smith, M. R. (1973, October). John H. Hall, Simeon North, and the milling machine: The nature of innovation among antebellum arms makers. *Technology and Culture, 14*(4), 573–591.

Smith, M. R. (1977). *Harper's Ferry Armory and the new technology: The challenge of change*. Ithaca: Cornell University Press.

Smith, E. A. (2010). Communication and collective action: Language and the evolution of human cooperation. *Evolution and Human Behavior, 31*, 231–245.

Smith, A., Cannan, E., & Stigler, G. J. (1977 [original 1776]). *An inquiry into the nature and causes of the wealth of nations*. Chicago: University of Chicago Press.

Smithurst, P. (2011). *The pattern 1853 enfield rifle*. Botley: Osprey Publishing.

Snatak, V. (1989). Lallulal. In A. Datta (Ed.), *Encyclopedia of Indian literature* (pp. 2241–2241). New Delhi: Sahitya Akademi.

Soldon, N. C. (1998). *John Wilkinson, 1728–1808: English ironmaster and inventor*. Lampeter: Edwin Mellen Press.

Somel, S. A. (2001). *The modernization of public education in the Ottoman Empire, 1839–1908: Islamization, autocracy and discipline*. Leiden: Brill.

Spence, M. (1973). Job market signaling. *Quarterly Journal of Economics, 87*(3), 355–374.

Spencer, H. (1981 [original 1884]). *The man versus the state*. Indianapolis: Liberty Classics.

Spilsbury, J. (2007). *The Indian mutiny*. London: Weidenfeld and Nicolson.

Spufford, M. (1979). First steps in literacy: The reading and writing experiences of the humblest seventeenth-century spiritual autobiographers. *Social History, 4*(3), 407–435.

Stein, D. (1994). Sorting out the variants: Standardization and social factors in the English language 1600–1800. In D. Stein & I. Tieken-Boon van Ostade (Eds.), *Towards a standard English 1600–1800* (pp. 1–17). Berlin: Mouton de Gruyter.

Stoye, J. (2007). *The Siege of Vienna* (New ed.). Vienna: Birlinn.

Sumner, M. (2015). The social weight of spoken words. *Trends in Cognitive Sciences, 19*(5), 238–239.

Sumner, M., & Samuel, A. G. (2009). The role of experience in the processing of cross-dialectal variation. *Journal of Memory and Language, 60*, 487–501.

Taillemite, É. (2005). *Henri-Joseph Paixhans et sa nouvelle force maritime*. Retrieved June 17, 2014, from Institut de stratégie comparée. http://www.institut-strategie.fr/PN4_TAILLEMITE.html

Tang, C., & van Heuven, V. J. (2009). Mutual intelligibility of Chinese dialects experimentally tested. *Lingua, 119*, 709–732.

Temperley, H. (1936). *England and the near East: Crimea*. London: Longmans, Green and Co.

Temple, R. (2007). *The genius of China: 3000 years of science, discovery & invention*. Rochester: Inner Traditions.

Tezcan, B. (2010). *The second Ottoman Empire: Political and social transformation in the early modern world*. Cambridge: Cambridge University Press.

Thomson, R. (2009). *Structures of change in the mechanical age: Technological innovations in the United States, 1790–1865*. Baltimore: The Johns Hopkins University Press.

Tilly, C. (1990). *Coercion, capital and European states*. Oxford: Blackwell.

Tönnies, F. (2001 [original 1887]). *Community and civil society*. Cambridge: Cambridge University Press.

Treadwell, M. (1998). The stationers and the printing acts at the end of the seventeenth century. In J. Barnard & D. F. McKenzie (Eds.), *The Cambridge history of the book in Britain, vol. IV, 1557–1695* (pp. 755–776). Cambridge: Cambridge University Press.

Trimble, W. R. (1950). Early Tudor historiography, 1485–1548. *Journal of the History of Ideas, 11*, 30–41.

Turchin, P., & Nefedov, S. A. (2009). *Secular cycles*. Princeton: Princeton University Press.

Uglow, J. (2002). *The lunar men: Five friends whose curiosity changed the world*. New York: Farrar, Straus and Giroux.

Ursinus, M. (2012). The transformation of the Ottoman fiscal regime, c. 1600–1850. In C. Woodhead (Ed.), *The Ottoman world* (pp. 423–435). London: Routledge.

Uyar, M., & Erickson, E. J. (2009). *A military history of the Ottomans from Osman to Atatürk*. Santa Barbara: Praeger Security International.

van Zanden, J. L. (2009). *The long road to the industrial revolution: The European economy in a global perspective, 1000–1800*. Leiden: Brill.

von Glahn, R. (2016). *The economic history of China: From antiquity to the nineteenth century*. Cambridge: Cambridge University Press.

Watson, W. J. (1968). İbrāhīm Müteferriḳa and Turkish Incunabula. *Journal of the American Oriental Society, 88*(3), 435–441.

Webster, A. (2009). *The twilight of the East India company: The evolution of Anglo-Asian commerce and politics, 1790–1860*. Rochester: Boydell Press.

Wickwire, F., & Wickwire, M. (1980). *Cornwallis – The imperial years*. Chapel Hill: University of North Carolina Press.

Williams, D. (2014). A St-Étienne Made Pattern 1853 Rifle Musket. *Arms & Armour, 11*, 40–43.

Williams, D. J., & Johnson, W. (2001). Schön's view of rifled infantry arms in the mid 19th century. *International Journal of Impact Engineering, 25*, 315–330.

Windle, J. (2012). Insights for contemporary drug policy: A historical account of opium control in India and Pakistan. *Asian Criminology, 7*, 55–74.

Wojciszke, B., Bazinska, R., & Jaworski, M. (1998). On the dominance of moral categories in impression formation. *Personality and Social Psychology Bulletin, 24*, 1245–1257.

Wolpert, S. (1993). *A new history of India* (4th ed.). Oxford: Oxford University Press.

Woodbury, R. S. (1960). The legend of Eli Whitney and interchangeable parts. *Technology and Culture, 1*(3), 235–253.

Woodhead, C. (2012). Ottoman languages. In C. Woodhead (Ed.), *The Ottoman world* (pp. 143–158). London: Routledge.

Worthing, P. (2007). *A military history of modern China: From the Manchu conquest to Tian'anmen Square*. Westport: Praeger.

Yadav, M. (2013). *Education in Mughal period during Akbar's rule – India*. Retrieved October 20, 2015, from importantindia.com. http://www.importantindia.com/5096/education-in-mughal-period-during-akbar-rule/

Yang, L.-S. (1954). Toward a study of dynastic configurations in Chinese history. *Harvard Journal of Asiatic Studies, 17*, 329–345.

Zeschky, M., Widenmayer, B., & Gassmann, O. (2011). Frugal innovation in emerging markets. *Research-Technology Management, 54*(4), 38–45.

Index

A

Abbasid Caliphate, 59
Abdul Hamid I (r. 1774–1789), 200
Abdülmecid I (r. 1839–1861), 230, 246, 247
Acemoglu, D., 10
Afghanistan, 44, 54, 111, 137
Africa, 11
Agra, 45, 48, 72, 111, 140
Ahmadnagar, 44, 45, 48
Akbar, Emperor (r. 1556–1605), 3, 31, 44–8, 54, 55, 71, 86, 87, 111, 137–41
akçe (Ottoman coin), 43
Allen, R., 11, 12
American System of Production, 192
Anatolia, 1, 39, 43, 54, 107, 108, 135, 136, 230
Anderson, B., 5, 132, 142, 209, 237, 271
Armstrong, W., 238, 239, 274
Arrow Incident (1856), 223
artillery, 17, 45, 140, 141, 146, 233, 234
  Armstrong gun, 23, 239, 240, 259, 260
  field gun, 45, 183, 233–5, 238, 246, 259
  Paixhans gun, 22, 231, 232, 237
  rifled, 16, 243, 274
  shell-firing, vii, 7, 17, 22, 220, 230
  siege train, 45, 235, 236
  smoothbore, 16, 168, 227, 229, 238, 239, 246
Ashoka, 85, 110
Asirgarh, 45, 48
Atlantic, The, 59, 61
Aurangzeb, Emperor (r. 1658–1707), 137–42
Auspicious Incident (1826), 245
Austria, 32, 39, 182, 195, 199, 216
Austrian Succession, War of the (1740–1745), 182, 199

B

Babur, 44, 111
Bada'uni, `Abd al-Qadir, 31
Baghdad, 59
Bahadur Khan II, 236
Bahadur Nizam Shah, 45, 48
Bahadur Shah II, 233, 234
Bakht Khan, 234, 235
Balaclava, 248
banner system, 51, 143
Barnard, H., 233–6

Battison, E., 187
Beijing, 1, 21, 51–3, 205–11, 238–41, 257–61
Bengal, 47, 140, 198, 232–7, 250–7
Bengal Gazette, 73
Bible, 19, 60, 66, 71, 82, 92, 94
Birmingham, 13, 155, 170, 171, 176, 250, 257
Black Sea, 2, 201, 231, 237, 248, 249
Black, J., 16
Blanc, H., 185
Blank, P., 102
Blount, C., Baron Mountjoy, 35
Blount, T., 104
BMW Motorrad, 14
Boston, 104
Bouchon, B., 12, 155
Boulton, M., vi–vii, 155, 162, 170, 171
Bowlby, H., 258, 260
Boyd, R., 13
Braj Bhasha, 111
Bramah, J., 171–3, 274
Bridgewater, Duke of, 159, 160
Bristol, 12
Brook, T., 112
Bruce, J., 8th Earl of Elgin, 239, 258, 261
bullet, 238, 239, 244

C

Cain, P.J., 197
Calcutta, 23, 224–6, 233
Calley, J., 154, 164, 274
Campbell, Sir Colin, 225, 254–6
Canning, C., 1st Earl Canning, 233
cannon borer, 167, 169
Canton. *See Guangzhou*
Carmichael-Smyth, G., 251
Carron Company, 154–9, 169
carronade, 216
cartridge, 23, 251
Catherine the Great, 205
Catholicism, 60
Cawnpore, 253–5
Caxton, W., 62, 103
Cecil, R., 37, 60
Censorship, 76
Chancery, 270
Charles I, 64, 127, 129, 132
Charles II, 66, 130, 132
Charlotte Dundas, 159, 162
Charlotte Dundas II, 159, 160
China, 1
  literacy in, 88–92
  mass-produced rifles in, 257–61
  printing in, 73–7
  in 1700, 142–6
  in 1793, 205–9
  shell-firing cannon in, 237–41
  in 1600, 48–53
  steam warships in, 220–4
Chongzhen Emperor, 91, 92, 143
Chuenpi, Second Battle of (1841), 222
civil service, Chinese, 35, 85, 88–92, 112, 114
Civil Wars, England, 10
cizye (poll tax), 43, 135
Clive, R., 199
Colt, S., 250, 257
communication, 4
compass, 9
competition, vii, 13, 15, 23, 62–4, 90, 146, 276, 277
Confucius, 94
Congress of Vienna, 1815, 22, 265
Convention of Beijing, 1860, 2
convergence, 100–7, 119, 120, 147, 210
  linguistic, 100–7, 119
cooperation, vii, 3–24, 37, 119, 170, 226, 232, 236
  and innovation, 164
  in military activities, 17
  role in innovation, 191
Cornwallis, C., 199, 204, 205

cotton gin, 186
Court of Chancery, 103
Cousin-Montauban, C., 239, 260, 261
Cressy, D., 82
Crimean War, 16, 225, 229, 230, 237, 241, 245–50, 257
Cromwell, O., 67, 130

D
Darby, A., 12
Dardanelles, 136, 246
debt
  long-term, 131
  short-term, 130
Deccan, 3, 44, 47, 54, 86, 127, 138–41, 203
Delhi, 1, 23, 47, 71, 86, 110, 111, 120, 139, 141, 224, 232–7, 251
Delhi Sultanate, 86, 111
Delhi, Siege of, 23, 236
Demologos, 163, 164
Devereux, R., 2nd Earl of Essex, 35
devşirme (boy slave) system, 40, 41, 84
dialect, vi, 4, 60, 71, 76, 77, 99–104, 112, 115–19, 133, 141–6, 271, 272
dictionary, vi, 6, 19, 95, 103, 104, 115, 116, 120, 133
  English, 4, 104, 119, 163
  English-Turkish, 109
  French, 4
  Hindustani, 72
  Literary Chinese, 95
  Ottoman Turkish, 109
  Turkish-Arabic, 68
  vernacular Turkish, 109
divergence, 4, 7, 11, 17–19, 21, 24n3, 24n5, 32, 107–20, 137, 142, 164, 210, 266, 278
  linguistic, 107, 110–19
Donglin Academy, 89, 91

Dundas, H., 196–8, 204, 206
Dundas, T., 1st Baron Dundas, 158, 159
Dupleix, J.-F., 141
dynastic cycle, 31, 32, 113, 127, 143

E
East India Company, 22, 71–3, 87, 88, 203–5, 208, 220, 221
  charter of 1600, 37
  charter of 1793, 196
  command and control, 232–7
  role of Enfield rifle in Rebellion, 250–7
  role of steamships in Rebellion, 224–6
Ebubekir Ratib Efendi, 201
Edict of Gülhane (1839), 246
Edinburgh, 154, 155, 157, 158
Edward III, 103, 270
Egypt, 8, 17, 44, 70, 107, 109, 167, 211, 218, 219, 231, 245, 249
Elizabeth I, 33–8, 54, 60, 63, 74, 128, 137
England, 4, 10–12, 18, 19, 21, 23, 32, 33, 35–754
  in 1700, 128–33
  in 1600, 33–8
English Stock, 63
eunuchs, 48, 50, 54, 90, 114, 116
Eurasia, 1–4, 7, 18, 20, 32, 33, 59, 78, 100, 108, 120, 127, 132, 167, 195, 196, 211, 238, 275
  balance of power, 1
Europe, 1–4, 6, 9–11, 15–23, 24n5, 34, 37, 42, 43, 50, 54, 59–62, 68, 73, 74, 77, 88, 92, 110, 116, 119, 120, 134, 141, 143, 152, 153, 164, 165n1, 168, 182, 186, 192, 196, 200, 202, 211, 215, 262, 265, 267–9, 271, 273
  balance of power, 1

examination system, Chinese, 89, 90, 114

F
factor prices, 11, 13, 18, 24
Falcon, J.-B., 12
Fauconnier, G., 7
firearms
   breech-loading rifle, 189, 238
   1819 Hall rifle, 238
   Enfield rifle, 23, 224, 244, 248, 256, 257
   flintlock musket, 243
   matchlock musket, 45, 209
   Minié rifle, 244, 247, 249, 259
   rifled musket, 238
   smoothbore musket, 16, 41, 156, 181, 185, 186, 189, 190, 207, 246
First Anglo-Maratha War (1775–1782), 203
Fitch, J., 161, 162
Forbidden City, 48–50, 143
Forth and Clyde Canal, 157–9
France, v, vi, 2–7, 12, 16, 17, 19, 23, 37, 61, 62, 68, 103, 109, 120, 131, 151, 155, 161–4, 181, 183, 195, 209, 211, 219, 223, 226, 230, 232, 241, 248–51
French, N., 191
Fujian, 76
Fulton, R., 152, 161–4, 175

G
Gay, J., 107
gazetteer, 76, 117
General Purpose Technologies, 12, 276
George III, 206, 209
Gilchrist, J., 71
Glasgow, 151, 157–9, 197, 224

Glasgow, University of, 155
Glorious Revolution, 10, 67, 131, 132
Gong, P., 260, 261
Gordon, R., 191
grammar texts, 6, 72, 103
Grand Alliance, War of the (1688–1697), 131
Grant, Sir Hope, 239, 259
Great Britain, 131, 162, 163, 208, 210, 211, 265
   in 1793, 196–9
Great Divergence, 9, 10
Great Game, 265, 266, 278
Great Powers, 2, 211, 249
Great Vowel Shift, 100
Greece, vii, 8, 22, 40, 107, 220, 245, 246
Greek War of Independence, vii, 22, 218
Gregory XIII, Pope, 70
Gribeauval, Jean-Baptiste Vaquette de, 183, 187, 238
Gros, Baron Jean-Baptiste Louis, 261
Guangzhou (Canton), 52, 206–9, 220–3
Gujarat, 47
Gutenberg, J., 60–2, 67, 69, 70, 73, 74, 279
Gwalior, 195, 203

H
Hai River, 223, 239
Hall, J., 21, 210
Hannas, W., 8
Harpers Ferry Armory, 189, 191
Hastings, Frank Abney, 230
Hastings, W., 73, 204
Havelock, Sir Henry, 254
Headrick, D., vi, 17, 220–2
Henry V, 270
Henry VIII, 35, 82, 128, 178

Heshen, 208
Hewitt, W., 252
Hideyoshi, 51
Hindu, 203
Hinduism, 46, 47, 85–8, 111, 138–42, 203, 234
Hoffman, P.T., vii, 268
Hong Kong, 24, 223
Hongwu Emperor (r. 1368–1398), 50, 52, 90
Hopkins, A.G., 197
Huntington, S., 9
hydraulic press, 173

I
Ibn Khaldun, 31
Ibrahim Pasha, 68, 69, 136, 218, 219
imperialism, v
India
  balance of power, 1
  cooperative warfare in, 232–7
  Government of India Act, 1858, 2
  linguistic divergence in, 110–12
  literacy in, 85–8
  mass-produced firearms in, 250–7
  printing in, 71–3
  in 1700, 137–42
  steamships in, 224–6
Indian Rebellion of 1857, 22, 224–6, 232, 236, 239, 250–7, 275
Industrialism, v
Industrial Revolution, vii, 3, 6, 10–13, 15, 20, 95, 167, 169, 171, 172, 181–92, 226, 262, 270, 279
information, vii, 6, 7, 13, 15, 63, 70, 92, 116, 132, 142, 191
  processing, 60
  transmission, 61, 62
Inglis, J., 253, 255
ink, 61, 74, 175

Inkerman, Battle of (1854), 237, 238
innovation, x, 6, 8–15, 41, 61, 167, 182, 183, 215
  Asia, 15, 18
  Chinese, 10
  and cooperation, 120, 210
  in France, 155
  Western, 9
Innovation Revolution, 7
institutions, 3, 4, 10–13, 18, 40, 42, 87, 130, 265, 276
interchangeable parts, vii, 13, 23, 181–8, 191, 241, 251, 261, 262, 274
Iran, 1, 3
Ireland, 19, 35, 54, 63, 129
Islam, 19, 31, 39, 40, 43, 46, 68, 77, 84–8, 109–12, 134–40, 224, 249
Itea, Battle of (1827), 216, 219, 227

J
jagir (land allotment), 46
Jahangir, 45, 139
James I, 19, 63, 66, 83, 92, 128, 129
  as James VI of Scotland, 37, 54, 63
James II, 67, 127, 224
Janissaries, 39–43, 54, 55, 84, 135, 136, 201, 202, 245
Japan, 3, 51, 53, 54
Jay, J., 185
Jefferson, T., 185
Jevons, S., 10, 11
Jiangnan, 76, 113, 145
Jiaqing Emperor, 210, 211
Johnson, S., 107, 210
Jones, E., 9, 134, 267
Jouffroy d'Abbans, Claude de, 151, 162, 164
Judaism, 39
Jurchen, 51, 142, 143

K

kafes (guilded cage) system, 40
Kangxi Emperor, 206
Kapikulu Corps, 202
Karteria, 22, 216, 219, 220
Keresztes, Battle of (1596), 39
Kipling, R., 225, 226
koine, 117, 118, 120, 146, 210
Korea, 3, 51, 53, 54
kowtow, 206

L

L'Estrange, R., 66, 67
language, 8, 9, 13, 19, 46, 51, 52, 59, 71, 113–17, 121, 127, 133, 137, 142, 146, 210, 237, 265–76, 278
  accent, 4, 175
  Anatolian Turkish, 108
  Arabic, 70, 85, 87, 108, 109
  Bengali, 72, 73, 110, 111
  Braj Bhasha, 110
  Chagatai, 108, 111
  Classical Arabic, 109, 211
  Classical Chinese, 94
  and cooperation, 262
  Dravidian, 110
  English, v, vi, 6, 11, 19, 62, 66, 70, 72–5, 77, 81–4, 88, 92, 94, 99–104, 111, 116, 119, 175, 210, 270
  English grammar texts, 210
  French, vi, 6, 62, 109, 116
  Greek, 102, 104, 109, 119, 154, 219
  Gujarati, 110
  Hindi, 71–3, 110
  Hindustani, 71, 111, 112, 120, 210, 237
  Indo-Aryan, 110, 112
  Indo-European, 9, 101
  Khariboli, 71, 112
  Latin, 59–63, 73, 82, 102, 104, 119, 154, 271, 272
  Literary Chinese, 76, 77, 115
  Manchu, 210
  Mandarin, 120
  Marathi, 110, 111, 253
  Middle-English, 100
  Ottoman Turkish, 85, 108, 109, 119, 120, 137, 211, 272
  Persian, 46, 71–3, 87, 108, 111, 112
  Prakrits, 110
  Punjabi, 111
  Republican Turkish, 108
  Rum, 108
  Sanskrit, 72, 87, 110, 142
  Scots, 100, 274
  Spanish, 109
  Standard Chinese, 94
  Standard Danish, 102
  Standard English, 9, 100, 119, 120, 210
  Standard Norwegian, 103
  Standard Swedish, 103
  Tamil, 71
  and technological divergence, 164
  Turkic, 111, 112
  Turkish, 69, 71, 108, 109
  Urdu, 71, 72, 112, 142
  vehicular, 120, 271, 272
  vernacular, 210
language standardization, v, vii, 3–7, 13, 18, 23, 104, 111, 133, 210, 237, 270–5, 278
  absence in Asia, 164
  and cooperation, 226, 236, 272
  and innovation, 23, 164
  vernacular, 21, 163, 262
language-standardization hypothesis, xii, 23, 266, 270, 278
lathe, 20, 167, 168, 171
Lawrence, Sir Henry, 252, 253

Levant Company, 37
Li Chengliang, 51
Liechtenstein, J.W., 182, 183, 238
Linguistic Revolution, vii, 6, 18, 270, 279
literacy, 9, 19, 22, 50, 61, 63, 111, 113–16, 120, 133, 137, 138, 142, 146, 175, 210, 227, 236
  in Britain, 81–4
  in China, 88–92
  in India, 85–8
  and language standardization, 272
  in the Ottoman Empire, 85
Little Ice Age, 36, 143
Liu Jin, 112
Livingston, R., 152, 161, 162
Loch, H., 258, 260
Long Turkish War (1593–1606), 3, 54, 135
Longqing Emperor, 48
Lucknow, 225, 252–6
Lunar Society, 170

M
M'Gee, R., 240
Macartney, G., 1st Earl, 21, 22, 205–9
Macau, 52, 91
machine tools, vii, 13, 171, 175–8, 186, 227, 229, 232, 238, 243, 261, 274
  absence of development in Asia, 167
MacLean, G., 81
macro-inventions, 12, 77, 261, 274
madrasa, 85
Mahadaji Shinde, 21, 195, 203, 204
Maharashtra, 203
Mahmud II, 218, 245–8
Maisse, André, sieur de, 33
Mamluks, 175
Manchester, 159, 175–8, 197
Manchu, 3, 51, 91, 118, 142, 143, 146, 206, 210

Manchuria, 51, 52, 127, 142, 144, 147
mansabdars (Mughal official), 45–7
Maratha, 15, 16, 21, 22, 86, 127, 138–42, 195, 203–6, 211
Marks, Steven, vii
Marx, K., 11
mass-produced firearms, vii, 274
Maudslay, H., 171–8, 210, 274
McNeill, W., 2, 265, 266
Meerut, 23, 224, 232, 233, 251, 252
Mehmed II, 108
Mehmed III (r. 1595–1602), 38–44, 137
Mencius, 31
metaphor, 7, 275
Metighe, T., 14
Middle Ages, 5, 7, 9, 20, 111, 116, 127, 132, 216, 227, 229, 238, 268
Middle East, 1, 3, 8, 15, 17, 32, 55, 68, 168, 195, 211
Middletown, Connecticut, 187
Military Revolution (First), 16, 146, 268, 274
Military Revolution (Second), vii, 7, 17, 270, 274, 279
Miller, P., 157, 158, 161, 274
milling machine, 187, 189
Ming dynasty, 3, 19, 32, 49, 50, 75, 77, 88–92, 116, 127, 143–6, 206
missionaries, Christian, 52, 71, 77, 78, 142, 208
Mokyr, J., v, 10, 12
Mongols, 51, 91
Mughal Empire, 1, 19, 20, 23, 32, 59, 71, 77, 86, 88, 111, 120, 127, 203, 210, 233, 237
  in 1700, 137–42
Muhammad Ali, 218, 245
Muscovy Company, 37
Mustafa III, 200
Mustafa IV, 245
Müteferrika, I., 68

N

Nakhimov, Admiral Pavel, 231
Nanjing, 52, 76, 89, 113, 117, 118, 145, 210, 223
Napoleon, 70, 162, 182, 211, 229, 247
nation state, v, vii
nationalism, v, 99, 100
Navarino, Battle of (1827), 22, 219, 246
Nemesis, 22, 221, 222
Neo-Confucianism, 49
Netherlands, 12, 36, 37, 131, 211, 272
network, vi, vii, 13, 14, 16, 19, 21, 42, 89, 99, 116, 120, 137, 158, 178, 191, 199, 210, 262
Newcomen, T., 151, 152, 154, 164, 274
news sheets, 75, 77
newsbook, 64
newspaper, 19, 64, 69, 72–8, 103, 159
Nicholas I, 230
Nicholas, T., 14
Nicholson, J., 235, 236
Nizam-i cedid, 202
Nobel Prize, 9
North, D., 10, 132
North, S., 21, 181, 182, 186–92, 210
Nurhaci, 51, 91, 142, 206

O

O'Brien, P., 129, 130, 132
O'Neill, Hugh, Earl of Tyrone, 35
Ochakov, Siege of (1788), 201
opium, 198, 208, 221, 223
Opium War
 First, 22
 Second, 2, 23, 237
Osman Pasha, 230, 231
Ottoman Empire, vii, 1–3, 21, 31–3, 37, 54, 55, 59, 77, 92, 95, 119, 147, 153, 164, 195, 211, 237, 241, 243, 271
 battles in Crimea, 245–50
 Black Sea Battles, 230–2
 linguistic divergence in, 107–9
 literacy in, 84–5
 in 1700, 137
 in 1793, 199–203
 as sick man of Europe, 202
 in 1600, 38–44
 vs. steam, 216–20
Outram, Sir James, 254, 255

P

Paixhans, H.-J., 218, 230
Palikao, Battle of (1960), 259
Palmerston, Henry John Temple, 3rd Viscount, 223, 232, 239
pamphlet, 19, 63, 64, 66, 69, 77, 84, 94
paper, 9, 59–61, 68, 69, 74, 76–8, 82, 86, 137, 142, 155, 175
Paris, 185
Parker, G., 16, 134, 268
Parkes, H., 258–60
patent, 14, 15, 24, 35–7, 151, 155, 157, 167, 169–72, 176, 177, 185, 189, 239
Peacock, Thomas Love, 220
Pearl River, 22, 52, 222
Peking Gazette, 75, 77
percussion cap, 243
periodical, 63–7, 73, 75, 77, 84
Persia, 32, 39, 255
Philadelphia, 13
Philip II, 34
Phillips, E., 104
Pitt, William, the Younger, 162, 196, 198
planing machine, 176
Pleading in English Act, 103, 270
Pomeranz, K., 11
Pondicherry, 141
Portland, Maine, 189
Portugal, 34, 35, 211

Powell, B., 8
Powell, W., 14
printing, 77
   block, 19, 59, 61, 68–71, 74, 75, 77, 115, 116
   bronze movable type, 10
   engraving, 61
   movable type, 6–10, 19, 59–64, 66–78, 86, 109, 115, 116, 120, 178, 270–2
Protestantism, 3, 33, 35, 60, 73
Punjab, 235

Q

Qianlong Emperor (r. 1735–1796), 21, 195, 205–10
Qing dynasty, 1, 15, 22, 75, 77, 118, 127, 142–6, 206, 208, 220–3, 243, 258, 271
Quran, 68, 85, 86, 109

R

Rajastan, 47
Raleigh, Sir Walter, 35
Reformation, v, 33, 82, 84, 128, 132, 133
Renaissance, 59
Rendel, J., 238, 274
revolution, vii, 8, 279
Ricci, M., 52, 74
Richerson, P.J., 13
rifled musket, 17
Roberts, M., 16
Roberts, R., 64, 174–8
Robinson, J., 10
Roebuck, J., 155
Russia, 1, 2, 22, 37, 195, 201, 219, 220, 229–33, 249, 265
Russo-Turkish War
   1768–1774, 201
   1787–1792, 201
   1828–1829, 246

S

Safavid dynasty, 3
sailing ship, 1, 16, 153, 220, 222, 227, 261
Sarah Sands, 22, 225, 226
Savannah, 215
scale economies, 62, 63, 268, 271
Schumpeter, J., 14, 15
Scotland, 19, 37, 63, 99, 100, 128, 132, 151, 154–62, 170, 210, 224
script
   Arabic, 19
   Bengali, 72
   Brahmi, 110
   Devanagari, 71, 72, 111
   Nagari, 72
   Perso-Arabic, 59, 69, 71, 78, 111, 112, 120
   Roman, 52, 72
   Semitic, 110
sebkan (irregular troops), 39
Selim III, 21, 195, 200–2, 245
sepoy, 23, 141, 233–5, 251, 252
Seton-Watson, H., v
Sevastopol, 237, 248, 249
Shah Jahan, 111, 137, 140
Shakespeare, W., 66, 100–2
ship
   oar-propelled, 153
   sailing, 153
Shivaji Bhonsle, 140, 142
signaling, 6, 13
Sikandar Bagh, Battle of, 1857, 254
Singapore, 3
Single Whip system, 51, 53, 144
Sinop, 1, 22, 220, 231
sipâhîs (feudal cavalry), 41, 42
Smeaton, J., 169

Smith, A., 13, 196, 198, 275, 278
Smith, E.A., 13
Smith, M.R., 191
social networks, 191
Song dynasty, 49, 53, 68, 115, 145
Spain, v, 10, 16, 32, 35, 54, 61, 64, 68, 83, 117, 130, 131, 211
   Armada (1588), 34, 62, 153
   tercios, 34
Spanish Succession, War of the (1701–1714), 131
specialization, 183
Spence, M., 13, 284
Spencer, H., 10
Spengler, O., 265
Spufford, M., 81
standardization, 183
Stationers' Company, 62, 63, 66
steam engine, vi, vii, 13, 20, 24, 226, 261, 274
   atmospheric, 151, 154, 156, 163, 168, 169, 171, 274
   Boulton and Watt, 152, 154, 156, 162, 169, 170
   marine, 175
   Symington's design, 156–9
steamboat, 152, 155, 158, 160–2, 164, 210, 211, 215, 220, 224, 243
   iron-hulled, 17, 22, 220, 261
   metal-hulled, 227
steamship, vii, 7, 16, 17, 20, 22, 215–20, 224, 225, 231, 243, 261, 274
   iron-hulled, 221, 224
   propeller-driven, 225
Stuart Dynasty, 127
Sûleymân the Magnificent, 41
Summer Palace, Beijing, 1, 260, 261
Symington, W., 162, 164, 175, 210, 274

T
Taiping Rebellion, 223
Taiwan, 3
Taku Forts
   First Battle of (1858), 223
   Second Battle of (1859), 223, 239
   Third Battle of (1860), 23, 239, 241, 258
Tang dynasty, 49, 89, 94
Tanzimat, 69, 246
taxation, 8, 31, 33, 35, 46, 47, 89, 99, 114, 115, 129–32, 199, 205, 267, 269
   avoidance, 53, 55
   in China, 144–6
   direct, 20, 129, 134, 135
   in England, 128–33
   evasion, 53
   excise, 53
   extraordinary, 43
   import duties, 36, 128
   in India, 137–41
   indirect, 20, 43, 144
   in kind, 20, 42, 43, 51, 52, 55, 129, 134, 135, 144
   land, 52
   in Ottoman Empire, 135–7
   poll tax, 43
   tax farm, 38, 42, 43, 246
Taylor, J., 157, 158
Terry, E., 183
Third Anglo-Mysore War (1790–1792), 204
Thomson, R., 191
Tianjin, 206, 209, 239, 241, 258, 259, 261
Tianqi Emperor, 91
Tigris River, 22, 59, 222
timar (feudal land grant), 40, 42, 43, 134, 135

Tipu Sultan, 204, 205
Topkapi Palace, 39, 85
tournament model, vii, 23, 266, 268, 270, 275, 276, 278
Tousard, Louis de, 187
Toynbee, A., 265
Trafalgar, Battle of (1805), 162, 218
Treaty of Adrianople (Edirne) (1829), 246
Treaty of Nanjing (1842), 222
Treaty of Paris (1856), 2, 249
Treaty of Salbai (1782), 203
Treaty of Tianjin (1858), 223, 239
Treaty of Utrecht (1713), 153
trust, 4, 6, 7, 85, 132, 133, 145, 146, 276
Tudor dynasty, 33, 127
Turkey, 1, 108, 109
Turner, M., 7

U
uniformity, 183
United States, v, 1–7, 14, 23, 24, 161–3, 165, 181, 183, 186, 187, 191, 215, 223, 226, 250, 251, 265, 273, 276, 279
Upper Paleolithic, 7

V
Venice, 37
Verbruggen, J., 169
Vergil, P., 32
vernacular, vi, 4, 6, 7, 15, 19, 22, 60–2, 67, 72, 73, 76, 87, 94, 95, 119, 120, 133, 146, 147, 164, 227, 269, 271, 272, 274
   divergence in China, 112–19
   standardization in Britain, 100–7, 111

Vigo Bay, Battle of (1702), 153
Villers-Cotterêts, Ordinance of, 271

W
Walker, J., 107
Wang Yangming, 89
Wanli Emperor (r. 1572–1620), 48, 54, 74, 89, 91, 112, 144
War of Greek Independence (1821–1832), 249
War of the First Coalition, 161, 195
War of the Second Coalition, 161, 181
War of the Third Coalition, 162
warfare, 4, 16, 23, 33, 41, 84, 134, 153, 158, 161, 182, 186, 218, 226, 227, 229, 247, 250, 257, 265–75, 278
warship, 1, 2, 20–2, 146, 163, 215, 216
Watt, J., vii, 151, 155, 157, 159, 169–72, 175
Wei Zhongxian, 91
Weingast, B., 10, 132
Wellesley, R., 72
West, 24, 92, 94, 115, 134, 135, 153, 205, 216, 224, 227, 243, 268, 269, 271, 272, 278, 279
Whitney, E., 21, 181, 182, 185–7
Wilkinson, J., 167, 169–71, 176
Wilson, A., 233, 235
women, 19, 76, 81, 83, 84, 88, 95, 104, 114, 116, 119, 120, 133, 146, 253
Woodbury, R., 186
writing, 5, 6, 8, 9, 61, 74, 81, 85, 88, 92, 100, 104, 108, 120, 146
writing system, 5, 6, 9, 59, 120, 146, 210, 262
   alphabetic, 62, 271
   alphasyllabary, 110
   Chinese, 74
   consonantal, 8, 69, 110
   Korean, 88

writing system (*cont.*)
   logosyllabic, 8, 9, 94
   Manchu, 51

Y
Yang Yinglong, 51, 53
Yangtze River, 76, 113, 117, 145, 146, 222, 223, 258

Yongle Emperor (r. 1402–1424), 52
Yorktown, Battle of (1781), 204
Yuanmingyuan, 260, 261

Z
zamindar (lineage head), 45, 138, 140, 141, 205
Zhengde Emperor (r. 1505–1521), 112

CPSIA information can be obtained
at www.ICGtesting.com
Printed in the USA
BVOW06*0721041017
496684BV00007B/9/P

9 781137 403179